Collective bargaining
in industrialised market economies:
A reappraisal

ν + νν

Collective bargaining in industrialised market economies: A reappraisal

Part I: A comparative study by John P. Windmuller

Part II: Country studies by W. Albeda
Lars-Gunnar Albåge
R. Blanpain
Guy Caire
Donald E. Cullen
Braham Dabscheck
Harry Fjällström
Friedrich Fürstenberg
Gino Giugni
John Niland
B. C. Roberts
Taishiro Shirai

International Labour Office   Geneva

ISBN 92-2-105606-6 (limp cover)
ISBN 92-2-105607-4 (hard cover)

First published 1987

Printed in Switzerland   ATA

PREFACE

In 1973 the ILO published *Collective bargaining in industrialised market economies*. A decade or so later it was apparent that developments in the countries concerned were such as to warrant an updating of both the country studies contained in Part II of that volume and of the comparative study by Professor John Windmuller which constituted Part I. In fact, the "updating" in most cases became in essence a new study of the situation, indeed a reappraisal of collective bargaining experience in the light of the significant economic and social developments which have taken place in the past decade. Thus we have the present volume for which we again have had the good fortune of Professor Windmuller's co-operation in the preparation of the comparative study.

It should perhaps be emphasised that this volume is mainly an analysis of methods and practices of collective bargaining and their evolution over the years in the light of changes in the various environments in which industrial relations operate. Thus it does not seek to deal with issues that might be the subject of bargaining in any real substantive manner. Of course such issues are referred to in the context, for example, of the expanding scope of collective bargaining, or as reasons provoking a change in bargaining practices and procedures. But the emphasis remains on methods and practices as such.

Moreover, questions concerning collective bargaining in the public service are not treated, or at least not treated separately. This is not because public service bargaining is not important. Indeed it is one of the more crucial issues currently facing many of our societies. But given the focus of the volume and the fact that the ILO has devoted a good deal of specialised work to the general question — including collective bargaining — of public service labour relations,[1] we did not feel it necessary in the present volume to afford special treatment to this important issue.

Nor are the means for dealing with labour disputes, including those arising out of impasses in collective bargaining, treated as such. Although the machinery for settling disputes can have a strong influence on the effectiveness of collective bargaining, they none the less involve measures and practices that are normally quite distinct from the bargaining process. Again it should be noted that work by the ILO in the field of labour disputes has not been lacking.[2]

I should add that since this volume must stand on its own, the discussions in both Parts I and II not only focus on situations at national, industry or enterprise levels in which collective bargaining has evolved, sometimes quite dramatically, during the period in question; they also include analyses of issues relating to certain practices and methods that have not necessarily changed greatly in the past decade.

Part I is John Windmuller's comparative study and Part II reproduces ten country studies which have appeared as articles in various issues of the *International Labour Review* between May-June 1984 and January-February 1986. Part I has of course made generous use of the national information contained in the various articles, but is based as well on substantial comparative research and analysis as regards the situation in industrialised market economies generally.

Comparative studies in industrial relations (even those limited to countries at relatively similar stages of development and with relatively similar socio-economic systems) are always a hazardous venture, but to my mind necessary if we are better to understand the workings of industrial relations systems, including our own. Comparative studies are also necessary if we are to be able to utilise international experience to serve the practical end of adapting or improving national practices. In this respect it is obvious that labour relations systems, or parts of those systems, are not easily or automatically transposable. These systems function and evolve within, and are heavily influenced by, a wider political, economic, social and cultural environment; moreover, they reflect particular historical patterns and exigencies. Nevertheless, international comparisons can and do provide inspiration for the adaptation and modification of existing systems. In a sense this is what the ILO is all about: performing this function through the collection, study, analysis and dissemination of international and comparative information and, taking things one step further, through the adoption — where this is feasible — of international labour standards. I hope and expect that the systematic comparative survey contained in Part I, as well as the national studies in Part II, will make a distinct and distinctive contribution both to understanding the institution of collective bargaining and to its development.

I should perhaps also note that the concept of collective bargaining, as reflected in this volume, is a wide one. The concept is not restricted to the negotiation of formal agreements, although this is of course a paramount thrust of the study, but includes also that wide range of collective contacts which involve elements of negotiation aimed at reaching consensus or an agreed decision. In other words, we are dealing with a phenomenon which goes beyond mere consultation. Having said this, it is of course evident that a procedure officially labelled as "consultation", but which does involve elements of shared decision-taking, may in fact be "bargaining" in the sense to which we are referring. In any event, it is the real nature of the phenomenon that counts, regardless of what it is called, and where that real nature is "bargaining" it is within the conceptual framework of this volume.

I should like to record here the debt owed to Alfred Pankert, Chief of the Labour Management Relations Section of the Labour Law and Labour Relations Branch, for his efforts — substantive, editorial and managerial — in co-ordinating the project that has resulted in this volume.

Alan Gladstone
Director,
Industrial Relations and
Labour Administration Department

Notes

¹ ILO: *Freedom of association and procedures for determining conditions of employment in the public service*, Report VII (1), International Labour Conference, 63rd Session, Geneva, 1977; Tiriano Treu et al.: *Labour relations and disputes settlement in the public service*, Study prepared for the ILO (forthcoming); E. Córdova: "Strikes in the public service: Some determinants and trends", in *International Labour Review* (Geneva, ILO), Mar.-Apr. 1985, pp. 163-180.

² ILO: *Conciliation and arbitration procedures in labour disputes: A comparative study* (Geneva, 2nd impression, 1984); Alan Gladstone: *Voluntary arbitration of interest disputes: A practical guide* (Geneva, ILO, 1984); ILO: *Conciliation in industrial disputes: A practical guide* (Geneva, 5th impression, 1985); idem: *Grievance arbitration — A practical guide* (Geneva, 3rd impression, 1985).

CONTENTS

Collective bargaining: A reappraisal

ABBREVIATIONS IN PART I

ACAC   Australian Conciliation and Arbitration Commission
ACAS   Advisory, Conciliation and Arbitration Service (United Kingdom)
AFL-CIO American Federation of Labor-Congress of Industrial Organizations
AUEW   Amalgamated Union of Engineering Workers (United Kingdom)
BDA   Confederation of German Employers' Associations (Federal Republic of Germany)
CGIL   General Confederation of Labour (Italy)
CISL   Italian Confederation of Workers' Unions
CNPF   National Council of French Employers
DA   Danish Employers' Confederation
DGB   German Confederation of Trade Unions (Federal Republic of Germany)
EETPU   Electrical, Electronic, Telecommunication and Plumbing Trades Union (United Kingdom)
ETUI   European Trade Union Institute
FMCS   Federal Mediation and Conciliation Service (United States)
IMF-JC Japan Council of Metalworkers' Unions
LO   Swedish Confederation of Trade Unions
NLRB   National Labor Relations Board (United States)
OECD   Organisation for Economic Co-operation and Development
PTK   Swedish Federation of Salaried Employees in Industry and Services
SAF   Swedish Employers' Federation
TUC   Trades Union Congress (United Kingdom)
TCO   Swedish Central Organisation of Salaried Employees
UIL   Italian Workers' Union
UIMM   Metal and Mining Trades Federation (France)

PART I

COMPARATIVE STUDY OF METHODS AND PRACTICES

John P. Windmuller (Martin P. Catherwood Professor of Industrial and Labor Relations, Cornell University, Ithaca, New York)

ORIGINS AND NATURE OF COLLECTIVE BARGAINING

1

Collective bargaining is a process of decision-making between parties representing employer and employee interests. Its overriding purpose is the negotiation and continuous application of an agreed set of rules to govern the substantive and procedural terms of the employment relationship, as well as to define the relationship between the parties to the process. As used here, therefore, collective bargaining should be understood to refer not only to the negotiation of formal collective agreements but also to other aspects of the collective dealings between the parties.

Although collective bargaining exists in many different societies and occurs in many different forms, its relative importance as compared with other ways of decision-making is greatest in those countries where industrialisation is far advanced, where product and labour markets operate with a substantial degree of freedom, and where employers and employees have been able to establish representative and self-governing institutions for the purpose of protecting and advancing their respective interests. On the whole, these conditions are most closely approximated in the group of countries commonly referred to as industrialised market economies. Although the specific institutional arrangements represented within this group are quite diverse, they share enough elements of fundamental importance in the domains of social, political and economic affairs to permit a comparative examination of the methods and practices of collective bargaining. While it undoubtedly remains true that, as Allan Flanders once noted, "many of the problems likely to dominate the future of collective bargaining can only be sensibly discussed in their specific national context", there is nevertheless a strong case for the proposition that certain insights into the operation of collective bargaining can best be gained by comparative analyses of the ways in which the different systems — with due regard to their unique features — respond to the challenges constantly generated by the dynamics of modern societies.[1]

As a mechanism for setting wages and other terms of employment, as a way of managing complex organisations, as a form of joint industrial government, and generally as a means of regulating labour-management relations, collective bargaining is constantly called upon to demonstrate its merits. In the final analysis the degree of public support which it will continue to command, if not its very survival, depends on its adaptability to the ever-changing character of its environment. The relevance of this observation has been reinforced in recent years by the impact on collective bargaining of the economic crisis whose beginning coincided with the sharp upturn in world oil prices in 1973. We shall return to this development later.

ORIGINS

This is not the place to trace in detail the history of collective bargaining. That task has already been undertaken with considerable success for certain countries, for example Great Britain,[2] although for quite a few others the historical record still remains to be illuminated.[3] Here only a few general comments can be made.

The emergence of collective bargaining is intimately linked to the social and political consequences of that complex constellation of economic, technological, demographic and related developments which is usually referred to as the Industrial Revolution — a phase in the development of modern societies that in some countries occurred as early as the second half of the eighteenth century but in others not until near the end of the nineteenth century. The dislocations and insecurities ensuing from the profound changes associated with this transformational period had a particularly unsettling effect on traditional relations between employers and employees — or masters and servants, to use the terminology of an earlier time. First in Great Britain, and not much later in other countries, workmen sought to protect themselves against the harsh effects of radical innovations in production methods and machinery, the loss of traditional skills and the intensity of competition in the labour market by forming organisations capable of representing their collective interests vis-à-vis their employers and the State. In the beginning the organisations best able to survive the vicissitudes of the business cycle, the adamant resistance of the masters and the sometimes hostile policies of the State were the ones set up by skilled workers. As a rule, only the craftsmen had the material and administrative resources and the leadership talents required to build solidly founded institutions. Viable organisations for less-skilled and unskilled employees lagged behind everywhere, but especially in the Anglo-Saxon countries, a fact that helps to account for the continuing relative importance of craft-based bargaining structures in Australia, Canada, Great Britain, New Zealand and the United States.

The first organisations of employees [4] were intended to meet diverse purposes. Some emphasised restrictions on entry into the trade to avoid an over-supply of qualified workmen, while others functioned mainly as mutual benefit societies, providing some protection against loss of income due to unemployment, old age, ill health or industrial disputes. Regulation of wages and other basic terms of employment was often the most important object, but there was no common pattern for achieving this aim. Some early trade unions tried to determine unilaterally the wage scales under which their members would work, while others sought to establish a "common rate" through negotiations with employers. The reactions of employers varied from a reluctant acceptance of some limits on their authority to set the terms of employment to an outright refusal to deal with employees except on an individual basis. At a fairly early stage, employers established associations to safeguard their common interests, in some cases through negotiations with unions, in others by seeking to eliminate them.

Thus, collective bargaining had no single, uniform origin. Sometimes it was the employers who sought to establish it in place of union-imposed "price lists"; sometimes the unions strove to overcome employer opposition to joint wage determination; and in still other instances, though perhaps more rarely, the impetus came from both sides. It would certainly be unjustified to neglect the role of employers and their associations in tracing the early development of collective bargaining,[5] but the main burden for securing its acceptance and expansion rested on workers and their unions, especially in those industries where the main body of the labour force consisted of unskilled and semi-skilled workers, for there the employers were often extremely reluctant to abandon the practice of unilateral rule making.

The resistance of many employers to engagement in joint dealings with their employees was for a long time powerfully reinforced by public policies which in several countries derived their philosophical justification from the anti-combination principles of economic liberalism. There is no question that restrictive legislation and the disabling judgements of the courts, often in the name of upholding the sanctity of the individual contract of employment, tended to weaken the unions, especially outside the crafts, and to retard the development of collective bargaining. However, in some countries — Great Britain for example — already well before the beginning of the twentieth century, public policy had begun to swing around to at least a benevolent tolerance of collective bargaining, while other countries followed during the 1920s and 1930s. In fact, one can even cite several instances of governments actively promoting collective bargaining during the period between the two World Wars, although admittedly the development as a whole was far from even. In some countries, employer resistance was deeply entrenched; in others, severe weaknesses and divisions among the unions created serious obstacles. Nevertheless, a major report on collective agreements prepared by the International Labour Office in the mid-1930s could properly take notice of —

... the increasing importance of the collective agreement as an element in the social and economic structure of the modern industrial community. The growth of the movement for regulating conditions of work by means of collective agreements has been particularly marked since the war [i.e. the First World War], and in many countries the collective agreement is now a recognised method of determining working conditions. The movement is primarily based on the desire of employers and workers to settle for themselves the conditions in their industries, but it has proved to be not inconsistent with various forms of the co-operation, the regulation or the control of the State. Although the collective agreement has become widely established in a large number of countries as an integral part of the industrial system, it has discharged its important functions on the whole so smoothly and efficiently that the full extent of its influence on national life is often overlooked.[6]

At the time these observations were made, the expression "collective bargaining" was already well established. The practice had, of course, existed long before the name. In fact, there was a time in the nineteenth century when collective bargaining was known as "arbitration" or "conciliation", even though no third parties took part in the proceedings.[7] Credit for first applying the term to negotiations in industry belongs to Beatrice Webb, who used it in 1891 in her study, *The cooperative movement in Great Britain*. But it took some years for the term to become part of everyday language. In the United States an official report, issued in 1902, still considered it a rarity:

This term, collective bargaining, is not often employed in common speech in the United States, but is gradually coming into use among employers and employees in Great Britain. It evidently describes quite accurately the practice by which employers and employees in conference, from time to time, agree upon the terms under which labour shall be performed.[8]

In non-English-speaking countries, particularly on the European continent, where the institution of collective bargaining has had an almost equally long history, the emphasis came to rest on the term "collective agreement" because the central objective of workers was not so much the procedure of bargaining itself as having collective agreements recognised and enforced as legally binding contracts.

In most of the countries covered by the present study, collective bargaining has become a pre-eminent method of industrial rule making. This is the case even in those relatively few countries where the proportion of workers covered by the terms of one or more collective agreements falls short of a majority of the total number of wage and salary earners. The reason for the pre-eminence is that the terms of employment negotiated under collective bargaining not only cover large numbers of employees but also tend to set a pattern in relevant areas of comparison, such as an industry, a region or some combination of the two. Often the pattern setting happens informally, as when enterprises not represented in collective bargaining decide to incorporate newly negotiated provisions into their own wage scales, working conditions, personnel policies or shop rules, as the case may be. Not infrequently such decisions stem from efforts to demonstrate to workers that they do not need to be represented by a union.

In a number of countries the pattern-setting dimension of collective bargaining has been adopted as public policy and has received a legal foundation of its own. One manifestation of it is the requirement, as embodied in the legislation of certain countries, that an employer who is a party to a collective agreement must apply its terms without discrimination to all categories of workers whom the agreement covers, whether or not they are members of the trade union which negotiated the agreement. In Canada and the United States a comparable obligation is imposed by law on the union certified as the exclusive bargaining agent to represent fairly the interests of all employees in the bargaining unit, whether or not they are union members.

A different form of recognition of collective bargaining as an instrument for setting socially useful standards is the legislation adopted by a substantial number of countries that provides for the possibility of "extending" the terms of an agreement to non-signatories by making it generally binding on all employers and employees within a given industry or region.[9] The administrative details of the "extension" procedure vary considerably from country to country and need not be reviewed here since a section examining the practice as it relates to collective bargaining is included in Chapter 5 on "The role of government".[10] But what does need to be noted is that trade unions, although generally supportive of "extension", have come to realise that the advantages of "extension", in terms of universalising the standards agreed to in collective bargaining, have countervailing disadvantages. While it is true that the principal purpose of "extension" is to prevent employers, who by virtue of non-membership in an employers' association are not bound to the terms of a collective agreement, from operating at a competitive advantage, it is also evident that workers who benefit from its application have that much less of an incentive to become union members.

Notwithstanding its importance, collective bargaining is by no means the only method of determining conditions of employment or regulating labour relations, and even where it predominates it always exists side by side with other methods. The chief alternatives are individual bargaining between an employer and an employee, government regulation through legislative or other means, or the unilateral imposition of the terms of employment by an employer or by a trade union. Unilateral determination has become relatively rare, though it is by no means non-existent, especially in industrial sectors where employers or trade unions occupy an exceptionally powerful position. It may even be the case that during the economic crisis of recent years the ability of employers to impose the terms of employment unilaterally has increased, although more likely it is their relative power in collective bargaining that has been strengthened.

Government regulation as an alternative to collective bargaining cannot be readily distinguished from government regulation as a supplement to collective bargaining. There are no countries in which the State abstains completely from legislating in the area of working conditions. However, until fairly recently the scope of such legislation varied enormously between countries, partly for the simple reason that whereas the North American countries generally adopted only a minimum of legislation on substantive working conditions, social legislation in many European countries covered a broad spectrum of issues that were also simultaneously the subject of collective bargaining. This disparity has narrowed considerably in recent years. Between 1960 and 1980 state intervention in the substantive terms of employment in the United States increased quite dramatically in areas previously left almost exclusively to determination by the parties to collective bargaining, notably in matters of industrial health and safety and collectively bargained pension programmes. Still more recently, however, there are indications that the period of increased government intervention has come to an end and that at least for the time being there will be no further expansion of regulation.

ATTRIBUTES

Any attempt to explain the vitality of collective bargaining must recognise that it is a complex institution which draws its strength from a variety of sources. It is, in the first place, a highly flexible method of decision-making, far more so than legislative, judicial or public administrative processes could be expected to be. Not only does collective bargaining allow for substantial inter-country variations, which indicate that it can adapt to a broad range of economic and political systems, but within a given national context it has shown itself able to adjust to the exacting requirements of many different industrial and occupational sectors, to the private as well as the public sector, to single-plant units as well as to an entire industry, and to the needs of unskilled manual operatives or service employees as well as to the expectations of the most highly skilled professionals.

Expressive of this flexibility is the diversity of agreements which emerge from collective bargaining negotiations. These may range from a purely oral understanding or the simplest and briefest of documents, containing barely more than an agreed wage scale, to the most complex master agreement not only covering a wide spectrum of issues but also allowing for the addition of supplementary agreements. General agreements with their customary provisions concerning wages, hours of work and working conditions may be supplemented by highly specialised agreements, as for example an agreement on the integration of a private supplemental retirement programme with a publicly provided pension scheme or on the retraining of workers whose jobs are being eliminated by the introduction of technological improvements. Supplemental agreements may also take the form of workshop-level agreements specifying rules of conduct and dealing with other workplace-oriented issues that cannot be efficiently settled at a higher level.

Another reason accounting for the prevalence of collective bargaining in contemporary industrial societies is its use as a means of applying widely shared notions of equity and social justice to the industrial setting and the labour market. Historically, as the conviction grew that individual workers could not adequately protect themselves against potential exploitation through individual dealings with their employers, there gradually developed a readiness in many societies to entrust a major share of the protective function to a process that would enable the collective strength of employees to match the bargaining power of the employer. Encouraged by public policies increasingly favourable to collective bargaining, workers' organisations pressed for, and in due course assumed, a shared responsibility for the proper operation of a joint rule-making system in industry. It may well be that the fear of even more radical solutions or a distaste for excessive paternalism underlying state regulation and private employer benevolence also played a significant role in helping to secure public acceptance of collective bargaining. The fact remains that the institution of collective bargaining became a major means of achieving social justice and fair treatment on the job.

Beyond its attributes of flexibility and equity, collective bargaining has from the very beginning also served as a channel for workers' participation in industrial decision-making. The notion that employees are entitled to participate in setting the terms under which they are to work, in other words the notion of industrial democracy, is inherent in collective bargaining, for even the most rudimentary form of collective bargaining involves a shift of certain issues, be it only wages, from the domain of unilateral to the domain of bilateral decision-making. In this sense collective bargaining represents a diminution of absolute management rights in areas which employers in the past considered to be exclusively under their own authority. In this sense, too, collective bargaining introduced democratic practices into the hierarchical relations that were once characteristic of virtually all industrial and many non-industrial organisations. It is also worth pointing out in this connection that over time the scope of collective bargaining has generally widened, though not without many disagreements and conflicts, and has generally done so in line with shifting ideas about the range of issues that are legitimately subject to joint decision-making.

Inherent in any employment relationship are both conflicting and joint interests between employers and employees. Collective bargaining cannot negate the conflictual element in the relationship since that is based, after all, on the existence of diverging goals, needs and aspirations. But it does provide an opportunity for an exchange of information tending to enhance the understanding of the parties for each other's positions, objectives and problems, both where they differ and where they coincide. Moreover — and this is very important — it provides an orderly procedure by which each side can present to the other the best possible case for the satisfaction of its particular demands. There is no guarantee of an agreed outcome, but the process of negotiations creates at least the possibility that each side will move closer to the attainment of its own separate objectives, while contributing to the attainment of objectives shared with the other side.

Another significant source of strength underlying bargaining is its ability to elicit the consent of those who have to live under the terms of the agreement which emerges from the bargaining process. Stability is an important element in the employment relationship, and "consent assures stability because parties who have accepted an agreement will live by its terms".[11] In so far as notions of democracy can be applied to the employment relationship, as indeed they have been on an increasing scale, collective bargaining helps to substitute freely given consent for grudging or blind obedience.

Finally, and without trying to give an exhaustive list of the attributes of collective bargaining, mention should be made of its usefulness for problem solving. The conventional view of collective bargaining emphasises its function as an adversary or "distributive" process, that is, as a means for resolving conflicts of interest in situations characterised essentially by a scarcity of resources relative to claims. In purely distributive bargaining, what one party gains the other loses. Another view of the possibilities inherent in collective bargaining, however, emphasises its use as an "integrative" or "creative" process from which both parties can derive benefit.[12] "Creative bargaining", as one observer has noted, "is practised when the parties adapt the bargaining process to their particular needs . . . in order to attack, in a meaningful way, the problems that face them, hopefully finding solutions that are to their mutual benefit and satisfaction".[13]

COVERAGE

One way of assessing the importance of collective bargaining in different countries is to determine the extent of its coverage. The question to be answered is: For what proportion of the workforce are the principal terms of employment set through collective bargaining? Unfortunately, here one has to rely largely on informed estimates instead of reasonably precise data. That is so because, in the first place, governments do not keep records of collective agreement coverage to the same extent as they usually maintain and publish a statistical series on trade union membership figures. In the second place, unless union membership is compulsory, there is no necessary identity between it and collective agreement coverage; as a rule employers apply collective agreements at enterprise level to all employees, whether they are union members or not. Likewise, in the case of negotiations conducted on a multi-employer or industry-wide basis, the number of employees to whom the agreement applies will often be substantially larger than the number of union members. Moreover, in several countries the legislation on extension of collective agreements, already referred to earlier, has contributed significantly to enlarging the gap between the two sets of figures even further.

Although there are some offsetting situations where union members are not covered by collective agreements, they are relatively rare. As a general rule, one may quite safely assume that the number of employees covered by collective agreements is almost always larger than the number of union members, and sometimes very much larger. This is the case particularly in countries where union membership is comparatively modest but where industry-wide bargaining and extension are widely practised. France would be an example of such a situation. On the other hand, in countries where collective bargaining is contingent on a demonstrable majority of union members among the employees, or where collective agreements often require union membership as a condition of employment, as in Canada, Great Britain and the United States, the gap between union membership and collective agreement coverage is likely to be quite narrow.[14]

To return to the main question, it appears that there are substantial inter-country differences. In Austria, Belgium and Sweden, as of about 1980 almost 100 per cent of employees were covered by collective agreements, in the Federal Republic of Germany 90 per cent, in the Netherlands 80 per cent, in Great Britain between 65 and 70 per cent, in Canada between 35 and 45 per cent, and in the United States between 25 and 30 per cent.[15] These are global figures, and as is usually the case with such figures they conceal substantial internal differences by sector and occupation, and also according to size of enterprise. Manufacturing, transport, communications and the utilities are ordinarily the sectors with the highest proportions of employees covered by collective agreements, but within manufacturing there are sizeable differences according to industry. Other service sectors and agriculture, particularly the latter, tend to rank substantially lower than manufacturing. Occupationally, collective bargaining coverage is strongest among blue-collar workers, less well established among white-collar employees, and weakest among professional, technical and managerial personnel. To cite only one example of occupational differences, a recent study of collective agreement coverage in Canadian establishments with 20 or more employees showed that, in 1983, 39 per cent of office employees were covered by collective agreements, compared with 73 per cent of non-office employees.[16] Yet it should also be noted that, according to the same study, the relative increase in collective agreement coverage among office employees for the period 1963-83 was much greater than among non-office employees (rising from 13 to 39 per cent for the former, but only from 61 to 73 per cent for the latter).

Size of enterprise is also a variable of considerable importance. Almost without exception, collective bargaining is more strongly entrenched among larger than among smaller establishments. (A major recent study of industrial relations in Great Britain showed that in the private sector the most important variable accounting for employer recognition of unions for collective bargaining was size of establishment. That was, however, not the case in the public sector.)[17]

While during the 1970s the overall trend in collective agreement coverage was generally upward — the United States and possibly Japan being the exceptions — the changes that have occurred since 1980 have gone in the opposite direction. That is so chiefly because employment in manufacturing, where collective bargaining was most strongly entrenched, has been declining, while employment in traditionally less well-organised sectors, particularly in services, has been increasing. Countering this downward trend has been a fairly steady increase in the public sector, as regards both the level of employment and collective bargaining coverage, although this development has not been of sufficient magnitude to offset the decline in manufacturing. When the data for the mid-1980s become available, one should expect them to register for most countries a decline in the number of employees covered by collective agreements as compared with 1980.

CONSULTATION AND COLLECTIVE BARGAINING

If there has recently occurred a decline in the number of employees covered by collective agreements — and together with it a subtle weakening in the position of collective bargaining as a decision-making process in industry — there has also occurred in a number of countries a substantial increase in organised consultative relations between employers and employees. That this increase is often linked to severe economic difficulties — or more precisely to expectations that consultation can be an important means for overcoming economic difficulties — can hardly be in doubt. In historical perspective the importance of consultation has usually increased during periods of severe strain on society: a sharp recession, a wartime emergency, difficult post-war readjustments, major technological innovations or similarly stressful situations. Conversely, consultation tends to decline with the onset of more settled times, although that is not necessarily the case when it becomes closely integrated into the national industrial relations system, as indeed it has in some instances.

The most recent upturn in many countries represented in this volume apparently began sometime in the late 1970s. Regarding Great Britain, for example, Professor Roberts has noted that after a significant decline of consultation in the 1960s there was an increase from 1977 onwards.[18] Of course there was no single impetus anywhere but instead a steadily growing recognition that traditional "distributive" collective bargaining no longer sufficed to cope with ever tougher economic challenges. Increasingly, management attempts to boost productivity converged with employee concerns about job security and were reinforced by government policies favourable to consultation.

The chief aim here is to outline the relationship between collective bargaining and consultation rather than to examine in detail how consultation operates. Consultation, or joint consultation as it is frequently called, differs from collective bargaining in that it is intended to be an advisory rather than a decision-making process and that it emphasises the co-operative rather than the adversary elements in labour-management relations.[19] More specifically, consultation is a forum for employers and employees to discuss, formally or informally but usually within an organised framework, matters of common concern and to exchange information as well as to explore ideas intended to help resolve common problems. Unlike collective bargaining, where decisions depend on the consent of both sides to the negotiations, the ultimate decision-making power in consultation is almost invariably retained by management. (In national economy-wide consultations of a tripartite character, ultimate decision-making power is retained by the government.)

While collective bargaining and consultation can both exist to the exclusion of the other, and in fact often do, the two also coexist, and it is not unusual for the same union (or unions) that represents employees' interests vis-à-vis management in collective bargaining to represent also the employee side in consultation schemes. A recent survey of a random sample of 3,300 establishments in Great Britain found that over half of the employees were employed in workplaces covered both by collective bargaining and joint consultation and that 37 per cent of all workplaces were in some way participating in joint consultation arrangements.[20] In some other countries, such as Japan, the equivalent figures are even higher. Already in 1977, according to a Ministry of Labour survey, 71 per cent of firms included in the sample, with 82 per cent of the employees, maintained standing committees for joint consultation.[21]

Where coexistence is practised, the terms of the relationship may emphasise either separation or integration. For many years Great Britain adhered to the principle of separation, and both sides saw to it that formal consultation procedures were kept apart from collective bargaining. But with the growth of plant-level bargaining in more recent decades, as Professor Roberts points out, the separation has become less clear-cut, although it has not disappeared.[22] In Japan, on the other hand, consultation and collective bargaining are sequentially integrated procedures in the sense that "in most enterprises where a joint labour and management council formally exists, issues concerning working conditions are initially discussed through this channel, and if the two parties fail to reach agreement on the issues the matters will be handed over to the collective bargaining machinery".[23] In other words, absent an agreed solution of the problem at hand through consultation, collective bargaining takes hold of it. That may be a somewhat oversimplified description, but there is no doubt that the dividing line is not readily discernible.[24] Professor Shirai even expects consultation to surpass collective bargaining in importance and in due course to "relegate collective bargaining to a minor role".[25]

Although this is only a prognosis and not a summary of established facts, it supports a concern about the consequences of consultation that is shared by a considerable number of union leaders and active union members in the United States. They believe that the application of current techniques to enhance productivity through union-management co-operation programmes, even when jointly implemented, may weaken — or may even be deliberately designed to weaken — the unions' bargaining power. Consequently, they view with concern the spread of quality of work life (QWL) and employee involvement (EI) programmes.[26]

Rather intricate is the relationship between consultation and collective bargaining in some of the countries where the employee side is represented in consultation by legally mandated works councils, but in collective bargaining by trade unions. In a formal sense a separation prevails, but in practice there is often a good deal of integration, not least because of the preponderant weight of union-sponsored members on the works councils and because of the support services which the unions provide for them. The problem is, of course, made even more complex by the fact that *de facto* the functions assigned to works councils in several countries are partly in the realm of consultation, partly in the realm of collective bargaining.[27]

In theory, consultation and collective bargaining are expected to address themselves to different, even if perhaps adjacent or overlapping issues, consultation being reserved especially for production and productivity issues, although by no means only these, and collective bargaining being employed for the determination of wages, conditions of employment and related matters. In practice, however, it has proved almost impossible to maintain a clear distinction, and though it may well be the case that production issues remain foremost on the agenda of consultative bodies, certain other issues that are associated primarily with collective bargaining — including wages and working conditions as well as health and safety matters, fringe benefits, and so on — also rank very high in consultation. By the same token certain issues have been introduced into collective bargaining that in earlier periods would probably not have been included, for example issues concerned with productivity. Further blurring the distinction is the fact that, notwithstanding the advisory character of consultation, a certain amount of decision-making almost inevitably becomes a part of the process, and conversely collective bargaining negotiations tend to become a forum for exchanging information on items not necessarily subject to bilateral decisions.

The lack of a clear distinction may well explain why some countries with a strong adversarial tradition in labour-management relations, notably the United States, have lagged in the development of consultation schemes. As Jacques Monat has put it:

The basic reason why United States employers and unions prefer collective bargaining to other forms of participation is that, in their opinion, it has the advantage of being a relationship which marks a very clear distinction between the respective functions of management and the unions, while other forms of participation [e.g. consultation] assume a relationship which ... limits the possibilities of genuine trade union action and sometimes blurs the distinction between management's functions and those of the union to such an extent that in their view there is actual incompatibility with collective bargaining.[28]

Up to this point the discussion has omitted to make clear that consultation, like collective bargaining, can operate at various levels, the most common ones being the individual plant or workplace, the enterprise, the industry and the national economy. Obviously the substantive content of the issues will vary from one level to another (as will the stature of the parties), although a certain amount of overlapping is to be expected. In general terms, workplace issues tend to centre on quality of work and productivity matters; enterprise issues are concerned with overall corporate plans and their likely impact on job security; industry-wide issues may well include impending changes in technology and foreign trade issues; and economy-wide consultation schemes almost always include broad policy questions concerning the labour market, the economy and the state of labour-management relations.[29]

Almost invariably the composition of consultative bodies at the first three levels is bipartite, except at industry level where formal tripartite mechanisms for consultation may occasionally exist. At the level of economy-wide consultation, however, the practice is to have tripartite bodies, the government usually being represented by the Ministry of Labour. An exception to this pattern is constituted by the Social and Economic Council in the Netherlands, where the neutral members consist almost entirely of government-appointed independent experts rather than of government officials.[30]

In some countries the relationship between collective bargaining and consultation has become so firmly institutionalised, with or without a legal framework, that no major changes should be expected in the next several years. In others, however, particularly where collective bargaining has in the past largely pre-empted the area of labour-management relations and where consultation is as yet only a modest supplement, the terms of coexistence are still open to substantial modification.[31] Much, though not all, will depend on the state of the economy. Continued adversity would be more likely than not to sustain the growth of consultative schemes — which may explain why in Great Britain the Trades Union Congress (TUC) late in 1984 resumed its participation in the consultative National Economic Development Council after an extended absence. On the other hand a sharp upturn in economic conditions could ease the constraints which have induced employers and employees to institute formalised consultation and could restore conventional collective bargaining to its former place.

Notes

[1] Allan Flanders: "The changing character of collective bargaining", in *Department of Employment and Productivity Gazette* (London), Dec. 1969, p. 1103. Richard Lester made the same point when he wrote: "The noteworthy fact about collective bargaining is how the institution differs in its various aspects from one country to another and in the same country from one period to another" (Richard A. Lester: "Reflections on collective bargaining in Britain and Sweden", in *Industrial and Labor Relations Review* (Ithaca, New York), Apr. 1957, p. 401).

[2] Throughout the comparative study, reference is made principally to the industrial relations system of England, Scotland and Wales (i.e. Great Britain), although many of the general comments apply equally well to Northern Ireland. Where "United Kingdom" is mentioned, Northern Ireland is specifically included.

[3] See, for example, E. H. Phelps Brown: *The growth of British industrial relations* (London, Macmillan, 1957).

[4] The term chosen in the English-language version of this study as the most comprehensive expression for the collectivity of wage and salary earners is "employee". The alternative would have been "worker", but that term has a blue-collar connotation which is absent from "employee". (See in this connection the definitions for "employee" and "worker" in A. I. Marsh and E. O. Evans: *The dictionary of industrial relations* (London, Hutchinson, 1973).) It should be made explicit, however, that the term "worker" remains the ILO's usual designation for the collectivity of wage and salary earners and also that the ILO's usual designations for the three elements of its tripartite structure are "Government", "Employer" and "Worker".

[5] "Today, with advantage of hindsight, it is easy to appreciate the inadequacy of any theory of either the nature or of the growth of collective bargaining which sees it only as a method of trade unionism and overlooks in its development the role of employers and their associations" (Allan Flanders: "Collective bargaining: A theoretical analysis", in *British Journal of Industrial Relations* (London), Mar. 1968, p. 3).

[6] ILO: *Collective agreements*, Studies and Reports, Series A (Industrial Relations), No. 39 (Geneva, 1936), p. 265.

[7] Vernon H. Jensen: "Notes on the beginnings of collective bargaining", in *Industrial and Labor Relations Review*, Jan. 1956, pp. 230-232.

[8] *Final Report of the Industrial Commission*, Vol. 19 (1902), p. 834, as quoted in Neil W. Chamberlain and James W. Kuhn: *Collective bargaining* (New York, McGraw-Hill, 2nd ed., 1965), pp. 1-2.

[9] For a comprehensive review of the origins of extension, see L. Hamburger: "The extension of collective agreements to cover entire trades and industries", in *International Labour Review* (Geneva, ILO), Aug. 1939, pp. 153-194.

[10] Otto Kahn-Freund (ed.): *Labour relations and the law* (London, Stevens, 1965), p. 12.

[11] Vernon H. Jensen: "The process of collective bargaining and the question of its obsolescence", in *Industrial and Labor Relations Review*, July 1963, p. 556.

[12] Richard E. Walton and Robert B. McKersie: *A behavioral theory of labor negotiations* (New York, McGraw-Hill, 1965), p. 11 ff.

[13] James J. Healy (ed.): *Creative collective bargaining* (Englewood Cliffs, New Jersey, Prentice Hall, 1965), p. 42.

[14] For the United States the most thorough analysis of the data on collective agreement coverage relative to union membership data is the one by Richard B. Freeman and James L. Medoff: "New estimates of private sector unionism in the United States", in *Industrial and Labor Relations Review*, Jan. 1979, pp. 143-174. For Canada, see Roy J. Adams: "The extent of collective bargaining in Canada", in *Relations industrielles* (Quebec), Vol. 39, No. 4, 1984, pp. 655-663.

[15] See the very similar proportions indicated in ILO: *World Labour Report 2* (Geneva, 1985), p. 36.

[16] W. D. Wood and Pradeep Kumar (eds.): *The current industrial relations scene in Canada 1984* (Kingston, Ontario, Queen's University at Kingston, Industrial Relations Centre, 1984), pp. 220-221.

[17] W. W. Daniel and Neil Millward: *Workplace industrial relations in Britain: The DE/PSI/SSRC Survey* (London, Heinemann Educational Books, 1983), p. 279.

[18] See Roberts below, p. 295.

[19] The term "consultation" is not in general usage in the United States. The closest American equivalent is "labour-management co-operation" or simply "co-operation".

[20] Daniel and Millward, op. cit., p. 178.

[21] See Shirai below, p. 247.

[22] See Roberts below, p. 295.

[23] OECD: *Collective bargaining and government policies in ten OECD countries* (Paris, 1979), p. 96.

[24] Kikuchi Kozo: "The Japanese enterprise union and its functions", in Tokunaga Shigeyoshi and Joachim Bergmann (eds.): *Industrial relations in transition: The cases of Japan and the Federal Republic of Germany* (Tokyo, University of Tokyo Press, 1984), p. 191.

[25] See Shirai below, p. 251.

[26] See for example Sanford M. Jacoby: "Union-management cooperation in the United States: Lessons from the 1920s", in *Industrial and Labor Relations Review*, Oct. 1983, pp. 18-33.

[27] For an analysis of the situation in the Federal Republic of Germany, see Wolfgang Streeck: *Industrial relations in West Germany: A case study of the car industry* (London, Heinemann Educational Books, 1984).

[28] ILO: *Workers' participation in decisions within undertakings* (Geneva, 1981), p. 171.

[29] Exemplifying the tasks usually assigned to national economy-wide consultative bodies are the provisions of the law that in 1977 created the Australian Labour Consultative Council: "The Council is to provide, in the public interest, a regular consultative machinery on industrial relations and manpower matters of national concern for representatives of the Federal Government, employers and workers." See *Social and Labour Bulletin* (Geneva, ILO), Dec. 1977, p. 295.

[30] Also exceptional about the Netherlands is the existence, parallel with the tripartite Social and Economic Council, of a bipartite body — the Foundation of Labour — whose terms of reference include consultation as well as collective bargaining.

[31] Regarding the United States, see Thomas A. Kochan et al.: *Worker participation and American unions: Threat or opportunity?* (Kalamazoo, Michigan, W. E. Upjohn Institute for Employment Research, 1984).

STRUCTURE AND ORGANISATION OF THE PARTIES

2

For collective bargaining to function effectively, or even to function at all, the parties engaged in it must maintain structures appropriate to the process. They must also be able to adapt their structures to ongoing changes in bargaining patterns. This chapter will review the principal elements of the structure on the employee and employer sides in so far as they are connected to and supportive of collective bargaining. Structural elements intended for purposes other than collective bargaining, for instance to promote the political or legislative concerns of employers' or employees' organisations, are beyond the confines of the discussion. The emphasis will be on such questions as the basis and extent of organisation, obstacles to organisational cohesiveness, the relations between different elements in the hierarchy of employees' and employers' organisations, trends and countertrends in centralisation, and the prevailing locus of decision-making. We shall begin with the employee side; it is unquestionably the more complex of the two.

THE EMPLOYEES

Employees are represented in collective bargaining chiefly by trade unions. Trade unions are, however, not the only representative entities. In several European countries works councils are the primary advocates of employees' interests at enterprise, plant and workshop levels, and though they are often closely linked to the trade unions, they lead for the most part an independent existence founded on the legislation that mandated them. Works councils will require separate discussion in this account. Mention should also be made of the associations which in several countries play an important role among certain categories of employees, such as teachers, nurses and government employees. Until fairly recently these associations emphasised the shared professional, as distinct from the common economic, interests of their constituents and avoided being identified as unions. In the past few decades, however, they have increasingly emphasised their claims-making and protective functions, and some of them have become virtually indistinguishable from trade unions, even to the extent of becoming affiliated with a national trade union centre. Moreover, many are nowadays classified as, or together with, trade unions in the official union membership statistics.[1]

Organisational characteristics and union strength

The ability of trade unions to participate effectively in collective bargaining depends to a substantial extent on their representativeness and their cohesiveness. Although many factors besides size of membership determine union strength and bargaining power, success (or failure) in attracting and holding members is probably the most important element.

Data on union membership are available for virtually all industrialised market economies, but they are not necessarily comparable or up to date and they usually present intricate problems of measurement, definition, data collection, reporting practices and the like. This is not the place to examine such difficulties; it has been competently done elsewhere.[2] But attention must be called to the probability that membership figures are subject to a margin of error. They should therefore be treated more as reasonable approximations than as certifiable quantities. This note of caution certainly applies to the data on "union density" or the "union penetration rate" provided in table 1. It must also be pointed out that aggregate density rates for an entire country represent no more than a weighted average of highly disparate situations in individual industrial sectors. In fact, in any one country the internal differences in membership rates, when broken down according to industry and occupation, can be astoundingly large.[3]

As table 1 indicates, union membership rates (based on all wage earners and salaried employees as reported by the Organisation for Economic Co-operation and Development — OECD) increased in most countries during the 25-year period from 1955 to 1980. The exceptions were the Netherlands and Norway, where the changes at five-yearly intervals were negligible, and the United States, which experienced a steady decline throughout the entire period — a decline made even more striking by the fact that the total figure for 1980 for the first time also included many associations not counted in previous years. It would have been even lower without them.

For many countries the year 1980, or perhaps 1979, marked a high point in the union density rate. Up to that time unions had been favoured by success in organising categories previously not well represented in their ranks, especially women, non-manual workers and in some countries — notably in North America — public service employees. Also up to that time they had been able for the most part to stem the adverse impact of a worsening economic situation. But ultimately the inflationary pressures unleashed by the so-called oil-price shocks of 1973 and 1979, and the steady decline of the traditional manufacturing industries which almost everywhere had long served as the historic strongholds of unionism, made their effects felt. After 1980 union density rates began to decline. In Great Britain, for example, the drop was from about 55 per cent in 1980 to less than 50 per cent by 1982. To be sure, the decline was not universal. In

Table 1. Union membership as an approximate percentage of all wage earners and salaried employees, selected years 1955-80

Country	1955	1960	1965	1970	1975	1980
Austria	60	60	60	63	67	65 [1]
Belgium	60	60	60	65	70	73
Canada	30	30	28	30	35	35
Denmark	60	62	62	64	70	72
Germany, Federal Republic of	38	37	36	36	39	41
Great Britain	44	44	44	50	53	56
Netherlands	44	43	41	40	42	41
Norway	62	62	63	62	61	62 [1]
Sweden	62	65	68	73	80	87
United States	32 [2]	31 [2]	28 [2]	27 [2]	25 [2]	25 [3]

[1] 1978.   [2] Exclusive of (professional) employees' associations. If they had been included, the figure for 1975 would have been about 29 per cent.   [3] Including (professional) employees' associations.

Sources: National statistical yearbooks, *OECD labour force statistics*, trade union reports and various secondary sources.

Australia, for example, the unions were able to maintain a fairly constant density rate. In Canada the rate may even have increased. But as more data become available for the first half of the 1980s, they will probably show a decline or at best a standstill for most countries.

Without seeking to pinpoint all the reasons for the decline, which would in any event vary from one country to another, the major ones include a reduction of employment in traditionally well-organised manufacturing industries (including publicly owned industries) and an expanding labour force in the less well-organised tertiary sectors; a parallel shift from blue-collar to white-collar occupations with corresponding adverse effects on density rates; more sophisticated attempts by employers to resist union recognition; and the uniform availability of the protective elements of social and labour legislation without regard to union membership.

There are, to be sure, some countervailing factors, such as the inroads which unions have made among female employees, formerly considered to be very difficult to organise; the advancing unionisation of the so-called cadre groups (supervisors, technicians, professionals and middle-level managers); and the very substantial representation of unions among employees in the civil services. The fact remains, however, that in the private sector a large portion of employment expansion is taking place in new industries, especially high-technology industries, where unions are as yet not well represented and where, moreover, they seem to have considerable difficulty in mounting effective organising drives.[4]

Unions have always striven for, but have not always been able to achieve, unity within their ranks in the justified belief that unity enhances bargaining power, whereas splits and divisions weaken it. Divisions based on ideology and

19

philosophy still account for the existence of plural unionism in Belgium, Canada (Quebec), France, Italy, Japan and the Netherlands, just as they did in the early 1970s. But some new internal developments do need to be mentioned. In the Netherlands the unification of the three major trade union confederations (socialist, Catholic and Protestant) became a distinct possibility in the 1970s, but the Protestant organisation decided in the end to maintain a separate existence. The socialist and Catholic unions merged their organisations, yet had to accept the formation of a separate new confederation for middle- and upper-level employees.[5] In Belgium the traditional lines of division between the Catholic and socialist trade union confederations have become even more complicated as a result of the federalisation of the country along linguistic lines. In the future this development might make the negotiation of national collective agreements a complicated task.[6] In Italy the three major confederations (communist/socialist, socialist and Catholic) co-operated for 12 years under the terms of a 1972 pact establishing a loose Unitary Federation. The pact, however, ceased to be applied in 1984 as a result of serious policy differences and may be regarded in practice as dissolved.[7] In Japan the two principal rival trade union centres are now co-operating more closely with each other than before in their search for a common strategy.[8]

Although divisions along ideological or philosophical lines are the most common basis for what is sometimes called "plural unionism", namely the simultaneous existence of several confederal trade union organisations in one country, other divisions of a rather different character, with emphasis on occupational or "professional" lines, have resulted in the formation of independent confederations for non-manual employees in France, the Federal Republic of Germany, the Netherlands and the Scandinavian countries. These organisations may in some instances themselves consist of separate bodies for white-collar and managerial-level (or academically trained) employees, as well as for public and private sector employees.

On the whole, confederal organisations based on separate occupational categories have been more successful than ideologically divided organisations in co-operating with each other for collective bargaining purposes. An apt example of a generally close co-ordination is the relationship developed between the blue-collar Swedish Confederation of Trade Unions — LO [9] — and the white-collar Swedish Central Organisation of Salaried Employees — TCO [10] (and particularly the TCO's co-ordinating body for the private sector, the Swedish Federation of Salaried Employees in Industry and Services — PTK [11]), but it must nevertheless be noted that even in this largely harmonious relationship the existence of somewhat divergent interests has from time to time caused serious friction, especially over so-called wage drift issues.

National confederations

The apex of the trade union structure everywhere is represented by a national trade union confederation. Where plural unionism prevails, two or more peak confederations, not necessarily of equal strength or importance, form the apex. National trade union confederations are composed of affiliated national unions whose number, as we shall see, varies greatly from one country to another. Almost all confederations derive their powers and functions from an act of delegation of authority by their affiliates, and as a rule the confederations' activities have to do largely with the maintenance of top-level relations with government agencies, political parties and the counterpart confederations on the employer side; the mobilisation of trade union influence on the legislative process; the dissemination of trade union views on public issues of special concern to labour; and occasionally the settlement of internal disputes that may arise between affiliated unions. For many trade union confederations, collective bargaining tends to be a peripheral activity; their affiliates almost invariably insist on retaining full control over this all-important task. They might, of course, provide certain important services which could range from economic research to the accumulation of a central strike fund. But except in a few countries, confederations do not as a rule regard collective bargaining as a central activity.

There are times, however, when a confederation does become directly involved in collective bargaining. The circumstances are quite varied, but four situations appear to stand out. One involves a concerted effort by a government to harmonise national economic policy goals with the outcomes of collective bargaining. Another occurs when governments encourage the central bodies on the employer and employee sides to help shape social policy in areas relevant to their concerns. A third occurs when the central organisations of employers and employees have decided to establish, by mutual agreement, certain basic rules to govern the relations between their respective constituents. And a fourth is likely to be the result of an agreement among the trade unions to co-ordinate their bargaining strength in pursuit of a common objective. We shall expand briefly on each one of these situations.

That governments prefer to win trade union support for their policies by dealing with a single authoritative body instead of having to persuade a large number of individual organisations representing divergent interests is hardly surprising. But it is not only a question of economy of effort. Governments also expect greater understanding for their aims and constraints from trade union leaders at confederal levels than from subordinate leaders, given the likely differences in perceptions and horizons. Under the impact of inflationary pressures in the 1970s, many European governments encouraged more centralisation of power in national trade union confederations in the expectation that strong confederations were in the best position to mobilise their constituents behind a policy of wage moderation. In a number of instances national trade union bodies concluded bipartite or tripartite "social contracts" which often embodied wage restraint measures — sometimes coupled with productivity improvement pledges — in return for long-sought social improvements, in Great Britain for example, in the area of employment security.[12]

Somewhat different in character has been the confederal role in helping to shape national social policies. The best example is probably offered by the situation in France where, ever since the late 1960s, the Government has encouraged the several central organisations on the employer and employee sides to negotiate "summit level" agreements on key issues of social policy, for example vocational training, maternity leave, severance pay, early retirement and the achievement of salaried status for hourly paid manual workers. In several instances the outcomes of these negotiations ultimately became the basis for government-sponsored legislation; that was in fact the understanding and the inducement for the negotiations in the first place. In others, the results became the framework for the substantive terms of the relationship between the organisations of employers and employees at industry and enterprise levels.

A related form of direct confederal participation in collective bargaining is constituted by the negotiation of so-called basic agreements which are of quite fundamental importance in a number of countries, notably Belgium, Denmark, Finland, the Federal Republic of Germany, Norway and Sweden.[13] Most basic agreements contain certain fundamental principles that are to govern the relations between the organisations of employers and employees. In this sense they are equivalent to basic national legislation or constitutional provisions, the chief difference being of course that the principles have been shaped by the parties themselves through their representatives at peak confederal levels instead of by a national legislature or constituent assembly. But not all such agreements are of a general character. Some are limited to a particular subject, for example in the Federal Republic of Germany, where the basic agreement deals only with disputes settlement procedures and has merely advisory standing instead of being binding. And in one case, that of Sweden, the once all-important Basic Agreement of 1938 has lost much of its significance to new legislation. Nevertheless, in quite a few countries basic agreements still constitute an important area of direct participation in collective bargaining by national trade union confederations and of course their counterparts on the employer side.

In several countries, particularly those where a high degree of centralisation is characteristic of industrial relations, trade union confederations have been granted negotiating powers by their affiliated constituents. In these situations the confederations have become directly involved in wage negotiations, either by actually concluding agreements that then serve as a framework for subsequent negotiations at subordinate (industry or enterprise) levels or by supervising and co-ordinating the bargaining activities of their affiliates. Either type of arrangement has at various times prevailed in Austria, the Netherlands and the Scandinavian countries. The situation has, however, been quite fluid and — Austria excepted — there have been no instances where national trade union confederations have been able to entrench themselves permanently as leading participants in collective bargaining.

Very likely there is a close relationship between government intervention in the economy and the acquisition of authority over collective bargaining by central trade union bodies. Not only do interventionist governments want to deal with representative agencies on the trade union and employer sides, but conversely trade unions also find that they can influence policy-makers in government more effectively through a single designated leading body.

Size of country also seems to be an important variable. The correlation is by no means perfect, but most of the countries in which trade union confederations are actively involved in collective bargaining are relatively small. Administrative factors and the constraints of the economy are likely to be the principal factors in this connection. Centralised authority in all institutions is more easily achieved, other things being equal, in a small than a large country. The pressure on the often relatively more vulnerable economies of the smaller countries to keep their cost levels — including labour costs — internationally competitive tends to promote the centralisation of authority.

But as already noted, authority relations do change, and in the current period most of the changes appear to favour decentralisation. Consequently the power of the national unions, whose role in collective bargaining will be reviewed next, has in many instances been strengthened relative to the authority of the confederations.

National unions

In virtually all industrially advanced countries national unions emerge at a certain stage in the development of labour organisations as the principal directive bodies for marshalling the collective interest of workers in more or less well-defined industrial or occupational sectors. This concentration of resources and power at national union level is undoubtedly aided by, but is not necessarily dependent on, the formation of equivalent national associations on the employer side. In the United States, for example, where most employers have chosen to administer their own labour policies and have refrained from establishing employers' associations for collective bargaining, national unions have nevertheless become the decisive organisations on the labour side.[14]

The factors which promote the rise of national unions and the rate at which their emergence occurs have, of course, varied considerably among different countries. They seem to thrive best in countries where workers consider collective bargaining to be the central activity of trade unions, but, conversely, to lag behind where political activities are given a higher priority. Likewise, where localist or enterprise-oriented tendencies among workers are strongly entrenched, the ability of national unions to assume a foremost role is sharply curtailed. The strength of localist forces explains why in some countries, such as France, the national unions remained for a long time primarily loose federations of essentially autonomous local union groups, whereas in other countries, by contrast, as for instance in nineteenth-century Germany, the national unions established their authority over local bodies at a relatively early stage in the development of labour organisations.[15]

An important exception to the pre-eminence of the national union in collective bargaining occurs in Japan, where the so-called enterprise unions have established themselves as the key organisations in a highly decentralised bargaining structure. Although national unions do exist, they are for the most part no more than loose federations of enterprise unions in particular industrial categories. The Japanese worker's close attachment to his or her enterprise, especially in large manufacturing companies, the recognised role of the enterprise as a social community and not merely as a place of employment, and the resistance of Japanese management to collective bargaining at levels beyond the individual enterprise are key factors accounting for this unusual situation.

During the formative period of trade unions, the structural principles which determined the make-up of their membership were often based on either craft or industry attachments. To these basic organisational categories others were added later, notably white-collar and general unions.[16] In some countries disagreements between unions over the appropriate structural principle turned into major controversies and gave rise, as in the United States, to the formation of separate confederations. In due course, however, industrial unions became, in most countries, the most widely followed base of organisation. The usual pattern was to have one national union for each industry, but there were many exceptions, for instance in countries like Australia, where the tradition of craft unionism was particularly strong, or Great Britain, where general unions encompassed a large proportion of total union membership.

In recent decades a new pattern has emerged. In many countries national unions of varying size and structural composition have merged their forces on a large scale to form multi-industrial or general unions whose membership extends over a substantial portion of the industrial spectrum. This consolidation movement extends to white-collar unions as much as it does to unions of blue-collar workers. In some countries the resulting reduction in the number of national unions has been quite dramatic. In Great Britain, for example, the total number of unions declined from 685 in 1956 to 393 in 1983. (The corresponding figures for unions affiliated with the TUC, the national confederation of unions, are 186 and about 100.) Similarly sharp reductions have occurred in the Netherlands, the Scandinavian countries, the United States and elsewhere. In the Netherlands it is actually the explicit aim of the two principal federations to reduce the number of their affiliates to six or seven each. That may be an extreme objective, but the trend is currently moving in that general direction.[17]

For the most part the mergers are intended to help unions cope with a variety of adverse developments, including membership declines, financial difficulties, changes in industrial organisation or technology, and most of all the negative consequences of all of these factors for union bargaining power. For some unions a merger with a stronger union has been the only alternative short of liquidation. By capitalising on the anticipated advantages of scale, unions expect to be able to achieve reductions in their costs of operation, enhance the services rendered to their members, improve their benefit programmes, and most of all strengthen their bargaining position vis-à-vis employers.[18]

National unions implement their crucial role in collective bargaining in many ways. In countries where industry-wide collective bargaining at regional or national level is the practice, it is their responsibility to define major bargaining objectives and policies — often on the basis of proposals emanating from local and regional levels — and to perform the research needed to support union negotiators' demands. Most of the time it is the national union that administers the organisation's strike fund. In the Federal Republic of Germany collective bargaining has become more and more the concern of the central leadership of the national unions, while members and local officials play for the most part only an advisory role, except for strike votes. The executive boards of most national unions affiliated with the central body, the German Confederation of Trade Unions (DGB),[19] are empowered by the by-laws to make all bargaining policy decisions, although in effect the policies are often made jointly by the central executive boards and the regional leaders.[20] In so far as there is a trend towards increasingly bureaucratic and legalistic approaches to labour problems, the resulting need for expertise would undoubtedly exert a centralising influence.[21]

In countries where bargaining is substantially more decentralised to local and regional levels, the national union will as a rule be represented in negotiations by one of its own officials whose presence serves to assist the local negotiators and simultaneously to ensure the observance of national bargaining policies. Or else it may rely on the officers and staff of its regional organisation to heed national union policies.

Intermediate co-ordinating organisations

National unions frequently establish regional or district bodies — or even both in very large countries where more than one layer of territorial subdivision is required for administrative reasons — to constitute an intermediate level of administration between themselves and their local branches. Among the principal reasons are more efficient internal operations, closer contacts with local union bodies and more effective collective bargaining.[22]

Better co-ordination of collective bargaining is an especially important reason for establishing subsidiary echelons in the union structure, but at least two somewhat different situations ought to be distinguished.[23] One reflects a structure of collective bargaining which is based on regional negotiations covering a particular industry or sector. A very large number of bargaining units in Western European countries, especially in the larger countries but not infrequently also in the smaller ones, reflect such regional boundaries. (In Australia the corresponding territorial lines are based on the individual states.) Where regional bargaining arrangements prevail, unions are virtually compelled to maintain a standing regional organisation. In the second case, the establishment of a subsidiary territorial level of union organisation results from a situation where two or more local unions belonging to the same national union function within the same product or labour market, as might readily occur in the United States, where bargaining units are often local in scope. In such situations the establishment by the national union of a local co-ordinating body, sometimes called a "joint board", has as its purpose to prevent the local unions from competing with one another over wages or other issues.

In countries where local unions are too small or financially too weak to support full-time paid officials at the local level, the regional or district organisation may be the lowest level at which a full-time paid official is employed.[24] In the Netherlands, which exemplifies this situation, the district officials' responsibilities include representation and assistance to the local organisations in collective bargaining as well as the provision of other union services.

There are striking differences both in the degree of autonomy granted by national unions to subsidiary regional bodies and in the degree of authority which they exercise over the local organisations under their jurisdiction. While they function in principle under the direction of the national union's central office, some regional bodies have acquired positions of considerable power in their own right, often derived from their role in regional collective bargaining. Others, however, are closely supervised by the national body. A similarly wide range of relationships characterises their position vis-à-vis the local unions, although in cases of conflicting pressures they are far more likely to conform to central office policies than to make themselves the advocates of the local bodies.

Intermediate negotiating bodies

In countries where industrial unionism is the prevailing principle of organisation, where therefore only one union represents the employees of a particular enterprise and industry (or other economic sector), and where the bargaining units are all reasonably homogeneous in composition, the major structural components on the union side should comfortably fit into a simple local-regional-national union pyramid, with the possible superimposition of a confederal level in circumstances already discussed. The reality is, however, rarely that simple. Aside from the proliferation caused by plural unionism based on ideology, industrial unions in many countries are flanked by craft, white-collar and general unions, and frequently more than one union is represented among employees in a given industry or enterprise. Because employers tend to resist solutions based on the establishment of multiple bargaining units — except for the usual separation of negotiations for white-collar employees from those for blue-collar employees — and because the unions themselves prefer to avoid potential competition and disunity in their own ranks, the unions have had to develop structures of their own capable of providing effective bargaining representation for their members within a context of multiple unionism and have had to do so in a way that ensures as much as possible the autonomy of the various unions concerned.[25]

Perhaps the simplest solution is the setting up of an ad hoc negotiating committee representing several unions with members in a particular industrial sector or enterprise. But this is usually only the forerunner of a more permanent arrangement, as exemplified in Great Britain by the creation of union federations for bargaining purposes. Federations are distinguished from ad hoc and similarly loose arrangements by the existence of an internal governing structure, a formal set of rules, separate officers and staffs as well as a headquarters office, and perhaps most of all by an expectation of institutional continuity. It is their chief purpose to co-ordinate the bargaining objectives of their constituent organisations and to consolidate their separate bargaining power. Depending on the diversity of their member organisations, some federations may even spread their activities over more than one industry.

Sometimes developments in different countries move in opposing directions, and the place occupied by bargaining federations may serve as an example. In Japan one of the most significant developments in recent years has been the formation of federations for bargaining co-ordination among major enterprise unions in broad-based industrial groupings and regardless of affiliation to a particular national confederation. The most important co-ordinating body is the Japan Council of Metalworkers' Unions, better known as the IMF-JC because it consisted originally of the Japanese affiliates of the International Metalworkers' Federation, one of the International Trade Secretariats. Similar councils, though not yet as well developed, exist in the food and chemical industries, also with ties to the respective International Trade Secretariats.[26] Another co-ordinating body, even more diffuse in the sense of having no industrial boundaries at all, is the recently established Trade Union Council for the Private Sector (Zenmin Rokyo).

On the other hand, while bargaining federations in Japan are flourishing, they have been "on the wane" in Great Britain in recent years, at least outside the public sector, and apparently in large part because the unions that at one time were their major constituents have merged with one another, thus obviating the need for the once so important co-ordinating functions of the bargaining federations.[27]

The increasing importance of multinational enterprises in the world economy has induced unions to create international structures of their own as a countervailing force aiming at the eventual establishment of bargaining relationships at international level. The adoption of so-called "international codes of conduct" for multinational enterprises by several international agencies, notably the ILO and the OECD, has reinforced this development. Particularly noteworthy has been the formation — under the sponsorship of the Internatonal Trade Secretariats — of "corporation councils" composed of national unions from different countries whose membership includes the employees of a particular multinational enterprise. Some of the most active councils exist in the automotive manufacturing industry. The long-term objectives of the corporation councils include collective negotiations with corporate world headquarters over issues of transcending importance, such as protecting the job security of employees against the adverse employment effects of plant closures or shifts in plant location, the retraining and re-employment rights of employees and the equalisation of major fringe benefits. It should be noted, however, that in no instance has any council yet succeeded in obtaining employer recognition as an international bargaining agent.[28]

Local unions

As a rule the basic administrative unit of trade union organisation is the local union or local branch — an organisation of workers who usually share at least one among the following three criteria: that they reside in a common locality (a city, county or other geographic area); that they work for a common employer (an enterprise, establishment or other workplace); or that they belong to a common occupational group (white-collar, blue-collar, skilled trade, etc.). These criteria will need elaboration, but first it should be pointed out that subsidiary units even below the local union level also exist, as exemplified by the *section syndicale d'entreprise* in France. (Where shop stewards are well integrated into the union structure and take their directions from the local union, they might also be considered as constituting a subsidiary echelon.) Legally mandated works councils, however, belong to a different category of organisation, and their specific relationship to the union structure will require separate discussion.

To bring out the existence of significant differences between and within countries as regards the local union's role in collective bargaining, distinctions in at least three important areas need to be drawn. The first pertains to the constitutional position of the local union within the larger entity, i.e. the national union, to which local unions in industrialised market economies almost invariably belong. (Except for a certain portion of the enterprise unions in Japan, fully independent local unions have virtually disappeared.) In some countries, notably in Japan and North America, where collective bargaining takes place mainly at the plant or enterprise level, the local union (respectively the enterprise union in Japan) often enjoys a high degree of autonomy. This means that, within certain limits set by the rule books of the national union or by custom, local unions have considerable freedom of action in helping to shape the terms of employment under which their members are employed. Freedom of action may extend to the negotiation and implementation of collective agreements with relatively little supervision by the national union, but the precise degree of local autonomy will, of course, vary substantially from country to country, from union to union, and even over periods of time.

Given the traditionally close correspondence between local union autonomy and a decentralised bargaining structure, one would expect that in countries where the prevailing structure of collective bargaining is industry-wide in national or regional terms — as is characteristic of most of the Western European countries — the local union is likely to have less autonomy and to operate more as an administrative arm of the national union of which it forms a part. In these situations local unions tend to concentrate on their administrative and service functions and to play only a subordinate and indirect role in collective bargaining. Change may, however, be in the offing. In response to an ongoing trend towards more decentralised collective bargaining, unions have sought to establish a presence of their own at the workplace, sometimes with the encouragement of legislation. Ordinarily one would expect such a development to result in more bargaining-related activity, and consequently in more autonomy, at local union level. Countering such a development, however, has been an increased need for trained union officials capable of handling ever more complex bargaining issues — and that need has had to be met largely by the national unions or their district organisation.

A second distinction among the various kinds of local unions identified above relates to their organisational base. In many countries, particularly in Western Europe, local unions tend to be geographically defined entities whose territory covers a particular city, town, county, department or similar governmental-administrative unit. Where membership in a local union is a function of the individual's place of residence, it is more than likely that the members of such a local organisation will be working for many different employers. The alternative principle of organisation is, of course, the plant or enterprise, or some other workplace-defined unit. Local unions based on territorial criteria predominate in Western European countries, including Great Britain, although this is by no means the only type.[29] They also exist in North America, especially among craft-based local unions, but they are considerably less characteristic of the North American union structure than local unions based on attachment to a given plant or other workplace. In Japan almost all organisations equivalent to a local union are formed on the basis of employment in a particular enterprise.

Workplace-based and territorially based local union structures, as Wolfgang Streeck has pointed out, "differ with regard to the type of interests they emphasise. While workplace-based structures tend to give preference to interests that are related to the special conditions in particular companies, plants, or workshops, territorially based structures are more likely to express those (general) interests of members that are independent of specific workplaces".[30] The distinction helps to explain why there are less likely to be works councils in countries with predominantly workplace-oriented local unions than in countries with territorially based local organisations.

The third distinction covers the occupational composition of local unions. At the extreme ends of the range, the membership of local unions may consist either of persons in a specific occupational category (e.g. teachers, bricklayers, locomotive engineers) in one or several workplaces, or else of all employees attached to an establishment or industry in a given locality regardless of occupation. In practice, the distinctions are rarely so clear-cut, but the fact remains that in countries with predominantly industrial unionism — as for example in Austria, the Federal Republic of Germany or Sweden — local unions tend to reflect the all-inclusive occupational structure of their parent organisations, whereas in countries with a mixed rather than uniform structure of unionism local unions will come in widely differing shapes: industrial, craft, white-collar, and so on. In the latter group, which consists predominantly of Anglo-Saxon countries, old-line craft unions exist side by side with occupationally mixed local unions, although it must be noted that the purely craft local union is gradually disappearing. Nevertheless, it is still entirely possible in these countries for a national union to accommodate within its ranks local unions of the most varied composition.

In countries where local unions have some degree of autonomy and have secured a firm foothold in the workplace, they often, even if not always, represent the vital link between the collective bargaining process and the individual worker, as for example in the United States. Where the local union or its equivalent is, however, not directly represented in the workplace, other ways may have to be found to establish the link. In general, there are three major ways in which unions can deal with situations in which they lack a secure and visible position at the workplace: they can leave workplace-centred tasks to other organisations; they can try to transform the basis of their membership from being essentially territory oriented to being workplace oriented; or they can seek to establish their own outposts in the workplace, but leave the territory-oriented union basis more or less intact.

The first solution is the traditional one in many countries of continental Europe. It relies on the presence in the workplace of works councils and analogous bodies whose legal status is distinct from that of the trade union organisations. Although this approach does not preclude the establishment of close links between unions and works councils, nor even a clear union dominance over the works councils, it does imply union acceptance of exclusion from the formal advocacy of worker interests at workplace levels. The functions of works councils and their relationship to unions will be reviewed below, but it should be indicated here that this particular approach has few advocates among unions nowadays.

The second solution has so far proved unattractive or excessively difficult, though developments in Sweden in the 1960s and 1970s come fairly close to exemplifying this approach. As of about 1960 the principal national confederation, the LO, contained a total of some 8,000 local organisations, distributed among the LO's national union affiliates. At about that time the LO and its national unions adopted a policy of concentration and consolidation at local level in order to correct what most union leaders regarded as excessive fragmentation and inefficiency. Besides encouraging local unions to join forces, the policy also envisaged the growth of sublocal organisations at workplace level. Over a period of about 20 years the number of local unions did indeed shrink to about 1,600. Coupled with a considerable increase in the LO's overall membership, the size of the average local union grew considerably, as did the capacity to employ a full-time local staff and to provide a wider range of services. At the same time the national organisations sought to improve the performance of the roughly 10,000 factory "clubs" or plant-level organisations which were already in existence.

The third solution, namely the establishment of union outposts at workplace level, is probably the most widely favoured one, even though it may create difficult problems of dual (or even multiple) representation resulting — quite aside from the proliferation caused by plural unionism — from the already well-entrenched position of works councils and equivalent bodies. Within recent decades the unions in Belgium, France, Italy and the Netherlands have made it one of their major aims to secure a recognised presence for themselves at the workplace, either by means of legislative support or through the conclusion of collective agreements at national or industry-wide levels, and have been successful in doing so. Of even longer standing than any of these is the workplace representation scheme in the Federal Republic of Germany, where it is particularly well developed in the metals sector.

It should be understood, of course, that these situations all differ from one another in important ways, not merely in terms of a legislative versus a contractual basis, but also in terms of involvement in collective bargaining.

In France the right of unions to maintain plant-level organisations and to seek employer recognition for them was embodied for the first time in the tripartite agreement of May 1968 (the so-called "Grenelle Agreement") and subsequently reaffirmed in the legislation of December 1968. Since then the number of plant sections has steadily increased and is currently approaching 40,000.[31] Their legal rights, particularly with respect to participation in collective bargaining at the level of the enterprise, have been considerably strengthened by the so-called Auroux laws of 1982.[32]

In Italy the precedent-making law enacted in 1970 (the so-called "workers' charter") provided for direct trade union representation at plant level. However, the intent of that legislation aimed more at the creation of facilities for the conduct of union business at the workplace than at the development of plant-level collective bargaining, not least because the unions themselves were opposed to any close definition of their bargaining rights at plant level for fear that this might in effect restrict their traditional freedom of action. While collective bargaining at plant level did make an important start in the first half of the 1970s, the unfavourable economic conditions of the second half led to what has been called "a major structural shift" in union decision-making from the local back to the national level.[33]

In the Netherlands, where the unions first recognised the need for closer relations with their members and consequently for more visible workplace activity in the early 1960s, the rules under which these activities are carried on have been incorporated into collective agreements, usually concluded at industry level. The rules apply to about three-fourths of all employees covered by a collective agreement.[34] They contain provisions focusing principally on the facilities which employers must provide (e.g. use of company-supplied office space and access to notice-boards), on protection of elected plant-level union representatives against dismissal, and on the relationship between union and works council.[35] They do not, however, assign to the union's workplace representatives any authority for the conclusion of plant-level agreements. In that respect, then, the situation in the Netherlands is comparable to practice in the Federal Republic of Germany which likewise does not confer on the union's plant representatives (the *Vertrauensleute*) any bargaining functions. But it clearly differs from the situation in Belgium, where one of the chief purposes of the "union delegation" in the plant is precisely to engage in collective bargaining over wages and working conditions (to be sure, within a two-tiered bargaining structure), as well as to handle individual grievances.[36]

A somewhat special case is that of Great Britain, where the rising importance of the shop steward under conditions of full employment in the decades immediately following the Second World War occurred independently of any deliberate effort to strengthen the position of unions at workplace level. In fact, although shop stewards are part of the union structure — even if not always a well-defined part — they derive their authority not only from the union (or unions) they represent but also from the members who elected them, and if anything more from the latter than the former. That ambivalence has been one of several factors enabling the stewards to act not infrequently with little regard to national union policy. Other factors have been the sizeable increase in the number of full-time shop stewards paid by the employer, the fact that the local branch to which union members belong is not as a rule based on the workplace but on place of residence, and, in firms with multiple union representation, the prevalence of joint shop stewards' committees. Joint shop stewards' committees are not directly answerable to a higher-level union body since they are composed of the stewards of several unions. Consequently, where an enterprise or establishment is large enough to support the development of a shop stewards' organisation, this body — i.e. the shop stewards' committee or the combine committee in multi-plant firms — will overshadow the branch as the principal locus of decision-making.[37]

There has always been considerable variation in the degree to which stewards depend on assistance by full-time union officials, but overall one might have expected the economic recession to increase the dependence, given the stewards' loss of bargaining power. Actually that has not happened, as Professor Roberts has pointed out, and not least because of the unions' need to conserve their resources under financial stringency.[38]

Works councils

Until fairly recently, as we noted above, trade unions in many continental European countries did not play a very active role at the workplace. Their focal point of operation was generally an industry-wide bargaining relationship with an employers' association, less frequently with a large individual firm. For historical reasons which have been explored elsewhere, the representation of employee interests at workplace level in Belgium, France, the Federal Republic of Germany, Italy, the Netherlands and other countries was exercised by specialised institutions whose name differs from country to country but to which we shall refer here uniformly as "works councils".

Works councils, as the term is used here, are not within the organisational structure of unions because they are not an integral part of the union hierarchy. They must be distinguished, therefore, from the shop committees or plant sections of a union and from North American or British shop stewards, which are an integral part of the union structure even when they appear to be acting rather independently of the policies of their organisations. Nor are works councils voluntary entities in the sense that they exist, as unions do, at the will of their members. Instead they are very often bodies whose existence is provided for by law or else, but less frequently, by collective agreements concluded between confederations of trade unions and employers' associations.

It must also be emphasised that works councils, unlike unions in certain countries, have invariably an all-inclusive representational responsibility. Their constituency is made up of virtually all employees in the enterprise or establishment except only for those at the very top, whether or not the employees are union members, and they are bound by law (or by collective agreement) to represent the interests of all employees without distinction. In this one respect they are comparable to unions in the United States which, in return for exclusive rights of representation, have a legally imposed obligation to represent all employees in the bargaining unit fairly and without distinction as to union membership.

In practice, of course, there can be — and indeed there are — many links between unions and works councils, and some of the links have achieved legal backing. For example, in a number of countries unions have an explicit legal right to present lists of candidates for election to works councils, but this right is generally not an exclusive one, for non-union groups may also present lists of candidates, or in some instances may do so after the first round of elections. Actually, most works council members are union members or become union members after their election. In the Federal Republic of Germany the proportion of union members elected to works councils has quite consistently been close to 80 per cent on a national basis. Other ties stem from the right of unions to attend works council meetings (in the Federal Republic of Germany, for example, on request of one-fourth of the members of the works council), the training and education programmes for works council members organised by unions, and the technical assistance which unions furnish to works councils.

Although there is no uniform set of functions with which all works councils are identified, historically two major sets of responsibilities have stood out. One was the promotion of a co-operative relationship between the employer (or management) and the employees, while the other was the representation of employees' interests. In some countries the emphasis was on co-operation, in others on advocacy, and in still others the situation was highly ambivalent. In general, the tendency during the past few decades has been in the direction of more explicit interest representation. This is strikingly exemplified by the Netherlands, where formerly the works councils were bipartite organs meeting under the chairmanship of the employer or his representative (as is still the case in such countries as Belgium and France) and doing so chiefly for consultative and informational purposes. Under 1979 amendments to the works council law, however, the employer's position on the works council has been eliminated, while at the same time the law has strengthened the protective and interest representational functions of the works council.

The increasing emphasis on interest representation has also been reinforced by the expansion of so-called co-determination rights which the legislation of several European countries grants to works councils. In many vital areas works councils have achieved equal or near equal standing with employers in making decisions of critical importance to the enterprise, particularly though by no means solely in matters concerning working conditions and employment policies, and at least advisory rights in such areas as investment or disinvestment decisions and plant location. Allowing for substantial variations by country and subject, works councils may have full co-determination rights, may be able to veto employers' decisions for at least a given period of time or may have the right to be consulted and to give advice.

As regards collective bargaining, which is of principal interest here, works councils have traditionally been in an ambivalent position. On the one hand, they have frequently been excluded by law, and sometimes by custom, from negotiating collective agreements in the sense defined by law because the trade unions have opposed any dilution of their exclusive right to engage in collective bargaining leading to the conclusion of legally valid collective agreements. (This does not necessarily prevent works councils from entering into agreements and understandings with employers that are called by some name other than collective agreement.) On the other hand, the works councils have frequently had an explicitly assigned responsibility for monitoring the proper application of collective agreements by the employer.

The balance of the relationship between trade unions and works councils was never a perfectly stable and harmonious one, but until fairly recently the established "division of labour" appeared to be the optimum solution to the problem created by the existence of two parallel systems of employee representation. The unions alone negotiated collective agreements and did so mostly at industry level, but because they lacked a workplace structure the implementation of the agreements became the task of the works councils which did have the requisite organisation.

In the past few years, however, a number of developments have occurred which raise doubts about the continued viability of the long-established relationship. So important are these developments that the European Trade Union Institute (ETUI), which is the research arm of the European Trade Union Confederation, has suggested that "in the long run there may be a need to review in depth the system of works councils. *In some cases it might even be wise to alter or even abolish the whole system.*"[39]

On the union side the most important innovation has already been pointed out, namely the establishment of a union base at workplace level in a sizeable number of countries, including France, the Federal Republic of Germany, Italy and the Netherlands. On the works council side the key development is the increase in activities that in fact constitute collective bargaining, even if that is not always the name attached to it. In other words, there is a reciprocal penetration of areas formerly kept more or less separate: unions at workplace level are taking on works council functions, while works councils are becoming engaged in work that unions have hitherto regarded as their sole prerogative. With this reciprocal penetration go certain changes in attitude, particularly in the transformation of works councils from essentially co-operative to claims-making bodies.

How the unions will try to resolve the problem is at this time not yet clear. For the unions to try to displace and absorb the works councils entirely is of course a possibility, as the ETUI suggests, but probably not more than remotely so since in most countries works councils are too strongly entrenched in law and practice. Moreover, such an attempt would probably run into determined employer opposition. More likely is a continued union effort to control the works councils and to monitor their activities by means of the unions' plant sections, together with an effort to reach an agreed demarcation of responsibilities. In practice, however, a certain amount of overlapping representation may be unavoidable.

THE EMPLOYERS

In all the countries here reviewed the representation of employers' interests in collective bargaining is shared between individual enterprises (or establishments) acting on their own behalf and groups of enterprises acting jointly through an association of employers. The division is, however, not equal. In Western European countries employers' associations are the predominant force, while in Japan and North America the enterprise or a subsidiary part of it occupies the leading position.

Employers' associations should be distinguished from trade associations. Trade associations represent employers' interests in "economic" matters such as industrial policies, tariffs, taxation and the like. Employers' associations, by contrast, specialise in representing the industrial relations interests of their member firms. Increasingly the two types of associations are combining their forces, but the concern here is in any event with employers' associations and the individual enterprise.

Employers' associations [40]

An outstanding characteristic of the industrial relations systems of Western Europe, and to some extent also of Australia, is the high degree of organisation and the readiness for joint action that one encounters among employers in the private sector. Although in recent years there has emerged a major trend towards bargaining at enterprise and establishment levels even in countries where association bargaining used to be almost the exclusive rule, a substantial difference still remains by comparison with the situation in Japan and North America.

Information on the membership of employers' associations is not as readily available as comparable data for unions, and no attempt will be made to present a comprehensive review. But in so far as data exist, they indicate that the rate of organisation among employers' associations equals or exceeds the corresponding rate for the trade unions. A few examples will illustrate the point. The Federation of Belgian Enterprises,[41] whose 48 industrial and sectoral associations contain some 35,000 enterprises, represents 75 per cent of all firms with ten or more employees.[42] In France, where the rate of organisation among employees has customarily been quite low, around 90 per cent of the 900,000 firms in the private sector are affiliated with the principal body of French employers, the National Council of French Employers (CNPF),[43] mostly through their membership of various CNPF-affiliated industrial and regional associations.[44] The central organisation for employers in the Federal Republic of Germany, the Confederation of German Employers' Associations (BDA),[45] encompasses through its 47 affiliated industry associations about 70 to 80 per cent of all privately owned undertakings, employing approximately 90 per cent of the relevant group of employees.[46] For Great Britain the most authoritative figures indicate that the Confederation of British Industries holds a total of about 300,000 member firms (mostly represented through industry and trade associations) which in turn employ some 12 million employees.[47] Finally, the Swedish employers' confederation for the private sector, the Swedish Employers' Federation (SAF),[48] is composed of some 37 member associations whose 38,000 affiliated firms employ a total of over 1.3 million workers.[49]

In seeking to account for the substantial degree of organisation, certain factors stand out. One is the search by employers for collective security, if necessary at the cost of having to exchange a certain portion of their individual freedom of action in return for the greater bargaining strength which comes from a consolidation of their separate forces. A second is the need for competent representation of employers' interests in relations with the State, the public at large and the media. A third is the provision of specialised services that, at least until recently, individual firms found too costly and too difficult to provide for themselves.

Typically, therefore, employers' associations encompass a wide range of functions: representational and lobbying activities in relation to the legislative and administrative branches of government; public information and public relations services to achieve effective dissemination of employers' viewpoints; research and data collection services as well as the provision of legal advice; education and training of specialists in personnel and industrial relations; and in particular a large variety of services related to collective bargaining and other dealings with unions, or the avoidance of such dealings. Prominent among the bargaining-related services are the formulation of common personnel policies, the analysis of the collective bargaining proposals of the unions, the development of an employer strategy in negotiations, the interpretation of the provisions of existing agreements, and the leadership of employers' actions in the event of industrial conflict.

In recent years the service functions have been affected by two rather contradictory trends. On the one hand is a growing demand for the services provided by employers' associations, which stems from the increasing complexity of industrial relations and in particular its legal and institutional contexts. That the larger firms' share in this demand is indicated by the findings of a British study according to which "most services [provided by employers' associations] have greater utilisation by large than small establishments".[50] On the other hand there has been a substantial increase in the number of firms, including medium-sized and even some of the smaller ones, that have established their own internal services to provide for their industrial relations requirements.

Most characteristic of the contemporary structure of employers' associations is its complexity. Among the major organising principles for the formation of associations are industrial attachment, geographic location, size of firm, ownership (i.e. whether publicly or privately owned), and even philosophical-religious beliefs (as in the case of the Netherlands, where Christian employers' associations exist alongside the non-denominational organisations). Any one of these criteria may be and indeed has been the basis for the formation of an employers' association. But for purposes of collective bargaining the industry-based associations are almost everywhere the most important ones, except in Italy and perhaps Australia, where associations based on territorial criteria play a more important role. Moreover, in most countries the industry associations constitute the most powerful echelon in the hierarchy of employers' associations.

The peak of the organisational pyramid among employers' associations is constituted in most countries by a confederation of employers' associations. As a rule there is only a single all-encompassing confederation. Among the exceptions are countries where the trade associations have a peak confederation of their own, and those others, like Canada and the United States, where no national federation can speak authoritatively in collective bargaining on behalf of all employers.

Most of the time the peak confederations are composed of two types of affiliates: industry associations and regional associations. However, in countries too small to have significant regional subdivisions, as in some of the Benelux and Scandinavian countries, the peak confederations consist almost entirely of industry associations. Some peak confederations also accept individual firms into membership. Peak confederations are far less involved in collective bargaining than industry associations. In fact, they may even be barred from it by their own rules or by the unwillingness of industry associations to permit transgressions on territory which they consider their own. Should a situation nevertheless arise which calls for the direct involvement in collective bargaining of a peak confederation, as occurred in France in the late 1960s, difficult negotiations may ensue between the confederation and its affiliates.

There are, however, some situations in which the peak confederations have become regular participants in collective negotiations. This is so especially in the Scandinavian countries, where the peak confederations have on many occasions concluded agreements with their counterparts on the trade union side not only over the establishment of the basic rules by which the system of industrial relations is to operate but also over the terms of employment, including basic wage agreements, which then become guide-lines for the negotiators at the next lower level, the industry association level. Even where they do not conclude framework agreements with their counterparts on the union side, the peak confederations in the Scandinavian countries exercise considerable authority over their affiliated employers' associations. In Denmark the central body — the Danish Employers' Confederation (DA) [51] — retains the right to approve all collective agreements negotiated by its member organisations, and at least one recent observer has concluded that, contrary to developments in Sweden, the trend in Denmark is towards the exercise of increasing central authority by the DA.[52]

Seen in a larger framework, current trends do seem to run in the opposite direction, that is, towards more decentralisation, although the industry-level employers' associations still occupy a key position in collective bargaining. In fact, in almost all countries where employers' associations occupy a foremost position in the industrial relations system the major bargaining activity on the employer side is carried on by industry associations. Generally, they exercise one of two roles in collective bargaining. If the basic negotiations are customarily conducted on an industry-wide basis and cover the entire country, the national association acts directly as the bargaining agent on behalf of its employer constituency. This tends to be the case especially in the smaller countries, for example in Denmark or the Netherlands, where there are no significant regional subdivisions. If, however, the basic negotiations are conducted on a regional or local basis, as is likely to be the case in the larger countries, the association will act more as a co-ordinating and resource body than as a direct party to the negotiations.

In joining an association, employers delegate the task of concluding collective agreements but retain certain responsibilities, especially those connected with the implementation of the agreement. Since employers' associations are not only coalitions whose members share certain vital interests but also alliances of competitors, maintaining the cohesiveness of the association is bound to be a primary association aim. That requires reasonably uniform adherence to the agreement, even if under certain conditions associations permit their members to negotiate supplemental terms. In any event, overly generous use of this possibility or deliberate attempts to undercut the agreement — as well as widely diverging applications of its terms — will almost certainly jeopardise the effectiveness or even the existence of the association.

Indeed, the disciplinary problems of employers' associations are substantial, given the often very large differences in size of firm, profitability and attitude towards unions, and if anything even greater during a period of decentralising trends in collective bargaining. Penalties for rule breakers are difficult to impose and may be counterproductive (in the sense of losing instead of retaining members), while reliance on peer pressure is especially unlikely to be effective during periods of labour shortages or sharpened competition in the market. Most associations are therefore forced to rely chiefly upon moral authority to maintain discipline, but of course they must also seek continually to enhance their usefulness. In this connection attention has been called to some recent developments in the Netherlands that may also be applicable to other countries:

First, the personnel of the associations is being more professionalised in order to make full-time experts available to employers ... Second, funds are being built up for supporting or reimbursing employers in serious conflicts with unions (a mutual employer-guarantee arrangement), and payments are being made to individual employers.[53]

Even when such efforts are successful, one should nevertheless expect association solidarity to remain subject to challenge, whether from employers unwilling to subject themselves to association discipline or whether from unions looking for weaknesses in association ranks.

Management and the individual enterprise

Whereas in Australia and in European countries the negotiation of collective agreements has, on the whole, been regarded as a matter external to the firm, in Japan and North America collective bargaining has developed as pre-eminently the task of the individual enterprise. The reasons for the difference are not entirely clear, but are likely to be connected with national traditions, policies and preferences. The strong competitive element in the American business ethos, reinforced by a long-standing national anti-trust policy, forms the background against which the predominance of individual enterprise bargaining in the United States needs to be appraised. By contrast, the sense of shared interests and solidarity among European employers and their greater willingness to submit to self-regulation in trade matters, which goes back to the guild era, probably helps to account for their willingness to act jointly in industrial relations.

Of course, there are exceptions to the generalisation. A considerable amount of single-enterprise bargaining has existed in European countries for many years, for example at Renault in France, Volkswagen in the Federal Republic of Germany, the Ford Motor Company in Great Britain and Philips in the Netherlands. Conversely, association bargaining is by no means unknown to Japan or North America. For example, in 1980 almost two-thirds of all agreements in the non-manufacturing sector of the United States resulted from negotiations in multi-employer bargaining units.[54] And as regards Japan, a recent study has pointed out that "Japanese employers have for years banded closely together in formally organised associations in order to develop common labour policies and collective bargaining positions".[55] Nevertheless, the basic difference remains.

That there is a particularly strong need for specialised management resources in industrial relations where enterprise bargaining is the practice hardly needs to be pointed out. What is perhaps less self-evident is the growing need for such specialisation even in countries where, to be sure, associations are chiefly responsible for collective bargaining but where the workplace has become an important secondary (sometimes even primary) arena for the negotiated determination of wages and employment conditions.[56]

That this is not yet everywhere fully realised is indicated by the findings of a British survey according to which the use of personnel specialists is still rather underdeveloped, although less so in the larger than the smaller firms, while many personnel or industrial relations officers are not specially qualified or trained for their responsibilities.[57]

Because it is in this respect unusually well advanced, the situation in the United States should be of special interest. As Quinn Mills has pointed out, specialists in industrial relations and personnel administration — two functional areas that are considered indivisible by some corporations, separable by others — are now represented in sizeable numbers in the managerial ranks of American business: "By 1979, unionised companies reported a ratio of one staff manager per 200 to 400 union-represented employees." [58] Moreover, they have also established themselves strongly at corporate headquarters level, where they have substantial access to senior management. Since staff executives in labour relations tend to spend their entire career in this function — fully four out of five top labour relations executives having passed their whole career in the industrial relations or personnel function, according to Mills — their seniority, bolstered by the relatively large number of people in the speciality, suggests that a high degree of professionalism has been achieved. Other observers have pointed out that in the past decade industrial relations specialists have moved up in status and are paid more than most other management specialists.

An important qualification, however, has recently been expressed by Kochan and McKersie who suggest that, in an environment characterised by increased international competititon, deregulation and other pressures, the labour relations professionals in some unionised corporations have become less influential and more isolated from strategic decision-making because of their concentration on traditional bargaining activities. Their position and influence have been captured, Kochan and McKersie conclude, by "new-style" human resource professionals whose concerns with long-term manpower planning, increased productivity and cost-reducing personnel policies are more attuned to the goals of top management and who sometimes follow "a very aggressive and sophisticated strategy of union avoidance".[59]

Public sector enterprises

Although, as already indicated, collective bargaining in the public service is not included in this overview, the arrangements prevailing in publicly owned industrial enterprises and boards are relevant to this discussion, especially since in some countries private and public enterprises coexist in the same sector of industry, as for example in automobile manufacturing in France, the Federal Republic of Germany and Great Britain. Formal authority over the key decisions of public sector enterprises is virtually everywhere vested in the government, but the degree to which it is exercised — and consequently the degree to which managers of publicly owned enterprises are able to take independent decisions in collective bargaining — is so variable that generalisations are not really feasible.

At one extreme is the situation in the Federal Republic of Germany, and even more so in Austria, two countries in which the government at national or individual state level is sole or part owner of numerous corporations in a wide variety of industries. In both countries the collective bargaining agreements for the various sectors, when concluded on an industry-wide basis, are applicable to the publicly owned corporations in the same way as they apply to private firms. By the same token the public corporations are subject to the same civil and labour laws that apply to private industry, so that their labour relations "have no relation whatever to public employment".[60] Sharply contrasting is the situation in Japan, where the employees of public corporations and national enterprises do have the right to bargain collectively (though not the right to strike), but where that right has little meaning because the enterprises "are under the strict financial control of the Treasury and their managements have no powers to negotiate pay increases with unions".[61]

The bargaining powers granted to public corporation managers in other countries fall somewhere in between. In France the Government engaged in a major effort in the 1960s and 1970s to foster collective bargaining in publicly owned enterprises and granted a corresponding degree of authority to managers to conclude agreements. Nevertheless, at least one critical observer concluded "that in practice the major decisions are taken by the Government itself, especially in very large undertakings . . . and that the state-owned undertakings [do] not enjoy any real independence save in respect of routine administration . . .".[62]

A similar ambivalence prevails in Great Britain, where ministers have used their powers over the boards of nationalised firms and industries sparingly, but where they nevertheless have great influence over them. Moreover:

Pay settlements in nationalised industries normally require the blessing of the Cabinet, if not its formal approval. For many years the Government tried to maintain the fiction that labour matters were within the managerial discretion of the boards, and board chairmen were required to support this pretence. However, since 1958 the secret has been less well kept. In that year, and again in 1962 and 1965, successive Prime Ministers themselves conducted the final stages of negotiations on railway pay, and in 1972 and 1974 another Prime Minister had to negotiate with the Mineworkers.[63]

The issue of ministerial intervention has several aspects. One is the complex problem of ministers having ultimate political responsibility for the operation of public enterprises and more broadly for the economy as a whole. Within limits this point always acts as a restraint on the freedom of action of managers in the public sector, but usually the question remains in the background until a particularly acute problem develops, as for instance a strike in a vital public enterprise. A second aspect is the role of treasuries and legislatures. In relatively normal times public enterprises that are able to balance their books are likely to have more freedom of action in collective bargaining than industries chronically in need of public subsidies. But during periods of financial stringency and restraints on expenditures, collective bargaining in all public sector industries becomes inevitably an object of close ministerial (and public) scrutiny.

The wide range of practices as regards collective bargaining has its parallel in the area of employers' association membership. Basically the question is whether institutions created for the defence of private employer interests can admit public corporations into membership without diluting their essence. In most instances employers' associations have answered the question in the negative, but there are many exceptions.[64] A singular exception because of its blanket character is the case of Austria, where the nationalised industries or enterprises are as a rule members of the statutory bodies representing the interests of employers by branch or sector. More commonly, however, it is at the level of the peak employers' confederation rather than the industry association that nationalised industries and the public sector corporations are granted admission, usually in the form of a special (i.e. second-class) membership. On the other hand, the Renault Company, one of the largest employers in France, does hold membership in the industry association for its industrial sector, the powerful Metal and Mining Trades Federation (UIMM).[65, 66]

Notes

[1] In the United States the Bureau of Labor Statistics began in 1965 to include employees' associations in its listing of trade union organisations and in its union membership statistical series, provided that the organisations were engaged in collective bargaining and related activities. See United States, Bureau of Labor Statistics: *Directory of trade unions and employees' associations*, Bulletin No. 1750 (Washington, DC, 1972), p. 58.

[2] See the introductory chapter of George Sayers Bain and Robert Price: *Profiles of union growth: A comparative statistical portrait of eight countries* (Oxford, Basil Blackwell, 1980).

[3] For the United States, see in this respect Richard B. Freeman and James L. Medoff: "New estimates of private sector unionism in the United States", in *Industrial and Labor Relations Review*, Jan. 1979, pp. 143-174. For Great Britain, see A. W. J. Thomson and L. C. Hunter: "Great Britain", in John T. Dunlop and Walter Galenson (eds.): *Labor in the twentieth century* (New York, Academic Press, 1978), p. 102. For the Federal Republic of Germany, see Wolfgang Streeck: "Politischer Wandel und organisatorische Reformen" [Political change and organisational reform], in *Gewerkschaftliche Monatshefte* [Trade Union Monthly] (Cologne), Oct. 1978, p. 633. For Japan, see Kikuchi Kozo: "The Japanese enterprise union and its functions", in Tokunaga Shigeyoshi and Joachim Bergmann (eds.): *Industrial relations in transition: The cases of Japan and the Federal Republic of Germany* (Tokyo, University of Tokyo Press, 1984), p. 173, table 2.

[4] Some American observers take the view that less than half of the decline in union membership in the United States can be attributed to structural shifts in the economy and the labour force. Their point is, of course, that any explanation of union membership decline must also take into account changes in the behaviour of the parties, for example greater employer resistance to unions. (See Thomas A. Kochan et al.: "Strategic choice and industrial relations theory", in *Industrial Relations*, winter 1984, p. 18.) See also Richard B. Freeman and James L. Medoff: *What do unions do?* (New York, Basic Books, 1984), pp. 224-243.

[5] See Albeda below, pp. 253-255.

[6] See Blanpain below, p. 178.

[7] See Giugni below, pp. 226-228.

[8] See Shirai below, p. 243.

[9] *Landsorganisationen.*

[10] *Tjänstemännens Centralorganisation.*

[11] *Privattjanstemannakartellen.*

[12] For other recent examples, see ILO: *Report of the Director-General*, International Labour Conference, 71st Session, Geneva, 1985, pp. 29-32.

[13] For a discussion of basic agreements, see the introductory chapter by Efrén Córdova in ILO: *Selected basic agreements and joint declarations on labour-management relations*,

Labour-Management Relations Series No. 63 (Geneva, 1983). The publication also contains verbatim texts of a large number of basic agreements.

14 For the most comprehensive analysis of the forces behind the growth of national unions in the United States, see Lloyd Ulman: *The rise of the national union* (Cambridge, Massachusetts, Harvard University Press, 1955).

15 For a detailed review of the early importance of national unions in Germany, see Klaus Schönhoven: *Expansion und Konzentration: Studien zur Entwicklung der freien Gewerkschaften im Wilhelminischen Deutschland 1890 bis 1919* [Expansion and concentration: Studies on the development of free trade unions in Wilhelmian Germany, 1890 to 1919] (Stuttgart, Klett-Cotta, 1980).

16 A general union is an organisation which recognises no limits by industry or occupation in its efforts to organise members but which recruits over a wide occupational and industrial spectrum. See the entry for "general union", in A. I. Marsh and E. O. Evans: *The dictionary of industrial relations* (London, Hutchinson, 1973).

17 Bram Peper and Gerrit van Kooten: "The Netherlands: From an ordered harmonic to a bargaining relationship", in Solomon Barkin (ed.): *Worker militancy and its consequences* (New York, Praeger, 2nd ed., 1983), p. 135 ff.

18 See John P. Windmuller: "Concentration trends in union structure: An international comparison", in *Industrial and Labor Relations Review*, Oct. 1981, pp. 43-57.

19 *Deutscher Gewerkschaftsbund.*

20 Joachim Bergmann and Walther Müller-Jentsch: "The Federal Republic of Germany", in Barkin, op. cit., pp. 240-241.

21 See Fürstenberg below, p. 212.

22 Studies of subsidiary levels in national unions are rare. For the Federal Republic of Germany, see Manfred Wilke: *Die Funktionäre: Apparat und Demokratie im Deutschen Gewerkschaftsbund* [Union officials: Machinery and democracy in the German Confederation of Trade Unions] (Munich/Zurich, Piper Verlag, 1979), p. 57 ff.

23 For distinctions between additional types of subsidiary organisations in the United States, see Edwin F. Beal and James P. Begin: *The practice of collective bargaining* (Homewood, Illinois, Irwin, 1982), p. 114 ff.

24 See the chapter on "Full-time trade union officials", in Anthony Carew: *Democracy and government in European trade unions* (London, Allen & Unwin, 1976).

25 For the British experience in this regard, see especially H. A. Clegg: *The changing system of industrial relations in Great Britain* (Oxford, Basil Blackwell, 1979), pp. 186-194. It should be noted that not all employers refuse to bargain separately with the various unions representing their employees. Clegg points out that the British steel industry "has traditionally dealt separately with each union representing production workers, of which there are now four [organisations]" (ibid., p. 189).

26 Solomon Levine: "Japan", in Albert A. Blum (ed.): *International handbook of industrial relations* (Westport, Connecticut, Greenwood, 1981), p. 337.

27 Clegg, op. cit., pp. 187-188.

28 See Herbert R. Northrup and Richard L. Rowan: *Multinational collective bargaining attempts* (Philadelphia, Pennsylvania, University of Pennsylvania, The Wharton School, Industrial Research Unit, 1979).

29 For Great Britain, see especially W. W. Daniel and Neil Millward: *Workplace industrial relations in Britain: The DE/PSI/SSRC Survey* (London, Heinemann Educational Books, 1983), p. 83 ff.

30 Streeck, op. cit., p. 17.

31 See Caire below, p. 195.

32 See for example *Social and Labour Bulletin* (Geneva, ILO), Mar. 1983, pp. 22-26.

33 Pietro Merli Brandini: "Italy", in Barkin, op. cit., p. 99.

34 *European Industrial Relations Review* (London), Dec. 1984, pp. 20-21.

35 See Albeda below, p. 260.

36 See Blanpain below, p. 187.

37 William Brown et al.: "Factors shaping shop steward organization in Britain", in *British Journal of Industrial Relations*, July 1978, pp. 139-159.

[38] See Roberts below, pp. 290-291.

[39] European Trade Union Institute: *Collective bargaining in Western Europe 1978-1979 and prospects for 1980* (Brussels, 1980), p. 154. Italics added.

[40] The following discussion is based in part on John P. Windmuller and Alan Gladstone (eds.): *Employers associations and industrial relations: A comparative study* (Oxford, Clarendon Press, 1984).

[41] *Fédération des entreprises de Belgique.*

[42] See Blanpain below, p. 179.

[43] *Conseil national du patronat français.*

[44] *European Industrial Relations Review*, Oct. 1978, p. 23.

[45] *Bundesvereinigung der Deutschen Arbeitgeberverbände.*

[46] See Fürstenberg below, p. 210. Cf. *European Industrial Relations Review*, Dec. 1978, pp. 8-9.

[47] Keith Sisson: "Employers' organisations", in George S. Bain (ed.): *Industrial relations in Britain* (Oxford, Basil Blackwell, 1983), p. 124.

[48] *Svenska Arbetsgivareföreningen.*

[49] Göran Skogh: "Employers' associations in Sweden", in Windmuller and Gladstone, op. cit., p. 159.

[50] William Brown (ed.): *The changing contours of British industrial relations* (Oxford, Basil Blackwell, 1981), p. 21.

[51] *Dansk Arbejdsgiverforening.*

[52] Colin Gill: "Industrial relations in Denmark: Problems and perspectives", in *Industrial Relations Journal* (United Kingdom), spring 1984, p. 47.

[53] Peper and van Kooten, op. cit., p. 139. See also Albeda below.

[54] Richard B. Freeman and James L. Medoff: *What do unions do?* (New York, Basic Books, 1984), p. 39, table 2-5.

[55] Levine, op. cit., p. 318.

[56] A particularly interesting attempt to document the rise of professionalism in industrial relations by quantitative methods has been made by John Niland in an article on "Research and reform in industrial relations", in *Journal of Industrial Relations* (Sydney, Industrial Relations Society of Australia), Dec. 1981, pp. 482-503. Niland bases his analysis on enrolment figures in university industrial relations courses and degree programmes, employer specifications for filling vacancies in industrial relations positions, and the formal qualifications of industrial relations specialists as indicated by the biographical data in the *Australian Industrial Relations Directory*.

[57] See Daniel and Millward, op. cit., Ch. V, and their summary on pp. 285-287. For a somewhat different perspective, see also John Purcell and Keith Sisson: "Strategies and practice in the management of industrial relations", in Bain, op. cit., pp. 95-120.

[58] D. Quinn Mills: "Management performance", in Jack Stieber et al. (eds.): *US industrial relations 1950-1980: A critical assessment* (Madison, Wisconsin, Industrial Relations Research Association, 1981), p. 120.

[59] See Thomas A. Kochan and Robert B. McKersie: "Collective bargaining — Pressures for change", in *Sloan Management Review* (Cambridge, Massachusetts), summer 1983, p. 64.

[60] William H. McPherson: *Public employee relations in West Germany* (Ann Arbor, Michigan, University of Michigan, Institute of Labor and Industrial Relations, 1971), p. 13.

[61] See Shirai below, pp. 245.

[62] See Jean-Maurice Verdier: "Labour relations in the public sector of France", in Charles M. Rehmus (ed.): *Public employment labor relations: An overview of eleven nations* (Ann Arbor, Michigan, University of Michigan, Institute of Labor and Industrial Relations, 1975), p. 91.

[63] Clegg, op. cit., p. 109.

[64] By law, public sector enterprises in Italy are prohibited from joining employers' associations in the private sector, but they do have their own associations.

[65] *Union des industries métallurgiques et minières.*

[66] Verdier, op. cit., p. 87.

RULES AND PROCEDURES IN BARGAINING

3

The time has passed when collective bargaining consisted of a relatively simple set of negotiations ending with the conclusion of an agreement. One observer even suggests, perhaps with over-emphasis, that "modern collective bargaining is a continuous and extremely complicated process; in fact, it has no end and no beginning".[1] However that may be, the aim of reaching an agreement is still central to the task. As one set of authors has observed: "In the drama of collective bargaining as a continuous process ... nearly all actions over time by management and union representatives are geared, consciously or unconsciously, to the period of actual contract negotiation."[2]

For collective bargaining to function effectively, the parties must address themselves to, and resolve, a number of procedural matters. They must have a means for resolving questions involving recognition, agree to meet at reasonable times and places to negotiate, determine an agenda and deal with a host of other issues vital to the proper functioning of the negotiations. This chapter will review several of the more significant procedural matters, not in order to single out the one "best" approach but rather to indicate the range and diversity of possible approaches.

RECOGNITION

In order that unions and employers, or associations of employers, may engage in negotiations leading to a collective agreement — and subsequently to co-operate in the implementation of the agreement — the parties must first acknowledge each other as legitimate and competent representatives of their constituents.[3] Thus, recognition must precede negotiations. That has rarely caused any problems in so far as union recognition of the employer side is concerned. After all, recalcitrant unions would only block themselves from engaging in what is probably their most important activity. But the reverse does not hold true: employers' refusal to recognise unions has often been a major issue of controversy. During the formative period of the contemporary industrial relations systems, disputes over the recognition of unions as the legitimate representatives of employees, or at least of those employees who chose to be union members, resulted in struggles which often involved the very existence of the trade union movement. Even nowadays, a controversy over recognition can from time to time escalate into a major conflict, although in most instances voluntary or statutory rules are in place to avoid that.

With some important exceptions to be noted shortly, the public authorities in European countries and Japan have generally refrained from adopting measures that would impose on employers a statutory obligation to recognise unions. For example, as Professor Delamotte points out, "French legislation has never made provision for the procedure of 'recognition' or approval of a trade union. Neither does it recognise the principle that the employees of a bargaining unit must be represented by a single trade union." [4] However, French law as well as Belgian law does contain the concept of "the most representative union", and unions which qualify for that designation are entitled to important privileges in collective bargaining.[5] Because of the general absence of statutory regulation, the extension of recognition of unions by employers has depended in most countries either on the economic power of unions to compel it or on the employers' voluntary acceptance of collective bargaining — and thus acceptance also of unions. In most countries, it would be fair to summarise, recognition came about only gradually, industry by industry, or sometimes enterprise by enterprise. Occasionally, however, a major event, as exemplified by the 1918 Revolution in Germany or the emergence of a Popular Front Government in France in 1936, or a joint employer-union effort to forestall government intervention, as in Sweden in the 1930s, led to recognition and negotiations between the peak federations on the union and employer sides which then became a signal for affiliated organisations at the subsidiary levels of individual industries and unions to follow the lead given to them by their parent bodies.

Conflicts over recognition arise mainly from the presence of one or several among the following situations: an employer's refusal in principle to accede to union demands for recognition; uncertainty or disagreement over the desire of the employees to be represented by a union; competing claims between two or more unions over recognition and representation rights; and disagreements about the proper area or territory for bargaining, i.e. about the shape of the so-called bargaining unit.

By and large, European countries have preferred to resolve recognition issues by voluntary action, that is by action of the parties themselves, as distinguished from the essentially legislative-administrative approach in North America. Several circumstances contributed to make that possible. One was the difference in the bargaining structure. As Professor Thomson explains:

Under centralised bargaining, recognition of unions as a prerequisite for collective bargaining is only of limited significance once a certain threshold density has been achieved. This is because the reach of collective bargaining is more determined by the extent of employer association membership than by the unionisation of any one plant or firm ... Under a decentralised structure, on the other hand, recognition is a vital issue at every plant in an industry. Even allowing for pattern-setting, there will be differences in terms and conditions between plants, and if the non-union sector is or becomes sizeable, it may significantly affect union bargaining power in the organised plants.[6]

A second factor had its basis in the fact that for the individual employer there was usually no need to make an explicit decision with regard to recognition because that was not how most unions approached the matter. For them, the appropriate counterpart was the association of employers, and if the association recognised the union it did so on behalf of all its members. Thus, it was the act of joining an association engaged in a bargaining relationship with the union (or unions) rather than an individual decision to grant or to withhold recognition that determined the position of the individual enterprise in the matter of recognition.

A third factor was the essentially industrial structure of unions which achieved predominance in the first few decades of the century. This obviated to a large extent — but certainly not entirely — those problems of recognition that stemmed from the conflicting claims of two or more unions. What it did not take care of, however, was the complication resulting from the existence of plural unions based on ideological beliefs. But that difficulty, as we shall indicate below, was not insuperable.

Finally, it was of great importance to the development of a voluntarist approach to recognition issues that in most countries the central or peak federations on both sides — employers and unions — had sufficient authority to settle any recognition disputes, including jurisdictional disputes, that might occur between their affiliates, and sufficient flexibility to settle among themselves any outstanding issues of principle.

By contrast, Canada and the United States have relied largely on legislative-administrative measures to resolve recognition disputes, and no doubt they have done so in large measure because, in contrast to the situation in most of Europe, the decision with regard to recognition was — and remains — largely a matter for the individual enterprise, because the mixed union structure has left ample room for conflicting claims to recognition, and because the peak federations have often not been strong enough to impose their authority in recognition disputes.

In the United States the union selected by a vote of a majority of the employees in a defined bargaining unit must be recognised by the employer as the exclusive representative for all employees in that unit. Several important elements are thereby resolved:

— the basic decision with regard to representation and recognition is made by majority rule in a secret ballot election;

— the employer must recognise the majority union as the exclusive representative for all employees in the bargaining unit;

— the majority union assumes an obligation to represent all employees and not merely its own members; and

— the boundaries of the bargaining unit are determined by an administrative agency if the parties fail to agree.

47

On the whole the system has done what its designers sought to achieve, namely to resolve recognition disputes without resort to open conflict. But that does not mean that the procedure has removed or lessened employer opposition to recognition. Many employers exercise the right actively to oppose the unionisation of their employees and to try to defeat union organisation campaigns by mounting counter-campaigns of their own for the purpose of convincing their employees that they do not need a union to represent their interests. Nowadays most of the so-called certification elections conducted in the United States to determine employee preferences apparently involve active opposition by the employer.[7] Union success in the elections already began to decline in the 1950s, but in the past few years the decline has accelerated.[8]

North American procedures to resolve recognition disputes also include the possibility of cancelling an established recognition by means of a so-called decertification election. Its purpose is to enable employees to rid themselves of a union whose services are no longer wanted. There are, however, far fewer decertification elections than certification elections.[9]

For recognition problems there is no parallel approach in continental Europe. Employers are as a rule not under a legal obligation to recognise a union, and the determination of the appropriate bargaining unit is, more often than not, a matter for the parties themselves to agree upon. Furthermore, instead of granting exclusive bargaining rights to majority unions, countries possessing pluralistic trade union movements, which are often based on divergent ideological orientations, have preferred pluralistic to unitary representation. In addition, it should be pointed out that in several countries a trade union represents in a legal sense only its members, although in practice an employer will almost invariably extend the terms of an agreement to all employees, whether or not they are union members.

Recent British developments regarding recognition deserve separate consideration. Until 1971 the tradition of voluntarism prevailed, which meant in practice that unions composed primarily of blue-collar employees were able to gain widespread recognition, but that the generally weaker unions of white-collar employees had considerable difficulties. In 1968 the report of the Donovan Commission,[10] which had been appointed to make a comprehensive review of the British industrial relations system, recommended the adoption of legislative provisions comparable with, but not identical to, North American procedures. Subsequently, a corresponding set of rules was incorporated into the 1971 Industrial Relations Act [11] which, however, lacked the compulsory feature of the American legislation. On repeal of the Act in 1974, somewhat more stringent rules were included in the Employment Protection Act of 1975.[12] Their unanticipated deficiencies were exposed in the course of a major recognition dispute at the Grunwick Company, and ultimately the 1975 provisions were repealed by the Employment Act of 1980. Currently, therefore, union recognition issues in Great Britain are again in the realm of voluntary rather than statutory action and thus coincide with the situation generally in effect in the continental European countries.[13]

THE DUTY TO BARGAIN

Behind the act of recognition lies the expectation that a bargaining relationship will ensue, leading in the first instance to the conclusion of a collective agreement and beyond that to its joint administration. Until recently the imposition of a legal duty to bargain on either or both sides was limited to countries which also provided for the legal regulation of recognition (the American model). Conversely, countries which left issues of recognition to the voluntary action of the parties likewise dispensed with attempts to apply parallel forms of regulation to the initiation of collective bargaining, but instead left that matter, too, to the decision of the parties (the European model).

This general characterisation has now become subject to some major exceptions. To be sure, the majority of European countries still adhere to the policy of leaving the establishment of collective bargaining to the parties. There is, for example, no duty to bargain under the legislation of Belgium, the Federal Republic of Germany or indeed most of the other countries, although there certainly is a considerable amount of ongoing bargaining.[14] But in France and Sweden laws have come into effect during the past decade which impose on employers an explicit obligation to bargain, while in Great Britain similar legislation (the Industrial Relations Act of 1971) was in force until its repeal in 1974. This suggests that there is a trend in the direction of requiring employers to engage in collective bargaining, no matter what their preference may be, and if so the question arises whether it is still possible to refer in general terms to a voluntarist European model.

However that may be, there have been no substantial changes since 1947 in the American approach to the duty to bargain. Under section 9 *(a)* of the Labor-Management Relations Act, both employers and unions are required to bargain *in good faith* "in respect to rates of pay, wages, hours of employment, or other conditions of employment".[15] In applying this provision, particularly as regards the obligations of employers, the agency charged with administering the law, the National Labor Relations Board (NLRB), has developed two sets of criteria — one procedural, the other substantive. The procedural provisions require individual employers or their representatives to meet the employees' bargaining representative at an agreed time and place and at reasonably frequent intervals. Employers must make a genuine effort to reach agreement and may not evade their obligations by, for example, going merely through the motions or refusing to present counterproposals to the union's demands. They may not try to deal directly with the employees over the heads of the union's negotiators, nor may they unilaterally improve or worsen the terms of employment. While employers are not under a legal obligation to reach an agreement at all costs, they must be willing to put any verbal agreement into writing and to sign it.

The substantive duty to bargain — as distinguished from its procedural counterpart — relates to the subjects that enter into the negotiations. Here the NLRB and the courts have devised three categories: mandatory, permissive and illegal subjects. Mandatory subjects are those which are directly related to the statutory provision that refers to "wages, hours, and other terms and conditions of employment". As regards these topics, the duty to bargain is in full operation, the only question being whether a marginal item falls just within or just outside the scope of the mandatory category. In the permissive category are all those items that the parties may bargain about if both sides wish to do so, but a refusal by either side would not constitute a violation of the duty to bargain. Quite the contrary, it would be a violation of the law for either side to insist on bargaining about a permissive item, nor could a union legally strike to enforce such a demand. Finally, certain issues cannot ever be legitimately raised and would therefore constitute an illegal category, as for example a union demand for pre-hire compulsory union membership (closed shop) which is prohibited by law.

What has been the effect of having a legal duty to bargain? Undoubtedly one of the consequences has been to involve the State more actively in collective bargaining. That was the conclusion drawn already in 1968 by the Canadian Task Force on Labour Relations when it called attention to the fact that the United States had "developed an elaborate jurisprudence on the issue of good faith bargaining, revolving largely around what subjects must be bargained, what may be bargained and what a party cannot insist be bargained".[16] To the question whether Canada should give legal force to the duty to bargain the Task Force gave a negative answer.

It reasoned:

We do not think it is useful to industrial relations in Canada to put the issue of good faith bargaining into such an elaborate jurisprudential container. The duty to bargain is not a duty to agree, nor does the right to bargain grant a right to a particular bargain. We see no reason why the subject-matter of bargaining should not include anything that is not contrary to law.

And it concluded by stating that it could not "envisage such a duty being amenable to legal enforcement, except perhaps to the extent of an obligation to meet and exchange positions".[17]

Until the early 1970s that was also the position of the unions in Sweden for whom the ideal role of the State in industrial relations had traditionally been one of minimal intervention. But having increasingly become concerned about the failure of collective bargaining to deal with workplace-centred issues and about management's insistence on preserving its right to make unilateral determinations in the areas of hiring, dismissals, direction of work and other matters, the unions prevailed upon the Government to appoint a Royal Commission to seek ways of introducing greater democracy at the workplace "on the premise that questions concerned with the right to direct work should be regulated in collective bargaining agreements" rather than by management alone.[18] The report of the Commission was followed by the enactment of the 1976 Codetermination Act which, among other things, imposes on employers at the level of the individual enterprise not only an obligation to respond to a union's request for negotiations but also to initiate negotiations before instituting any major changes involving the reduction or enlargement of the workforce, the closure of facilities, the subcontracting of work and related matters.[19] If the parties fail to reach an agreement, the (local) union may refer the matter to its national body for further negotiations, possibly involving the employers' associations. In that event the employer must postpone the contemplated action until negotiations at higher levels have run their course. Although these provisions seem to go even further than their American counterparts, it should be emphasised that, as in the United States, the employer's duty to bargain does not include a duty to reach an agreement. Employers may ultimately proceed to implement their intentions if negotiations fail.

A not dissimilar innovation was introduced into the French industrial relations system with the enactment, in November 1982, of a law [20] (the third in a series of four so-called Auroux laws) imposing on employers for the first time a duty to bargain annually. The duty applies both to the level of the industry (or sector) as well as to the individual enterprise, or more specifically to all enterprises with ten or more employees in which at least one trade union has established a plant section. It has been estimated that out of some 100,000 enterprises with ten or more employees, about 25 per cent have union representation.[21] At the industry level all organisations covered by an existing agreement must hold meetings at least once a year to negotiate on wages and at least once every five years to review job classifications. At the enterprise level, the employer is obligated to engage in annual negotiations concerning actual (as distinguished from minimum) wages, the length of working time and the organisation of work. Other subjects may be included at the option of the parties. But, as in Sweden and the United States, the duty to bargain does not imply a duty to agree.

The preceding review of existing practices with regard to recognition and the duty to bargain leads to several observations. A distinction can still be drawn between countries with predominantly enterprise-centred bargaining systems and countries with industry-wide bargaining systems, but it has lost some of its validity. In the former category issues of recognition and the duty to bargain are covered primarily by legislative-administrative regulations, whereas in the latter the chief reliance has traditionally been placed on the voluntary action of the parties themselves. There are now, however, countries in the second category which have introduced a statutory duty to bargain. That would appear to be a major change of public policy, and in a sense it is. But it must be kept in mind that both in France and in Sweden the main thrust of the legislation is the individual enterprise rather than the industry although, to be sure, the French legislation does specifically refer to the industry as well as to the enterprise.

It is the concentration on the individual enterprise that explains the shift in public policy regarding a statutory duty to bargain. There was no need for an explicit rule to this effect as long as bargaining proceeded almost entirely at the industry level where the representation of employers' interests was entrusted to associations. For employers' associations, collective bargaining was not — and is not — a threat but an opportunity, in fact a *raison d'être*. They are unlikely to resist it, at least not in principle. To individual employers, however, and particularly to those that have in the past dealt with unions only indirectly through the buffer mechanism of their associations, collective bargaining at the plant or enterprise level constitutes an imminent threat to management's freedom of action, a threat which they believe has to be resisted if possible. That is why governments intent on the promotion of collective bargaining at enterprise level have considered it necessary to reinforce their purpose by means of legislation on the duty to bargain.

STANDING BARGAINING MACHINERY

The development of machinery for collective bargaining and the characteristics of that machinery are the outcome of the particular needs and circumstances existing at country, industry and enterprise levels, to mention only those three. In no country has the machinery become standardised across the various bargaining units, and even if that were possible — which it probably is not — it would be undesirable because of the adverse impact on what are justly considered to be among the outstanding advantages of collective bargaining: its adaptability and flexibility. Some distinctions can, however, be reasonably made, and one is between standing (or permanent) and ad hoc machinery.

In most countries the negotiations leading up to the conclusion of an agreement proceed under ad hoc machinery, which of course does not mean that the bargaining machinery is haphazard or disorganised or unstable. In some countries, however, there is standing machinery, either under a privately agreed or under a publicly legislated "charter" or "constitution" which designates the parties, defines the main purposes, outlines the procedures, and may also indicate the functions of the full-time staff, if any. Standing machinery is most prevalent at the industry level but may also cover, as it does in Belgium and the Netherlands, the entire national economy.

Belgium best exemplifies permanent bargaining machinery established by national legislation for individual industries and for the economy as a whole.[22] At industry or equivalent level there are nearly 100 joint committees which cover virtually the entire private sector. They are composed of equal numbers of representatives from both sides, i.e. the employers' associations and the representative trade unions, and they meet under the auspices of an independent chairman. Each committee has its own secretariat which provides continuity and administrative services.

The main task of the committees is to negotiate industry-wide collective agreements, although a certain amount of bargaining also occurs outside the joint committee framework in ad hoc negotiations and particularly at enterprise level. Some committees are concerned only with the terms of employment for blue-collar or white-collar employees, while others have a mixed constituency.

For the economy as a whole there is a bipartite National Labour Council, also presided over by an impartial chairman, whose principal function is to act as a consultative body in relation to the Government but which may also conclude collective agreements on economy-wide issues.

Similar in general purpose but less inclusive than its Belgian counterpart is the standing machinery at industry level that has been established in Great Britain by voluntary action of the parties (not by legislation) under the impact, chiefly, of the reports of the Whitley Committee published in 1917-18.[23] Although the joint industrial councils (the name varies) are based on a single constitutional model, there is nevertheless a great deal of variety in their structure and even in the nature of their activities. While a few concern themselves only with wage negotiations — and a few others do not engage in any negotiations at all — most of them go beyond the negotiations themselves and tackle other problems related to their industry. There are considerable variations with regard to the size of the councils, the frequency of their meetings (but as a rule once per quarter) and the presence of a network of subsidiary councils at regional level.

A somewhat different kind of standing machinery is represented by the Foundation of Labour in the Netherlands. The Foundation, which came into existence in 1945 to aid in the reconstruction of the war-shattered economy, includes the major confederations of trade unions and employers' associations. It has a written constitution, a permanent secretariat and an agreed set of procedures. While at first not intended to be chiefly a forum for centralised national bargaining, that is in fact what it became. But after the collapse of the highly centralised wage negotiation system in the mid-1960s the key role of the Foundation as a guide-line setting body diminished, though it never entirely disappeared. To a substantial extent its continued usefulness as a consultative mechanism has compensated for its declining role in collective bargaining.[24]

In answer to the question whether standing bargaining machinery has intrinsic advantages over ad hoc or conventional forms, several points might be made. Aside from its continuity, whose value is likely to be considerable, standing machinery probably offers the parties an incentive to undertake joint research on issues of common concern, the expectation being that the outcome would constitute an agreed basis for bargaining. Standing machinery may also be a useful mechanism for the joint implementation of agreements, particularly where other devices to administer the agreement, as for example a grievance procedure, do not exist or exist only in a rudimentary state. Moreover, depending on the quality of the relationship between the parties, permanent machinery may become the instrument for joint approaches to problems outside the usual boundaries of collective bargaining. Admittedly these advantages, apart from continuity, can in all likelihood also be secured in the absence of standing machinery, at least as regards an industry-based system of collective bargaining, if not an enterprise-centred one.

FORMULATING BARGAINING POSITIONS

One of the habitually neglected subjects in research on collective bargaining is the negotiating process itself, as well as the preparatory work that almost invariably precedes it. Little has been done to correct this neglect. What Professor Blanpain has repeatedly observed about his own country is applicable to many others. He writes: "Hardly any research has been done in Belgium on the actual procedure of collective bargaining . . .".[25] Why the gap exists has been plausibly explained by Beal and Begin, who suggest that the neglect, relative to other aspects of collective bargaining which have been thoroughly examined, is not as surprising as it might seem:

Negotiations usually take place in private. Until they crystallise in the final, formal agreement, they remain fluid, tentative and usually informal. Once reached, the agreement captures attention and diverts interest from the preceding activity that produced it. Those whom it affects start thinking about what it will do to them in the future. All the time and talk and sweat that went into that final result becomes, except perhaps to the participants, as water over the dam: Gone and forgotten; unimportant and overshadowed; of only what is called "academic" interest.[26]

None the less the subject is of considerable importance, all the more so because a good deal more is involved than the actual negotiations themselves. Both sides must prepare for the negotiations well before they begin, and this requisite has policy (or political) aspects as well as technical aspects that are inter-related but are best discussed separately.

Taking the political aspects first, each party to collective bargaining faces a problem of achieving an internal consensus on its basic bargaining position, for without it negotiations would be exceedingly difficult if not impossible. The ability to reach a consensus is linked to several factors, but two seem to stand out. One is the mix of constituencies and constituency interests which the leaders on both sides must take into account in order to present a reasonably coherent and unified stance at the bargaining table; the other is the range and complexity of issues that constitute the substance of the negotiations. Other things being equal, the greater the heterogeneity of constituencies and interests and the greater the range and complexity of the issues, the more difficult it will be to achieve a consensus. These observations apply fully as much to the employer side as to the union side, though the internal political problems on the union side may appear to be the more difficult ones.

Yet even if elusive, the subject remains important, extending as it does well beyond the negotiations themselves to include the preparations and the immediate post-negotiation phase. In recent years the time set aside by the parties to prepare for bargaining, at least in the case of major negotiations, has steadily lengthened, due largely to the increasing number of issues and the ever greater complexity attached to many of them. It is thus no longer exceptional for the time allotted to preparations to extend from six months to a year or even more. "Most experienced union and management negotiators agree", according to the current edition of a standard treatise on collective bargaining, "that the time to begin preparing for the next contract negotiation is immediately after the current agreement has been signed and put into effect." [27] The preparations themselves involve complex issues which can only be sketchily discussed here. To divide them into policy (or political) and technical aspects, as though these were the only categories or as if they could be neatly separated, is admittedly an oversimplification that is here resorted to only for expository reasons.

Taking the employer side first, it may fairly be assumed that it will consist of either a single enterprise or an association, although within these broad categories there is room for considerable variation. In a multi-plant firm the problems faced by the various units are likely to be quite divergent in terms of the organisation of production, the local labour market, the skill mix of the labour force and other major variables, and these differences must be taken into account in preparing for negotiations. [28] Plant managers and their industrial relations staffs will of course need to be consulted in the process leading to the determination of the firm's bargaining position. Whether in single or multi-plant enterprises, supervisors and department heads are often brought into the initial deliberations in view of their knowledge of the application of the existing agreement and their key role in implementing any changes. It would certainly be a miscalculation to count on an easily achieved consensus on the employer side. Different attitudes and priorities, based partly on differences in functions and responsibilities, are almost as likely to develop among management representatives as among employees and their unions.

Among employers' associations, achieving a consensus on bargaining goals and strategy becomes particularly difficult when there are substantial differences among member firms in regard to size, market position, efficiency of operations, financial resources, location and other factors. To overcome the problem, employers' associations often seek to negotiate terms that can be met by their most marginal members. This aim preserves the existence of firms that might otherwise be forced out of business (or out of the association) — and also preserves jobs — while leaving the more profitable firms free to extend improved terms to their employees, whether by unilateral decision or as a result of supplementary bargaining at enterprise level. [29] Preserving the cohesiveness, or in an extreme case the very existence, of the association may permit no other course. Since the difficulty of reaching internal agreement among association firms generally becomes greater as the complexity of the issues that are the subject of bargaining increases, employers' associations tend to prefer to limit the range of issues to be negotiated. The problem of adhering to a united bargaining posture may become particularly acute when the association is faced with a choice between a strike or a settlement that the better-situated member firms can afford, but that is beyond the ability-to-pay of the marginal enterprises.

On the union side the formulation of bargaining strategy is profoundly affected by the dual character of unions as efficient instruments for the protection and advancement of their members' interests and as democratically operated mass organisations. What this duality means for the authority of union negotiators will be spelled out in a later section of this chapter. Suffice it to note here that some unions may have special difficulties in determining their bargaining position because of the heterogeneous make-up of their membership. It then becomes the responsibility of the leaders to put together an initial set of demands — and in due course to negotiate a set of terms — that meets the expectations of the various constituencies: skilled and less skilled, low seniority and high seniority, hourly paid and incentive workers, young and old, male and female, manual and white-collar employees (if covered by the same negotiations), and all the while to manoeuvre deftly enough to keep all of them reasonably content with the performance of their organisation and their leaders. Other things being equal, that demanding task is made somewhat easier when the bargaining unit is confined to a single enterprise and the employees are represented by a single local union, as is often the case in North America, and easier still if the workforce is relatively homogeneous. Before drawing up the list of demands for presentation to the employer, many unions solicit "inputs" from the membership, whether at regular or special meetings, through surveys of the membership or by means of contacts between union leaders and the union's workplace representatives.

Special problems may arise when local unions, in formulating their negotiating positions, must conform to the general policy set by the national organisation with which they are affiliated, and of course even more so when governments issue guide-lines or impose controls that restrict the freedom of action of unions as well as employers. Instructions from the national union office do not always suffice to compel adherence to national union policy, and consequently national unions may insist on being represented in local negotiations by their own designated representatives whose presence, whether they simply act as observers or take a leading role in the negotiations, is intended to guarantee that national union policies are incorporated in any settlement entered into by the local body.

Eliciting membership opinion when bargaining takes place at levels above the individual plant or enterprise is, of course, a more difficult task. Because of the longer lines of communication and the concentration trends among many unions nowadays, the tendency at regional and national bargaining levels has sometimes been to rely more heavily on the judgement of union officers and activists and correspondingly less on the opinions of rank-and-file members. But beginning in the late 1960s a strong current favouring more internal union democracy emerged in quite a number of countries, and one of its effects was the introduction of procedures that facilitated membership participation in the formulation of union bargaining demands, even in situations where that had previously not been the case.

In any event, union officials are well advised to find ways of discovering the wishes and preferences of the membership and to incorporate them into a coherent package of bargaining demands. In the metals industry of the Federal Republic of Germany proposals are put forward in membership meetings and officers' meetings and then screened by an internal negotiating committee before a formal demand to open negotiations is placed before the employers' association some four weeks before the termination of the agreement.[30] In the Belgian metals industry trade union demands are usually formulated first at local or regional level in meetings of union delegates and then forwarded to the executive committee of the national unions which must decide whether to incorporate the demands into the bargaining programme. Since plural unionism prevails in Belgium, the different national unions in the metals industry must still work out a common set of demands, which may mean having to harmonise conflicting positions. As a rule they manage to do so.[31] In the United States unions preparing for negotiations in a major enterprise, as in the case of one of the large multi-plant automobile manufacturing firms, may call a special conference to decide on a basic list of demands or may do so at one of their regular national conventions.

If faced with a profusion of diverse and possibly conflicting proposals, unions have a tendency, more so than employers' associations in similar situations, to incorporate a large number of demands into their package rather than risk antagonising a portion of their constituency by rejecting in advance certain clearly unrealisable demands. The decision to include, rather than sift out, marginal items is traceable most of the time to the leadership's reluctance to offend sections of the membership in circumstances where it is easier to abandon low-priority items in the course of the negotiations themselves. Similar considerations apply, more or less, to seeming exaggerations in the size of certain demands. What occurs, in effect, is that the union postpones the difficult and sometimes politically hazardous task of judging the relative merits of various proposals and perhaps also of taking sides with regard to the conflicting interests represented among the membership. In general terms, the complexity and intractableness of this task tend to increase in proportion to the diversity of the constituencies represented at the bargaining table.

RESEARCH AND PREPARATION

It remains an arguable question whether the outcome of a particular set of negotiations is significantly influenced by the care which the parties have devoted to the technical preparation of their case. There are those who maintain that bargaining is chiefly a contest of economic force, powers of persuasion and dissimulative skills, while others maintain that successful negotiations must be based on a realistic and above all a well-researched assessment of past performance, current circumstances and future prospects if the agreement which eventually emerges is to be perceived as fair and workable by both parties. Both views command some plausibility, but the emphasis has been shifting towards more careful and thorough preparation of the increasingly complex and technical issues that are at the centre of much contemporary bargaining, particularly in industries under pressure of the economic crisis. With the aid of trained professionals — above all economists but also engineers, accountants and other experts — employers and unions are spending substantial amounts of time and resources to construct well-substantiated arguments for their bargaining positions. In this endeavour they are often able to rely on steadily improving sources of data.[32]

There are, of course, certain kinds of agreements that do not require this kind of preparatory technical investigation. An example would be the Basic Agreement in Norway between the Employers' Confederation and the Federation of Trade Unions, the most recent version of which was negotiated in 1982.[33] Agreements of this sort are not intended to establish specific terms and conditions of employment, but instead reflect the outcome of deliberations involving fundamental principles and procedures in industrial relations, as negotiated with the participation of the very top representatives on both sides — and sometimes with government officials as well, in which case the outcome would probably be a tripartite agreement. Such agreements address basic aspects of labour-management relations instead of being concerned with the terms of employment and the underlying economic conditions pertaining to a particular industry, or a part of it.

In many countries extensive research efforts by both parties precede the negotiation of collective agreements embodying wages and working conditions. To prepare for such negotiations unions and employers' associations (or individual enterprises) rely on their research staffs — or if necessary on outside specialists when highly technical materials are at issue — to supply them with the information and arguments required to support their bargaining aims and strategy.

In recent years the parties have been making increasing use of the storage, sorting and retrieval facilities made possible by the rapidly growing availability of computers to marshall their data and arguments for negotiations. Nevertheless, specific information on the use of computers to prepare for collective bargaining is still surprisingly scarce.[34] Computers are able to produce almost instantaneously the kind of regional, industrial or enterprise-by-enterprise comparisons of wages and related fringe benefits on which negotiators base their bargaining positions. Computers can also rapidly "cost out" alternative settlement packages and compute the monetary cost of individual items under various assumptions. But the technical possibilities offered by computers do not necessarily eliminate differences between the negotiators about the data base or the results of the computations. That may not matter very much if each side in the negotiations relies on its own computerised data for the purpose of preparing only its own case. But the situation changes if there is an attempt at joint use. As one group of observers of a computer-aided set of negotiations expressed the problem:

Computer print-outs based on data compiled and programmed by one side will not be readily accepted as valid by an opponent. This mean[s] that a program to use the computer in collective bargaining must begin when facts are first fed into the data bank. Only data which both sides agree are accurate can be allowed into the bank, and if there is disagreement, the difference must either be negotiated out with the assistance of a "programmer mediator", or else the range of difference must be narrowed and put into the bank with the differences indicated.[35]

The importance of thorough and competent research increases even more when public authorities are involved in collective bargaining in an adjudicatory or regulative capacity for the transparent reason that public authorities must seek to form their decisions on the basis of demonstrated merit. The Australian system of arbitration and conciliation, with its intricate combination of direct negotiations and hearings before arbitration tribunals, represents a particularly apt example of the reliance on research in a quasi-collective bargaining situation. In the belief, no doubt based on years of experience with the system, that a case based on thorough research is best capable of enlisting the sympathetic attention of arbitration tribunals, unions and employers' associations have long made it a practice to prepare voluminous briefs in support of their case. Yet it does appear to be the case that unions lag behind employers in the quality of their research facilities and in the amount of resources which they devote to the effort, and they seem to be generally aware of the need to improve their research capacity.[36]

In the Netherlands the importance of research as an integral part of bargaining preparations increased substantially during the period of centralised wage determination in the 1950s and the first half of the 1960s because the parties were expected to present to the wage control agencies a rational and well-documented case for requests involving wage changes. Also contributing to the rising importance of research was the Government's approach to collective bargaining, which relied heavily on the forecasts of the Central Planning Bureau as a general guide to economically allowable wage levels.

Although the importance of competent technical preparations for collective bargaining has been on the increase almost everywhere, the trend has generally not yet reached a point at which the parties would be willing to rely on jointly gathered information. There are, however, some exceptions, and one of the more striking ones, as indicated in the following passage from a study of Swedish employers' associations, is the co-operation that developed in Sweden in the period following the Second World War from joint reliance on wage data, first, at the industry level and, subsequently, at the central national level:

In 1949 the ... Swedish Engineering Employers' Association and the Iron-Mill Employers' Association on one side and the ... Federation of Metal Trade Unions on the other agreed on devising a set of common wage statistics. A large number of similar agreements covering other industries were signed during the following years, and by the 1960s most employers' associations were covered by such agreements. Until 1970, however, there was no agreement on the preparation and use of common statistics for negotiations at the central level. LO [the central trade union federation] argued that the employers, as the producers of statistics, had an unfair advantage and suggested that the compilation of wage statistics should be entrusted to a separate institution controlled by both parties. After further negotiations, however, it was agreed that SAF [the central federation of employers' associations] should continue to collect the statistics, and nowadays LO has access to these data for its own use.[37]

The general point remains valid, however, in the sense that research for collective bargaining still tends to be undertaken separately by each party and that it is designed chiefly for the purpose of strengthening the case of either side. As Chamberlain and Kuhn pointed out some years ago: "After deciding on its bargaining position, each side makes selective use from among available data of whatever will support its demands . . . Facts are regarded as 'bargaining cards' to be played or withheld as tactical considerations warrant." [38] Yet a strong case could be made for the proposition that a more objective use of relevant data would improve both the process and the outcome of bargaining, and in several countries efforts in that direction have been stimulated by the economic crisis. The need for co-operation in the interest of preserving jobs has motivated the parties to de-emphasise the conflictual aspects of negotiations and to accentuate the collaborative ones. A recent ILO study has summarised the impact of economic pressures on the bargaining process in these terms: ". . . employers were forced to accept certain forms of communication and participation while unions tended to forego some of their most militant aspects as protest organisations".[39] Ultimately, the problem is one of shifting the emphasis from what Walton and McKersie have called "distributive bargaining" to "integrative bargaining" or, expressed differently, from bargaining as a way of competitively dividing limited resources to bargaining as a means for solving problems of common concern and in the common interest of the parties.[40] In order for this to happen on a large scale, there must be not only a change in the economic context but also in attitudes, and evidently that will take time.

EMPLOYER DISCLOSURE OBLIGATIONS

Although a substantial portion of the data required for effective collective bargaining is in the public domain or at least generally accessible to the parties, some of the factual information is exclusively within the possession of the employer side. This is a particularly important factor in situations characterised by enterprise-level bargaining, but it also applies to industry-wide bargaining units. Unions frequently assert that employers are unwilling to share vital information and that, consequently, they are severely handicapped in representing the interests of their constituents by reason of their inability to verify independently the allegations of employers about the economic position of the industry or the firm, as the case may be. The defences used most often by employers to justify withholding the desired information is that meeting the request would be excessively burdensome, time-consuming and costly, and also that the information sought by the union is confidential and could be used by business rivals to the competitive disadvantage of the firm. Behind these considerations, according to Bellace and Gospel, "lies the pervasive apprehension of increasing union bargaining power and control vis-à-vis management", but they also note that "some more sophisticated managers have welcomed greater disclosure as a channel of communications with employees and as a means of obtaining their co-operation in the enterprise".[41]

Until fairly recently the issue of what information, if any, the employer side could be compelled to share with the union side was regulated most explicitly in the United States, where the cumulative decisions of the federal courts and the NLRB created a network of fairly detailed rules. In European countries there were no statutory requirements in this respect until the enactment in Great Britain of the Industrial Relations Act of 1971, at least not as far as employers' dealings with trade unions — as distinguished from dealings with works councils — were concerned. The absence of rules was in large part the result of the diminished importance for unions of detailed enterprise-by-enterprise economic information under a system of industry-wide collective bargaining which, as already noted, aims frequently at the conclusion of collective agreements embodying minimum instead of actual terms of employment. The relevance of this explanation is reinforced by the legislative treatment accorded to works councils (or equivalent bodies) which by law were granted — and still have — extensive rights in many countries with regard to information about the current and anticipated economic position of the individual firm, as well as a good deal of other information. (Although the employer is privileged to designate the information as confidential, it may nevertheless be assumed that much of it finds its way to the union, considering that most works council members have close ties to the union which conducts the bargaining.) It must, of course, be kept in mind that the general perception of the employer-works council relationship has always emphasised its collaborative aspects, as distinguished from what has historically been the predominantly adversarial relationship between trade unions and employers or their associations.

There has been, however, a considerable change recently regarding employers' obligations to supply information to unions. Within the past 15 years several countries — notably France, Great Britain and Sweden — have introduced detailed regulations concerning the obligations of management to provide information to the union. As a result the disclosure gap that existed for many years between European countries and the United States has begun to narrow considerably, although by no means entirely.

As regards the situation in the United States, the employer's obligation to disclose information which the union can show to be "relevant and necessary" to its preparation for collective bargaining is derived from the statutory obligation to bargain in good faith. This is by now well established. On the whole, both the NLRB and the courts have given a broad interpretation to the obligation, procedurally and substantively. In particular, the NLRB has applied a so-called "liberal discovery type standard", which means that a union is entitled to any information that will aid it in discovering facts that are in some way relevant to preparing for negotiations, processing a grievance and administering the agreement.[42] Regarding financial information, for example, a union is entitled to data that may include production and sales records, costs of raw materials and operating expense figures in order to verify an employer's claim of financial inability to meet a wage demand.[43] The courts have also supported the NLRB in holding that an employer's failure promptly to provide relevant information is tantamount to a refusal to bargain and, furthermore, that there is a statutory obligation for the employer to provide information to the union throughout the life of the collective relationship so as to enable it to participate in the administration of the agreement.[44] In sum, as Bellace and Gospel have pointed out, "the right of American unions to seek information related to bargaining has a firm legal basis and is easily enforceable".[45]

In Great Britain the Industrial Relations Act of 1971 contained for the first time a statutory provision establishing an employer's obligation to disclose information for bargaining purposes, but the Act was repealed (1974) before implementation had begun. Subsequently, the obligation was restored in the Employment Protection Act of 1975 which is still in effect and which provides that the employer is required to disclose information without which the union's ability to engage in collective bargaining would be materially hindered, as well as information whose disclosure is in line with adherence to "good industrial relations practice".[46]

There was also a major change in Sweden in the mid-1970s with regard to disclosure rules. For several decades disclosure requirements had been limited to the relationship between enterprises or plants and their works councils. The obligation had taken the form, characteristic of Sweden, of a private agreement rather than a law. The agreement was concluded in 1946 between the peak confederations on the employer and trade union sides. It was renewed and expanded several times, but was ultimately found to be insufficient by the unions. Its place was then taken by provisions incorporated in the 1976 Act respecting co-determination at work, and particularly by section 19, which imposed on employers an obligation to provide a considerable amount of information to the union. Thus, the law grants unions the right to be kept continuously informed of all developments affecting the plant or enterprise that might affect the interests of the employees and to have access to the employer's books as well as other relevant documents. Special disclosure provisions regulate the use by the employer of subcontractors. Only a few areas of information, for example those concerning the enterprise's strategy in an impending industrial dispute, are exempt from disclosure.

Still more recently, France has joined the list of countries requiring the disclosure of certain information. Under the law of November 1982, the third of the four Auroux laws, French employers at enterprise as well as at industry level are required, in connection with the mandatory negotiations that are to take place every year and every five years respectively, "to furnish the union organisations with the information they need in order to be fully informed concerning the subject-matter of the negotiations".[47] A separate requirement compels individual employers to supply the unions "with information permitting a comparative analysis and explanation of the relative position of men and women in the workforce with respect to employment, qualifications, wages, hours and organisation of work time", presumably for the purpose of assisting the unions in bringing about greater equality in conditions of employment through collective bargaining.[48]

From an overall viewpoint, the advance of legislation on disclosure is only one aspect of evolving government policies designed to foster more effective collective bargaining. Three guiding ideas are particularly significant in this respect, although they are not necessarily of equal weight in all the countries concerned. One is the expectation that a common factual base, brought about if necessary by pressure on the employer to share relevant information, will lead to more realistic bargaining strategies and more responsible bargaining outcomes. Walter Reuther, for many years among the most highly regarded American trade union leaders, once expressed this point by urging that —

... we need to recognise that in a free society bargaining decisions should be based upon economic facts and not upon economic power. I hope the day will come in America when, in collective bargaining problems and other problems that bear upon economic interest, decisions can be based upon the power of economic persuasion rather than upon the persuasion of economic power.[49]

Closely related is the idea that disclosure should serve as a means of enlarging the area of joint union-employer decision-making by providing unions with access to the same information base that is available to management. This consideration was historically of great importance in the various laws establishing works councils and defining their rights vis-à-vis management. It also explains why the legislative provisions with respect to employer disclosure requirements in Sweden are incorporated in a statute whose overall aim, as reflected in the title of the law, is the extension of co-determination at work.

Finally, the trend towards more legislatively required information-sharing has also been influenced by public policies designed to bring collective bargaining into closer rapport with the workplace through strengthening plant-level and enterprise-centred negotiations as distinguished from industry-level negotiations. This is true of all the countries concerned, but nowhere more so than in Sweden: "One of the weaknesses of the Swedish law on disclosure", write Bellace and Gospel, "is that it assumes [the existence of] bargaining at plant level. *Indeed this is what it was expressly designed to encourage.*" [50] It need hardly be pointed out that this objective has a number of wide-ranging ramifications, for example as regards the structure of unions, some of which will be explored in a subsequent chapter.

NEGOTIATING PATTERNS

Negotiation is the essence of collective bargaining, but nowhere in the process do the differences associated with the national culture, the special characteristics of an industry or enterprise, or even the personalities of the leading negotiators show up more strikingly than in the varied ways by which the parties periodically seek to reach agreement on future conditions of employment and the terms of their relationship with one another. Whether to wear the other side down through interminable meetings or aim for a quick settlement, whether to open the negotiations with maximum feasible demands or begin by offering terms not far from the minimum acceptable settlement, whether to enlist the media as part of one's bargaining strategy or negotiate in strict seclusion — these are questions to which no certain answers can be offered since so much, indeed everything, depends on vast differences in traditions, circumstances, objectives, government policies and other factors.

Generalisations are made even more difficult by the fact that the level at which bargaining occurs has a decisive effect on the nature of the negotiations. There is an enormous gap — and not only in terms of the issues that happen to be on the table — between the almost daily confrontations that occur at workplace level between shop stewards or local union representatives and lower-level supervisors, and the highly formalised meetings, scheduled long in advance, between the plenipotentiaries of the national peak confederations of employers' associations and trade unions. Yet to many observers both sets of negotiations are encompassed by the term "collective bargaining".

Since it is not practicable to include here all conceivable kinds of labour-management negotiations, the emphasis will be placed on those negotiations that are intended to establish as nearly as possible the actual terms and conditions of employment for workers covered by collective agreements. In Japan and the North American countries that generally means the individual enterprise or plant, less frequently an industry or part of one. As to the other countries, notably the Western European ones, it used to refer rather uniformly to an entire industry, but due to the ongoing decentralisation of the bargaining structure it might nowadays also refer to an individual company or plant.

Negotiations proceed by stages.[51] Their number and duration depend on such factors as the complexity of the issues to be negotiated, the heterogeneity of the parties represented at the bargaining table, the degree of authority granted to the negotiators, the intervention and skilfulness of the conciliation and mediation services and the experience of the negotiators. In case of an already established bargaining relationship, with an agreement that may be about to expire, negotiations are usually started when one party notifies the other of its intention to terminate the existing agreement and to negotiate a new one. (In a new relationship the same purpose is accomplished by notice of the initiating party, usually the union, to the other party of its desire to negotiate an agreement.)

The rules regarding notice may be specified by law, agreement, custom or some combination of these. Tendering notice of intent to terminate the existing agreement is frequently required regardless of legal stipulations. In countries where bargaining tends to follow a well-established cycle, as in the Netherlands and Sweden, the date of notification has become fairly uniform over the years. Thus, for Swedish agreements expiring at the end of the year, as many do, the usual time for giving notice is 30 September. Before or at the actual start of negotiations the parties usually agree on the rules of procedure. In established relationships they will be guided mainly by precedent. Illustrative of the questions that arise are the selection of a chairman, if any, the maintenance of a verbatim transcript, and the meeting-place. These questions are not necessarily of vital importance to the progress of the negotiations, but deserve some consideration since they might influence them to some extent.

As regards chairing the negotiations, the main possibilities are having no chairman, appointing a single chairman from one of the parties, rotating the chairmanship among the parties or bringing in an outside chairman. Many —

perhaps most — negotiations take place without an explicitly designated chairman and proceed without hindrance. It is sometimes considered useful, however, especially when the number of negotiators is sizeable, to have someone who is responsible for maintaining an orderly discussion, knows when to call a recess, can keep tempers under control and is able to steer the talks towards the goal of reaching an agreement. A chairman furnished by one of the parties tends more often than not to be a member of the employer side and must of course act with absolute impartiality to avoid forfeiting acceptability. Rotation of chairmen is infrequent because it may interrupt the continuity of discourse which a capable chairman knows how to promote. An impartial chairman brought in from the outside has the advantage of not being identified with either party but may not be familiar with the issues central to the negotiations, the technological and economic constraints of the industry or enterprise and the personalities of the leading negotiators.

As a rule, verbatim transcripts of negotiations are not kept. They do have the advantage of constituting an accurate record to which the parties can refer to resolve conflicts of memory, as for example about interim agreements already reached on specific items, and may have the additional advantage of helping to resolve future interpretation disputes. But except in highly formalised settings or in circumstances where the parties have little trust in one another, the awareness of a stenographic record being made may inhibit the negotiators from expressing themselves freely, and this as well as the considerable costs is usually considered to be a sufficiently important drawback to outweigh the advantages.

Selecting a place for negotiations involves a choice between using the premises of one of the parties or meeting in a neutral location. If the parties maintain a permanent bargaining machinery with adequate facilities, these would be an obvious choice. But that is not often the case. Many negotiations take place at the seat of an employers' association or the main office of an individual enterprise, as the case may be, because they can provide suitable quarters at little or no cost. Where the relationship between the parties is characterised by considerable friction, or where the union side is concerned about adverse membership reaction to negotiations being held on the employers' territory, a neutral location is clearly indicated. In European countries the ministries of labour are often able to make a neutral location available. In North America the bargainers are more likely to choose a hotel. Major negotiations that have reached a critical stage are sometimes shifted at government request to a place where the negotiators are more easily accessible to persuasion attempts by highly placed public officials.

Other things being equal, publicity tends to have an adverse effect on ongoing negotiations, for example by making it difficult for the parties to retreat without loss of face from an announced position. For that reason the parties to a mature bargaining relationship often agree in advance to make no unilateral statements to the media about the course of the negotiations and to withhold comment until the negotiations have either resulted in an agreement or have reached an impasse. Nevertheless, the use of publicity as a means of exerting pressure in the course of negotiations is by no means unheard of, especially through information leaks.

Once the negotiations get under way, each side should have an understanding on how they are to be conducted and how interim decisions are to be made as particular points come up. Negotiators usually designate a single spokesman, who is almost invariably the senior member of the negotiating team, through whom all statements are conveyed to the other side at the bargaining table. In other cases, however, it is acceptable for other members to participate freely in the discussions or for the presentation of highly technical points to be entrusted to specialists. Where only a single union or single employer participates in the negotiations, there should be no difficulty in reaching internal agreement on the choice of a spokesman or other procedural matters. But where either side is a composite of different, more or less autonomous entities, such as a group of unions or an employers' association, consent may have to be negotiated. Actually it is in just such situations that a single spokesman would be most useful in order to maintain an appearance of unity when differences in the group arise that the other side might be able to exploit in the hope of creating divisions and weaknesses. This possibility arises more often on the union than the employer side, especially in those European countries where several unions affiliated with different national confederations participate in the negotiations, yet also compete with one another for members and pre-eminence. Similar problems can arise in the context of multi-union bargaining in Great Britain, even when there are no ideological differences separating the participants.

Employers' associations usually find it easier than unions to keep their disagreements to themselves and to let a single spokesman express their views, most likely either the principal full-time official of the association or a senior management member of an affiliated enterprise.

Negotiations begin most of the time with the formal presentation of the union's proposed changes in the agreement, although they may already have been communicated previously to the other side. If the employer side has had no previous information on the union's demands it may at this point request time to study them for the purpose of preparing a response at some future meeting. Alternatively, the employers may want to express a preliminary reaction to the union's claims and may also want to place on record their own initial bargaining position by indicating the changes which they wish to introduce into the agreement. The extent to which these initial bargaining positions are far removed from, or close to, the minimum acceptable settlement terms of the negotiators varies a good deal between and within countries, as does the forcefulness or emphasis with which the initial demands are presented.

The actual bargaining that ensues in what might be called the middle stages may range from brief and simple sessions, with agreement or deadlock quickly reached, to extremely time-consuming and complex endurance contests. Again there seems to be some variation in national patterns, with the negotiations in Great Britain and in most of the continental European countries being usually of relatively short duration in terms of total time consumed and number of sessions held, whereas in North America and Sweden the negotiations can stretch out long enough to tax the physical and emotional stamina of the negotiators. One observer of collective bargaining in the United States regards these middle stages as an opportunity for each party to develop an estimate of the relative importance which the other party attaches to the various outstanding issues, calculate the likelihood that an agreement can be reached without an impasse and convey to the other side which issues might be amenable to compromise at later stages of bargaining.[52] In sum, it is during this period that the parties seek to test out their respective priorities, potential concessions and latent flexibility.

As the negotiations progress, it may also be advisable, if technical subjects are under consideration, to form expert subcommittees whose findings are to be reported to the full group. At a certain point it may become useful for the leading negotiators to meet informally and in private since any departures from positions previously described as firm are easier to concede in such meetings. It is also likely that the negotiations will have to be interrupted from time to time to allow each negotiating committee to meet by itself. Especially when the bargaining covers a wide range of issues and when many different constituencies of employees and employers are represented, there are almost certain to be unresolved internal differences which need to be reconciled. There must also be opportunities for each side to reappraise its bargaining objectives and strategy as the position of the other side becomes clearer.

A highly structured pattern has developed in the metals industries in the Federal Republic of Germany. This is of special interest because the outcome of the negotiations often becomes the standard for other bargainers in the private and even the public sector and also because the dominant union, the Metalworkers' Union,[53] is the largest labour organisation in the Western world. Here the union's initial demands are conveyed to the employers four weeks before the termination of the agreement.[54] Actual bargaining begins two weeks before and continues four weeks beyond the agreement's expiration, in other words for a total of six weeks. Only then are the parties free to impose coercive measures on each other, and only then may either side declare a breakdown of negotiations. This might be followed, subject to agreement, by submission of the dispute to the jointly operated conciliation machinery.

Rather different is the pattern of bargaining in Japan, where strikes are more likely to be called at the beginning of collective bargaining than as a result of a breakdown, but these are of course demonstration strikes and not strikes to the finish:

It is still usual for the union to call a work stoppage at the onset of negotiations rather than wait until an impasse is reached. The Spring Offensive itself draws heavily upon this approach before hard bargaining develops. Use of the strike to signal the beginning rather than the breakdown of negotiations demonstrates primarily the union's seriousness about its demands and union member support and solidarity.[55]

It must also be noted, however, that for Japan as a whole the number of labour disputes, of workers involved and of working days lost have sharply declined since 1974.[56]

At a certain stage outside assistance by impartial third parties may become necessary, but the role of mediation, conciliation and other forms of dispute settlement will not be dealt with here. It should, however, be stressed that the possibility of a work stoppage, with its potentially heavy cost for both parties, is often a compelling factor inducing the negotiators to seek agreement, or in any event to compare the cost of a settlement with the estimated cost of a dispute of uncertain duration. In certain bargaining relationships a tradition has developed according to which employees do not work if there is no valid agreement in effect. The imminent expiration of an agreement gives rise, therefore, to what is known as "deadline bargaining", in which the parties strain to reach a meeting of minds before a work stoppage occurs, although it seems that in the current economic difficulties unions have been less insistent on observance of this tradition. In other bargaining situations the pace of negotiations may be more leisurely, and although tentative strike deadlines may exist, they are subject to change if the parties wish to give themselves more time to explore areas of potential agreement and disagreement.

AUTHORITY OF NEGOTIATORS

Collective bargaining is conducted by negotiators acting on behalf of constituents or principals. The question is bound to arise, therefore, how much authority is entrusted to the negotiators. Do they have authority to conclude an agreement binding on their organisations or does the ultimate authority to determine the acceptability of the agreement remain somewhere among the people whose interests they represent? In effect, there is no uniformity of practice at all, especially not on the union side where widely shared principles of internal democracy may sometimes be difficult to reconcile with the exigencies of the bargaining process.

Employers

To begin with the employer side, one has to distinguish between enterprise bargaining on the one hand and association or multi-employer bargaining on the other. Although further subdivisions exist within these categories (for example, an enterprise whose several plants bargain separately), the two major distinctions suffice to bring out the salient points.

The least complicated case is that of the single enterprise (or plant). In so far as it concerns companies with widely diversified shareholdings, the well-known separation that has arisen between corporate ownership and control precludes shareholders from having any direct influence on collective bargaining. Corporations do not regard themselves as democratic institutions, nor do shareholders expect to be consulted on bargaining strategy or specific issues. Boards of directors or supervisory boards often do become involved, but as a rule only for the purpose of providing operating management with general guidance on the shape of an acceptable settlement or possibly, but not very likely, to consider the costs and consequences of a strike or lockout. In any event, effective responsibility for, and control over, the negotiations is almost invariably in the hands of the highest levels of management, even where the actual conduct of the bargaining sessions is delegated to second-echelon executives, for example a vice-president for industrial relations in an American corporation (or possibly an executive with line instead of staff responsibilities).

The authority of the principal negotiators for the employer side may range from, at one extreme, full power to conclude a binding agreement to, at the other, serving as messengers between the negotiating room and the executive suite. It is far more likely to be nearer the first than the second alternative, but there are instances when top management may wish to avoid a situation where negotiators have to make on-the-spot decisions on matters whose full implications may not be clear at the time of the transaction, especially if the parties are acting under the pressure of deadline bargaining. For that very reason, top managers often prefer not to be present at the bargaining table but to let themselves be represented by trusted subordinates so that they can make decisions on complex problems while insulated from the pressures of the bargaining process. Invariably, however, unions strongly prefer to deal face to face with managers who have authority to make decisions as issues come up for consideration, anything less being considered highly unsatisfactory. Given these contradictory preferences, management negotiators are sometimes allowed an intermediate range of authority, being able to come to terms on some items or at least to enter into preliminary understandings, but obliged to refer back to their superiors on the more important ones.

More complex is the problem of negotiating authority in the case of employers' associations, although reliable information about it is exceedingly scarce. Since it is usually not practicable for all member firms of an association to have a place at the bargaining table, associations must make arrangements for setting up negotiating teams. As a rule they will seek to muster both the professional and technical talents of their full-time staffs and the authority and stature of the leading employers in the association. The representativeness of a negotiating team is also an important consideration. The various industrial branches and regions which make up the association expect to be adequately represented, and if there is a mixture of large and small firms, due account needs to be taken of that fact, too. Negotiating teams may be led either by the chief official of the association or by a senior executive of one of the major member firms. In the United States employers' associations sometimes entrust the actual negotiations to a lawyer, or to a firm of lawyers, already serving as their legal adviser.

Employers' associations tend to confer on their negotiators relatively ample powers to conclude agreements, certainly more so on average than in the case of unions, although sometimes they designate a representative group of member firms to which the negotiators are expected to turn for guidance and instruction on knotty problems. Quite generally, associations seek to avoid having to make decisions by ballot and try to rely instead on internal consultation for a solution satisfactory to all concerned. Therefore the preferred procedure for deciding what stand to take on a contentious issue of bargaining strategy is to seek a consensus rather than to take a vote, for that would allow internal differences to be exposed for possible exploitation by the bargainers for the union.

Unions

Although there are certain parallels between employers and unions with regard to the degree of authority delegated to their negotiators, the problem becomes more complex on the union side. On the one hand, in order to be credible, union negotiators need not only master the requisite technical expertise but must also have — or must at least be perceived to have — sufficient authority to enter into understandings as the negotiations proceed. Like their counterparts among employers, union representatives must have the requisite discretion to judge when the proper moment has come to demand or to concede, to stand firm or to hint at willingness to compromise, to probe for openings or to close a deal. All this requires skills, judgement and mental agility, but negotiators who for lack of authority cannot do much more than act as messengers on behalf of their constituents will be under a severe handicap.

On the other hand, unions do pride themselves on the democratic character of their decision-making, which may take the form of direct membership participation in deciding vital issues (instead of leaving such decisions to periodically elected leaders and representatives) or may mean representative democracy. Even where representative democracy is generally accepted as appropriate, union members may still insist that decisions on the acceptance of collective agreements are too important to be delegated to negotiating committees. The relative importance attached to considerations of bargaining efficiency versus participatory democracy varies not only from country to country but also from union to union. Consequently, a range of practices have evolved with regard to the authority entrusted to union negotiators.

Although trends are difficult to spot with any certainty, some general observations may be hazarded. Unions with decentralised internal structures tend to limit the authority delegated to their negotiators by requiring that agreements must be approved either by the relevant membership or by an elected body of members, such as a policy committee. Conversely, unions that have adopted a substantial amount of centralisation in their administration are more likely to entrust their negotiators with considerable authority, sometimes even to the extent of enabling them to conclude binding agreements.

Illustrative of the latter situation is the policy of the largest peak confederation in Sweden, the LO. Within the context of a relatively highly centralised system of industrial relations, the LO's rules specify that affiliated unions must assign the right to make all final decisions concerning collective bargaining to their own national executive boards, including the termination of existing agreements, the acceptance or rejection of newly negotiated agreements, and the question of engaging in industrial action. Without such a provision in its constitution, a union presumably cannot remain affiliated to the confederation. But at the same time the statutes of the confederation also encourage affiliates to find ways to consult their members, by referenda or delegate conferences, about issues to be raised in collective bargaining.[57] Whatever the means used, any voting that is held may have only an advisory effect, so as to preserve the executive board's final decision-making power.

A sharply contrasting situation is presented by the much more decentralised industrial relations system in Japan. In that country, where the authority of the national unions over their constituent enterprise union affiliates is extremely limited, neither the negotiators nor the members of the enterprise union's executive board are normally authorised by the membership to make final decisions in collective bargaining. Instead the decisions of the negotiators have only a preliminary character and are subject to periodic review by general delegate meetings as the bargaining proceeds.

Another important factor determining the degree of authority conferred on union negotiators was identified by Shirley Lerner, who pointed out that "the degree of popular participation in determining an agreement to a considerable extent varies inversely with the size of the geographic area for which the bargain is conducted".[58] This would certainly help to explain the restrictions on the authority of union negotiators that frequently exist in the United States with its single-firm and single-plant bargaining units. In part the prevalence is of course also due to widely accepted notions about the importance of direct membership participation for the effective functioning of trade union democracy. Moreover, the absence, by and large, of multi-union (or coalition) bargaining from the industrial relations system in the United States — as contrasted with the situation in several European countries — has prevented any build-up of pressure to attenuate existing restrictions on the authority of union negotiators, for there is no doubt that direct membership participation in decision-making is more easily accommodated in a system of single-union than multi-union bargaining.

Ratification of agreements

As the preceding section has implied, questions about the authority of negotiators are closely linked to the practice with regard to required membership ratification of the agreement, especially on the union side. In so far as information is available about ratification procedures in different countries, it seems to be in general accord with the criteria mentioned above. In countries such as Austria, Belgium and Sweden, where centralised union structures, industry-wide negotiations and (at least in some instances) multi-union bargaining arrangements tend to reinforce each other, ratification by the union's membership is rare.[59] By contrast, ratification is commonplace, even if not universal, in countries such as Canada, Japan and the United States, where union structures are on average more decentralised, negotiations tend to be enterprise centred, and single-union bargaining representation is the general rule.

An intermediate position is held by countries such as France, the Federal Republic of Germany, Great Britain and Italy, some tending towards the first group, others towards the second. There are no ratification votes in France at industry level, but in those relatively infrequent instances where bargaining takes place at enterprise level (as in the case of Renault), agreements may be submitted to general assemblies of the employees. British unions follow widely diverging practices, some submitting their agreements to membership approval, while others (probably the majority) follow procedures that do not include a membership ratification vote. In the Federal Republic of Germany the general practice is to allow an advisory vote by the wage policy committee (*Tarifkommission*), but the final decision is made by the union's national executive board. Balloting by the general membership occurs as a rule only if a strike — or a settlement to end a strike — has been recommended.[60] In Italy union negotiators often make final acceptance of an agreement dependent on workers' approval (i.e. not only union members) at workplace meetings.

Difficult problems arise for both unions and employers if a preliminary agreement is rejected by the ratifying employee constituency. (No doubt difficulties of at least equal magnitude would arise in the event that the membership of an employers' association were to reject an agreement concluded by its negotiating committee, but that hardly ever happens.) Only the main ones will be mentioned here. First, since the ratification vote on a new agreement usually occurs close to the terminal date of the previous agreement, or even after its expiration if by mutual consent the date has been extended, a negative vote in some countries, notably in North America, may signify an immediate cessation of work. Should the rejection be unexpected, both sides may find themselves in the midst of a strike for which neither was prepared and which presumably neither side wanted.

Second, to renegotiate an agreement on the basis of improved terms after the initial version has been rejected in a ratification vote may be regarded as proof that the employers' allegedly final bargaining position in the negotiations may not have been the final position after all. This implies that the union's negotiators did not obtain the best possible agreement on their first attempt. The creation of such impressions may lead to serious complications in future negotiations, once a precedent exists that seems to demonstrate that a refusal to ratify results ultimately in a better agreement. Precisely to avoid such a situation the employer may decide to withhold his best offer until after the anticipated first rejection. For their part, the union negotiators may become reluctant to commit themselves to any settlement before first having heard from their members.

Third, rejections of preliminary agreements tend to undermine an established relationship because in certain circumstances they may cast doubt on the good faith of the negotiators. The employer in particular may suspect, for example, that as a means of extracting additional concessions the union's negotiators failed to exert their best efforts on behalf of ratification or, alternatively, may believe that the union's leaders are not attuned to their members or are not in control of them.

If these are some of the adverse consequences that may ensue from a negative ratification vote, there are also strong reasons that support the practice. Perhaps chief among them is the point that collective agreements are so important in setting the conditions under which employees spend their working lives that they ought to be demonstrably acceptable to them. The only valid test of acceptability, so the argument continues, is by direct expression of the wishes of employees themselves. Indirect expressions, as indicated by the opinions of negotiating committees or delegate conferences, are insufficient for this purpose. It is also held that agreements which have stood the test of membership ratification are more likely to be regarded as fair and proper by those to whom they apply, therefore more likely to be respected and less likely to lead to dissension, disruption and disregard. Improved communications are cited as another important advantage in the sense that the need for a favourable ratification vote will induce union negotiators and union leaders to devote more attention to ascertaining rank-and-file expectations and to explaining more carefully the reasons behind the terms of the tentative agreement at the time it is submitted for ratification.

Those who believe that full authority to make commitments on behalf of the union should be vested in the negotiating committees or the organisation's officers often maintain that ratification votes lend themselves to abuse in the sense that they can become part of a union's negotiating tactics, that most members lack a realistic appreciation of all the elements that enter into the complex process of negotiating an agreement and that only those who actually participate in the bargaining can fully understand the economic constraints bearing upon the settlement.

It is difficult to estimate how widespread the problem of negative ratification votes is and whether there are any trends upward or downward. Statistical data for the United States, covering the period 1964-81, provide a certain amount of information, but the figures pertain only to settlements negotiated with the assistance of the Federal Mediation and Conciliation Service (FMCS), not to the total number of settlements. Table 2 indicates year by year the number and percentage of settlements rejected by the members of the bargaining unit after an agreement had been tentatively negotiated. Although there was an increase in the absolute number of rejections in the late 1970s, which might be related to the economic difficulties of that period and to members' discontent with the agreements reached, the corresponding percentage figures for these years do not support the conclusion that there was a distinct upward trend.

The Norwegian approach to the problem is worth special mention. That the matter is important to the parties in that country is indicated by the fact that they decided to incorporate the relevant provisions in the Basic Agreement which is applicable to all affiliates of the central organisations.[61] Not only does the Agreement contain separate provisions for ratification votes by employees and, interestingly enough, by employers as well, but it is founded on the principle, agreed to by the peak confederations on both sides, that a ratification vote should

Table 2. United States: Number and percentage of closed FMSC joint meeting cases involving rejection of tentative settlement, 1964-81

Fiscal year	No. of cases rejected	% rejected
1964	629	8.7
1965	746	10.0
1966	918	11.7
1967	1 019	14.2
1968	893	11.9
1969	991	12.3
1970	843	11.2
1971	795	9.9
1972	732	10.1
1973	697	9.6
1974	1 050	12.4
1975	976	11.1
1976	876	9.8
1977	1 208	11.5
1978	1 145	11.9
1979	1 219	11.9
1980	1 101	10.7
1981	832	8.9

Source: Federal Mediation and Conciliation Service: *Annual Reports*, various issues.

be a representative vote. That is why the employees' voting procedure specifies that "All members [of the trade union concerned] having the right to vote have the duty to vote".[62] Failure to do so may result in forfeiture of financial assistance from the union. If, nevertheless, so few members vote that the results do not adequately reflect majority opinion, the national union's executive board may order a new ballot.

DURATION OF AGREEMENTS

With the conclusion of a collective agreement, or upon its ratification where that is customary or required, the parties establish the terms and conditions of employment that are to be in effect for the agreed duration. The length of that duration is by no means uniform. Not only are there substantial inter-country differences as well as changes in response to changed circumstances, but within any particular country the nature of the agreement often determines its duration. Central or basic agreements, concluded between peak confederations for the purpose of establishing general principles or guide-lines for labour-management relations, are usually concluded for a substantially longer period than industry-level or enterprise-level wage agreements and may even be concluded for an indefinite period, subject to cancellation by either party. At industry or enterprise level, if distinctions are made between procedural agreements and substantive agreements, as in Great Britain, procedural agreements are likely to be open-ended, while substantive agreements will probably contain a specific expiration date.

The emphasis here will be on collective agreements which determine the conditions of employment and which normally contain provisions related to wages, hours of work and other items. In most countries agreements of this kind are negotiated for a fixed duration, but in some, notably in Belgium, France and Great Britain, there are still agreements of indeterminate duration. The French situation is particularly noteworthy. While it is normal practice to conclude agreements for a fixed period, usually one year, the parties often tend to operate as though the agreements were of indefinite duration, for it is understood that expiring agreements will automatically be prolonged if they are not renegotiated. Existing legislation supports this understanding by providing that, unless otherwise agreed, a fixed-term agreement becomes, on expiration, an agreement of indefinite duration and provides further that a cancelled agreement remains in effect for one more year, unless superseded by a renegotiated agreement.[63] Yet even in these three countries fixed-term agreements have become increasingly the rule, and it would be reasonable to assume that this is so because, on balance, they offer greater advantages to the parties. This is certainly so for employers, who have a strong interest in regard to their need for forward calculations of wage costs, production planning, submission of bids on prospective orders, and other business activities that are dependent on foreseeable wage and fringe benefit costs. Employees, for their part, are protected against a sudden abrogation of the gains they have achieved through collective bargaining which could result from an employer's decision to cancel an agreement without fixed duration. From the point of view of the public interest, as well as the interest of the parties themselves, the maintenance of industrial peace for a definite and predictable period, which is implicit in a fixed-term agreement, may be regarded as an important advantage.

Fixed-term agreements have become unquestionably more common than open-ended ones. But how long is a fixed term? Until about ten or perhaps 15 years ago, one-year agreements probably predominated in most countries, but there was also a noticeable trend then towards two-year and three-year agreements in a substantial group of countries, both in North America and Western Europe. That trend was probably most pronounced in the United States, where already in the late 1960s half of all major agreements were concluded for a period of three years, and an additional 20 per cent for even longer. As Thomson later pointed out:

One noticeable development in the US which has had no real parallel in Europe has been the shift to the longer term contract since 1950, such that the great majority of contracts last three years. This has given an additional amount of predictability to the employer. This has held up remarkably well during inflation, although the widespread COLA [cost-of-living adjustment] clause does help here.[64]

Although there was perhaps "no real parallel" to this development in Western Europe, the proportion of two-year and three-year agreements in several countries and in Canada did increase significantly in the 1960s.

That trend has now been reversed everywhere except in the United States. In Canada and in most countries of Western Europe most industry-wide or enterprise agreements are nowadays concluded for one-year periods, and central agreements for two years. Thus, table 3 indicates strikingly what happened to the duration of major agreements in Canada in a 16-year period. Evidently there occurred a remarkable shift away from long-term agreements and towards much shorter durations, especially toward one-year terms. Current data for the Federal Republic of Germany indicate that of all new agreements concluded in 1983 those negotiated for one year covered 73.7 per cent of a total of 17,628,000 employees.[65]

The reasons for the reversal of direction are not far afield. In a period of economic uncertainty unions are reluctant to commit themselves to long-term agreements, especially if the agreements do not contain adequate protection against the erosion of the living standards of their members. In a context of government wage restraint programmes and declining inflation, unions came under pressure to make concessions on the cost-of-living adjustment provisions in collective agreements, but in return they insisted on shorter durations. Similar considerations led to parallel results in quite a few European countries.

Only in a few countries is there a longer modal period for industry-wide agreements, for example two years in Denmark and three years in Italy. In such instances there are sometimes wage reopener provisions which become effective if the rate of inflation exceeds a predetermined level. It must also be pointed out, however, that in other countries, for example Great Britain and Japan, a distinction is made between wage agreements and agreements to set other terms; and where that is the case the duration of the wage agreements is likely to be the shorter of the two. Additionally, there are now some indications that British wage agreements are once again being negotiated for a longer period, as indicated by the conclusion of several important two-year agreements in 1984-85.[66] The relatively low inflation rate of about 5 per cent may be the major reason.

Table 3. Duration of collective agreements in Canada, 1967 and 1983 (percentages)

No. of years in major new settlements	1967	1983
	(N = 227)	(N = 624)
1	17.6	55.7
2	52.4	30.8
3	30.0	13.5
	100.0	100.0

Source: W. D. Wood and Praedeep Kumar (eds.): *The current industrial relations scene in Canada 1984* (Kingston, Ontario, Queen's University at Kingston, Industrial Relations Centre, 1984), p. 424.

In the United States the outcome was rather different. According to a 1983 study of the Bureau of National Affairs, which compares the contents of 400 major collective agreements at four-year intervals, 77 per cent of agreements were concluded for three years, as compared with 73 per cent in 1979 and 70 per cent in 1970 — a noticeable increase.[67] The 1983 study also showed that 4 per cent of agreements were concluded for four years, 17 per cent for two years and only 1 per cent for one year. The fact that three-year agreements retained such a strong position was due partly to the continued inclusion of compensatory cost-of-living adjustment provisions and built-in wage increases for the second and third years, but in part also to the relatively greater bargaining strength of employers. Aided by the rapid decline of inflation in the early 1980s and by the emphasis which American unions increasingly placed on job security in their collective bargaining objectives, American employers were able to obtain long-term agreements — and the stability and predictability generally associated with long-term agreements — on a far larger scale than most of their European counterparts.

Notes

[1] Nils Elvander: "Sweden", in Benjamin C. Roberts (ed.): *Towards industrial democracy: Europe, Japan and the United States* (London, Croom Helm, 1979), p. 134.

[2] Harold W. Davey et al.: *Contemporary collective bargaining* (Englewood Cliffs, New Jersey, Prentice Hall, 4th ed., 1982), p. 108.

[3] For a comparative review of the issues involved in recognition, see Alan Gladstone and Muneto Ozaki: "Trade union recognition for collective bargaining purposes", in *International Labour Review* (Geneva, ILO), Aug.-Sep. 1975, pp. 163-189.

[4] Yves Delamotte: "Recent trends in the statutory regulation of industrial relations in France", in *Labour and Society* (Geneva, IILS), Jan. 1985, p. 8.

[5] For France, see Michel Despax and Jacques Rojot: "France" (1979), in R. Blanpain (ed.): *International encyclopaedia for labour law and industrial relations* (Deventer, Kluwer, 1977 onwards), Vol. 4, pp. 127-129.

[6] Andrew Thomson: "A view from abroad", in Jack Stieber et al. (eds.): *US industrial relations 1950-1980: A critical assessment* (Madison, Wisconsin, Industrial Relations Research Association, 1981), pp. 302-303.

[7] D. Quinn Mills: "Management performance", in Stieber et al., op. cit., p. 115.

[8] Detailed information on the outcome of elections between 1950 and 1978 appears in Edwin F. Beal and James P. Begin: *The practice of collective bargaining* (Homewood, Illinois, Irwin, 1982), p. 195, figure 6-1. For the period 1978-83, see W. D. Wood and Pradeep Kumar (eds.): *The current industrial relations scene in Canada 1984* (Kingston, Ontario, Queen's University at Kingston, Industrial Relations Centre, 1984), p. 226, table 6.

[9] Beal and Begin, op. cit., pp. 196-197 and figure 6-2. Also Wood and Kumar, loc. cit.

[10] United Kingdom, Royal Commission on Trade Union and Employers' Associations, 1965-68: *Report* (The "Donovan Report"), Cmnd. 3623 (London, HM Stationery Office, 1968).

[11] See *Legislative Series* (Geneva, ILO), 1971 — UK 1.

[12] ibid., 1975 — UK 2.

[13] For a brief review of these developments, see Henry Phelps Brown: *The origins of trade union power* (Oxford, Clarendon Press, 1983), pp. 215-216. Cf. Roberts below, pp. 284-285.

[14] For present purposes we exclude the legal prescriptions that establish a *de facto* bargaining relationship between employers and works councils since most countries consider this relationship *de jure* to be outside the domain of collective bargaining.

[15] See *Legislative Series*, 1947 — USA 2. Emphasis added.

[16] Canada, Privy Council Office: *Canadian industrial relations: The report of the Task Force on Labour Relations* (Ottawa, 1968), p. 163.

[17] ibid.

[18] Lennart Forsebäck: *Industrial relations and employment in Sweden* (Stockholm, Swedish Institute, 1981), p. 40.

[19] For an English translation of the law, see Act respecting co-determination at work dated 10 June 1976, *Legislative Series*, 1976 — Swe. 1.

[20] Act No. 82-957 concerning collective bargaining and the settlement of collective labour disputes. For an English translation, see *Legislative Series*, 1982 — Fr. 2 D.

[21] See *Social and Labour Bulletin*, June 1983, pp. 185-186. Cf. *European Industrial Relations Review*, Jan. 1983, p. 8 ff. Also Delamotte, op. cit., pp. 7-26, and Mary Ann Glendon: "French labor law reform 1982-1983: The struggle for collective bargaining", in *American Journal of Comparative Law* (Berkeley, California), summer 1984, pp. 449-491.

[22] See Blanpain below, pp. 182-183.

[23] See United Kingdom, Advisory, Conciliation and Arbitration Service: *Industrial relations handbook* (London, HM Stationery Office, 1980), p. 99; also H. A. Clegg: *The changing system of industrial relations in Great Britain* (Oxford, Basil Blackwell, 1979), p. 229.

[24] John P. Windmuller: *Labor relations in the Netherlands* (Ithaca, New York, Cornell University Press, 1969), pp. 282-286.

[25] See Blanpain below, p. 183. But see Thomas A. Kochan: *Collective bargaining and industrial relations: From theory to policy and practice* (Homewood, Illinois, Irwin, 1980), Chs. 5 and 6.

[26] Beal and Begin, op. cit., p. 210.

[27] Davey et al., op. cit., p. 109.

[28] For a checklist of specific items to be reviewed by managers preparing for bargaining, see Davey et al., op. cit., p. 112.

[29] Thomson goes so far as to maintain that "European employer organisations essentially exist to protect the marginal firm". Thomson, op. cit., p. 309.

[30] See Fürstenberg below, p. 215.

[31] See Blanpain, below, p. 183.

[32] As regards the United States, it has been noted that "the substantial improvement in 'official' data has reduced the need for self-help in this area. The bargaining can be more objective when both parties are agreeable to arguing their cases in terms of data published by the Bureau of Labor Statistics, the Federal Reserve Board, or a state agency whose information is jointly regarded as reliable" (Davey et al., op. cit., p. 111).

[33] For the text of this agreement and examples of others similar to it in objective, see ILO: *Selected basic agreements and joint declarations on labour-management relations*, Labour-Management Relations Series, No. 63 (Geneva, 1983).

[34] Still the most comprehensive work on the subject is Abraham J. Siegel (ed.): *The impact of computers on collective bargaining* (Cambridge, Massachusetts Institute of Technology, 1969). See also Clive Jenkins and Barrie Sherman: *Computers and the unions* (London, Longman, 1977), especially Ch. 8.

[35] Emanuel S. Savas et al.: *Computers in collective bargaining: The Adelphi experience*, Report to the Carnegie Corporation (New York, n.p., Jan. 1974), p. 5.

[36] John Niland: *Collective bargaining and compulsory arbitration in Australia* (Kensington, New South Wales, Australia, New South Wales University Press, 1978), pp. 95-97.

[37] Göran Skogh: "Employers associations in Sweden", in John P. Windmuller and Alan Gladstone (eds.): *Employers associations and industrial relations: A comparative study* (Oxford, Clarendon Press, 1984), pp. 254-255.

[38] Neil W. Chamberlain and James W. Kuhn: *Collective bargaining* (New York, McGraw-Hill, 2nd ed., 1965), p. 75.

³⁹ ILO: *Collective bargaining: A response to the recession in industrialised market economy countries* (Geneva, 1984), p. 8.

⁴⁰ Richard E. Walton and Robert B. McKersie: *A behavioral theory of labor negotiations* (New York, McGraw-Hill, 1965).

⁴¹ Janice R. Bellace and Howard F. Gospel: "Disclosure of information to trade unions: A comparative perspective", in *International Labour Review*, Jan.-Feb. 1983, p. 58.

⁴² Harold C. White and Lynn M. Meyer: "Employer obligation to provide information", in *Labor Law Journal* (Chicago, Illinois), Oct. 1984, p. 644.

⁴³ ibid., p. 646.

⁴⁴ See particularly *NLRB v. Acme Industrial Co.* (1967), 385 US432, as cited ibid., p. 643.

⁴⁵ Bellace and Gospel, op. cit., p. 63.

⁴⁶ See Howard F. Gospel: "Trade unions and the legal obligation to bargain: An American, Swedish and British comparison", in *British Journal of Industrial Relations*, Nov. 1984, pp. 349-350. Cf. Roberts below, p. 296. See also Roger Hussey and Arthur Marsh: *Disclosure of information and employee reporting* (London, Gower, 1983).

⁴⁷ Article L.132-12 of Act No. 82-957, quoted in Glendon, op. cit., p. 472. Cf. Delamotte, op. cit., p. 17.

⁴⁸ Glendon, op. cit., p. 473.

⁴⁹ Walter P. Reuther: "Labor's role in 1975", in Jack Stieber (ed.): *US industrial relations: The next twenty years* (East Lansing, Michigan State University Press, 1958), p. 63.

⁵⁰ Bellace and Gospel, op. cit., p. 71. Emphasis added.

⁵¹ Published descriptions of actual negotiations are still relatively rare. Among recent publications, see Klaus Wohlert: "Vergleich des Tarifverhandlungssystems in Schweden und der Bundesrepublik Deutschland" [Collective bargaining systems in Sweden and the Federal Republic of Germany], in *WSI Mitteilungen* [WSI Information] (Cologne), Aug. 1976, pp. 465-475; Wolfgang Streeck: *Industrial relations in West Germany: A case study of the car industry* (London, Heinemann Educational Books, 1984), especially Chs. 5, 6 and 7; and Kochan: *Collective bargaining . . .*, op. cit., pp. 245-248.

⁵² Kochan, op. cit., p. 246.

⁵³ IG Metall.

⁵⁴ See Fürstenberg below, pp. 215.

⁵⁵ Solomon Levine: "Japan", in Albert A. Blum (ed.): *International handbook of industrial relations* (Westport, Connecticut, Greenwood, 1981), p. 344.

⁵⁶ See Shirai below, p. 251.

⁵⁷ Developments in the Netherlands are relevant here. In that country, with a history of ample powers delegated to the negotiators, both parties (i.e. unions and employers' associations) have increasingly resorted, in the negotiations of recent years, to consulting their members (through so-called *kaderbijeenkomsten*) and have tried to take their views into account. European Communities: *Problems and prospects of collective bargaining in the EEC member states* (Luxembourg, 1980), p. 19.

⁵⁸ Shirley W. Lerner: *The impact of technological and economic change on the structure of British trade unions*, Paper submitted to the First World Congress of the International Industrial Relations Association, Geneva, 4-9 September 1967 (doc. IC-678-3, mimeographed), p. 3.

⁵⁹ For Belgium, see Blanpain below, p. 183.

⁶⁰ Manfred Wilke: *Die Funktionäre: Apparat und Demokratie im Deutschen Gewerkschaftsbund* [Union officials: Machinery and democracy in the German Confederation of Trade Unions] (Munich/Zurich, Piper Verlag, 1979), p. 67.

⁶¹ ILO: *Selected basic agreements and joint declarations on labour-management relations*, Labour-Management Relations Series No. 63 (Geneva, 1983), pp. 181-182.

⁶² ibid., p. 181.

⁶³ Jean-Claude Javillier: *Droit du travail* (Paris, Librairie générale de Droit et de Jurisprudence, 1981), p. 626.

⁶⁴ Thomson, op. cit., p. 321.

⁶⁵ Michael Kittner (ed.): *Gewerkschaftsjahrbuch 1984* [Trade union yearbook] (Cologne, Bund-Verlag, 1984), p. 80, table 3.

[66] *LLE Journal* (London, Labour Line Europe Ltd.), Apr. 1985, pp. 14-17.

[67] United States, Bureau of National Affairs: *Collective bargaining negotiations and contracts* (Washington, DC, 1983), section 36. See also United States, Bureau of Labor Statistics: *Characteristics of major collective bargaining agreements, January 1, 1980*, Bulletin No. 2095 (Washington, DC, 1981), p. 2, chart 1.

THE BARGAINING STRUCTURE

4

Whenever collective bargaining becomes established as the process by which decisions of considerable importance to those affected are made about the terms and conditions of employment, there develops a network of institutionalised relationships which is referred to as the bargaining structure. The term applies in particular to the often highly complex horizontal and vertical segmentations which divide and subdivide industrial relations systems into hierarchical layers and compartments, and to the relations that exist between them.

Bargaining structures are not easily portrayed in an orderly way even if the term "structure" seemingly implies certain qualities of symmetry, hierarchy and neatness. The leading authority on American bargaining structures has cautioned that "In view of the diversity of collective bargaining in the United States, generalisations about bargaining structure can be made only with some peril." [1] All the greater is the hazard of generalising about a group of rather heterogeneous countries. But this much can be said. Bargaining structures evolve in response to certain common variables, for example economic or market factors, the emergence of communities of interest or the direction of government policies. These are generally long-lasting influences with long-lasting consequences, and change tends to come about only gradually. Thus, neither the enterprise-centred bargaining structure of Japan nor the industry-centred (regional) bargaining structure of the Federal Republic of Germany is likely to undergo a basic transformation, at least not in the near future. But this does not mean that bargaining structures are impervious to change when circumstances alter. The best recent example is that of Great Britain, where the dominance of industry-wide bargaining has been in decline ever since the end of the Second World War, but especially since the appearance of the Donovan Report in 1968 which recommended, among other things, the development of "comprehensive and authoritative collective bargaining machinery to deal at company and/or factory level with the terms and conditions of employment which are settled at these levels".[2]

The British case is not the only one. In several other countries important changes in bargaining structure have occurred during the past several years, most of the time, but not always, in the direction of greater decentralisation. It is, however, by no means clear yet whether these changes will be enduring or whether they represent only a temporary adaptation to market forces, and more particularly to a shift in the balance of bargaining power between unions and employers.

Because there is no commonly agreed definition of the term "bargaining structure", nor even a common terminology, a comment on the meaning given to it here is necessary.[3] The two principal but closely related concepts are the bargaining level and the bargaining unit. The bargaining level refers to the hierarchical and horizontal layers which are characteristic of the bargaining structure in virtually all countries. Schematically, and in descending order of comprehensiveness, the principal layers are commonly understood to be the economy as a whole, the industry and the individual enterprise. But this three-tiered division is in practice much too crude, for there are additional layers in which bargaining takes place, including the individual plant or workshop, the regional subdivision of an industry, a composite of several related industries, and so on.

In a substantial number of countries the terms and conditions of employment under which work is performed are the outcome of two or more agreements concluded at different levels. The following description of British practice illustrates the point:

... in most industries there continue to be negotiations on a limited range of issues between employers' organisations and trade unions at the national or industry level. Below this level bargaining may take place at the district or local level and at the level of the enterprise or plant. In many industries there is bargaining at all these levels.[4]

In countries where this is the case, the negotiations conducted at the higher level — whether that be the economy as a whole, an industry, an enterprise or some other entity — usually establish general guide-lines or minimum standards, or both, as the case may be. Agreements concluded at subsidiary levels then have as their purpose one or more of the following: they may selectively contain improvements over the minimum conditions, they may provide for the implementation of already agreed rules or they may deal with issues not yet covered.

The relationship which connects the various levels at which bargaining takes place constitutes an important aspect of the bargaining structure. As new levels of bargaining are added to those already in existence, for example through legislatively mandated bargaining at enterprise level, or as the relative weight and significance of any given level changes, for example with the abandonment of central nation-wide agreements, that also changes the relationship between the levels of the bargaining structure. If agreements concluded at enterprise level overtake those at industry level in importance, as may be happening in Great Britain, that should be taken as evidence of a decentralising trend. Conversely, if plant-level bargaining is largely subordinated to enterprise-wide bargaining or if, due to a reversal of trends, industry-wide bargaining should become once again subsidiary to economy-wide bargaining, that would signify a change towards greater centralisation. Below we shall review the directions that these trends have actually taken in recent years.

The concept of the "bargaining unit" — or, to use the terminology in section 9 of the United States Labor-Management Relations Act of 1947, the "unit appropriate for the purposes of collective bargaining"[5] — originated in the North American industrial relations systems, but it can be applied usefully to other systems as well.[6] The bargaining unit comprehends the groupings of employees and employers who are represented in collective negotiations and who are subject to the terms embodied in the agreement.[7] Each of the two parties — employees and employers — represents a variable dimension of the bargaining unit. On the employer side the grouping may be as small as an individual enterprise (or an even smaller unit, such as a plant, workshop or department), or it may be as large as a major group of enterprises at regional or national level. It may therefore contain no more than a single employer, or it may encompass hundreds of separate enterprises held together by an employers' association.

The grouping on the employee side can be equally variable. It may contain no more than a small number of craftsmen in a single enterprise who share a certain skill and exercise a common function, or it may be as comprehensive as the workforce attached to an entire industry. Between these two poles, many different possibilities are conceivable because the employee grouping can vary in size, occupational status and function, and in other respects. There may be joint units for production and office employees, or these categories may negotiate separately from one another. Likewise, there may be joint units encompassing highly skilled maintenance employees and semi-skilled assembly line operators, or they may negotiate in separate categories.

DETERMINANTS OF THE BARGAINING STRUCTURE

The structure of collective bargaining that becomes attached to, and an integral part of, a particular industrial relations system is the result not so much of a series of coincidences or historical accidents as of the cumulative effect of identifiable factors. That is why behind virtually every bargaining unit there can be found a deliberate decision to establish that particular unit rather than some other unit, whether the outcome came about by agreement of both parties, by the superior power of one of them or by the decision of an appropriate government agency. To illustrate, the enterprise-centred bargaining structure in Japan emerged from a series of implicit agreements between the parties rather than from a contest of wills. On the other hand, Deaton and Beaumont conclude that while in Great Britain decisions as to the appropriate bargaining structure are mostly dominated by management, equivalent decisions in the United States are more often the result of a power struggle between the two parties, but a struggle in which the union's wishes typically prevail.[8]

83

That the general configuration of the bargaining structure and the specific shape of a particular bargaining unit is of vital interest to the parties themselves is self-evident. Different kinds of units have different consequences in terms of bargaining power and ultimately in terms of bargaining settlements. But governments are not disinterested bystanders in these matters. They too have a stake in the bargaining structure, in part by virtue of their growing role as employers, and in part of course because of their responsibility for stable industrial relations and a sound economy. But aside from the United States, where a specialised government agency has long had an authoritative role in determining the shape of bargaining units, it is only in the quite recent past that governments have begun to concern themselves actively with bargaining structures, as shown by the precedent-making decisions in France and Sweden to institute mandatory bargaining over defined subjects at the level of the individual enterprise.

A number of questions pose themselves at this point. How are the overall differences in bargaining structure between national industrial relations systems to be explained? Why do some countries adhere to a structure which is predominantly composed of industry-wide bargaining units (in some form or other), while others have constructed a more decentralised structure or are in the process of doing so? And what is currently happening to bargaining structures? Although definitive answers to these questions are beyond the scope of this work, the following analysis is intended to provide a better understanding of some of the major points.

Historical bargaining patterns

In most European countries the emergence of trade unions was followed by efforts on the part of employers to meet union collective action with collective efforts of their own, either to break the unions or to negotiate with them. "Many associations were formed only in reaction to the impact of unionism, or it was that impact which brought latent combination into action." [9] Where the decision was to negotiate, employers tended to do so in organised fashion, either by enlarging the functions of an already existing trade association or by creating an organisation especially for negotiations, even if they did so reluctantly, for many would undoubtedly have preferred to act on their own and without the constraints imposed on them by joining with their fellow employers. Although the beginnings of collective bargaining were mostly on a local level at a time when product and labour markets were still local, bargaining expanded to regional and district levels as the extent of markets expanded, and in the smaller countries even to national levels. But the important point here is not whether one level or another predominated, but rather that virtually from the earliest period bargaining involved groups of enterprises instead of individual firms or plants.

In Great Britain multi-employer bargaining dates back to the early part of the nineteenth century, and in some trades possibly even before then. Although most of the time the main initiative came from the unions, employers' associations sometimes took the lead, for example in ironworking and hosiery.[10] Where they did, it was as a result of the perception that there were considerable advantages in multi-employer bargaining as compared with going it alone. Multi-employer bargaining reinforced the employers' individual bargaining power, provided only that group solidarity was maintained, prevented cut-throat competition by pegging wages at levels commonly bearable by the marginal firms, helped to avoid or resolve industrial conflict, and blocked the unions from direct interference with what would nowadays be called managerial prerogatives.

Employers on the European continent were motivated by similar considerations: "Negotiating with unions came to be the decisive reason for the formation of employers' associations in Germany, although this reason was neither uniformly perceived nor quickly accepted by employers." [11] Like their counterparts in Great Britain, they reasoned that if bargaining *per se* was unavoidable, then they preferred multi-employer bargaining units to dealing with unions in their plants. Most of the time they were indeed strong enough to defeat union efforts to penetrate into the individual enterprise for bargaining purposes.

On the whole, European unions were willing to accept multi-employer bargaining units. Regional or national negotiations served to set a minimum wage level which kept union members from competing with one another for available work, and to some extent acted as a substitute for protective labour legislation in establishing a body of work rules of general application. There was also an ideological side to the unions' preference for multi-employer bargaining. Many unions regarded themselves as integral parts of a broader working-class movement struggling for a fundamental reconstruction of society. From that point of view, enterprise-centred bargaining brought to the fore job-related issues which only tended to obscure the ultimate goal. As Kassalow has pointed out:

The employer tendency to favour the industry type of bargaining was reinforced by the broad socialist, class consciousness of major European unions which probably led them to favour this approach, since it would engage "employers through mass class action", and also extend protection to a larger part of the workforce.[12]

Developments in North America took a rather different turn. To be sure, in some economic sectors the level of bargaining was regional and the bargaining units often multi-employer, for example in coalmining, clothing and the railways. But on the whole, the trend favoured single-enterprise bargaining units, and did so for reasons to be found mainly on the employer side. The competitive spirit and the trust in the superiority of individual initiative were even stronger than among European employers, so strong indeed that there was not even the required minimum of willingness to co-operate with other employers for the common benefit. But without it an employers' association — as distinguished from an ad hoc group of employers — is not viable. Public attitudes against cartelisation, powerfully reinforced by anti-trust legislation, contributed to a setting inhospitable to the formation of multi-employer bargaining units. Moreover, the rise of giant firms in some of the basic industries conferred on the employer side a high degree of self-sufficiency in dealings with any conceivable combination of employees. The hostility of most employers towards collective bargaining and their economic power to enforce their views meant that no collective bargaining of any great significance took place in the mass-production industries until public policy became explicitly supportive of collective bargaining in the 1930s. When it did, the rules, as embodied in the legislation and as interpreted by the NLRB, tended to favour the establishment of a bargaining structure based on enterprise-by-enterprise and plant-by-plant relationships.

Interestingly enough, most North American unions, unlike their European counterparts, tended to favour limited as against broad-based bargaining units, although the preferences were by no means uniform. But many unions found that under existing legislative and administrative rules it was often easier to organise and win bargaining rights by concentrating their resources on the most promising enterprises — or parts of them — instead of tackling an entire industry at one time. Moreover, the largely pragmatic philosophical orientation of most American unions concentrated their attention not on the fundamental reconstruction of society but instead on gradual yet steady improvements in wages and working conditions and, wherever possible, on job control. These aims, the unions realised — and particularly the aim of job control — could be attained only by organisations that had gained secure positions inside the enterprise. Based on that understanding, North American unions, unlike their counterparts in European countries, insisted with remarkable success on entrenching their presence at the work site itself and not merely outside the plant gates. And that policy, in turn, contributed to the establishment of a far more decentralised bargaining structure than prevailed in most European countries.

It does not diminish the importance of historical influences on the shape of contemporary bargaining structures to point out that there are limits to the explanatory powers of the past. Other factors also act powerfully upon the bargaining structure, some tending towards centralisation, others towards decentralisation, while still others might oscillate in either direction. Before reviewing their impact it is important to note that there is no uniformly established union or employer position favouring in principle a particular kind of bargaining unit or seeking as a matter of standing policy to establish the primacy of a particular kind of bargaining level. In so far as preferences do exist, they are predominantly the outcome of assessments by the parties of how their interests — that is, their relative bargaining power — will best be served. It is, for example, not the case that unions will invariably press for more and more inclusive bargaining units or for ever higher bargaining levels, nor is it true that employers always aim for the opposite outcome. A bargaining unit of skilled craftsmen will almost certainly oppose any attempt to become integrated into a more comprehensive bargaining unit if such integration is likely to reduce the bargaining power of the trades concerned. Likewise, an industrial employers' association engaged in national bargaining with an industrial union may be expected to condemn any attempt by one of its member firms to leave the association for the purpose of establishing a single-enterprise bargaining relationship if the severance threatens to weaken the solidarity and bargaining power of the employer side.

Markets

Both unions and employers are influenced in their bargaining structure policies by the nature of the product and labour markets within which they operate. Historically, as markets have expanded, unions have usually sought to protect established positions by correspondingly extending the bargaining structure to preclude wage competition and to ensure wage equalisation among their members, or among all affected employees, whether union members or not.

The "standard rate" is one of the oldest principles of trade unionism; the Webbs devoted an entire chapter to it in their classic study, *Industrial democracy*.[13] More recently Kochan summed it up again by pointing out that

... unions will always seek to take wages out of competititon by organising as much of the product market as possible and ensuring that equal wages are paid to workers performing the same work within the relevant market. *One of the major mechanisms for ensuring that wages are taken out of competititon is to expand the formal or informal bargaining structure to correspond with the scope of the market.*[14]

Despite the continuing importance of this link, its universal applicability has recently been undermined by the conclusion of several collective agreements providing for dual wage scales in certain American industries, notably some of the major airlines. Responding to severe competitive pressures, several companies have insisted with success on the adoption of compensation systems under which new employees receive substantially lower pay than current employees in the same job categories.[15] In other words, the unions signing these agreements were not strong enough to insist on the standard rate so as to ensure that equal wages would be paid to workers performing identical work in the same bargaining unit.

Competitive pressures in the market are also continuing to affect the shape of the bargaining structure. Although there is no uniform direction to the thrust, the general tendency in most countries is towards greater decentralisation in the bargaining structure. In countries long accustomed to central economy-wide bargaining, notably in Sweden, there has been some decentralisation to the individual industry level, although it is by no means yet clear whether this is a change with long-term prospects or only a temporary adjustment to accumulated dissatisfaction with decentralisation. Similar shifts to lower bargaining levels (from industry to enterprise, from enterprise to the individual plant) are occurring on a relatively wide scale in several other European countries, even to the point that in some instances one can almost refer to a fragmentation of the bargaining structure. As the 1980 collective bargaining report of the ETUI observed:

There has, for some time, been a remarkable development as regards the level at which bargaining takes place; where trade union organisations are largely in favour of a solidary approach to collective agreements and, consequently, high level bargaining ... the level ... is, in actual fact, moving more and more towards the enterprises and even the factories themselves.[16]

It should not be assumed, however, that current attempts to change the existing bargaining structure are an entirely unprecedented reaction to the contemporary challenge of keen economic competition. Already 20 years ago Chamberlain and Kuhn cited the case of —

... a manufacturer of flat glassware who has long negotiated with the union on a company-wide basis [but] is now seeking plant-by-plant bargaining. He believes that in order to compete effectively, he cannot allow old work rules and already established wage payment systems to spread to his new plants. Competition from other materials and new forms requires him to make full and flexible use of the latest equipment and production techniques.[17]

This has a very modern ring.

Issues

Within the context of market factors, the nature of the issues figuring in negotiations also exerts a strong influence on the bargaining structure. Some issues are inherently of such a broad character that, if they are to be regulated through collective bargaining at all, they can be handled only at the most inclusive bargaining level. For example, if the question whether it should be national policy to add a week of paid vacation to the already existing standard is referred to collective bargaining for resolution, it can be resolved uniformly only through collective bargaining at the economy-wide national level. The alternative would be legislation. On the other hand, questions related to the specific timing of vacations do not require national bargaining, indeed do not even lend themselves to a comprehensive agreement, and are instead best negotiated at enterprise or plant levels or their equivalent. The fact that the issues arising in collective bargaining are, as a group, sufficiently varied to contain both centralising and decentralising elements explains why it is not always entirely clear whether a particular industrial relations system is moving towards more centralisation or decentralisation. It also explains the contemporary trend towards multi-tiered bargaining levels, particularly in those European countries which are fostering the development of enterprise-level and plant-level bargaining while often simultaneously seeking to retain industry-wide and even economy-wide bargaining.

Of course the existence of several levels of negotiation raises questions not only about the proper allocation of issues to the most appropriate level, but also about co-ordination between the various levels, both on the union and on the employer sides. Articulated bargaining is a very difficult process, and as Efrén

Córdova has pointed out, attempts to match issues with levels have met so far with only limited success.[18]

Community of interests

Bargaining units represent bilateral communities of interest, although this is perhaps more obvious on the employee than on the employer side. A variety of factors can stimulate the development of a community of interests strong enough to lead to the creation of a bargaining unit. On the employee side, the relevant criteria may be, illustratively, employment in the same plant or enterprise, attachment to the same industry, exercise of the same occupation or skill, dependence on the same labour market or any one of several other cementing links. Equivalent criteria operate on the employer side, including common ownership of subsidiary units or plants, attachment to the same industrial branch or sharing the same scale of operations.

There is no way of measuring the specific weight of any particular factor, but it is obvious that the differences between as well as within countries are considerable. The varying position of white-collar employees makes this clear. In some countries, for example in the Federal Republic of Germany, where collective bargaining occurs predominantly at the regional industry level, or in Japan, where by far the most important level of bargaining is the individual enterprise (or a subsidiary), white-collar employees are frequently represented by unions which simultaneously represent blue-collar employees, although admittedly in the Federal Republic of Germany fairly substantial numbers of white-collar employees are also represented by unions of their own. In other countries, however, as for instance in Sweden, white-collar employees in industry have formed bargaining units strictly separate from those for blue-collar employees and are represented in negotiations at all levels by their own unions and their own peak national confederation, although this top-to-bottom separation does not preclude a certain amount of co-ordination between the unions concerned.

The distinction might be generalised in these terms. In Japan the community of interest between white- and blue-collar employees created by dependence on employment in the same enterprise, and in the Federal Republic of Germany the similar community of interest created by attachment to the same industry or group of industries, count for more, at least for purposes of collective bargaining, than do conventional occupational or status distinctions. In Sweden, however, occupational identification has until now been the stronger factor. Yet even in that country, technological developments are increasingly blurring the traditional distinctions. Consequently, it is becoming more and more difficult to identify particular jobs or tasks as belonging clearly to the white-collar or blue-collar category. In the long run that trend is likely to lead to a shift in the perceived community of interests and, ultimately, in the bargaining structure.

But many distinctions will remain, both on the employer and employee sides. Among employers the formation of alliances for bargaining purposes is often beset by problems based on major differences in the scale of operations. In extreme cases, the special needs and constraints of "small" firms, as contrasted with "large" ones, may lead to the formation of a separate community of interest by size of firm, and consequently to separate bargaining units. Among employees the distinctions between skilled and process workers, or even between different categories of skilled workers, will continue to have an impact on the bargaining structure, as will the other factors that lead to the emergence of separate communities of interest, even if the specific impact does vary considerably from one country to another.

In this connection it should be noted that structural changes among employers, and to a certain extent among unions, are also likely to produce corresponding changes in the bargaining structure. Growth in the size of business units leads sooner or later to growth in the size of the bargaining unit, certainly in countries such as Canada, Japan and the United States, where the enterprise constitutes the principal unit of bargaining. Likewise, business mergers tend to result, perhaps after a certain interval, in a corresponding merger of bargaining units. The amalgamation of unions may have the same consequence, especially if the merging organisations operate in the same industry and cover identical or related groups of employees.

Government policies

Until fairly recently, most governments did not become directly and consistently involved in questions related to the bargaining structure. Their policy of non-intervention was in conformance with a more general conviction that the parties should be left to work out for themselves the terms of their relationship, including questions of recognition, bargaining units and other procedural matters of mutual concern.

There are, however, two important exceptions. First, two North American Governments, Canada and the United States, have taken a very active and sustained part in adjudicating issues and controversies related to the bargaining structure. One of their chief aims has been to avoid industrial conflicts resulting from disputes between employers and unions or between different unions over the determination of the specific bargaining unit. Put in different terms, their concern has been the establishment and maintenance of industrial stability, and we shall indicate below how they have gone about it.

Second, a fairly substantial number of governments have intervened occasionally and tangentially in matters related to the bargaining structure, particularly during periods of adverse economic developments and particularly when governments have sought to initiate high-level negotiations intended to produce agreed — rather than government-imposed — solutions to problems of inflation and unemployment. Their chief objective might then be, for example, the formulation of a national incomes policy based on the co-operation of employers and unions at the highest levels and aimed at moderation all the way down the line in wage and price movements. Attempts to achieve wage restraint by intervening at the very highest level of bargaining — involving the national confederations of trade unions and employers' associations — have at various times been of considerable importance in such countries as the Netherlands and Norway. In those countries the bargaining structure has in effect been extended to include centralised negotiations, although the extension was not necessarily of an enduring nature.

The situation in Canada and the United States has been rather different. In both countries specialised administrative bodies, created by legislation, have had wide authority to determine the appropriate unit for collective bargaining.

As a recent study of the Canadian system noted:

Bargaining unit determination has been the primary influence shaping the collective bargaining structure. . . . Labour boards have been given a general power to determine "the unit of employees appropriate for collective bargaining" qualified only by legislative instructions relating to certain types of employees such as those who belong to established crafts or professions.[19]

It is, of course, no accident that it was the North American governments which have taken an active role in matters concerning the bargaining structure. In both Canada and the United States governments asserted their interest at a time of widespread industrial unrest, namely the 1930s, and behind that unrest was not only a bitter struggle between unions and employers over union recognition and bargaining rights but also an equally bitter dispute between craft and industrial unions over the proper unit for collective bargaining. Moreover, in both countries unions had traditionally struggled for recognition not against employers' associations representing entire industries but in a much more fragmented way against individual employers. It was the complexity of the issues, the fierce inter-union rivalries and the quest for industrial peace that led to the legislation which staked out a decisive role for government in determining the appropriate unit for collective bargaining.

Thus, for the past five decades, specialised government agencies in Canada and the United States, acting within the framework of legislation, have been directly involved in decisions that have had a fundamental effect on the development of the bargaining structure in specific industries and, cumulatively, in the country as a whole. The criteria, which of necessity have been flexible, have included the notion of a community of interest among the employees, the history of collective bargaining, the custom in the industry, the wishes of the parties, and at least in Canada, the public interest in the maintenance of stable labour-management relations. Some observers hold to the view that the specialised government agencies have on balance leaned towards forming more centralised units in making their decisions. One of the most recent assessments of Canadian developments refers to a general bias "in the direction of defining more comprehensive units", in other words a bias towards more centralisation.[20] Similarly, according to Professor Kochan, the decisions of the American agency, the NLRB, "have encouraged the movement toward greater centralisation in the structure of collective bargaining".[21] That view is, however, by no means universally shared.

Although for reasons mentioned at the beginning of this section there are as yet no situations in European countries comparable to the broad authority of North American governments over the bargaining structure, the gap may have begun to narrow, even if only by indirection. In France the Auroux law of November 1982, which requires individual enterprises to engage in annual bargaining with the plant sections of the unions, has in effect mandated the establishment of bargaining units in many thousands of firms. Of course this is bound to have a decentralising effect on a bargaining structure which has always been oriented towards industry-wide negotiations. In Sweden the 1976 Act respecting co-determination at work, already referred to in an earlier chapter, will have broadly similar results, although perhaps not quite to the same extent because bargaining at the level of Swedish enterprises has already been fairly well established.

In Great Britain any attempt to bridge the gap that may have occurred has turned out to be only temporary. The Industrial Relations Act of 1971, repealed in 1974, gave explicit recognition to the concept of the bargaining unit (section 44a) but did not go so far as to invest a public agency with the power to determine what constituted an appropriate bargaining unit. The Employment Protection Act of 1975 entrusted the Advisory, Conciliation and Arbitration Service (ACAS) with certain functions in recognition disputes which included the determination of a bargaining unit, but this law, which in practice turned out to be flawed, was repealed by the Employment Act of 1980. At present, therefore, the Government is not directly involved in issues concerning the bargaining structure.

These issues of general significance need to be given additional consideration, but this can be done more profitably after a review of recent centralising and decentralising trends in the bargaining structure of several individual countries.

CURRENT TRENDS IN SELECTED COUNTRIES

Australia

Although collective bargaining is not entirely absent from the Australian system of industrial relations, it is not one of its central features. That position belongs to conciliation and arbitration through industrial tribunals established by federal and state governments. (The term "federal" refers here to jurisdictions covering the country as a whole and the term "state" to a jurisdiction limited to one of the six states that constitute the Australian Commonwealth.) Thus, the Australian system differs in this respect from the systems of other industrialised market economies in a fundamental way. To examine the structure of collective bargaining in Australia would, therefore, not be a productive exercise. Nevertheless it is still relevant to inquire whether the system of industrial relations is itself becoming more or less centralised, and that will be attempted here. First, however, a few general observations need to be made.

For almost all Australian employees, whether members of a union or not, basic wages, hours of work and other key terms of employment are set by one of the six or seven principal tribunals which give the lead to a further 100 or so other industrial tribunals. The most important tribunal is the federal Australian Conciliation and Arbitration Commission (ACAC). Decisions of the tribunals are called "awards", and at present approximately 50 per cent of workers are covered by state, 40 per cent by federal, awards.[22] Some of these are consent awards where the tribunals endorse collective bargaining agreements; that is, they issue awards based upon what the parties privately work out, if requested to do so.

Although procedures vary somewhat, usually one of the parties — almost invariably from the union side — presents the other with a set of demands, the implication being that failure to accept them within a certain time will lead to the dispute being submitted to a federal or state tribunal for decision. Subsequently, there may be an attempt by the tribunal to conciliate the dispute, but unresolved issues will be arbitrated and result in an award. Additional "collective bargaining" may then occur at the level of the enterprise if the union (or unions) concerned seeks to extract further concessions from the employer — i.e. the so-called "over-award" negotiations.

In the kind of system briefly sketched here, the question of structural centralisation really resolves itself into two parts: *(a)* what has been the trend in the relative importance of federal and state tribunals, the assumption being that if federal tribunals are in the ascendancy the system is moving towards greater centralisation; and *(b)* what has been the trend within the federal system itself as regards the different levels — national, industry and enterprise — of decision-making?

Concerning the first part, the federal system has gradually gained a position of pre-eminence that is due to several factors: the ACAC's leadership role in national wage policy; the weight of the Federal Government as an employer; the growth of unions across inter-state lines; and certain constitutional decisions by the High Court, the supreme judicial body. Dabschek and Niland describe the Court's decisions as favouring "the Federal Government first and the Arbitration Commission second, to the detriment of the influence of state-based bodies — both legislatures and tribunals. The effect of these cases is to make centralism easier to sustain".[23] Other observers have expressed virtually the same point in somewhat different terms: "Few people who have wanted to be covered by Federal Awards ... have been disqualified on the constitutional grounds of want of jurisdiction." [24]

In sum, there does not seem to be much disagreement on the conclusion that there has been a decided shift towards the predominance of the federal over the state systems.

There is, however, considerably more uncertainty about the second part of the question, namely whether there has also been a steady trend towards more decentralised decision-making within the federal system itself, at least during the past decade.[25]

From 1975 to 1981 the ACAC followed a policy of centralised wage setting under which the Commission made quarterly adjustments to all wages covered by federal awards, the basis for the adjustments being the movements of the consumer price index. However, by mid-1981 the index-linked policy — supported by most unions but objected to by the employers who wanted the linkage to be based on productivity changes rather than the price level — succumbed to a build-up of various pressures, including those resulting from several "over-award" collective agreements. For the next couple of years wage determination became more decentralised in the sense that wage changes were left to be determined by a combination of collective bargaining and the awards of individual federal and state tribunals. A build-up of adverse economic conditions led the ACAC by the autumn of 1983 to initiate a resumption of centralised wage determination. That policy reversal was ushered in by a general Accord between the new Labor Government, which had taken office earlier in 1983, and the Australian Council of Trade Unions, and soon after by the conclusions of a National Economic Summit Conference. In an effort to achieve more centralised decision-making, both the Federal Government and the ACAC are currently emphasising national wage cases and downgrading, or discouraging, industry wage cases as well as over-award negotiations at the level of the individual enterprise. In practice, the ACAC adjusts wages on a semi-annual basis in accordance with the consumer price index; unions benefiting from these periodic adjustments are required to undertake not to seek increases outside the centralised wage-indexation system.

Currently, therefore, the federal system must be regarded, in the Australian context, as once again internally centralised. In view of the several changes of direction that have occurred in recent years, it would not be advisable to consider the present centralisation as a permanent feature. Nevertheless it is remarkable that Australia, unlike other countries, has sought to resolve its economic problems by means of centralising, rather than decentralising, its decision-making processes in industrial relations.

Belgium

Collective bargaining in Belgium has operated historically within a highly structured institutional framework. Negotiations used to be regarded as taking place on three principal levels: the economy-wide or national level; the level of the various branches and industries, no doubt by far the most important one; and the level of the individual enterprise. In a sense, that categorisation may still be valid. Given, however, the country's increasing linguistic and ethnic bifurcation "with its ever more marked social and economic overtones",[26] several observers have identified the regional industry as a separate fourth level, interposing it between the branch of industry level and the enterprise level.[27]

Until the mid-1970s, two distinguishable kinds of collective agreements were being negotiated at the economy-wide national level (also called the inter-occupational level).[28] One was a series of inter-industry agreements, first concluded in 1960, which from time to time stipulated certain overall changes in wages and working conditions, usually at two- or three-year intervals. These so-called "social programming" agreements were concluded independently of any formal institutional structure — in fact, strictly speaking they were not collective agreements but recommendations intended to be implemented by collective agreements at industry level — yet they were generally observed and set the overall direction for labour-management relations in the entire country. They were particularly attractive to the unions because they tended to make the terms of employment more uniform and enabled employees in economically weaker industries to obtain benefits which they would probably not have been able to secure by themselves. The social programming agreements fell victim to the severe recession that began in the second half of the 1970s. The last one was concluded for the period 1975-76. An attempt to negotiate an additional one in 1977 failed for lack of agreement on the issue of a national ceiling on wages. Since then no new ones have been voluntarily negotiated, at least not on major issues, but under the threat of legislated wage restraints the central parties did reach a national-level agreement which was in effect during all of 1981 and 1982.

Under these circumstances the major forum for collective bargaining at the economy-wide level and for the conclusion of rather more conventional kinds of collective agreements is now the National Labour Council, a body composed of 22 members representing the employers' associations and the main trade union federations, which meets under an independent chairman. Legally it has been able to conclude collective agreements since 1968, although that is not intended to be its main function. (The main function is to advise the legislative and executive branches of government on general social policies and social problems.) Among topics covered in recent years by nationally applicable agreements are the prior consultation rights of employees' representatives in case of mass lay-offs, adjustments to cost-of-living clauses in collective agreements, employees' rights in case of plant relocation, minimum monthly compensation for minors and earnings levels for handicapped employees. Some agreements concluded in the National Labour Council are intended for enactment into legislation, and in so far as they have bipartite support they are virtually certain to be adopted.

The problems which led to the demise of "social programming" agreements at the level of the economy as a whole have also affected collective agreements at the industry level. The principal negotiating bodies at this level, the joint industrial committees, first appeared after the First World War but did not gain legal status until after the end of the Second World War. Composed of equal numbers of employer and union representatives, these committees, of which there are currently about 100 (actually substantially more if one also includes the regional committees and subcommittees), have served as forums for the negotiation of collective agreements, advisory bodies to government and agencies for dispute resolution. The traditional separation between white- and blue-collar employees still persists in a large number of industries, and as a rule bargaining is separate for these two groups. Currently about half of the joint committees cover blue-collar employees, one-fourth white-collar employees and the remaining fourth both categories.

For many years the industry committees were at the centre of the Belgian bargaining structure, for the key wage bargains were usually concluded at this level, particularly in the committees for the most important industries, such as the metals industries.[29] But while in some sectors national agreements are still being concluded, for example in textiles and retailing, others have found the negotiations so difficult for economic as well as regional-linguistic reasons that the level of bargaining has in many instances been shifted downward to the regional or provincial level, or even further to the level of the individual enterprise. Although unions as a whole are ambivalent about the decentralisation process, those unions which operate in the more prosperous sectors, such as chemicals, reflect the views of a membership that does not want to have its wages and working conditions determined chiefly by the ability-to-pay of the marginal industries or marginal firms. One of the more important results of the increase in enterprise- and plant-level bargaining is, of course, a considerable widening of inter-industry and intra-industry disparities in wages and working conditions.

Canada

Despite changes that have occurred in collective bargaining in Canada during the past 15 years — and there have indeed been some important ones, such as the expansion of public sector bargaining — the bargaining structure in the private sector has remained substantially decentralised and in fact remarkably stable.[30] Most collective bargaining agreements involving 500 or more employees (the only category for which official data are available) are negotiated at the level of the individual enterprise, representing either a single- or a multi-plant operation. Multi-employer agreements, including those concluded by employers' associations, are a distant third, usually covering in any one year no more than one-fifth or one-sixth of all employees in collective bargaining involving units of 500 persons or more.[31]

Since the agreements resulting from negotiations involving 500 or more employees number only approximately 1,000 out of a total of 18,000 agreements, and since the other 17,000 agreements by definition all cover a smaller number of employees, it may be taken as likely that the bargaining structure is even more decentralised than the above data indicate.[32] This seems to be so despite the fact that the Government's anti-inflationary policies in the second half of the 1970s, which included the use of wage and price guide-lines, could have been expected to promote more centralisation in collective bargaining by encouraging unions to institute more formal and informal co-ordination of their bargaining strategy. The actual impact appears, however, to have been relatively small. Any centralisation that may have occurred was generally limited to a few industries, such as transportation and construction, and resulted at most in province-wide bargaining arrangements.

Of seemingly greater long-term importance has been the role of administrative agencies in determining the appropriate unit for collective bargaining. Since only about 15 per cent of the Canadian labour force is attached to industries under federal jurisdiction, the share of collective bargaining that is conducted within nationally determined bargaining structures is rather small by comparison with the much larger number of units determined by provincial labour relations boards.[33] Consequently, the impact of the several provincial boards has been particularly important, and in general they have tended to favour single-employer or single-plant units. However, with respect to situations involving the interests of several competing unions, the aim of the labour boards has been to avoid excessive fragmentation, and in such instances their bias has been, as already noted, "in the direction of defining more comprehensive units".[34]

By contrast with the general expansion of collective bargaining during the 1960s and 1970s, there has more recently occurred a significant slow-down, and the rise in unemployment as well as the elimination of thousands of jobs have been reflected in major declines in the size of many existing bargaining units.[35] It would, therefore, be reasonable to conclude that the impact of the recession on the already fragmented Canadian bargaining structure has either been largely neutral or has tended, if anything, towards even more decentralisation.

France

More so than in almost any of the other countries, the bargaining structure in France has become potentially subject to major changes. They are contained in the legislation enacted by the Government which took office in 1981 — the so-called Auroux laws of 1982 [36] — and not only mandate new subjects for inclusion in collective bargaining at the level of the enterprise and industry, but also stipulate the levels at which collective bargaining is henceforth to take place, instead of leaving such decisions to the parties. Although it is too early to draw firm conclusions about the specific impact of the laws, it is at least possible that they will mark a significant departure from the situation that had developed within the framework of previous legislation, particularly the law of 1950 and its subsequent amendments.

In common with the majority of European countries, the principal level of negotiations that developed in France under the basic legislation of 1950 was the "*branche d'industrie*", that is, an industry, sometimes also categorised as an occupation or *profession*. Depending primarily on the preferences of employers, as expressed through their associations, and also but to a much lesser extent on the wishes of the unions, the negotiations at industry level occurred either on a nation-wide or on a regional basis. The decision was influenced by such factors as the number of enterprises involved, the extent of diversity in the labour and product markets between different regions, the presence (or absence) of particularly large enterprises, the state of technology and similar considerations. Most frequently it was — and still is — the pattern of organisation on the employer side which determined the occupational and territorial coverage of collective agreements.[37] In any event it would be fair to judge that under the 1950 legislation the industry level — whether national or regional — indeed occupied "a privileged place . . . as the setting for negotiations".[38]

Hence until the late 1960s collective bargaining at the level of the individual enterprise was of only minor importance. Nor was the inter-industry or economy-wide level of much significance, especially since most employers' associations were keen on retaining their authority over collective bargaining rather than ceding any portion of it to their central federation. However, a certain amount of collective bargaining did occur above and below the industry levels. At the enterprise level, a "wave" of agreements, which in the end turned out to be a rather weak wave, followed the conclusion of the first enterprise agreement at the Renault automobile company in 1955, while a first inter-industry agreement on unemployment insurance was negotiated between the principal confederation of employers' associations, the CNPF, and the major trade union federations in 1958.

A genuine surge of top-level bargaining did, however, follow in the 1960s and early 1970s. With considerable encouragement from the Government, the CNPF and the trade union federations negotiated a significant number of inter-industry agreements on a large array of subjects, including for instance employment security, vocational training, income maintenance in cases of business failure, and maternity pay. The terms of some agreements were subsequently incorporated into legislation. Other agreements became eligible for "extension" to non-signatory firms under provisions of legislation passed in 1971. In response to increasing rank-and-file pressure for local bargaining, the 1971 legislation also gave enterprise-level agreements equal juridical status with industry-level agreements in order to encourage collective bargaining at the enterprise level.[39]

But the Auroux Act of November 1982 goes considerably further in seeking to stimulate bargaining at the workplace. As perceived by Professor Delamotte, it is "intended to bring the centre of gravity of the bargaining system closer to the base by laying down the obligation for the enterprise to bargain every year", but without abandoning bargaining at the industry level.[40] In principle, that very same aim had also been the thrust of the innovations introduced by legislation in 1968 and 1971, on the basis of which several venturesome observers predicted somewhat prematurely that the enterprise would be moving to the forefront of the French bargaining structure.

Initial results produced so far indicate that caution is once again advisable in estimating the ability of legislation to modify deeply entrenched patterns and practices that have for so long asserted the centrality of industry-level rather than enterprise-level negotiations. A citation by Professor Delamotte about the prospects of enterprise-level bargaining seems particularly appropriate: "The introduction of the obligation to negotiate [at enterprise level] implies . . . a far-reaching change in behaviour that cannot be brought about in the space of a year." [41] And perhaps not even in several years.

Federal Republic of Germany

The bargaining structure in the Federal Republic of Germany has remained relatively unaffected by the economic downturns of the 1970s and 1980s. Now, as before, there are two principal levels. One is the individual industry, which more often than not is subdivided by region; the other is the plant or workplace level. Although the link between the two levels is probably becoming closer, the two still reflect quite different types of relationships, operate on different assumptions, rely on different parties to represent the employer and employee sides, and derive their legitimacy from different sets of legislation. [42]

The legislation which governs collective bargaining at the industry level is the Collective Agreements Act of 1949, as consolidated in 1969. [43] Pursuant to this law, the parties that are eligible to engage in negotiations over the terms of employment are individual employers, associations of employers and trade unions. In practice, most collective bargaining takes place, region by region, between the regional organisation of an employers' association for a particular industry and the regional body of a national union for that industry. Agreements concluded in one region tend to set a pattern for the others, particularly if a region contains leading segments of the industry. The co-ordinating role of the national organisations on both sides also contributes substantially to the practice of pattern-setting.

Two "deviations" from the regional industry norm must be registered. In some industries the negotiations are conducted on a genuinely national basis, for example in building construction, several manufacturing industries, and such service sectors as banking and insurance. At the other end there is also a certain amount of collective bargaining between individual enterprises and unions, resulting in perhaps one-third of all agreements, but the parties on the employer side are for the most part relatively small firms which have chosen not to belong to the employers' association for their sector. One of the major exceptions is the Volkswagen Company, which has for many years negotiated its own agreements.

Conceivably in future years there may be an expansion of collective bargaining involving individual enterprises, particularly the large and profitable ones. At least that appears to be the aim of several unions. [44] Targeted employers and their associations will most likely resist such an effort. The employers' associations will seek to preserve their cohesiveness, while the stronger individual enterprises have an interest in maintaining the present situation because it enables them to offer terms of employment that are significantly better than the minimum terms negotiated in industry-wide bargaining, where the ability-to-pay of the marginal firm must be taken into account. Nor do all unions necessarily favour an expansion of enterprise-based negotiations at the expense of industry-wide bargaining. Some are concerned about the adverse effects on worker solidarity that might be brought about by the ability of a few among their own group to extract unusually favourable terms of employment from highly profitable enterprises.

The total number of agreements of all kinds registered with the Federal Ministry of Labour as of March 1985 was slightly in excess of 45,000. This appears to be a rather high figure for a country in which the key wage negotiations are usually conducted at (regional) industry level. In explanation it should be pointed out, however, that the figure includes a relatively large number of individual enterprise agreements (over 15,000), that separate collective agreements are often concluded for distinct segments of the workforce (white-collar employees, plant guards, etc.), that wage agreements are often negotiated separately from agreements dealing with general terms of employment *(Manteltarifverträge)*, and that a substantial number of supplemental agreements — each one negotiated separately and counted separately — deal with single issues, such as performance evaluation, the introduction of technological changes, job security, supplemental retirement pay, holiday bonuses, disputes settlement procedures and quite a few others.

Although there is no summit-level bargaining in the Federal Republic of Germany similar to the top-level negotiations that are held in France and the Scandinavian countries, the confederations of employers' associations and trade unions, the BDA and DGB, do consult each other from time to time on issues of major importance and have even concluded a model agreement on disputes settlement procedures for voluntary adoption by their affiliated bodies.[45]

If a basically adversarial position is expected of the trade unions and employers' associations engaged in industry-wide collective bargaining and is even built into the relevant legislation, a basically co-operative attitude — "a spirit of mutual trust" — is enjoined upon management and works councils which deal with one another at the level of the individual plant or workplace. The applicable legislation here is the Works Constitution Act, originally adopted in 1952 and amended in 1972.[46] It mandates the establishment of elected works councils in virtually all establishments and confers on them extensive rights of participation in management. Many of the rights can be implemented only through collective negotiations, and as a matter of fact one of the rights explicitly granted is the conclusion of so-called "works agreements".[47] The content of the works agreements covers not only the large array of subjects declared by law to be within the defined scope of employee participation in decision-making but also any other items agreed between works council and management. However, because of a possible overlap, or even conflict, between works agreements and collective agreements concluded at industry level, the law provides that "works agreements shall not deal with remuneration and other conditions of employment that have been fixed or are normally fixed by collective agreement".[48] Under this restriction, on which the unions insisted, works agreements are not supposed to trespass on items that are ordinarily subject to negotiations between unions and employers' associations (or individual enterprises) unless the collective agreement itself expressly authorises the inclusion of such items in the works agreement.

Not all works councils and plant managements have taken advantage of the opportunity to conclude works agreements. A recent survey found that one out of eight establishments with 200 or more employees had failed to do so and seemingly preferred to rely on less formal arrangements to register their understandings. If the survey had included smaller establishments as well, the proportion of establishments without a works agreement would probably have been considerably higher.[49]

The proper relationship between the two levels of collective bargaining is one of the continuing questions in the industrial relations system of the Federal Republic of Germany. In a sense they are supposed to complement each other, and often they do. But they emerge (at least theoretically) from quite different contexts, one being essentially adversarial, the other essentially integrative. So far the two have been kept in delicate balance. It is conceivable, however, that in the future the demonstrated ability of unions to dominate most works councils, among which on average the candidates elected from union lists hold almost 80 per cent of the seats, will lead increasingly to an emphasis on the role of works agreements as supplements to industry-level agreements rather than as independent and functionally separate accords. If so, the process may well be aided by the fact that an increasing number of industry-wide and regional agreements now include a so-called "opening clause" which explicitly recognises the possibility of adapting the collective agreement to the plant level.[50]

Great Britain

During the past two to three decades the bargaining structure in Great Britain has become extraordinarily diversified and complex, probably more so than that of any other country represented in this study. A vivid description of the current situation is contained in a recent survey of British industrial relations:

There are negotiations between employers' associations and trade unions at the national or industry level. There is bargaining at the company level between a particular employer and the trade unions he recognises. ... At lower levels, multi-employer bargaining sometimes takes place at regional or district levels and company bargaining at divisional levels. Beyond that there is often a further stage of negotiations at the workplace. ... Frequently there remains a final level of bargaining at shop floor level . . .[51]

This is not an exceptional view. A similar assessment of the complexities of the bargaining structure has been made by Roberts:

Many employers continue to belong to employers' organisations and in most industries there continue to be negotiations on a limited range of issues between employers' organisations and trade unions at the national or industry level. Below this level bargaining may take place at the district or local level and at the level of the enterprise or plant. *In many industries there is bargaining at all these levels.*[52]

Even before the onset of the current economic difficulties in the 1970s, the importance of industry-wide bargaining had begun to diminish considerably and the significance of bargaining at enterprise levels (or sub-enterprise levels) had begun to increase. These trends were reinforced by the report and recommendations of the Donovan Commission, which expressed serious doubts about the sufficiency of the established industry-wide bargaining structure (the formal system). In particular, the Commission urged an expansion of the bargaining structure through the articulation of plant and workplace agreements (the informal system) with agreements concluded at the industry level.[53]

Since then the trend towards single-employer bargaining has gone very far. Single-employer agreements, whether at plant or enterprise level, have largely replaced multi-employer agreements as the major determinants of wages and working conditions in many private sector manufacturing industries. Where both levels — or several levels — coexist, the national negotiations are likely to be increasingly marginal in their effect on the wages and working conditions of employees because the major decisions are now generally made at enterprise or establishment level. In fact, already by 1978 a survey of manufacturing industries showed that the most important level for wage bargaining for over half of all manual and non-manual employees was the single employer.[54]

What this means, for example, is that there are now a large number of formal bargaining committees at plant or enterprise level, that the unions' workplace organisations have become more structured, that there are far more full-time shop stewards then there ever used to be (possibly a four-fold increase in the past decade), and that local union branches or shop stewards rather than national or district union organisations take the initiative in making claims on behalf of their members to management at enterprise or workplace level.

Where the major decisions in collective bargaining continue to be made through industry-wide or multi-employer bargaining, the sector concerned is likely to be either in the non-manufacturing category (for example, construction), under public ownership (coalmining), or a highly competitive manufacturing industry characterised by a relatively large number of small and medium-sized firms seeking to pool their modest individual bargaining power. In the public sector in particular, industry-wide bargaining continues to be of great significance, and in some industries multi-employer agreements still specify important minimum standards.

Although decentralisation is without doubt the dominant trend, in a certain sense the bargaining structure may be in the process of becoming recentralised. Some current research seems to indicate that where plant bargaining has become the most important level of bargaining, there are definite pressures towards centralisation at the enterprise level.[55] And indeed in some of the larger multi-plant enterprises, plant-level collective bargaining is being superseded or controlled by enterprise-wide bargaining, although the reverse also occurs.[56] Much depends on management strategy and union power, but it is no doubt true that "the levels at which collective bargaining takes place both reflect the balance of power between managements and trade unions and are a major influence on it".[57] In other words, the dominant level depends on which side is stronger and can best impose its position. Under present circumstances this more often than not is likely to be the management side.

Multi-unionism is still very widespread, and the practice has endured of different unions at industry and enterprise levels not only representing different sections of the workforce — which is not unusual — but also claiming to represent the same sections. Although multi-unionism is gradually being reduced by union mergers, this is a very slow process. More significant at present is the combination of multi-unionism with single bargaining units, in other words the formation of a joint bargaining structure designed to enable the several unions commonly represented in one enterprise to retain their separate identities but to pool their bargaining power and perhaps also to reduce inter-union rivalry. The advantages for management are no less significant: greater bargaining efficiency and less union pressure to engage in wage leap-frogging.[58]

An even more recent development affecting the bargaining structure — and possibly the entire system of industrial relations — is the emergence of a type of exclusive bargaining agency arrangement in which management recognises a single union as the representative of the entire workforce in return for, among other things, a no-strike pledge with binding arbitration. The initiative in introducing this innovation (for Great Britain) has been taken on the employer side by the subsidiaries of several multinational corporations and on the union side by the Electrical, Electronic, Telecommunication and Plumbing Trades Union (EETPU). Other unions, such as the Amalgamated Union of Engineering Workers (AUEW), are also moving in this direction. No doubt, union participation in this untraditional arrangement must be viewed in the light of the United Kingdom's high rate of unemployment and the country's need for foreign investment. It is a major departure from past practice, and if it spreads it may produce a significant modification in the British bargaining structure.

Italy

Whether Italy has a three- or four-tiered bargaining structure depends on where one draws the dividing line between the several levels at which collective bargaining takes place. It is rather generally agreed that the central (or interconfederal) level and the industry level constitute two distinct categories for collective bargaining, but some observers regard enterprise and plant (or establishment) bargaining as a joint third level, while others prefer to view them as two separate — i.e. third and fourth — levels.[59]

Interconfederal bargaining between the major confederations of trade unions (the General Confederation of Labour — CGIL, the Italian Confederation of Workers' Unions — CISL and the Italian Workers' Union — UIL)[60] and the principal employers' confederations (the Confederation of Industry — Confindustria — for the private sector and after 1956 Intersind and ASAP for the public controlled enterprises) dates back to the early years of the post-war period, when "All matters of major importance . . . were regulated by central agreements applicable to large sectors of the economy or even the whole of industry. [61] Some important agreements emerged from the negotiations at this level, for example the 1953 agreement on the establishment of works councils (the so-called *commissioni interne* which in the meantime, however, have been almost entirely disbanded and replaced by factory councils). But beginning in the late 1950s the substantial role once played by economy-wide bargaining diminished, although it did not entirely cease, and industry-wide as well as enterprise bargaining increasingly moved into a leading position. In some economic sectors the region or province also became an important level in collective bargaining.

The decentralisation in bargaining that took place at this time was closely associated with the economic growth and general modernisation that became such important features of the 1960s and early 1970s. From this time on and until the mid-1970s, "industry-wide agreements regulated the most important conditions of work . . ., but also delegated a number of specific issues to enterprise or plant-level bargaining . . .".[62] Referring to this period, one observer wrote that "any matter can be bargained at any level and at any time".[63] Subsequently, however, and principally as a result of the economic difficulties that began in the 1970s, interconfederal bargaining again assumed a position of foremost importance, and not only because of the large number of interconfederal agreements signed but also because of the importance of the matters dealt with.[64]

An apt example of interconfederal bargaining is the Interconfederal Agreement on Labour Costs and Productivity of 1977, addressed chiefly to the goal of enhancing the competitive position of Italian industry.[65] This Agreement, together with other central agreements, supports the view that in Italy, by contrast with quite a few other countries, the response of the industrial relations system to a major economic crisis has been to centralise the structure of collective bargaining and to concentrate the decision-making power of the parties at central level.[66] The unions, in particular, "seem to realise that centralisation of major decisions and of wage differential negotiations is of major importance in an era of high inflation".[67] It is not clear at this point, however, whether the renewed importance of central bargaining in the 1980s can withstand the recent breakdown of the loose alliance that has linked the three trade union federations ever since 1972. If they continue to disagree over such key questions as the linkage of wage increases to the cost of living, the survival of interconfederal negotiations will be in serious doubt.

The outcome could well have a major effect on national and enterprise bargaining. National agreements have continued to play an important role in establishing minimum conditions for employees in major industry groups such as the diffuse metals sector. But, relatively speaking, they lost some of the importance which they had acquired in the 1960s when industry-level agreements, usually lasting three years, were the principal means for setting wages and working conditions. If central agreements cease to be concluded or if their reach is diminished because of the absence from the bargaining table of the largest of the three trade union federations (CGIL), industry-wide agreements should then be expected to help fill the gap.

Considerable progress was made in the late 1960s and throughout most of the 1970s in collective bargaining at enterprise and plant levels. Agreements concluded at this level between managements and the factory councils to supplement industry-wide agreements mounted into the thousands every year, and by 1976 about 50 per cent of all industrial workers (some 3.5 million altogether) were covered by enterprise agreements.[68] More recently, however, the expansion ceased, largely as a result of the recession. The economic problems faced by many companies forced a halt to the pattern-setting bargaining that in an earlier period had made of the individual enterprise a platform for the development of new provisions in collective agreements, which subsequently were often extended to the national level. The new agreements became exercises in difficult efforts to reconcile the imperatives of company restructuring and the overall maintenance of employment levels.[69] A tripartite central agreement, in whose negotiation in 1983 the Government participated, suspended for a period of 18 months the negotiation of enterprise wage agreements. But that was before the breakdown of the triple union alliance. If central agreements will no longer be concluded, one should expect the importance of the company level, together with the industry level, to increase once again, provided only that the overall balance of bargaining power does not shift overwhelmingly in favour of the employers in a context of severe economic difficulties.

Japan

By far the most important level of bargaining in Japan, both in terms of the number of agreements concluded and the number of workers covered by them, is still the individual enterprise. In this respect, the Japanese bargaining structure continues to show a remarkable degree of stability.[70]

A similar degree of stability also characterises the structure of organisations on the employer and employee sides. Central to the union structure are the enterprise unions which function as largely autonomous and self-sufficient bodies, even when they are loosely affiliated with one of the national industrial unions (also called industrial federations). Most enterprise unions exercise close control over the major functions of collective bargaining, disputes strategy and the handling of grievances, but some of them may accept a certain measure of co-ordination, policy guidance and assistance in industrial disputes from their national union. Actually not many more than about one-tenth of all enterprise unions allow outside national union officials to participate in their collective bargaining.

A similar relationship prevails between industrial enterprises and their employers' associations. Here, too, the links are tenuous, and most enterprise managements engage in collective bargaining without the participation of their association. Thus on both sides — employers and unions — the role of the intermediate industry-level organisations, which in many other industrialised countries occupy a foremost place in collective bargaining, has remained fairly limited, and neither their authority nor their functions have been allowed to intrude significantly. Nor, for that matter, do the peak confederations of trade unions and employers' associations participate in collective bargaining. In sum, the centre of gravity in collective bargaining is unquestionably at the enterprise level.

Yet this account would be incomplete if it did not take note of some major exceptions and modifications in the largely decentralised bargaining structure. In the first place there are certain sectors in which multi-employer or multi-enterprise bargaining at national or regional levels occurs regularly. These are not inconsiderable sectors, for they include shipping, where industry-wide bargaining has a long history, as well as coalmining, chemicals, textiles and the privately owned railways. Second, informal bargaining at industry level is practised in several other industries, notably in iron and steel, shipbuilding, automobiles and electrical appliances — all very important components of the Japanese industrial system — although the implementing agreements are concluded at enterprise level.[71]

A third but more indirect centralising influence is exerted by the outcome of the tripartite discussions of general economic conditions that have been carried on since about 1970 under the auspices of the Industry-Labour Council.[72] Several times each year this body brings together top officials from the employer and labour sides and from government, as well as several leading scholars, for informal discussions that are designed to achieve a common perspective on the economic context within which bargaining will be taking place and to foster a common point of departure. These conferences, which may be regarded as pre-bargaining sessions, have served as a model for similar meetings at regional, industry and even enterprise levels.

Separately from the tripartite meetings, bipartite discussions on broad issues of industrial relations have been held since the early 1970s between the Japan Federation of Employers' Associations[73] and the principal labour federations. Like the tripartite meetings, these consultative gatherings represent a significant counterweight to the highly decentralised enterprise-by-enterprise system of industrial relations.[74]

Although one cannot point to a clearly profiled trend, it appears that the Japanese bargaining structure is gradually acquiring some moderately centralising features. However, efforts to speed up the process are likely to encounter strong opposition from enterprise unions and enterprise managements — the unions because they are not prepared to tolerate any diminution of their autonomy and the employers because of the many advantages which they derive from being able to deal with unions inside the enterprise.

The Netherlands

During the past ten to 15 years the foremost level in the Netherlands bargaining structure has been the individual industry (which here is understood also to include a few very large enterprises customarily bargaining separately, such as Philips). The central or economy-wide level has, however, retained a considerable amount of importance, and the level of the individual enterprise or plant has achieved considerably more significance than ever before.

Centralisation used to be the hallmark of the Netherlands industrial relations system. During the first 15 years of hardship and reconstruction after the Second World War, the structure of collective bargaining was perhaps more highly centralised than that of any other industrialised market economy, as indicated by a high degree of government involvement in wage setting and by the dominant role played by the central organisations of employers and trade unions in collective bargaining. In the ensuing years from the mid-1960s to the mid-1970s, which in general were years of prosperity and full employment, the rising importance of industry-wide bargaining was accompanied by a decline in the role of government and the central organisations. Beginning in the mid-1970s, however, this phase was followed by a period of severe economic difficulties which have not yet abated.

In the three-tiered bargaining structure that has by now become firmly established, negotiations always begin at the central level. Each year for nearly all of the past two decades the parties at this level — the confederations of trade unions and employers' associations, joined together in their own consultative body, the Foundation of Labour — have attempted to reach a central wage agreement as an authoritative guide-line or framework for the negotiations of their affiliated organisations at industry level. In this endeavour they have had before them the economic analyses and forecasts of the official Central Planning Bureau, the reports and recommendations on major issues of social and economic policy of the tripartite Social and Economic Council (in which they themselves play a leading role), and usually the tacit encouragement of the Government. Yet only once, in 1972, did they succeed in concluding for one year a so-called "social agreement".

The repeated failure to reach a consensus at central level has had several consequences. First of all, the negotiations at industry level have acquired special importance, especially those in the leading industries, such as the metals industry and building construction, which tend to set the pattern for the others. In most years the broad outlines of the discussions at the central level have been taken into account in the separate negotiations in the various industries, so that even when the central negotiations failed to reach their ultimate objective — which was most of the time — they still had an important effect.[75] Furthermore, against the background of a worsening economic situation the Government has frequently made extensive use of its powers under the Wage Determination Act of 1970 [76] and other legislation to impose wage control measures designed to arrest or to slow down the increase in labour costs, often over the opposition of both parties deeply concerned about infringements of free collective bargaining. These measures have, of course, had a centralising effect.

A centralising impact may also be attributed to the (so far exceptional) central agreement that the peak federations of trade unions and employers' associations concluded in 1982 to deal with the unemployment problem.[77] This agreement, which should not be confused with conventional central agreements containing guide-lines for wages and working conditions for a defined period of time, envisages among other things a reduction in hours of work through the negotiation and renegotiation of collective agreements and through various forms of work-sharing designed to create jobs.

While the 1982 agreement may eventually become the signal for a rejuvenated effort at economy-wide bargaining and thus lead to greater centralisation,[78] some of the most dynamic changes have recently been occurring at the level of the individual plant or enterprise. On the whole these changes have tended towards greater decentralisation. As in other continental European countries, the unions in the Netherlands for many years neglected the development of plant-level organisations and more or less accepted (or were too weak to counteract) employer resistance to their presence at the workplace. Instead they relied heavily on the statutory works councils to be responsible for representing job-related employee interests, even though until fairly recently the works councils had only consultative rights and conducted their meetings under the chairmanship of the employer.

One of the major changes has been a considerable enlargement of the rights of the works council and a transformation of its status. The employer has been removed from its midst, and instead of being purely an advisory body the works council has been given specific functions to represent employee interests. In certain areas generally identified as "social and personnel matters" (pension programmes, profit-sharing plans, working hours, holiday rosters, health and safety measures, etc.), the employer must now obtain the consent of the works council before acting, and that often requires negotiations which are the equivalent of collective bargaining. In other areas the works council retains consultative rights, but these rights, too, have been enlarged to the point where works councils are now entitled to be heard in such disparate but vital matters as corporate reorganisation or mergers, major lay-offs, work rules, systems of wage payment, and employment and training policies.

Paired with this development has gone the creation of a union structure at the enterprise level. By means of collective agreements concluded for the most part at industry level between employers' associations and national trade unions, the unions have gained the right not only to a recognised presence in the enterprise but also to specific facilities (meeting rooms, clerical assistance, etc.) and to protection of their representatives against disciplinary actions or discriminatory treatment. It is mostly in the larger and medium-sized enterprises that the unions have established their plant sections, and one of their key functions is to improve the lines of communication between unions and their members. Participation in the determination of working conditions at plant level is another important task. As van Voorden has noted: "Negotiations at the plant level, either to reach a collective agreement or to fill in the details of a collective agreement already reached for an entire branch of industry, are becoming more frequent, and plant-level collective agreements for senior staff are on the increase."[79]

Obviously the tendency to decide more aspects of the employment relationship by local collective agreements results in greater decentralisation of the industrial relations system. But what the unions must still decide is whether they will use the statutory works council, over which they can often wield considerable influence, or their own relatively new plant sections as their principal chosen instrument to influence the decision-making process in the enterprise.

Sweden

Since the mid-1950s centralisation has been the outstanding characteristic of the structure of collective bargaining in Sweden. Centralisation has meant that economy-wide agreements concluded between the peak confederations of employers' associations and trade unions have outlined the basic changes in wages and conditions of employment for a specified period, usually one to two years, and these agreements have then served as authoritative guide-posts for the negotiations in individual industries or groups of industries and eventually for still further negotiations at the level of the enterprise. Under this system, the national unions and the corresponding employers' associations usually carry on their own negotiations during the period of central bargaining and of course particularly afterwards, the main subject being the distribution of the global wage increases that have been centrally negotiated. Further negotiations at enterprise level then determine how the changes are to be applied at that level.[80]

It ought to be noted that although the degree of centralisation is considerable it has been neither absolute nor all-encompassing. Instead of just one central bargaining unit there are several central units: one for blue-collar and another for white-collar employees in the private sector, as well as several public sector units. Centralised bargaining for white-collar employees in the private sector is of more recent vintage than central negotiations for blue-collar employees. It is, therefore, not yet quite as well organised. However, because of the steadily rising share of white-collar employees in the total labour force, this sector is becoming ever more important. In recent years, moreover, the two central trade union federations have developed channels for continuous contacts and information exchanges which operate not only in preparation for negotiations but also while they are in progress.

In some of the industry and enterprise negotiating units vigorous bargaining occurs as regards the adaptation of the central agreement to the specific conditions prevailing at their levels, and over supplemental substantive provisions. Moreover, prior to each national bargaining round the central organisations on the employer and employee sides must obtain from their constituents, the industrial employers' associations and the national trade unions, a renewal of their negotiating mandates.

In recent years the employers have become concerned about what they regard as the excessive rigidities of the centralised system. In the 1982-83 bargaining rounds the industrial employers' associations in the private sector, led by the powerful Metal Trades Employers' Association,[81] withheld their bargaining authorisation from their own peak confederation, the SAF, and for the first time in decades insisted on separate negotiations with their counterparts on the trade union side from which a separate industry agreement emerged. Subsequently, the other private sector unions affiliated to the LO negotiated a central bargain with the SAF for 1983. In 1984, however, each union concluded its own agreement.[82]

It is not yet possible to determine whether the employers' decentralising initiative will ultimately lead to a more decentralised bargaining structure in the private sector, or whether the negotiations in the first half of the 1980s will be viewed retrospectively as an exceptional period. In any event, after the Government had made clear its aim to limit inflation in 1985 to a maximum of 3 per cent, the negotiations reverted to the long-established pattern of central negotiations, subsequently followed by industry-level and enterprise-level negotiations.[83]

A series of top-level talks about the negotiating procedures *per se*, which the Government first convened in early 1984, may be expected to continue. In these talks the employers have taken the position that the centralised negotiations (which the unions prefer to call "co-ordinated bargaining rounds") have become too detailed and too inflexible and that the agreements that have emerged from them have not provided sufficient room for adaptation to the specific circumstances prevailing at industry and enterprise level.[84] Some employer groups consider the only effective remedy to be the elimination of economy-wide bargaining; others, however, seem willing to retain a modified form of central negotiations under which individual industries would have greater leeway to negotiate wages and working conditions. The LO has left no doubt about its continued support of central bargaining as an essential element in its policy of wage solidarity, but it too has expressed a willingness to consider a looser form of central bargaining.[85]

One other set of negotiations of economy-wide scope needs to be mentioned. In the course of the past four to five decades the central organisations in the Swedish labour market have from time to time concluded agreements on specific subjects in order to achieve a uniform approach. The first agreement of this kind — the Saltsjöbaden Agreement (1938) — defined the basic nature of the relationship between the parties themselves and might well be described as a form of private legislation. Other agreements have dealt with such items as works councils, industrial training and safety at work. The most recent agreement of this type was concluded in 1982 between the main private sector employers' and trade union organisations (SAF and LO) on the subject of the development of Swedish industry and constitutes an effort to implement one of the more important provisions of the 1976 Act respecting Co-determination at Work. It is intended to provide a basis for joint regulation "in matters concerning both the overall [or long-term] development of the enterprise and its day-to-day development".[86] The intention here, as in the case of the perennial wage negotiations, is for implementing agreements to be concluded at industry and enterprise levels.

United States

That the role played by government in framing the bargaining structure is probably more important in the United States than in other countries has already been brought out in previous sections of this chapter. The NLRB has the power to determine the appropriate unit for collective bargaining, and its impact is particularly great in those instances where the parties disagree on the delineation of the appropriate unit. Conversely, where the parties do agree, the NLRB will usually accept their decision. For the purpose of linking its decisions in disputes over the configuration of the bargaining unit to predictable criteria, the NLRB has developed over the years a series of guiding factors, among them particularly the wishes of the employees, the history of the bargaining relationship, the presence of a "community of interest" among employees in the prospective unit and the extent of union organisation.

By comparison with most other industrialised market economies, the bargaining structure in the United States continues to be characterised by a high degree of decentralisation. Indeed, "on the whole", as Thomson has noted "the configuration of the bargaining structure in the United States in 1980 is not vastly different from that in 1950, although there are of course significant changes in the balance of individual sectors, most notably the public sector".[87] There is no economy-wide bargaining between representatives of peak confederations of employers' organisations and trade unions, not even on an occasional basis, nor is multi-employer bargaining a major factor in manufacturing industries. Most agreements are concluded at the local or enterprise level between a single trade union and a single employer, although a fairly substantial amount of multi-employer bargaining does occur in non-manufacturing industries. Indeed, in so far as the economic problems of the past decade have had an impact on the bargaining structure, it has been generally in the direction of even greater decentralisation, as seen for example in the employer-induced decline of pattern bargaining and the reduced significance of coalition or co-ordinated bargaining. On the other hand, the substantial amount of multi-employer bargaining that goes on in the non-manufacturing sectors has not changed under the pressure of economic developments.

The most recent authoritative estimate of the number of collective agreements puts the total for 1978 at about 178,000.[88] This figure is not strictly comparable with the equivalent figure of 155,000 for 1969 because the more recent data include agreements negotiated by employees' associations which were excluded from the 1969 survey. The total number of employees covered by the 178,000 agreements was estimated to be about 25 million, but in view of the steadily shrinking trade union membership figures in the first half of the 1980s, it may reasonably be assumed that several million fewer employees are currently covered by collective agreements than was the case in 1979.[89]

111

Although the aggregate figures conceal many different kinds of bargaining arrangements for which statistical breakdowns are not available, a fairly recent set of data does exist for 1,550 so-called "major collective bargaining agreements", each one covering 1,000 workers or more.[90] In 1980 the total number of employees covered by the 1,550 agreements was 6.6 million, thus indicating that even though in an overall sense the United States bargaining structure is highly decentralised, it also shows a paradoxically high degree of concentration since fewer than 1 per cent of all agreements cover nearly one-third of all employees working under collectively bargained terms of employment. Approximately 60 per cent of the agreements and close to the same portion of the 6.6 million workers were found to be in single-employer units (which are here not further subdivided into single-plant and multi-plant units), while the remainder were in multi-employer units. This is almost exactly the same distribution as in 1973, the first year when data were collected for agreements covering 1,000 workers or more.

When the current (1980) figures are separated into manufacturing and non-manufacturing industries, an interesting reversal of proportions emerges. Of the 750 major collective agreements in the manufacturing sector, 86 per cent and a virtually identical percentage of the 3 million workers covered by agreements in manufacturing were found to be in single-employer units, while multi-employer units accounted for only a small fraction (14-15 per cent) of the total. On the other hand, of the 800 major agreements in the non-manufacturing sector — which among others includes construction, transportation other than airlines and railways, services, and retail and wholesale trade — almost two-thirds had been concluded in multi-employer units, covering slightly more than two-thirds of the 3.6 million employees in these industries. It must be noted, however, that the construction industry by itself accounted for well over half of the non-manufacturing multi-employer units, both in terms of the number of agreements and the number of employees.

In summary, the manufacturing sector in the United States is dominated by single-employer agreements (which usually means single-enterprise or single-plant agreements), whereas multi-employer bargaining, at either local or regional but only rarely at national industry-wide level, tends to prevail in major portions of the non-manufacturing sector.

In general, multi-employer bargaining has been associated with certain definable characteristics. It tends to exist primarily in industries where —

(a) the number of individual enterprises is relatively large;

(b) the average number of workers per enterprise is relatively small;

(c) there is significant geographical concentration among enterprises, usually in a metropolitan area;

(d) competition among enterprises is vigorous; and

(e) the rate of unionisation is above average.

Where these conditions are present, either fully or substantially, multi-employer bargaining is likely to be an important factor, regardless of whether the industry in question belongs to the manufacturing sector or the non-manufacturing sector.

Although certain developments have tended towards more centralisation in the American bargaining structure — for example the continued concentration of business organisations and the parallel concentration in the union structure [91] — the overall trend is moving in the opposite direction. As Barbash has pointed out, "the tendency here is towards decentralising bargaining structures away from large industry and multi-employer units, to bring the bargaining closer to the circumstances of the individual employer and plant".[92] The initiative has come mainly from the employer side, motivated particularly by competitive pressures from foreign imports and domestic non-union firms. This development has adversely affected not only pattern bargaining, where the most recent termination occurred in the steel industry after a history of nearly 30 years, but has also inhibited the practice of coalition or co-ordinated bargaining in multi-plant corporations.[93] In coalition bargaining a group of unions with members and bargaining rights in a large multi-plant corporation tries to overcome the weakness of fragmentation in its ranks by seeking agreement on common bargaining objectives and a common bargaining strategy, and usually joint negotiations as well. However, this effort to neutralise or to match the advantages of a unified employer side has failed to spread in the face of employers' opposition and of problems on the union side brought on by differences in union organisational style, leadership and approach to bargaining.[94]

On the whole, then, in so far as the already highly decentralised bargaining structure is undergoing further change, it is moving towards more rather than less fragmentation. There are, of course, exceptions to the overall trend, and not the least among the more recent ones has been the maintenance of industry-wide bargaining in coalmining. But it is difficult to agree with the conclusion, contained in a standard treatise on American collective bargaining, that "The long-term trend toward centralised bargaining structures should continue, notwithstanding some resurgence of local union initiative." [95] Most of the current evidence seems to point in the opposite direction.

COMPARATIVE ASSESSMENT

The foregoing review of recent trends in the structure of collective bargaining makes no claim to comprehensiveness, but it does provide a basis for several observations of a general nature.

Surely the first one must be to stress once more the great diversity in national bargaining structures. Even among countries that might justifiably be regarded as having in common a centralised or a decentralised structure, as the case may be, structural parallels are limited to overall appearances and do not hold up well under close examination.

The basic features of the national bargaining structure, once put in place, tend to persevere. An essentially centralised (or decentralised) structure will probably retain its basic shape over a long period of time. In this sense, relative stability is one of the outstanding characteristics of the bargaining structure. But that does not mean that the structure is immune to pressures for change. On the contrary, bargaining structures are able to adapt readily to significant changes in the market context of industrial relations, in the rules imposed by governments and in the balance of power of the parties, but more often than not the changes are gradual and cumulative rather than sudden and revolutionary.

In most cases neither employers nor trade unions are bound to a predetermined "ideal" bargaining structure. Instead they tend to deal on an ad hoc basis with specific situations in a way that is most conducive to meet their needs and interests as they perceive them. By and large, neither side is inherently committed to maintaining a particular configuration of bargaining units, although there is some tendency for trade unions to seek more centralisation as the most effective means to achieve standard terms of employment and for employers to prefer more decentralisation in the hope of achieving greater flexibility in the exercise of entrepreneurial and managerial tasks. Where union commitments to policies of wage solidarity are unusually strong, as in Sweden, adherence to the preservation of a centralised bargaining structure is likely to be correspondingly firm, although not necessarily rigid.

On the whole most governments have considered it neither necessary nor desirable to become involved in issues affecting the structure of bargaining. There have, of course, been exceptions, such as the already noted adjudicatory role of Canada and the United States in determining the appropriate unit for collective bargaining. Another exception has occurred in situations where governments have instituted incomes policies as part of a more generally activist role in the management of the economy. The most efficient way of obtaining the co-operation of employers and trade unions in policy formulation and implementation has usually been to work through the national confederations of employers' associations and trade unions, and sometimes through institutionalised tripartite bodies; this tends to have a centralising effect on the bargaining structure. Even more recent instances of government actions affecting the bargaining structure are, of course, the decisions by the French and Swedish Governments to institute and reinforce respectively the bargaining structure at the level of the individual enterprise.

Although it would be difficult to identify a consistent pattern, most of the changes in bargaining structure that have occurred within the past ten to 15 years have tended towards greater decentralisation. To be sure, some countries have experienced virtually no change, as for example the Federal Republic of Germany and Japan, and in one or two others — Australia and perhaps Italy — the trend has been towards greater centralisation. But the dominant tendency has been towards the decentralisation of the bargaining structure, even if not everywhere in identical terms, for decentralisation can have quite different meanings. In systems traditionally emphasising industry-wide collective bargaining, as in Great Britain, it may refer to the development of negotiations at plant and enterprise levels. In countries with highly centralised structures on the employer and trade union sides, such as Sweden, it may involve the assertion of greater independence from the restraints of national central authority by employers' and workers' organisations at individual industry levels. And in situations traditionally characterised by pattern-setting (or co-ordinated) bargaining, as in the steel industry of the United States, it may mean a shift from bargaining over master agreements to negotiations based essentially on the competitive circumstances of the individual enterprise.

The reasons for the general trend towards decentralisation are complex and certainly not identical from one country to another. In some countries government policies have been of considerable importance. Thus, in France, the Netherlands and Sweden, and possibly also in Belgium, it has become an explicit government objective during the past decade to encourage more local decision-making, more plant-level bargaining, and more emphasis on the claims-making and protective functions of works councils or their equivalents. The overall aims have been to associate employees more closely with decsion-making at the workplace, to respond to demands for a greater share of workers' control over working conditions, to foster greater job satisfaction, and ultmately perhaps to improve productivity and efficiency. These decentralising changes, brought about by legislation or administrative policies, have generally been supported by the trade unions and often opposed by the employers. In fact, without sustained trade union pressure they might not have come about at all.

Another impetus towards decentralisation of the bargaining structure has come mainly from recent competitive pressures in product and labour markets and the introduction of new technologies, but in these instances the positions of the parties have been reversed. Under the conditions of full employment that prevailed in the latter part of the 1950s and the 1960s, unions often used their enhanced bargaining power to consolidate or to enlarge existing bargaining units and in this way to achieve a more centralised bargaining structure.[96] The economic reverses of the second half of the 1970s and the first half of the 1980s led employers to seek ways of reducing costs (including of course labour costs), achieving greater flexibility in wage payment (incentive) systems, modernising production methods and equipment use, and generally securing more flexibility in the assignment of work and more independence in management decision-making. The effort to link employees' compensation more closely to individual performance had a significant decentralising effect on the bargaining structure, but the consequences went further than that. Some employers severed their ties with employers' associations so as to avoid the contractual obligations associated with membership; others made a deliberate effort to devolve responsibility for industrial relations from the enterprise to individual establishments by delegating authority to plant managers to engage in local bargaining with representatives of their employees; and still others attempted to operate without a collective agreement, at least in portions of their enterprise. Unions usually resisted the fragmentation of existing bargaining structures into independent negotiating units because they anticipated, correctly, a reduction in their bargaining power, but given the state of the labour market they were often unable to do so effectively.

Notes

[1] Arnold R. Weber: "Stability and change in the structure of collective bargaining", in Lloyd Ulman (ed.): *Challenges to collective bargaining* (Englewood Cliffs, New Jersey, Prentice-Hall, 1967), pp. 13-14.

[2] United Kingdom, Royal Commission on Trade Unions and Employers' Associations, 1965-68: *Report* (The "Donovan Report"), Cmnd. 3623 (London, HMSO, 1968), p. 45.

[3] Readers may wish to see for themselves the diverging approaches of several authors to the problem of articulating a definition of the bargaining structure. Weber identifies the "informal work group", the "election district", the "negotiation unit" and the "unit of direct impact" as the four main components of the concept (Weber, op. cit., p. 14). Kochan defines the bargaining structure as "the scope of the employees and employers covered or affected by the bargaining agreement" and also distinguishes between the formal and informal bargaining structure (Thomas A. Kochan: *Collective bargaining and industrial relations: From theory to policy and practice* (Homewood, Illinois, Irwin, 1980), pp. 84-85). Farnham and Pimlott differentiate between "bargaining levels", "bargaining units", "bargaining forms" and "bargaining scope" as the relevant entities of the bargaining structure (David Farnham and John Pimlott: *Understanding industrial relations* (London, Cassell, 2nd (revised) ed., 1983), pp. 222-227). Bean equates the bargaining structure with "regularised patterns of union-management interaction" (Ron Bean: *Comparative industrial relations: An introduction to cross-national perspectives* (London, Croom Helm, 1985), p. 73).

[4] See Roberts below, p. 289.

[5] See *Legislative Series* (Geneva, ILO), 1947 — USA 2.

[6] Still the best discussion of the bargaining unit in the American context of labour-management relations is the one by Neil W. Chamberlain and James W. Kuhn: *Collective bargaining* (New York, McGraw-Hill, 2nd ed., 1965), pp. 233-263.

[7] According to Chamberlain and Kuhn, a "bargaining unit identifies those employees and employers to whom the negotiated terms of a collective agreement apply" (ibid., p. 233). This definition fits the situation in the United States but becomes too restrictive when applied elsewhere because it does not take into account those European countries where it is possible, by administrative action, to "extend" the terms of a collective agreement to employers and employees not represented in the negotiations.

[8] D. R. Deaton and P. B. Beaumont: *Determinants of bargaining structure: Some large scale survey evidence for Britain* (Coventry, United Kingdom, Warwick University, 1979).

[9] Henry Phelps Brown: *The origins of trade union power* (Oxford, Clarendon Press, 1983), pp. 102-103.

[10] E. G. A. Armstrong: "Employers associations in Great Britain", in John P. Windmuller and Alan Gladstone (eds.): *Employers associations and industrial relations: A comparative study* (Oxford, Clarendon Press, 1984), p. 46.

[11] Ronald F. Bunn: "Employers associations in the Federal Republic of Germany", ibid., p. 170.

[12] Everett M. Kassalow: "Industrial democracy and collective bargaining: A comparative view", in *Labour and Society* (Geneva, IILS), July-Sep. 1982, p. 216.

[13] Sidney and Beatrice Webb: *Industrial democracy* (London, Longmans, Green, 1920), pp. 279-323.

[14] Kochan: *Collective bargaining . . .*, op. cit., p. 97. Emphasis added.

[15] George Ruben: "Modest labor-management bargains continue in 1984 despite the recovery", in *Monthly Labor Review* (Washington, DC, United States Department of Labor), Jan. 1985, pp. 3-12. Ruben notes that in 1984 two-tier systems were introduced into agreements covering 200,000 employees in the United States. For additional observations, see John J. Lacombe II and James R. Conley: "Major agreements in 1984 provide record low wage increases", in *Monthly Labor Review*, Apr. 1985, pp. 39-45.

[16] ETUI: *Collective bargaining in Western Europe 1978-79 and prospects for 1980* (Brussels, 1980), p. 191.

[17] Chamberlain and Kuhn, op. cit., p. 248.

[18] Efrén Córdova: "Collective bargaining", in R. Blanpain (ed.): *Comparative labour law and industrial relations* (Deventer, Kluwer, 1982), pp. 228-229.

[19] H. W. Arthurs et al.: "Canada" (1984), in Blanpain (ed.): *International encyclopaedia for labour law and industrial relations* (Deventer, Kluwer, 1977 onwards), Vol. 3, p. 193.

[20] ibid., p. 195.

[21] Kochan: *Collective bargaining . . .*, op. cit., p. 100.

[22] See Dabschek and Niland below, p. 163. Besides relying on this source, the general comments here are also based in part on D. Plowman et al.: *Australian industrial relations* (Sydney, Allen & Unwin, 1980); Braham Dabschek and John Niland: *Industrial relations in Australia* (Sydney, McGraw-Hill, 1981); and Norman F. Duffy: "Australia", in Albert A. Blum (ed.): *International handbook of industrial relations* (Westport, Connecticut, Greenwood, 1981), pp. 3-36.

[23] See Dabschek and Niland below, p. 164.

[24] Plowman et al., op. cit., p. 119.

[25] For a brief review as far back as the 1950s, see Dabschek and Niland below, pp. 167-168.

[26] See Blanpain below, p. 184.

[27] ibid., p. 183.

[28] Thérèse Beaupain: "Belgium", in Solomon Barkin (ed.): *Worker militancy and its consequences* (New York, Praeger, 2nd ed., 1983), pp. 154-155.

[29] One recent observer still takes the position that "the most important level of bargaining in Belgium is industry-wide bargaining", but he adds that "in certain industrial sectors, bargaining traditionally takes place at the plant level" (Guy G. Desolre: "Belgium", in Blum, op. cit., p. 42).

[30] The most comprehensive review of the Canadian bargaining structure is the chapter by John C. Anderson on "The structure of collective bargaining", in John Anderson and Morley Gunderson (eds.): *Union-management relations in Canada* (Don Mills, Ontario, Addison-Wesley, 1982), pp. 173-195.

[31] ibid., p. 179, table 1. Somewhat different figures, but basically indicating the same direction and derived from the same official sources, are contained in Alton W. J. Craig: *The system of industrial relations in Canada* (Scarborough, Ontario, Prentice-Hall, 1983), pp. 152-153.

[32] OECD: *Collective bargaining and government policies in ten OECD countries* (Paris, 1979), p. 22.

[33] Anderson and Gunderson, op. cit., p. 184.

[34] Arthurs et al., op. cit., p. 195.

[35] W. D. Wood and Pradeep Kumar (eds.): *The current industrial relations scene in Canada 1984* (Kingston, Ontario, Queen's University at Kingston, Industrial Relations Centre, 1984), p. 321.

[36] For an English translation of these Acts, see *Legislative Series*, 1982 — Fr. 2 B-2 E.

[37] OECD: *Collective bargaining . . .*, op. cit., p. 43.

[38] Yves Delamotte: "Recent trends in the statutory regulation of industrial relations in France", in *Labour and Society*, Jan. 1985, p. 16.

[39] François Sellier: "France", in John Dunlop and Walter Galenson (eds.): *Labor in the twentieth century* (New York, Academic Press, 1978), p. 222.

[40] Delamotte, op. cit., p. 17.

[41] ibid., p. 23.

[42] Not all authorities acknowledge the negotiations at the second level as constituting collective bargaining. A recent study of collective bargaining sponsored by the OECD does not refer to the plant or workplace level in the Federal Republic of Germany and deals exclusively with the industry level (OECD: *Collective bargaining . . .*, op. cit., pp. 58-67).

[43] For an English translation of this Act, see *Legislative Series*, 1969 — Ger.F.R. 4.

[44] Hans Günter and Gerhard Leminsky: "The Federal Republic of Germany", in Dunlop and Galenson, op. cit., p. 175.

[45] ILO: *Selected basic agreements and joint declarations on labour-management relations*, Labour-Management Relations Series No. 63 (Geneva, 1983), pp. 91-93.

[46] For an English translation of this Act, see *Legislative Series*, 1972 — Ger.F.R. 1.

[47] Section 77 (2) provides among other things: "Works agreements shall be negotiated by the works council and the employer and recorded in writing."

[48] Section 77 (3).

[49] The survey was conducted by the Social Research Institute in Saarbrücken for the Federal Ministry of Labour. See *European Industrial Relations Review*, Dec. 1983, pp. 14 ff.

[50] Günter and Leminsky, op. cit., p. 175.

[51] W. W. Daniel and Neil Millward: *Workplace industrial relations in Britain: The DE/PSI/SSRC Survey* (London, Heinemann Educational Books, 1983), p. 177.

[52] See Roberts below, p. 289. Emphasis added.

[53] See United Kingdom, Royal Commission on Trade Unions and Employers' Associations: *Report*, op. cit., especially Chs. 3 and 4.

[54] William Brown (ed.): *The changing contours of British industrial relations* (Oxford, Basil Blackwell, 1981), p. 8, table 2.1, and p. 12, table 2.3.

[55] N. J. Kinnie: "Single employer bargaining: Structures and strategies", in *Industrial Relations Journal*, autumn 1983, p. 77.

[56] See Roberts below, p. 290.

[57] John Purcell and Keith Sisson: "Strategies and practice in the management of industrial relations", in George S. Bain (ed.): *Industrial relations in Britain* (Oxford, Basil Blackwell, 1983), p. 109.

[58] Daniel and Millward, op. cit., pp. 46-47.

[59] Gino Giugni identifies three levels in his chapter on "The Italian system of industrial relations", in Peter B. Doeringer (ed.): *Industrial relations in international perspective* (London, Macmillan, 1981), pp. 326-327. But a four-tiered categorisation is suggested in "Italy: Industrial relations in context", in *European Industrial Relations Review*, Mar. 1979, pp. 19-20. One author even identifies five levels, the fifth in his view being the negotiations between the three major union confederations and the government on topics of social reform. See Thomas Kennedy: *European labor relations* (Lexington, Massachusetts, D. C. Heath, 1980), pp. 191-192.

[60] *Confederazione Generale Italiana del Lavoro, Confederazione Italiana Sindicati Lavoratori* and *Unione Italiana del Lavoro*, respectively.

[61] Alberto Martinelli and Tiziano Treu: "Employers associations in Italy", in Windmuller and Gladstone, op. cit., p. 267.

[62] ibid., p. 268.

[63] Tiziano Treu: "Italy" (1981), in Blanpain (ed.): *International encyclopaedia . . .*, op. cit., Vol. 6, p. 137.

[64] See Giugni below, p. 232.

[65] For the text of the Agreement, see ILO: *Selected basic agreements . . .*, op. cit., pp. 129-133.

[66] Tiziano Treu: "Italy", in Benjamin C. Roberts (ed.): *Towards industrial democracy: Europe, Japan and the United States* (London, Croom Helm, 1979), pp. 96-97.

[67] ibid., p. 97.

[68] OECD: *Collective bargaining . . .*, op. cit., p. 72.

[69] See Giugni below, p. 236.

[70] For an account of the origins of the enterprise as the focal point of Japanese collective bargaining, see Kazutoshi Koshiro: "Development of collective bargaining in postwar Japan", in Taishiro Shirai (ed.): *Contemporary industrial relations in Japan* (Madison, Wisconsin, University of Wisconsin Press, 1983), pp. 208-212.

[71] See Shirai below, p. 244.

[72] *Sangyô Rôdô Konwakai — Sanrô-Kon.*

[73] *Nikkeiren.*

[74] Solomon Levine: "Employers associations in Japan", in Windmuller and Gladstone, op. cit., p. 346.

[75] William van Voorden: "Employers associations in the Netherlands", in Windmuller and Gladstone, op. cit., p. 227.

[76] For an English translation of this Act, see *Legislative Series*, 1970 — Neth. 1.

[77] *Social and Labour Bulletin*, Mar. 1983, p. 57.

[78] See Albeda below, p. 263.

[79] Van Voorden, op. cit., p. 228.

[80] Göran Skogh: "Employers associations in Sweden", in Windmuller and Gladstone, op. cit., p. 154.

[81] *Verkstadsföreningen.*

[82] *LO News* (Stockholm), No. 2, 1984; Scott Lash: "The end of neo-corporatism? The breakdown of centralised bargaining in Sweden", in *British Journal of Industrial Relations*, July 1985, pp. 222-223.

[83] *European Industrial Relations Review*, Apr. 1985, pp. 9-10.

[84] See Albåge; Fjällstrom below, p. 273.

[85] *Industrial Relations Europe* (Brussels), Oct. 1984.

[86] *European Industrial Relations Review*, June 1982, p. 12.

[87] Andrew Thomson: "A view from abroad", in Jack Stieber et al. (eds.): *US industrial relations 1950-1980: A critical assessment* (Madison, Wisconsin, Industrial Relations Research Association, 1981), p. 307.

[88] United States, Department of Labor, Bureau of Labor Statistics: *Directory of National Unions and Employee Associations, 1979*, Bulletin 2079 (Washington, DC, 1980), p. 75, table 21.

[89] For recent trends in trade union membership figures, see Courtney D. Gifford: *Directory of US Labor Organizations: 1984-85 edition* (Washington, DC, Bureau of National Affairs, 1984), p. 2, table 1.

[90] United States, Department of Labor, Bureau of Labor Statistics: *Characteristics of major collective bargaining agreements, January 1, 1980*, Bulletin No. 2095 (Washington, DC, 1981), p. 19, table 1.8.

[91] See John P. Windmuller: "Concentration trends in union structure: An international comparison", in *Industrial and Labor Relations Review*, Oct. 1981, pp. 43-57.

[92] Jack Barbash: "Trade unionism from Roosevelt to Reagan", in *Annals of the American Academy of Political and Social Science* (Beverly Hills, California) (Special edition on *The future of American unionism*, edited by Louis A. Ferman), p. 14.

[93] For an account of the end of pattern bargaining in the steel industry, see William Serrin's reports in the *New York Times*, 4 and 6 May 1985.

[94] Jack Barbash: "Collective bargaining: Contemporary American experience — A commentary", in Gerald G. Somers (ed.): *Collective bargaining: Contemporary American experience* (Madison, Wisconsin, Industrial Relations Research Association, 1980), p. 583.

[95] Harold W. Davey et al.: *Contemporary collective bargaining* (Englewood Cliffs, New Jersey, Prentice Hall, 4th ed., 1982), p. 105.

[96] It should be noted, however, that full employment may tend to strengthen decentralising tendencies in bargaining structure, as shown particularly in Great Britain during the years of full employment by the enhanced ability of shop stewards to bargain informally with plant managers for improvements in wages and working conditions in excess of nationally negotiated terms.

THE ROLE OF GOVERNMENT

5

The purpose of this chapter is to review the role of government (or the State) in the collective bargaining process. Considerable attention has already been given to that role in preceding chapters, as for example in connection with government influences on the bargaining structure, but here the place and policies of government will be central to the discussion rather than subsidiary.

At issue is the role of government as guardian of the public interest, as arbiter and rule maker — in brief, as sovereign — rather than its role as an employer of civil servants or of employees in public utilities and industrial enterprises, though the two sometimes do overlap and though no doubt the role of government as an employer is of increasing importance in many countries. The ILO has elsewhere examined the special problems of collective bargaining which arise when the State acts as the employer.[1] In so far as they differ substantially from the problems arising in the private sector, some have already been reviewed in a preceding section of this study.[2]

EVOLUTION OF PUBLIC POLICIES

An examination of government in its third-party capacity is best begun with a brief review of the evolution of public policies towards collective bargaining. As long as governments perceived their primary responsibility to be the protection of the freedom of the market-place and the sanctity of the individual contract of employment, and as long as they considered trade unions to be a major threat to both, the purpose of intervention by the public authorities was the suppression, or at the very least the tight containment, of unions. During this early period the courts frequently played a decisive role in defining public policies by promulgating rules that blocked attempts by unions to organise and bring employers to the bargaining table. Under such conditions collective bargaining had neither public sanction nor a legal foundation for development. Only rarely was it able to establish itself in the early stages of industrialisation. One instance was among skilled craftsmen in Great Britain in the first half of the nineteenth century; their bargaining power was often strong enough to induce employers to recognise their unions and to participate in the collective determination of wages and the basic terms of employment. More commonly, however, it was the individual contract of employment which constituted the only socially approved and legally recognised agreement between employers and employees.

An important change in public attitudes and policies towards at least a limited form of tolerance of unions, and therefore also of collective bargaining, occurred on a relatively widespread scale in about the last quarter of the nineteenth century or soon afterwards. Its most visible expression was the removal, by legislation, of many former obstacles to trade union organisation. In Great Britain Parliament adopted the Trade-Union Act of 1871 and the Conspiracy and Protection of Property Act of 1875, and later the even more important Trades Disputes Act of 1906, which together conferred important immunities from prosecution on trade unions and their members and officers; [3] in France the long-deliberated law of 1884 granted freedom of association; and in Imperial Germany the Reichstag in 1890 allowed the suppressive anti-socialist legislation, first enacted in 1878, to expire. But legislation was not the only instrument through which unions gained new rights. In Sweden it was under the collectively negotiated Compromise of December 1906 that the principal organisation of employers recognised the right of unions to organise, though that concession was made conditional on union acceptance of extensive management rights.

Public policies explicitly concerned with the methods and procedures of collective bargaining first emerged after the turn of the century, and in the ensuing decades became a widely recognised subject for legislation, especially during the period between the First and Second World Wars when a substantial body of legislation intended to regulate collective bargaining — and sometimes even to promote it as an effective form of industrial self-government — was entered in the statute books. Frequently included were provisions defining the rights and mutual obligations of the parties, the legal status and enforceability of the agreement, the substantive issues to be negotiated, and in some countries the procedural rules to be followed by the parties. Also covered, sometimes by separate legislation, were the rules to be followed in the event of the parties failing to reach agreement and the establishment of public disputes settlement machinery.

Of the inter-war decades one may say that in most countries the governments conceived their role in collective bargaining to be an important but a subsidiary one, centring chiefly on the maintenance of industrial peace and stability, the facilitation of bargaining machinery, the legal protection of employees in the exercise of their freedom of association and their right to bargain collectively, and the enforcement of collective agreements through administrative or judicial tribunals. The major responsibility for making collective bargaining work was supposed to be left to the parties. Aside from providing conciliators and other specialised services to resolve disputes, as for example the labour courts, governments sought to refrain from intervening, barring of course a critical downturn in the economy or sometimes a breakdown in major negotiations when protection of society from serious harm to the national economy or to the public health and welfare became a paramount consideration. In most countries governments were also expected to provide a minimum level of wages, social benefits and social insurance programmes that in some other countries were left to the negotiations between the parties.

This limited view of the proper role of government in collective bargaining might be regarded as the classic conception. It was adhered to most closely in Great Britain and perhaps in Sweden (in the former the term "voluntarism" was used to describe the relatively subordinate role of the law and the State), largely but somewhat less closely in most continental European countries with a more activist legislative and judicial tradition, and not at all closely in some of the other countries. In fact, in Australia, Canada and the United States quite different conceptions were gaining, or had already gained, acceptance.[4] In Australia a government-operated arbitration system became as early as 1904 a major instrument for setting the terms and conditions of employment in those instances where conventional bargaining between employers and trade unions had failed to produce agreement. What was particularly noteworthy about the Australian approach was its emphasis on the adjudicatory role of government in the determination of substantive issues, especially of wages but also of other key terms of employment, although it should also be noted that the compulsory arbitration system was not intended to become a complete substitute for collective bargaining.

In the United States the declared public policy, as reflected initially in the National Labor Relations Act of 1935 as subsequently amended by the Labor-Management Relations Act of 1947, assigned to the Government itself a major responsibility for fostering and consequently for regulating collective bargaining as a socially desirable form of decision-making in industry and as a means for reducing industrial strife. A specialised administrative agency — the NLRB — was established for the purpose of applying the quite detailed terms of the law to the negotiations and the relations between trade unions and employers, and in a relatively short period the collective bargaining system in the United States became subject to a far more complex network of administrative and legislative rules than could be found in almost any other industrialised market economy. On the other hand, the activist government role in the procedural aspects of collective bargaining had no parallel in a similar activism towards substantive matters. In this area the Federal Government for many years followed a policy of abstaining from legislation and left the determination of issues very largely to the negotiations between the parties.

Responding to the increasing importance of collective bargaining in the period between the two world wars, the ILO published its first major study of collective agreements in 1936. The concluding section of its report contained a prescient comment about the rising importance of collective agreements in the years ahead:

123

If, as seems likely, collective agreements are destined to play an increasingly important part in the future, and if industrial self-government is still to be more firmly established, it is clear that the State will allow the collective agreement to play an increasingly large part in the regulation of conditions of work. Such a development could not fail to have important consequences for the establishment and enforcement of international labour legislation.[5]

The adoption by the International Labour Conference of a series of international instruments shortly after the end of the Second World War indeed helped to foster the continued development of collective bargaining. The chief instruments were the Freedom of Association and Protection of the Right to Organise Convention, 1948 (No. 87), and the Right to Organise and Collective Bargaining Convention, 1949 (No. 98). To these were subsequently added the Workers' Representatives Convention, 1971 (No. 135), and the Collective Bargaining Convention, 1981 (No. 154). In addition, the Conference adopted specialised Conventions concerning collective bargaining for employees in the public service and rural workers, and several Recommendations.[6] One should also add here the resolutions, conclusions and other texts emanating from ILO regional conferences and meetings of Industrial Committees.[7] They are referred to not so much for their substance as for the general influence which they may have had on the attitudes of many governments towards collective bargaining in the years following the Second World War, for this period became a time, in several countries, for reassessing the operation of the collective bargaining system, and particularly in the case of the Federal Republic of Germany, Italy and Japan for reviving a once-prohibited and atrophied institution. Thus the Italian Constitution of 1947 recognised free collective bargaining as one of the keystones of a pluralist industrial relations system; [8] the Federal Republic of Germany enshrined freedom of association in its Basic Law of 1949 [9] and reintroduced free collective bargaining through Acts passed by the legislature in 1949 and 1952; while the Japanese Constitution guaranteed workers the right to organise, bargain and act collectively as fundamental and inviolable human rights.

In several other countries, too, the immediate post-war period became a time for legislative reform, partly as a reaction to the controls imposed during the Second World War or immediately afterwards. In France the collective bargaining law of 1950 [10] removed some of the restrictive controls imposed in 1946 under the pressure of the severe economic constraints of the immediate post-war period and sought to initiate — somewhat prematurely as it turned out — the widespread conclusion of collective agreements. In the United States the National Labor Relations Act underwent major revisions in 1947, including several that responded favourably to employers' complaints about unequal treatment.

During the first two to three decades following the Second World War, collective bargaining proceeded within a context of generally favourable public attitudes and rising economic prosperity, yet not without considerable differences in the role of government. "In some countries", as Oliver Clarke has pointed out, ". . . the principle that industrial relations are regulated, within the law, by unions and employers themselves has been generally maintained." [11] In many others, however, the conviction gained ground — brought on by a widening conflict between the outcome of collective negotiations and the economic goals of governments — that government could not properly discharge its responsibility to safeguard the public interest if it were to limit its presence in the domain of collective bargaining to the functions of making and applying the procedural rules, helping to maintain industrial peace and stability, and providing certain useful services. To limit government's concern merely to the smooth functioning of the machinery for collective bargaining, as this line of thought went, no longer corresponded to the needs of an era characterised by severe inflationary pressures, increasingly keen competition associated with rapid changes in technology and the internationalisation of product markets, and the rise of powerful employer and trade union groupings capable of inflicting serious harm on the economy. Consequently, according to this view, governments now had to become much more closely concerned not only with negotiating procedures but also with the substance of collective bargaining and the economic context in which bargaining takes place.

And indeed that is what occurred in a substantial number of countries. Depending, at least in part, on their general philosophical orientation, some governments relied chiefly on monetary and fiscal policies to shape the bargaining context rather than the actual outcomes, while others inserted themselves more directly into the negotiations in order to determine — through statutory wage measures, price controls, emergency regulations and tripartite accords — the actual terms of settlement.

It should, however, not be assumed that the increase in government intervention in collective bargaining was attributable only to the perceived impact of wage settlements on the effective functioning of the economy. To be sure, governments committed to the aims of economic growth, price stability and full employment — as most of them were and are — understood already perfectly well before the onset of the economic crisis associated with the first oil price shock of 1973 that they could not afford to neglect the impact of collective bargaining on the economy, and if anything these convictions were strongly reinforced after the onset of the economic crisis in the 1970s. But other considerations also played a role. The far-reaching obligation to offer to negotiate on a wide range of issues that Swedish legislation imposed on employers in the mid-1970s was not linked to the state of the Swedish economy but was instead the result, at least primarily, of trade union pressure to redress the balance of bargaining power at local level. Likewise in Great Britain the short-lived Industrial Relations Act of 1971, which introduced a far greater degree of government intervention in industrial relations than ever before instituted in that country, was only in part inspired by attempts to resolve the difficulties of the British economy; basically, it constituted a major attempt to reform the bargaining system and the bargaining structures and institutions associated with it more or less according to the North American model.[12] To be sure, this legislation was repealed in 1974, but the laws that took its place in the 1980s have also, in large measure, "led to increased legal regulation of industrial bargaining and industrial action".[13]

All in all, and allowing for the ever-present differences between countries, it would be difficult to disagree with the proposition that the State has in recent decades assumed a more active role in collective bargaining by promulgating more rules, imposing more restraints and becoming a more active participant in negotiations.

The remaining sections of this chapter will be concerned, first, with the continuing or traditional roles of government in collective bargaining, notably with regard to procedural and substantive issues, matters of implementation and service functions; and second with more recent efforts by governments to harmonise collective bargaining with the constraints imposed by the severe economic problems of the post-1973 period.

THE NEGOTIATING PROCESS

Since a number of procedural questions likely to arise in the course of the bargaining process have already been reviewed in an earlier chapter, the discussion here will be brief and will focus on the role of government. Matters considered to be procedural include, illustratively, employers' recognition of unions, the duty to bargain in good faith, the determination of appropriate bargaining units, the obligation of employers to disclose information relevant to the negotiations, and other non-substantive but sometimes potentially controversial matters.[14]

Basically, governments may adopt one of two approaches to procedural questions. They may either confine themselves to the formulation of a few essential rules, thus leaving it mainly to the parties to develop the details of their relationships, or they may decide to formulate a body of quite specific legislative prescriptions and prohibitions which will almost certainly require an administrative or judicial enforcement mechanism. Aside from some major exceptions and qualifications that will need to be emphasised, the first approach has been characteristic of most continental countries of Western Europe, while the second one has been identified with the North American countries. To be sure, the absence of legislation does not necessarily mean the absence of any form of public regulation. For example, the fact that the statute law of the Federal Republic of Germany has nothing to say about the actual process of collective bargaining or about the settlement of procedural disputes has resulted in certain matters being referred to the courts, and the rulings of the courts have of course grown into an important body of precedents and guide-lines for the parties. Also, a limited amount of procedural legislation actually does exist in some Western European countries, exemplified in Belgium and France by the statutory designation of "most representative" for qualifying trade union organisations which enjoy important privileges, including the privilege of concluding collective agreements eligible for "extension" to an entire industry. Still, it remains true that by far the largest amount of legislative and administrative rule making on bargaining procedures has occurred in the North American countries.

Why should that be so? It is at least conceivable that systems of collective bargaining which have traditionally focused on the establishment of minimum wages and other minimum terms of employment through industry-wide negotiations between comprehensive bodies of employers and trade unions have afforded fewer occasions for procedural disputes than systems of bargaining at enterprise or establishment level from which effective and detailed conditions of employment are expected to result. That may be so because negotiations over a relatively limited number of standard issues between an association of employers and a national union (or a group of unions) offer less of a direct threat to the preservation of managerial prerogatives and managerial flexibility than the item-by-item bargaining characteristic of the North American countries, where the outcome is much closer to actual wages and working conditions. The distinction would help to explain why employers in North America have historically offered stronger resistance than their European counterparts to union demands for recognition as bargaining agents, why this resistance has extended to almost every step of the bargaining process and why the resulting level of industrial conflict over procedural matters was sufficiently pervasive to require intervention by the State.

If this is a well-founded explanation, one would expect to find an increase in government regulation of bargaining procedures in those countries where for whatever reason — government policy, union initiatives or other considerations — the enterprise becomes a key focus of collective bargaining and of employee interest representation, while at the same time certain issues become subject to discussion and bargaining that impinge directly on managerial functions which were previously immune to challenge. And that is indeed what has occurred, as a few examples will show.

In France detailed provisions about the rights of unions in the individual enterprise were already contained in the legislation of December 1968,[15] although that law did not yet directly address the question of plant-level collective bargaining. That was left to the third of the four so-called Auroux laws (November 1982) which specifies, among other things —

(a) that in an enterprise where a trade union is present — or where several are present — the head of the enterprise is obliged to arrange for negotiations every year;

(b) that the items to be negotiated must include real wages *(salaires effectifs)*, actual working hours and the organisation of working time;

(c) that agreement must be reached in the first meeting on the underlying information to be supplied by the employer to the trade union negotiators and the date on which that information will be conveyed;

(d) that the information will be such as to enable a comparative analysis to be made of the position of men and women employed in the enterprise as regards jobs and skills, wages, hours of work and the organisation of working time; and

(e) that as long as the negotiations are being held, the employer shall not, except in case of urgency, take any unilateral decisions on matters under discussion.[16]

Equally detailed, or even more so, are the legal regulations governing the procedural relations between managements and works councils encountered in the legislation of such countries as the Federal Republic of Germany and the Netherlands. Admittedly, these relations are not formally considered to be in the domain of collective bargaining, although *de facto* they would be hard to differentiate. Not only are the laws in these countries on plant-level relations incomparably more specific than the legislation on what is essentially industry-level collective bargaining, but their content also resembles in several respects — rights of the parties, employers' obligation to furnish relevant information and so on — the statutory and administrative rules that deal with bargaining procedures in the North American countries.

The general proposition supported by these examples is that the degree of government regulation of the procedural aspects of collective bargaining — or more broadly of the industrial relations system as a whole — tends to increase as the level of negotiations moves closer to the workplace. It would not be prudent, however, to claim universal validity for the relationship. The experience of Japan indicates that it is possible to combine an essentially enterprise-oriented bargaining system with only a moderate degree of government involvement in bargaining procedures. In the past few decades the overriding aim of the Japanese Government has been the promotion of voluntary collective bargaining with only a limited role for government, and there has been little effort by the Government to prescribe procedural rules for negotiations.

To a certain extent the contrasting structure of union organisation may also account, at least historically, for some of the observed differences in the degree of government intervention. In industrial relations systems generally characterised by industrial unionism, as in Western Europe, the potential for inter-union conflict disruptive of collective bargaining has been rather less than in systems where, as in North America, competition between unions has been fostered by the uneasy coexistence of several structural types of unionism. In this regard Great Britain is in part an exception. While certain features of British trade unionism have been closer to the North American than to the continental European pattern, such as the presence of different types of unions, the ability of British unions to work out arrangements for joint representation in collective bargaining has made government intervention for the sake of settling inter-union conflicts infrequent.

In so far as unions have devised procedures for peacefully settling among themselves disputes over representation in collective bargaining, the pressure for government intervention in certain kinds of "jurisdictional" or "demarcation" disputes declines correspondingly. In most European countries the central bodies of the trade union confederations have had the requisite authority to resolve such controversies. However, by the time unions in North America had made equivalent arrangements and had worked out the necessary principles and processes to settle their competitive claims, an administrative procedure under public law had already become firmly established to adjudicate representation disputes involving two or more unions. That procedure is based on the principle of exclusive representation — i.e. one union per bargaining unit — as determined by a majority of employees voting by secret ballot in a defined bargaining unit. As Professor Kahn-Freund once explained, the policy to limit the representation of employees to a single labour organisation per bargaining unit, which is virtually unique to the North American countries —

... must be understood against the background of a society in which union practice is hardly influenced by the idea of working class solidarity and in which the intense competition between unions extends into the field of collective bargaining in a way unknown even in those countries (such as Belgium, France, Italy and the Netherlands) whose unions are divided by political and religious differences. In America the law had to create a union monopoly of representation in each bargaining unit.[17]

Since current trends in the structure of European trade unionism are generally tending more towards consolidation than towards fragmentation and competition — a trend which incidentally is also characteristic of developments in North America — there are no grounds to expect increased government intervention for this particular reason. Significant exceptions exist only with respect to white-collar employees and scientific, technical and managerial staffs where rival organisations do at times press their conflicting aspirations for representation in collective bargaining and where there has been a certain amount of ad hoc government intervention. Normally, however, such disputes are resolved through mutual accommodation among the unions themselves.

SUBSTANTIVE ISSUES

In countries which rely upon collective bargaining as the key instrument for determining the conditions of employment, it has long been the rule that the parties themselves should be free to determine the issues subject to negotiation as well as the terms of settlement. Professor Blanpain's observation that "the social partners in Belgium enjoy a quasi-total autonomy in the fixing of wages and working conditions in the broadest sense of the phrase" applies most of the time to most of the other industrialised market economies.[18] The reasons are readily at hand. From a legal point of view, the parties enjoy freedom of contract as long as they do not violate the mandatory provisions of any applicable legislation. From the point of view of practical labour relations, the parties are in a better position than any public authority or other outsiders to assess their respective needs and resources and to let that assessment be reflected in the subjects which form the substance and outcome of their negotiations. If an irreconcilable disagreement were to develop, for example over the addition of an item to the bargaining agenda, most governments would probably treat it as they would treat any other industrial conflict. Depending on the circumstances, they might invoke conciliation procedures, suggest voluntary arbitration, let the parties settle their disagreement by resorting to a test of economic force, or perhaps proceed in some other fashion. But they would ordinarily not impose their judgement to resolve the dispute unless so requested.

There are, however, important exceptions to the general rule of non-intervention, some forms of intervention being indirect, others direct. Indirect intervention consists of pre-emption by substantive legislation. It occurs when the State establishes through social and labour legislation substantive rules that could have been determined — and often are determined — through collective bargaining. As pointed out with regard to France in one recent study —

... large numbers of questions which might, elsewhere, have become matters for collective bargaining, have been the object of politics, legislation and state regulation in France. The length of the work week, vacation time, many aspects of job security (hiring/firing/seniority/job classifications), fringe benefits of many kinds, in addition to more ordinary matters like the minimum wage, have become direct state concerns.[19]

It needs to be emphasised, however, that the sometimes far-reaching role of government in the determination of substantive issues may well have not only the endorsement but also the participation of the parties. In Italy government intervention has resulted in the adoption of numerous laws through "negotiated" legislation; they were drafted on the basis of collective agreements already reached beforehand between the trade unions and employers' associations, or in consultation with them, or sometimes in consultation only with the trade unions.[20] Much the same also applies to France and to several other countries in Western Europe.[21]

Until about 1960 the balance between substantive rule making by collective bargaining and by state action was tilted in favour of collective bargaining in North America and — allowing for substantial inter-country differences — in favour of the State in Western Europe. But between 1960 and 1980 the traditional role of government in the United States as regulator of the process of rule setting, not of its outcomes, changed dramatically as government regulation of the terms and conditions of employment expanded.[22] During the 15-year stretch from 1960 to 1975, for example, the number of regulatory programmes administered by the United States Department of Labor tripled from 43 to 134.[23] Evidently the industrial relations systems of the United States and Western Europe were in this particular respect moving towards much closer convergence than had previously been the case. It now remains to be seen, however, whether the trend towards substantive government intervention in the United States will recede. The recent deregulatory measures of the current administration constitute a sharp reversal of direction and may establish a new balance between intervention and regulation.

The more direct forms of intervention, though still exceptions, are of a different kind. The first and probably most far-reaching direct intervention is represented by the case of the United States, where the statutory law defines certain items — "wages, hours and other terms and conditions of employment" — to be mandatory subjects for bargaining and where an administrative agency, the NLRB, has been given broad powers to interpret the legislative language.[24] The NLRB recognises three categories of issues — mandatory, permissive and prohibited subjects, each one with its own set of rules. Mandatory subjects are those that the NLRB holds to be within the explicit language of the statute; both parties are required to negotiate about them "in good faith", a formulation which in itself is subject to interpretation. Permissive subjects are considered by the Board to be outside the terms of what the law requires; neither side may seek to compel the other to bargain about permissive subjects, let alone insist on agreement about them. Prohibited subjects are those few items that the legislature, on grounds of public policy, has declared to be inappropriate for inclusion in a collective agreement. Over the years the NLRB's interpretations have resulted in a gradual expansion of the mandatory subject-matter for collective bargaining, mainly through a shift from the permissive to the mandatory category.[25]

While it can readily be argued that the freedom of the parties to define the scope of their negotiations has been severely circumscribed, the procedure does have the advantage of ensuring the peaceful settlement of the preliminary question of what is and what is not negotiable, which might otherwise have had to be resolved through a test of economic strength. It could also be argued with some plausibility that the need for an administrative mechanism to resolve controverted issues of negotiability in collective bargaining is greater in a system such as that of the United States, where the scope of subjects included in negotiations at enterprise level is rather large, than in systems essentially oriented towards industry-level bargaining where the range of bargainable issues is likely to be more limited and more geared towards agreements embodying minimum rather than actual terms. If this is indeed the case, the observation has important implications for industrial relations systems in which plant-level bargaining is becoming more widespread and in which the issues in negotiations are becoming more numerous and more specific.

A different but not entirely dissimilar type of government regulation of which substantive terms should be covered in collective bargaining is represented by French collective bargaining legislation as enacted in 1950.[26] The law provides that if it is the intention of the parties to conclude an agreement which is eligible for "extension" (a topic covered below), the agreement must contain provisions related to a very large number of specifically named subjects. They need not all be enumerated here, but among them are provisions related to minimum wages, premium pay for dangerous or difficult work, paid holidays, severance pay and many more items. The law does not prescribe how the issues should be resolved; that is left for the parties themselves to decide. But it does compel them to address each one of the mandated items. The parallel with

American practice goes one step further. The French law of 1950 contains a supplemental list of "permissive" provisions which the parties may but need not include in their negotiations.

Exceptions of a less sweeping character to the general rule of non-intervention than is contained in the legislation of France and the United States appear with some frequency in many industrialised market economies, usually in the form of mandated exclusions from the array of bargainable subjects, but occasionally in the form of mandated inclusions. Some exclusions are intended to be permanent, or at any rate to be in effect until there is a major change in public policy as normally expressed in legislation; other exclusions are intended to be temporary, either with or without a specified length of time.

High on the frequency list of banned provisions are agreements which in some form require union membership as a condition of initial hiring (closed shop) or as a condition of continued employment (union shop). Usually associated closely with this prohibition is a ban on contract clauses that reserve certain benefits or terms of employment for union members and exclude non-members from their application. Examples abound. Thus the Basic Law of the Federal Republic of Germany contains a provision on freedom of association which has been interpreted not only as precluding the parties from agreeing to compulsory union membership provisions (i.e. freedom to associate being considered to include freedom not to associate), but also as narrowly circumscribing the ability of the parties to limit certain provisions of collective agreements, for instance supplemental retirement benefits, to union members. In the United States federal legislation not only prohibits the closed shop but also leaves the individual states free to impose within their own jurisdiction additional restrictions on the freedom of the parties to enter into union shop agreements.[27] Recent British legislation, while not prohibiting compulsory union membership agreements, has imposed important restrictions on both employers and unions in dismissing employees for reasons of non-membership.[28] In the Netherlands the Collective Agreements Act of 1927 declares to be void any negotiated provisions which impose on the employer an obligation "to engage or not to engage workers of a specific religious persuasion or political opinion *or members of a specific trade union*".[29] Unlike the rules promulgated in other countries, the Netherlands statute does not prohibit a contractual union membership requirement *per se*. It only precludes the linkage of such a requirement to membership in a particular union — an understandable measure in a society long characterised by plural unionism, although not to the same extent now as formerly.

A few countries prohibit or limit the inclusion of wage indexation clauses in collective agreements — an unusual measure because such clauses are often among the more important sections of collective agreements and also because here the prohibition reflects standing public policy rather than a short-term attempt to overcome a particular economic emergency. In the Federal Republic of Germany the linkage, while perhaps not illegal — opinions on this point diverge — at the very least requires the approval of the central bank *(Deutsche*

Bundesbank). The restriction is apparently acceptable to the central trade union federation (DGB) and its affiliates on the ground that indexation clauses represent in principle an undesirable limitation of the right to bargain collectively *(Tarifautonomie).*[30] A similar prohibition in France on tying wages to a cost-of-living index dates back to the economic stabilisation measures taken by the Government in 1958-59 but appears in practice not to have been uniformly observed.[31]

Turning now to required inclusions, those few that are intended to express standing public policy tend to be motivated by government attempts to improve available methods for applying the terms of an agreement rather than to intrude on the content of the substantive provisions. Thus, legislation in Canada and Finland makes it compulsory for agreements to include grievance procedures, while New Zealand "requires each collective agreement to contain provision for the final and conclusive settlement of all disputes of rights".[32]

In contrast to the above-mentioned interventions which are expressive of long-term public policy rather than ad hoc attempts to handle a particular situation, government interventions in the substantive terms of collective agreements are almost invariably occasioned by efforts to overcome serious but presumably not permanent economic difficulties. They consist of statutory limits, or outright freezes, on negotiated wage (and price) increases, controls over commonly negotiable items affecting labour costs such as improvements in paid holidays, attempts to link wage increases to productivity improvements, severance of wage movements from cost-of-living indices, and other limitations on collective bargaining. In so far as such restrictions form part of government efforts to master the economic problems of the current era they will be covered in a separate section of this chapter.

APPLICATION OF COLLECTIVE AGREEMENTS

While it is generally agreed at least in principle — but circumscribed in practice by many exceptions — that the State should not become involved in determining or resolving the substantive issues of collective bargaining, an equivalent limitation does not govern the application of collective agreements. To be sure, the parties themselves always bear the initial responsibility for assuring the proper execution of their agreement, and for that purpose they will almost invariably establish appropriate machinery as part of their agreement. But should the machinery prove unable to do the job, they are likely to turn to the State to secure assistance, protection or justice. In terms of degree and scope of involvement, the role of government in the application of collective agreements is sufficiently extensive to require a review of representative practices. No attempt will be made, however, to deal with complex questions of legal interpretation or to explicate the status of collective agreements under the laws of various countries.

Two major areas will be reviewed in this section. One concerns the role of the State in extending the coverage of a collective agreement to non-signatories.

The other deals with the enforcement of the rights and obligations embodied in the agreement.

Extension

As a general rule, the provisions of a collective agreement apply only to the parties — i.e. the employers or organisations of employers and of employees, and of course their members — that participated or were represented in the negotiations and subsequently indicated their willingness to adhere to the agreement by affixing their signature, sometimes in conjunction with a ratification procedure.[33]

Where the negotiations take place at industry level, and where the employer side is fully inclusive of the industry in the relevant geographic area — whether an entire country or a particular region — the agreement will correspondingly apply to all employers and employees in the industry or branch concerned. If, however, the degree of representativeness is less than complete, some employers and their employees will obviously not be covered. Under certain circumstances, their position as outsiders may confer an important competitive advantage on them. This is so if the terms of the agreement impose on covered employers labour costs, mostly in the form of negotiated wage or wage-related items, which are higher than the costs borne by non-covered employers. At times the cost differential may be wide enough to jeopardise the ability of covered employers to stay in business and consequently jeopardise the jobs of their employees. When this occurs the disadvantaged parties will seek relief. If they cannot obtain it by bringing their competitors under coverage of the agreement and thus equalise the cost differential, they may look to the State for a remedy on the ground that the institution of collective bargaining is an important social good which deserves to be protected against being undermined by unfair competition. The threat of undercutting may become particularly acute during periods of economic hardship, which explains why a number of governments first responded to requests for protection in the depression years of the 1930s.[34] Their response was to enact legislation which "extends" the terms of an agreement to all non-signatories or, in the language of some countries, which declares the terms of an agreement to be generally binding on non-covered employers and their employees.

Currently, such legislation prevails in several countries, including Belgium, France, the Federal Republic of Germany, Italy, the Netherlands and Switzerland. It is, however, not found in the Scandinavian countries, and this mostly because the level of representativeness on both sides of the bargaining table is so high that the coverage of collective agreements often approaches the entirety of the industry concerned. Extension is also absent from the industrial relations systems of North America (except for the Canadian province of Quebec) because it is not readily adaptable to systems based chiefly on enterprise bargaining.[35] It is normally through industry-wide bargaining that employers and employees can best be brought under the terms of an agreement in proportions sufficiently large to justify the extension of an agreement to an entire industry. That probably explains why the existing legal provisions on extension in Japan, where the individual enterprise is the dominant bargaining unit, are seldom utilised.

Procedures for extension vary from country to country and need not be examined in detail here. Usually a request must be made by one or more of the signatory parties to a designated government authority, probably the Minister of Labour, who may be assisted by a bipartite advisory body. The parties to the agreement are expected to be widely representative of the industry (or trade) to which the agreement is to be extended; normally the coverage before extension must include the employers of at least half of the employees in the industry. The requesting party or parties (many requests are made jointly by the representatives of employers and employees) must demonstrate that the public interest will be served by extension. This is an important, even if elusive, requirement because the declaration of extension transforms an originally private agreement between independent private parties into a kind of common law or common set of rules for an entire industry. In other words, before extension occurs the agreement binds only the members of the organisations which signed it. Afterwards it binds all employers and employees within its industrial and geographic scope, and it becomes subject to enforcement by appropriate public agencies, e.g. the labour inspectorate.[36]

Although the practical importance of extension and the frequency with which extension requests are submitted and approved vary considerably between countries and periods of time, extension can be an exceedingly important element in a national industrial relations system. Belgium is an apt example; by means of extension most workers are covered by collective agreements, and the non-observance of collective agreements declared generally binding by Royal Decree is penally sanctioned. "It is quite obvious", notes Professor Blanpain, "that such a system [of extension] obliges employers, certainly the more important ones, to join employers' associations in order to be able to influence the agreements which the association is negotiating and which are going to have an effect on the firm whether the employer is a member or not."[37]

Enforcement

A review of disputes settlement procedures is beyond the assigned scope of this study; the ILO has dealt with the subject extensively elsewhere.[38] But some general observations need to be made since one of the important functions of government in collective bargaining is the enforcement of the terms of collective agreements. Enforcement is not exclusively a governmental function; in several countries public measures exist alongside arrangements established by the parties themselves, such as private arbitration. Nor do all governments regard the enforcement of collective agreements as one of their proper responsibilities; in at least one country — Great Britain — a collective agreement is usually not considered to be, and not intended by the parties to be, a legally enforceable contract.[39] Nevertheless, in the large majority of countries and under a variety of circumstances, the parties will at some point turn to the State for enforcement of their claims under an agreement.[40]

Collective agreements create rights and obligations for both sides. That is why disputes about them are often referred to as "rights disputes", as distinguished from "interest disputes" or disputes involving the negotiation or renegotiation of an agreement. But rights and obligations are not usually implemented by themselves. During the life of an agreement either party may have reason to believe that the other side has infringed upon a contractual right or has failed to live up to an express or implied obligation; or else the two sides may in good faith place different interpretations on a particular provision of their agreement. Such situations are quite common; it would in fact be most unusual for a collective agreement to be so lucidly drafted that no room were left for divergent interpretations. Less common but by no means inconceivable is an outright refusal by one side to abide by the terms of an agreement, but this does happen.

Whatever the impetus, the rights and obligations created by the agreement must be implemented — and if possible implemented without recourse to open conflict and interruptions of work. In this process, what in particular is to be the role of the State? There are no uniform answers. In fact, diversity and choice are the rule.[41] In most countries the initial responsibility belongs to the parties themselves, but when the parties are unable to resolve disagreements over the application or interpretation of their agreement through procedures of their own devising, almost all countries make available a judicial procedure, usually through specialised boards or labour courts but not infrequently also through the ordinary courts.

In most continental European countries the legal enforceability of collective agreements is of relatively long standing, in Switzerland since 1911, and in most of the other countries since the 1920s or 1930s.[42] The Collective Agreements Act of 1927 in the Netherlands, to cite only one instance, permits either party to a collective agreement to compel faithful performance of its contractual obligations by the other party through the order of an ordinary court and allows suits for damages to be brought if damages result from a breach of the agreement. Either the contracting parties themselves or their members — i.e. individual employers or individual union members — may seek enforcement and recovery of damages.

Similar provisions are found in the legislation of the United States, where collective agreements are declared enforceable in the ordinary federal courts by means of suits "for violation of contracts between an employer and a labour organisation representing employees in an industry affecting commerce . . .".[43] Although the language is broad enough to cover any contract provision, most court cases involving contract disputes in the United States deal with the meaning and application of the arbitration provision in the collective agreement. The reason is, of course, that in the United States a very large percentage of rights disputes are resolved by voluntary resort to private arbitration under provisions included in almost all collective agreements. Consequently, the cases brought before the courts tend mostly to be appeals against arbitrators' decisions reached under the arbitration procedure rather than issues involving the substantive terms of employment.

RESEARCH, INFORMATION, ADVICE AND EDUCATION

Several governments among the countries included in this study give support to, or themselves engage directly in, activities for the general purpose of improving the functioning of collective bargaining through guidance, information and other forms of assistance to the parties. Unlike mediation, conciliation, arbitration, fact-finding and related services to which governments resort in specific situations to settle a dispute or to help the parties define more precisely their negotiating positions, the activities considered in this section are intended to serve a broader and longer-term purpose. They aim at enhancing the information base available to the parties, improving the negotiating skills of their representatives, conveying a more informed understanding of the economic context within which bargaining takes place, enlightening the constituencies represented in the negotiations, and generally reducing potential sources of conflict that are founded on lack of skills and information, mis-understandings and other remediable shortcomings.

Far-seeing governments tend to regard investment in activities designed to reduce these shortcomings as an investment in industrial peace.[44] But it is necessarily a long-run venture. The results are rarely as immediate and dramatic as, for example, the successful settlement of a major dispute in an industry vital to the national economy. Yet failure to develop sustained programmes of research, information and education may be costly.

More solidly established among the various responsibilities of governments than any other is the area of research and information. It has become routine for most governments to collect and disseminate information of direct usefulness to the parties in collective bargaining and often to go beyond fact-gathering by providing high-quality analyses of important issues. Informational areas covered most frequently in statistical series or other suitable ways include:

— trends in wages, earnings, fringe benefits, hours of work and related data, usually broken down by industrial, occupational, geographic and other subdivisions;
— labour force and labour market data, including changes in occupational distribution, employment and unemployment;
— changes in price levels (particularly in consumer price indices) and in productivity;
— negotiations of collective agreements currently in progress, contents of agreements, work stoppages and extension of agreements; and
— important decisions of courts and administrative tribunals.

Some governments have also undertaken or have commissioned in-depth studies of the entire national industrial relations system or of certain key segments. Probably the best known among the comprehensive studies is the above-mentioned report of the Royal Commission on Trade Unions and Employers' Associations (1968) in Great Britain, better known as the Donovan Commission Report.[45] A more current but less comprehensive review, conducted with financial support from the British Government and designed partly as a follow-up to the Donovan Report, is the recent survey, *Workplace industrial relations in Britain* (1983), jointly undertaken by the Department of Employment, the Policy Studies Institute and the Economic and Social Research Council.[46] Others could readily be cited: the report by Professor Gérard Adam in France (1978), commissioned by the Minister of Labour to inquire into the consequences of the 1950 legislation on collective bargaining; [47] the report by a government-appointed commission under the chairmanship of Professor Kurt H. Biedenkopf in the Federal Republic of Germany (1970) to investigate the workings of the system of worker participation in management; [48] and the report of the "Hancock Committee of Review into Australian Industrial Relations Law and Systems", whose work has been described as "the first wide-ranging review of the formal system [of industrial relations] since its inception some 80 years ago".[49] These reports often include specific recommendations addressed either to the parties for joint or separate action or to the legislative and administrative agencies of government to improve the workings of the industrial relations system.

The need for additional research initiated or financially supported by government and removed as far as possible from the immediate pressures of ongoing negotiations would seem to be particularly acute at the present time when marked shifts are occurring in the industrial relations systems of virtually all industrialised market economies. In particular, more attention than before needs to be paid to the service sectors of the economy because they are experiencing the most rapid rise in employment and because in the past a large proportion of studies have been mainly concerned with manufacturing industries.

But whatever insufficiencies there may be in government research efforts related to collective bargaining, the fact remains that, in terms of resource allocation, governments put far more emphasis on data collection, research and dissemination of information than on education and advice. That may be so because the parties themselves, as well as certain other institutions, notably universities, already meet some of the educational and consultative needs. However that may be, government support of formal educational programmes in collective bargaining and related areas has become an accepted notion only fairly recently. In Great Britain the Employment Protection Act of 1975 required that all employers who recognise trade unions should allow employees who are unpaid union officials compensated time off from work for industrial relations training.[50] Also, since 1976 the British Government has made available funds towards the cost of trade union educational facilities provided by the central body, the TUC, and its affiliated organisations.[51] In 1978-79 the grant for this purpose from the Ministry of Education and Science amounted to US$2 million. It should also be noted that while the inception of the programme occurred during the tenure of a government led by the Labour Party, the programme was continued after the Conservative Party took office. Governments in other countries, including France, have also been making direct subsidies for educational programmes available to the trade unions. Other countries achieve the same purpose by means of indirect subsidies enabling educational institutions to offer programmes on collective bargaining and related subjects to trade union and employer groups.

In some countries, notably Great Britain and the United States, the principal mediation services maintained by the national government also perform educational and advisory services in collective bargaining. In Great Britain a staff of professional advisers was appointed as far back as 1945 in what was then called the Ministry of Labour and National Service but is now the Department of Employment.[52] That work has been performed since 1975 by the ACAS, an independent public agency not answerable to the government in office but supervised by a tripartite council.[53] The ACAS is responsible for a range of activities, including particularly the resolution of industrial disputes through conciliation and arbitration but also the provision of advice to the parties on industrial relations and the development of effective personnel practices. It has also issued several codes of practice containing practical guidance on the improvement of industrial relations. Advice is given free and includes short advisory visits as well as in-depth work. The advisory work of the ACAS appears to be particularly influential in relatively small companies that are not able to employ personnel management specialists.[54]

In the United States the FMCS has also long been aware of the need to promote the development of sound and stable labour-management relations. To this end it offers educational programmes to help the parties improve their relationships under circumstances free of the pressures of the bargaining table and negotiating deadlines. In recent years it has concentrated on the formation of labour-management committees and particularly on a programme called Relationships-by-Objective (RBO), introduced in 1975 as a successor to an earlier "preventive mediation" programme. The RBO is intended "to get key labour and management leaders in companies with poor labour-management relations to analyse what they are doing wrong, and then work together to effect changes", the aim being to bring about a co-operative problem-solving attitude at the workplace.[55]

WAGE BARGAINING UNDER SEVERE ECONOMIC CONSTRAINTS

The various activities of government which have been reviewed up to this point indicate the main tendencies that shape the relationship between the public authorities and the parties to collective bargaining. With due allowance for a considerable range of differences, the generally accepted terms of the relationship allocate — or at least have in the past allocated — to the government a paramount position in prescribing and often also administering the basic procedural rules, while they leave to the parties the principal responsibility for framing the substantive conditions of employment. To summarise the situation in this way is, of course, to some extent an oversimplification. In some countries governments have been a major force in determining substantive issues in the employment relationship, and in several countries the procedural rules promulgated by the parties themselves have been of greater day-to-day importance in resolving procedural issues than the rules fashioned by the public authorities.[56] Yet at least until fairly recently, most governments in countries where collective bargaining was reasonably well developed acted on the proposition that, leaving aside periods of national emergency, the determination of wages and conditions of employment was chiefly a matter for bargaining between representative organisations on both sides. In the past ten to 15 years, however, there has been a substantial increase in government intervention, and the period 1980-83 has been described as a time when —

... governments played a more active role in affecting the outcome of collective bargaining than ever before in peacetime. There were several wage freezes, or statutory limitations on increases, of varying duration. Almost everywhere that there was a national practice of indexing wages on prices, the mechanism was halted, or its consequences limited or its implementation postponed. Pay increases for workers in the public service were cut back in several countries, as governments sought to limit the burden of budget deficits — and in some cases to set an example of desirable levels of increases for the private sector.[57]

It is not asserted here that everywhere there has been a relentless and unvarying expansion of the role of government in collective bargaining. The evidence is, in fact, quite to the contrary. It shows intermittent rather than continuous intervention, with periods of relatively unmonitored collective bargaining succeeded by periods of more or less close supervision. There are of course also remarkable differences between countries. But the overall long-term tendency does seem to be in the direction of an increasingly activist governmental role, and this for reasons that have already been explored elsewhere in considerable detail.[58] Here a summary will suffice.

A major change in the economic context for collective bargaining was inaugurated by the substantial increase in the world price of oil during the decade of the 1970s. The increase was followed in most countries by a major recession, accompanied by the highest unemployment rates since the end of the Second World War, especially among young workers. The sharp decline in the rate of economic growth was accompanied in most countries by strong inflationary pressures, mounting budget deficits and chronic balance-of-payments difficulties. The adverse impact of the recession, particularly on unemployment, was aggravated severely by what Professor Roberts has described as "a collapse of manufacturing capacity in the steel and engineering industries" [59] (sometimes referred to as the "smokestack" industries), which also happened to be almost everywhere the most highly unionised industries with a strong tradition of collective bargaining. The nearly universal decline of traditional manufacturing industries in the older industrialised countries was directly related, in turn, to a sharp increase in international competition, resulting partly from the arrival of several newly industrialising countries seeking markets for their products, and partly from an unusually rapid acceleration of technological and labour-saving changes. Cumulatively, these developments have presented a powerful challenge to governments seeking to contain inflation, maintain economic growth, restore the balance of payments and reduce unemployment.

The full range of government responses has been extraordinarily varied. It has included, among others, the following measures:

— the use of fiscal and monetary policies;
— the development of special incentives to stimulate productivity and to encourage investment;
— reductions in public expenditures for social programmes;
— cuts in subsidies for nationalised industries and in some instances a decision to reprivatise them;
— the use of improved techniques in the management of labour markets;
— the relaxation of one or another among the already mentioned key policy objectives; and
— varying degrees of intervention in collective bargaining.

Here we shall be concerned only with the last item.

Broadly speaking, three kinds of government attempts to intervene in collective bargaining for the purpose of affecting the outcome of wage negotiations may be distinguished: persuasion; direct or indirect participation; and controls. There are also certain other possibilities, for example government insistence on wage restraint in the public sector as a model for wage negotiations in the private sector, which in view of the growth of the public sector has sometimes been an important factor.

Persuasion can take various forms. At its weakest it consists of exhortatory statements, often by leading government officials, that are designed to impress upon the parties the urgent need to take macro-economic factors into account in their negotiations. Because exhortation has only rarely been successful, several governments in the 1960s and 1970s adopted informal or voluntary wage guide-lines at various times as a way of meeting the dual goals of preserving reasonably unfettered collective bargaining and still holding wage increases within economically tolerable limits.

That a guide-lines policy goes beyond mere advocacy of restraint is evident. Besides enlisting the force of public opinion behind wage moderation, it sets up a more or less specific target or ceiling and thereby confronts the parties to collective bargaining with the need to make a choice between visible support for national economic capabilities and goals as defined by government, or some form of evasion, defiance or outright rejection.

Most governments pursuing a guide-lines policy strive for the endorsement and support of the central confederations of trade unions and employers' associations. They do so in the expectation that the moral authority of the central bodies will reinforce the appeal to the bargainers at industry and enterprise levels to exercise restraint. Since the support of the central bodies is usually obtainable only, if at all, through consultation on the substance and administration of the guide-lines, one of the potential consequences of a policy promulgating guide-lines is the emergence of tripartite bargaining at top national levels. That process not only exerts a centralising effect on collective bargaining by strengthening the authority of the central organisations, but also promotes the second of the three types of government intervention mentioned above, namely direct or indirect government participation in negotiations.

Rare are the guide-lines policies that have endured more than a few years. Even under favourable circumstances, it is difficult to reconcile for any length of time the practice of free collective bargaining with self-imposed restraints, especially for the leaders of organisations whose tenure in office depends on periodic renewal of membership support through democratic procedures. That is one reason why some governments have shifted the focus of their restraint policies to the formation of tripartite structures or more active use of already existing ones in the expectation that a thorough exchange of views and a common base of information will result in a consensus about economic constraints and prospects. If so, the outcome will serve as a basis for bargaining at industry and enterprise levels within already agreed limits, or else the top-level meetings will themselves become the forum for the conclusion of a national inter-industry agreement (i.e. a kind of framework agreement), to be followed by more detailed bargaining at subsidiary enterprise and industry levels.

An apt example of tripartism as a discussion forum was the institution of *Konzertierte Aktion* (concerted action) which in the Federal Republic of Germany served for a decade as a means for periodic reviews of the Government's economic analyses and forecasts. It was instituted in 1967 and consisted of two to four meetings per year between leading representatives of government agencies (including the central bank and the Council of Economic Advisers), employers' associations and trade unions.[60] The aims of the meetings were to discuss relevant information provided by the Government on the economic situation and the economic outlook of the country and to provide an opportunity for the voluntary co-ordination of official policies and private collective bargaining. The meetings were discontinued in 1977 when the trade unions decided to cease their participation for reasons not directly connected to the purpose of concerted action. Recently the possibility of reinstituting them has been raised.[61]

There are many other institutions for regular tripartite consultation in matters affecting the context for collective bargaining: the Central Economic Council in Belgium, *Sanrô-kon* in Japan, the Social-Economic Council in the Netherlands, the Contact Committee in Norway, and others. To be sure, they have widely varying mandates. Moreover, in some countries regular consultations may occur without a formal institutionalised framework. But they are all founded on more or less the same aim, namely reducing the conflict — actual or potential — between national economic exigencies and collective bargaining, and integrating or reconciling the various interests involved.

A more activist form of tripartism has emerged in several European countries, as described in this passage from the ILO's *World Labour Report*:

Since the beginning of the last recession, wages policy in these countries has often been determined in central framework agreements (that is to say agreements that lay down only general principles to which a more explicit form is given later in collective agreements concluded at lower levels). The governments have made a decisive contribution to the working out of these central agreements, although they have not always been parties officially. The signature of most of these agreements, indeed, has been possible only because the governments, along with the employers and workers, also accepted certain commitments aimed, for example, at creating employment or at reducing taxes on wages and the employers' contributions to social security.[62]

Exemplifying the commitments that governments have had to make to achieve the conclusion of tripartite agreements are the negotiations that occurred in Sweden in the mid-1970s which, while providing for wage restraint, also included reductions in direct income taxes in order to correct a situation in which exceedingly high marginal income tax rates prevented increases in money wage rates from having any significant effect on increases in real wages.[63] Another instance is the tripartite national agreement concluded in Italy in 1983 which provided for a limitation on automatic wage indexing — a concession agreed to by all the major trade unions in order to help control inflation in return for certain social improvements.

Similar tripartite national accords reflecting an effort to accommodate simultaneously the national economic policy goals of governments as well as the aspirations of the parties to collective bargaining have been concluded in recent years in Australia, Norway and Spain, usually by means of so-called "package deals". But still one of the most successful and long-lived examples of tripartism is the case of Austria, where tripartite negotiations on wages and prices have been held ever since 1957 under the aegis of a tripartite Joint Council on Wages and Prices composed of high-level representatives of the Government and the central organisations of the private parties. Central to the deliberations in this system of negotiations, to which the term corporatism or neo-corporatism has often been attached, as it has to similar systems elsewhere, have been macro-economic considerations, with special emphasis on the attenuation of inflationary pressures and the maintenance of Austria's international competitiveness. The survival power of this system demonstrates the long-term feasibility of shared decision-making between government and organised private interest groups, although the particular social and political conditions in Austria that have contributed to the success of the system can hardly be replicated easily in other countries.[64]

Neither the actual presence of government representatives in central negotiations nor their signature on the agreement is an essential condition for the results to be consonant with government policy objectives. Bipartite agreements can serve the purpose perfectly well. In the Netherlands the Government has frequently, even if most of the time unsuccessfully, urged the parties to conclude bipartite central agreements that could serve as a framework for the conclusion of collective agreements at industry and enterprise levels. On the one occasion in recent years when the leading organisations of employers and trade unions succeeded in negotiating a bipartite central agreement, its expression of support for measures designed to speed economic recovery, secure stable price levels and strengthen the ability of employers to increase employment by improving the competitive position and profitability of industry closely reflected government economic objectives.[65]

Since voluntary approaches, whether by persuasion or participation, have often fallen short of resolving the problems of collective bargaining under severe economic constraints, several governments have in recent years resorted to various kinds of controls on the freedom of the parties to bargain collectively. There are considerable variations in the nature, incisiveness and duration of these measures, but the more frequent and more important ones have included outright freezes on wages (often also on prices), usually for a stipulated period, as in Belgium; legislated suspensions of wage indexation, as in Denmark, or negotiated suspensions, as in Italy; ceilings on allowable wage increases, particularly for employees in the higher earnings brackets (or alternatively special provisions for low-paid employees); and prohibitions or limitations on improvements in fringe benefits that are likely to increase labour costs, such as more days of paid holidays or collectively bargained supplements to public social insurance programmes, as in the Netherlands. It is, of course, entirely possible for more than one measure to be applied at the same time. When the French Government introduced its austerity programme in 1982 it imposed a wage freeze to last for four-and-a-half months and at the same time prohibited wage indexing — all this at a time when, as Guy Caire points out, Parliament was debating the Government's Bill compelling employers to engage in annual wage negotiations.[66]

The overall range of specific controls has become quite broad, and the above listing is by no means an exhaustive one. Account should also be taken of the fact that governments have achieved some of their aims through measures that largely (but not always) bypass collective bargaining, such as reductions in social insurance benefits and increases in social insurance contributions. Sometimes legislated restraints on wage changes are linked to certain social policy requirements, as for example the stipulation that the payroll savings which employers in Belgium realise from government-imposed limits on allowable wage increases are to be used for the creation of new jobs.

On balance the conclusion seems inescapable that in recent years the extent of government intervention in wage bargaining has increased considerably, although an exception must be made for those countries, notably Great Britain and the United States, whose governments have chosen to rely heavily on monetary controls, deregulation and competition to achieve their aims — and in Great Britain also on selected legislation to curb the power of unions — rather than on direct controls over wage bargaining.

Notes

[1] See, for example, ILO: *Freedom of association and procedures for determining conditions of employment in the public service*, Report VII (1 and 2), International Labour Conference, 63rd Session, Geneva, 1977.

[2] See Ch. 2 above, pp. 19-21.

[3] See the section on "Legal policy: Historical development" in Roy Lewis: "Collective labour law", in George S. Bain (ed.): *Industrial relations in Britain* (Oxford, Basil Blackwell, 1983), pp. 362-368.

[4] See the chapters on Australia, Canada and the United States in Henry Phelps Brown: *The origins of trade union power* (Oxford, Clarendon Press, 1983), pp. 194-279.

[5] ILO: *Collective agreements*, Studies and Reports, Series A (Industrial Relations), No. 39 (Geneva, 1936), p. 268.

[6] For a brief discussion of the content of the Conventions and Recommendations, see N. Valticos: "International labour law" (1984), in R. Blanpain (ed.): *International encyclopaedia for labour law and industrial relations* (Deventer, Kluwer, 1977 onwards), Vol. 1, pp. 47-51.

[7] For the texts of these documents up to 1973, see ILO: *International standards and guiding principles, 1944-1973*, Labour-Management Relations Series, No. 44 (Geneva, 1975).

[8] However, as Professor Treu has pointed out, the constitutional model was not fully implemented, so that Italian industrial relations during the 1950s and 1960s developed largely outside the scope of legal regulation. Tiziano Treu: "Recent development of Italian labour law", in *Labour and Society* (Geneva, IILS), Jan. 1985, p. 28.

[9] For an English translation of this law, see *Legislative Series* (Geneva, ILO), 1949 — Ger.F.R. 1.

[10] Act No. 50-205 respecting collective agreements and proceedings for the settlement of collective labour disputes; ibid., 1950 — Fr. 6 A.

[11] Oliver Clarke: "The development of industrial relations in European market economies", in *Proceedings of the Industrial Relations Research Association, 1980* (Madison, Wisconsin, 1981), p. 171.

[12] Lewis, op. cit., p. 370.

[13] Lord Wedderburn: "The new industrial relations laws in Great Britain", in *Labour and Society*, Jan. 1985, pp. 58-59.

[14] See Ch. 3.

[15] Act No. 68-1179 respecting the right of association in undertakings. See *Legislative Series*, 1968 — Fr. 1.

[16] ibid., 1982 — Fr. 2, p. 46. Cf. Jean-Claude Javillier: *Les réformes du droit du travail depuis le 10 mai* (Paris, Librairie générale de Droit et de Jurisprudence, 1984), pp. 369-375. Also Yves Delamotte: "Recent trends in the statutory regulation of industrial relations in France", in *Labour and Society*, Jan. 1985, pp. 16-18.

[17] Otto Kahn-Freund (ed.): *Labour relations and the law* (London, Stevens, 1965), p. 8.

[18] Roger Blanpain: "Belgium" (1985), in Blanpain (ed.): *International encyclopaedia . . .*, op. cit., Vol. 2, p. 230.

[19] Peter Lange et al.: *Unions, change and crisis: French and Italian union strategy and the political economy, 1945-1980* (London, Allen and Unwin, 1982), p. 71.

[20] See Giugni below, p. 230.

[21] See Caire below, pp. 203-204.

[22] Thomas A. Kochan et al.: "Strategic choice and industrial relations theory", in *Industrial Relations*, winter 1984, p. 19.

[23] Andrew Thomson: "A view from abroad", in Jack Stieber et al. (eds.): *US industrial relations 1950-1980: A critical assessment* (Madison, Wisconsin, Industrial Relations Research Association, 1981), p. 328.

[24] *Legislative Series*, 1947 — USA 2, section 8 *(d)*.

[25] For examples of issues that have moved from the permissive to the mandatory category, see Harold W. Davey et al.: *Contemporary collective bargaining* (Englewood Cliffs, New Jersey, Prentice Hall, 4th ed., 1982), pp. 50-51. It is, of course, conceivable that a change in the

philosophy of the NLRB may result in a reverse movement and a contraction of the mandatory subject-matter for collective bargaining.

[26] *Legislative Series*, 1950 — Fr. 6 A. Cf. Michel Despax and Jacques Rojot: "France" (1979), in Blanpain (ed.): *International encyclopaedia . . .*, op. cit., Vol. 4, pp. 189-190.

[27] Some 21 states have taken advantage of this possibility. It should be noted that when a union in the United States becomes the certified exclusive bargaining agent for a group of employees it must represent fairly the interests of every employee, whether union member or not, and it may not discriminate between members and non-members.

[28] A summary of the relevant provisions of the Employment Act of 1982 is provided in *Social and Labour Bulletin*, Mar. 1983, pp. 34-35.

[29] M. G. Levenbach: "The law relating to collective agreements in the Netherlands", in Kahn-Freund, op. cit., p. 107. Emphasis added. For an English translation of the Collective Agreements Act, see *Legislative Series*, 1927 — Neth. 2.

[30] See "Indexierung wirtschaftlich relevanter Grössen" [Indexation of relevant economic factors], in *Recht der Arbeit* [Labour Law] (Munich), No. 5, 1975, pp. 310-312. Cf. Herbert Wiedermann and Hermann Stumpf: *Tarifvertragsgesetz* [Collective Agreements Act] (Munich, C. H. Beck'sche Verlagsbuchhandlung, 5th ed., 1977), pp. 91-92.

[31] See Jean Rivero and Jean Savatier: *Droit du travail* (Paris, Presses universitaires de France, 1970), p. 441. Cf. J. Pélissier: *Documents de droit du travail* (Paris, Editions Montchrestien, 1971), p. 733.

[32] Efrén Córdova: "A comparative view of collective bargaining in industrialised countries", in *International Labour Review* (Geneva, ILO), July-Aug. 1978, p. 432.

[33] See Ch. 3, "Ratification of agreements", above. Actually the matter is not quite that simple since the agreement is often intended to apply to all employees of the employers represented in the negotiations, whether or not they are members of the trade union(s) represented in the negotiations.

[34] The classic treatise on extension is still the article by L. Hamburger: "The extension of collective agreements to cover entire trades and industries", in *International Labour Review*, Aug. 1939, pp. 153-194.

[35] However, for workers employed on construction projects financed or financially aided by the Federal Government in the United States, the Davis-Bacon Act (1936) provides in effect for a kind of extension by requiring that the wages and fringe benefits paid to workers by their employers be no less than are found by the Secretary of Labor to be "prevailing" in the area concerned. Almost invariably the Secretary finds the wages fixed through collective bargaining to be the prevailing wages for the area and industry concerned.

[36] See for example Despax and Rojot, op. cit., p. 192.

[37] Roger Blanpain: "Belgium" (1985), in Blanpain (ed.): *International encyclopaedia . . .*, op. cit., Vol. 2, p. 235.

[38] See for example ILO: *Conciliation and arbitration procedures in labour disputes* (Geneva, 1980).

[39] After the passing of the Industrial Relations Act of 1971 it became the rule in Britain that any new collective agreement "shall be conclusively presumed to be intended by the parties to it to be a legally enforceable contract" unless the parties provided in writing to the contrary. In practice the Act made no difference since the parties almost invariably took advantage of the exemption opportunity. When the Act was repealed in 1974 the matter lost its practical significance.

[40] For a review of enforcement practices in a large number of countries, see Benjamin Aaron: "Arbitration and the role of courts: The administration of justice in labor law", in *Recht der Arbeit*, Sep.-Oct. 1978, pp. 274-291. (The same article also appeared in *Comparative Labor Law* (Los Angeles, University of California), fall 1979, pp. 3-30.)

[41] A survey of 21 countries found "one common feature: in none of the reporting countries is reliance placed exclusively on one particular procedure for resolving disputes over rights; each permits the use of one or more other procedures in some circumstances". ibid., p. 275.

[42] For Switzerland, see Friedrich H. Heither: *Das kollektive Arbeitsrecht der Schweiz* [The collective labour law of Switzerland] (Stuttgart, Gustav Fischer Verlag, 1964), pp. 93-94.

[43] *Legislative Series*, 1947 — USA 2, section 301 *(a)*. The "commerce" referred to in the law is so-called inter-state commerce (i.e. commerce between the states of the United States) or

foreign commerce. Its existence is constitutionally required to establish the jurisdiction of the federal courts.

[44] Alan Williams: "International perspective: Labor education and labor relations in New Zealand", in *Labor Studies Journal* (New Brunswick, New Jersey), May 1976, pp. 76-77.

[45] United Kingdom, Royal Commission on Trade Unions and Employers' Associations, 1965-68: *Report* (The "Donovan Report"), Cmnd. 3623 (London, HM Stationery Office, 1968).

[46] W. W. Daniel and Neil Millward: *Workplace industrial relations in Britain: The DE/PSI/SSRC Survey* (London, Heinemann Educational Books, 1983).

[47] Gérard Adam: "La négociation collective en France: éléments de diagnostic", in *Droit social* (Paris), Dec. 1978, pp. 420-451.

[48] *Mitbestimmung im Unternehmen: Bericht der Sachverständigenkommission* [Co-determination with the enterprise: Report of the Commission of Experts] (Biedenkopf Report) (Deutscher Bundestag — 6. Wahlperiode, Drucksache VI/334).

[49] See Dabschek and Niland below, p. 174-175. The reference is to *Australian industrial relations law and systems*, Report of the Committee of Review (Canberra, Australian Government Publishing Society, 1985), 3 vols.

[50] Higdon C. Roberts, Jr.: "Steward training in Great Britain", in *Labor Studies Journal*, spring 1979, p. 17.

[51] John A. McIlroy: "Education for the labor movement: United Kingdom experience past and present", ibid., winter 1980, p. 209.

[52] For an account of the work of the advisory service between 1945 and 1960, see M. Towy-Evans: "The personnel management advisory service in Great Britain", in *International Labour Review*, Feb. 1960, pp. 125-139.

[53] The Employment Protection Act of 1975 under which the ACAS was established provides that "the Service shall not be subject to directions of any kind from any Minister of the Crown as to the manner in which it is to exercise any of its functions under any enactment". See *Legislative Series*, 1975 — UK 2.

[54] Eric Armstrong: "Evaluating the advisory work of ACAS", in *Employment Gazette* (London, Department of Employment), Apr. 1985, pp. 143-146. This article reviews some findings of a book by Eric Armstrong and Rosemary Lucas: *Improving industrial relations: The advisory role of ACAS* (Beckenham, Kent, Croom Helm, 1985) which was not yet available when the manuscript of this volume was in preparation.

[55] United States, Federal Mediation and Conciliation Service: *Annual Report 1979* (Washington, DC, n.d.), pp. 28-29.

[56] It should be noted that not all governments look with tolerance on private procedural rule making. For example: "Arbitration plays no part in Belgian labour law and labour relations. There is a deep distrust of arbitration; a feeling that the employer will try to impose his own arbitrator and that the Labour Courts should settle disputes. Arbitration is consequently practically outlawed" (Roger Blanpain: "Belgium" (1985), in Blanpain (ed.): *International encyclopaedia . . .*, op. cit., Vol. 2, p. 136).

[57] Oliver Clarke: "Collective bargaining and the economic recovery", in *OECD Observer* (Paris, Organisation for Economic Co-operation and Development), July 1984, p. 19.

[58] See for example Robert J. Flanagan et al.: *Unionism, economic stabilization and incomes policies* (Washington, DC, The Brookings Institution, 1983).

[59] See Roberts below, p. 282.

[60] See for example Michael Hudson: "Concerted action: Wages policy in West Germany, 1967-1977", in *Industrial Relations Journal*, Sep.-Oct. 1980, pp. 5-16.

[61] *Industrial Relations Europe*, Oct. 1984.

[62] ILO: *World Labour Report 2* (Geneva, 1985), pp. 42-43.

[63] Nils Elvander: "Sweden", in Benjamin C. Roberts (ed.): *Towards industrial democracy: Europe, Japan and the United States* (London, Croom Helm, 1979), p. 138.

[64] Recent publications on the Austrian experience include Peter J. Katzenstein: *Corporatism and change: Austria, Switzerland and the politics of industry* (Ithaca, New York, Cornell University Press, 1984); Joseph Mire: "Industrial relations in Austria", in *New Zealand Journal of Industrial Relations* (Wellington), Dec. 1981, pp. 139-149; "Austria: The 'economic and social partnership'", in *European Industrial Relations Review*, Aug. 1984, pp. 20-22. See

also ILO: *The trade union situation and industrial relations in Austria* (Geneva, 1986).

[65] For the content of the agreement, see *Social and Labour Bulletin*, Sep. 1981, p. 298.

[66] See Caire below, p. 207.

SUMMARY AND PERSPECTIVES

6

The preceding chapters constitute an attempt to examine comparatively the principal methods and practices of collective bargaining in the private sector of a group of leading industrialised market economies. This chapter will summarise the major findings and suggest some directions that future developments might take. Because the wide-ranging diversity of institutional arrangements among the different countries precludes making any universally valid generalisations, the most that one can reasonably hope to achieve is a set of close approximations, with a generous margin for exceptions, variations and even contradictions. Moreover, since the basic units of comparison in this study consist of national industrial relations systems, in other words of entire countries, adequate recognition of the considerable intra-country diversities among industrial sectors and individual enterprises is not possible.

1. The extent to which collective bargaining has become the principal means for setting the terms of employment ranges from nearly complete coverage in several of the smaller European countries to a relatively small portion of the economy in the United States. (Yet because of wide intra-country variances, some industrial sectors in the United States are almost fully blanketed by collective agreements. Moreover, the impact of collective agreements often reaches beyond the unionised sectors.) On the whole, current trends in bargaining coverage and in union membership rates are generally downward, mainly because the manufacturing industries where collective bargaining has long been a firmly established institution have experienced rapidly shrinking employment, while other sectors — especially in the services and the so-called high-technology industries — with a weaker tradition of collective bargaining and a lower overall rate of union membership are expanding. This trend has become a major challenge to the trade unions and has been recognised as such in many countries, but perhaps nowhere more explicitly than in the United States, where the American Federation of Labor and Congress of Industrial Organizations (AFL-CIO) recently published the results of a two-year study of the problems faced by trade unions and a set of recommendations to help overcome them.[1]

149

2. Historically, one of the consequences of severe economic dislocation and of periods of decline in collective bargaining has been an increase in the importance of consultation at the several levels of the industrial structure. Consultation differs from collective bargaining first of all in its emphasis on the shared rather than the separate and distinct interests of employers and employees and their organisations, and second in its use principally as an advisory rather than a decision-making process. Consultation and collective bargaining often coexist, but the terms of coexistence may vary from relatively strict separation by subject-matter and approach on the one hand to such close integration on the other that the dividing line between the two becomes blurred. In countries where consultation has not become firmly institutionalised through usage, the extent to which the parties will rely upon it to help solve their problems will tend to vary inversely with the state of the economy.

3. Although collective bargaining is only one of the activities carried on by trade unions, it is usually of such central importance that the prevailing structure of collective bargaining has had a decisive influence on the structure and government of trade unions.[2] Consequently, where collective bargaining becomes a centralised process with direct participation by the confederations of trade unions and employers' associations, as for example in response to government pressure on behalf of wage restraint, the authority of the central bodies over their affiliates will rise correspondingly. This is especially likely to occur in relatively small countries, in part because their special vulnerability in the international economic system tends to induce the parties to collective bargaining to tolerate a high degree of centralised authority.

4. In practically all countries the dominant position on the union side in collective bargaining is occupied by the so-called national unions which are based on more or less well-defined industrial and occupational categories. (Currently it might be more accurate to say "less and less well-defined" because ongoing concentration trends among unions have led to the widespread formation of multi-industrial and general unions and have overturned many of the former lines of demarcation.) It is the task of the national unions to define bargaining goals, undertake research to support bargaining demands, conduct or monitor the negotiations with the employer side, and if necessary mobilise membership support in the event of an impasse in negotiations. Rare exceptions aside, national unions may be expected to retain and perhaps even to strengthen their dominant position in collective bargaining.

5. In industries or major enterprises where the representation of employees is shared by two or several unions — an occurrence which is not unusual in countries not adhering to the principle of exclusive bargaining representation — the potentially weakening effects attributable to division and multiple representation create pressures for the co-ordination of union bargaining activities. One result is often the formation of ad hoc negotiating committees which may be followed by the establishment of more permanent linkages through joint councils, bargaining federations and similar bodies. Whatever the

device, its purpose is not only the consolidation of union bargaining power but also the simultaneous preservation of the autonomy of the participating organisations. While co-ordinating bodies have up until now existed chiefly at the national level, where their importance is to some degree being diminished by the trend towards outright union mergers, the growth of multinational companies has promoted the formation of similar co-ordinating instruments at the international level. As yet, however, none of the international union councils has succeeded in establishing bargaining relations with the counterparts on the employer side.

6. Virtually without exception it is the local unions that form the basic link between individual members and their organisation. But in countries where industry-wide bargaining structures predominate, their role in negotiations has usually been eclipsed by their administrative role, partly because of the pre-emptive authority of national unions and their regional and district organisations over collective bargaining, and partly because of the quasi-bargaining functions assigned by statute or custom to works councils, shop stewards and similar workplace institutions. It is only in countries where collective bargaining is decentralised that local unions are deeply engaged in negotiating the terms of employment. This distinction, however, although still valid, appears to be losing force as a result of tendencies in a substantial number of countries towards a more decentralised structure of bargaining and a more visible union presence at the workplace. In fact, establishing union outposts at the workplace through legislation or agreements with employers is currently one of the major aims of unions seeking to strengthen relations with their rank-and-file members.

7. As this effort develops, it will increasingly bring to the fore an unresolved and difficult problem of overlapping functions at the workplace between trade union organisations on the one hand and works councils or similar forms of employee representation on the other. There are important differences between the two. Unions are voluntary institutions, while works councils exist either by statutory mandate or occasionally as a result of a collective agreement between confederations of trade unions and employers' associations. Only union members participate in the election of their leaders, while all employees regardless of union membership are eligible to vote in works council elections. Beyond these distinctions is the fact that some works councils are acting more and more as vigorous representatives of employees' interests vis-à-vis the employer — in other words acting more like unions and sometimes doing so with legislative encouragement — and are correspondingly de-emphasising their historical mission of chiefly promoting labour-management co-operation. Although unions may eventually try to take the place of works councils, that attempt appears so difficult and is so unlikely to succeed that they will more probably seek instead to control them.

8. Employers' interests in collective bargaining are everywhere represented both by associations and by individual enterprises, but associations are of special

importance in Australia and Western Europe, whereas in Japan and North America the individual enterprise tends to predominate. Typically, employers' associations do not limit their activities to collective bargaining but, like unions, engage in a large array of related services such as public and governmental relations, consulting and research. When employers join an association, they delegate to it an important measure of authority required for the effective negotiation and administration of collective agreements. To this extent, they have important interests in common which they pursue through their association. Employers are, however, also competitors with manifestly conflicting interests, and it remains one of the major tasks of employers' associations to maintain the cohesiveness of their members despite the presence of forces that tend to pull them apart. The task has always been a difficult one because employers' associations have few effective disciplinary measures at hand. It may become even more difficult in the future if the trend towards decentralised collective bargaining loosens the cohesiveness of employers by shifting the emphasis from association-led, industry-wide bargaining to enterprise- or plant-level bargaining.

9. As a rule, public sector industrial enterprises maintain collective bargaining agreements of their own, for aside from scattered exceptions they are either not admitted to industrial associations composed of employers in private industry or they are by law or otherwise prevented by government from joining them. (They may, however, be allowed to join the peak confederations of employers' associations, and if so usually in a special membership category.) Moreover, the ability of public sector management to determine key bargaining policies and bargaining strategy is often circumscribed, directly or indirectly, by ministerial intervention and direction, especially in circumstances characterised by a major industrial conflict, whether imminent or actual, or by government efforts to follow an active incomes policy.

10. It is a prerequisite of collective bargaining that the parties recognise each other as the legitimate representatives of their constituencies. For obvious reasons there have rarely been difficulties about unions recognising employers or employers' associations, but employers' refusals to recognise unions are not uncommon, especially in countries with fragmented trade unions and a bargaining structure based largely on the individual enterprise, in other words a bargaining structure that may impinge directly on the authority of the employer. In most countries the public authorities have refrained from regulating recognition disputes on the ground that the parties themselves can best resolve their differences, and this has indeed largely been the case, particularly where the peak federations have been granted sufficient authority to settle internal demarcation conflicts. In countries with decentralised bargaining structures, however, governments have often imposed detailed rules designed to avoid or reduce conflicts over representation and recognition. Should the current trend towards decentralisation in collective bargaining continue, it is likely that more governments will issue rules regulating recognition, especially where the trade

unions are not united or where employers refuse voluntary recognition. In fact, that has already begun to happen.

11. Only a minority of countries have ever sought to define by law what is to be understood by "the duty to bargain" and specifically what the reciprocal obligations of the parties are with respect to the procedures as well as the subjects for negotiation. The major reason probably lies once again in the consequences of different bargaining structures. Employers' attitudes towards collective bargaining in a structure based on industry-wide units are likely to be more accommodating (or less resistant) than in a bargaining structure based on the individual enterprise or plant. In industry-wide bargaining units the representation of employers' interests is entrusted to an employers' association which can act to some extent as a buffer mechanism. This is not so, however, in the case of enterprise-level bargaining, which tends to be perceived by employers more readily as a direct threat to their freedom of action and is therefore more likely to lead to employers' resistance, first of all to the very notion of bargaining itself and, should that question not be at issue, to the bargaining agenda. Here, too, the trend towards more decentralised bargaining is likely to produce more government intervention to settle disputes over issues of procedure and negotiability or to avoid them in the first place.

12. In most cases collective bargaining is an ad hoc process, which means that the parties meet at intervals to negotiate an agreement, the length of each interval usually being determined by the duration of the agreement. Normally the parties do not meet again until the next round of negotiations, which may be a year or more away. In some countries, however, the negotiators (or in some instances the government) have established standing machinery, mostly at the level of an industry but in some instances also for the entire national economy. The advantages of standing machinery include greater frequency and continuity of relationships (which is an intangible but potentially a very important factor), opportunities for joint fact-finding as an agreed base for collective bargaining and the availability of a mechanism for the joint administration of the agreement. Permanent machinery tends to fit best into systems of industry-wide bargaining. Consequently, the spread of more decentralised bargaining may turn out to be an adverse development for the future of standing machinery.

13. In preparing for negotiations, each side is compelled to achieve an internal consensus on its bargaining position, that is, on its overall strategy, specific demands, priority rankings and eventual concessions. As a general rule, the greater the diversity of interests among the constituents of the negotiators and the more complex and wide-ranging the items to be negotiated, the more difficult it will be to reach a consensus. For employers' associations the difficulty of the task is proportionate to the range of differences among the member firms with regard to profitability, scale of operations, market position, geographic location and other critical factors. For trade unions the difficulty increases with greater heterogeneity in the composition of the membership, especially with respect to occupational categories, skill levels, age or seniority and systems of

remuneration. Employers' associations frequently seek to resolve their problem by limiting the range of issues introduced into the negotiations and by holding out for settlements embodying terms that can be met by even the marginal firm, the expectation being that the more favourably situated firms are free to improve on the association minimum through unilateral decision or through supplemental bargaining. Trade unions, by contrast, have a tendency to achieve the aim of not offending any constituency group by presenting a larger number of demands than they expect to be seriously discussed.

14. Although the distribution of power between the parties may be a more decisive element in governing the outcome of collective bargaining than the quality of the pre-bargaining research, most negotiators are persuaded of the importance of thorough preparation for discussions of issues that are becoming increasingly technical and complex. Yet it remains common practice for each side to conduct its own research, the main purpose being to provide factual support for arguments designed to persuade the other side. Jointly organised fact-finding ventures are still quite rare, even though a strong case could be made for the proposition that the quality of bargaining relationships would gain from the development of mutually acceptable data through a shared research effort or jointly hired independent experts. In this respect the increasing sophistication of the research tools, although greatly increasing the range of available data, does not necessarily increase the confidence of one side in the accuracy or validity of the data presented by the other.

15. Unions often express themselves as being dissatisfied with the adequacy of the information supplied by employers in conjunction with negotiations and complain that their ability to represent effectively the interests of their members is impaired by employers' refusals to supply relevant information. Employers respond that the information sought by unions is burdensome to compile, often not relevant to the negotiations and potentially helpful to competitors. Until fairly recently, legally mandated disclosure requirements were confined chiefly to the North American countries, but now a growing number of countries have adopted legislation requiring employers to disclose a substantial body of information to unions. Often the new rules are also important in defining the rights of works councils to obtain information about corporate developments affecting the interests of the workforce. Unions will continue to press for information needed in negotiations, especially if and as collective bargaining becomes more decentralised.

16. In order to conduct negotiations effectively, the negotiators need authority to negotiate. But they are not necessarily granted full power to conclude a binding agreement. Frequently it is the principals who retain the ultimate decision over what constitutes an acceptable agreement, although practice in this respect varies greatly. In single-enterprise bargaining top-level corporate officials will probably reserve for themselves the final power to approve an agreement, although the actual negotiators are likely to be given a substantial measure of discretionary authority. This may allow them to enter into

154

preliminary understandings or even to make binding commitments as regards less crucial items, while requiring them to consult their corporate superiors on the most important ones. In the case of employers' associations negotiating committees may have full authority to arrive at an agreement, but it is by no means unusual for associations to require that the agreement receive final approval from a representative assembly of member firms or from a smaller body to which the final decision has been delegated. Trade unions are in a particularly difficult situation, for more so than their opposites they must resolve an inherent conflict between two valid objectives: bargaining efficiency and democratic decision-making. They tend to rely more heavily on direct membership participation in decentralised systems of collective bargaining and, conversely, to entrust their negotiators with considerable authority in industry-wide or centralised systems. One should, therefore, expect that the further expansion of decentralised bargaining will probably result in a corresponding increase in union rules which require direct membership participation in determining the acceptability of a collective agreement, in other words which lead to more ratification votes.

17. In most countries collective agreements to set wages and working conditions — as distinguished from procedural agreements or certain kinds of central agreements — are concluded for a fixed rather than an indeterminate period because both sides perceive important advantages in such an arrangement: employers for planning and cost calculations, and generally for stable labour-management relations, and employees for protection against sudden loss of collectively secured benefits and entitlements. Until the early 1970s the average duration of collective agreements had been on the increase, but inflationary pressures have reversed that trend. In most countries one-year or at most two-year agreements have become the general rule. Where longer-term agreements are in effect, unions may insist on wage reopening or cost-of-living escalator clauses. If the rate of inflation stabilises and if confidence in continued stability persists, one should once again expect the conclusion of longer-term agreements.

18. In every national system of industrial relations the development of collective bargaining leads to the formation of a network of institutionalised relations which is commonly referred to as the bargaining structure. The configuration of any particular bargaining structure is the outcome not of a series of accidents but of identifiable factors. Thus, the historical context in which trade unions developed explains, at least up to a certain point, the contrasting rise of a structure based on multi-employer bargaining in Western European countries and of a predominantly single-employer bargaining structure in North America. Pressures of competition in product and labour markets have often been a prime consideration in shaping employer and trade union policies with regard to the kind of bargaining structure for which they have striven. And while the introduction of certain issues into collective bargaining — supplemental pension plans, for example — tends to have a centralising impact on the bargaining

155

structure, others may well have the reverse effect. With some important far-reaching exceptions, governments until quite recently refrained from adopting policies designed to exert a direct influence on bargaining structures, although the adoption of incomes policies has usually resulted in greater centralisation.

19. Once established, the basic features of a national bargaining structure tend to remain in place over a long period. Consequently, just as industry-wide bargaining has retained its predominant position in most European countries, so enterprise- and plant-level bargaining has maintained its foremost position in Japan and North America. However, the underlying stability has not precluded the bargaining structure from adjusting to important changes in context, and in the recent past these changes, at least in Western Europe, have pointed predominantly in the direction of greater decentralisation. The reasons are complex and vary from one country to another, but often include *(a)* competitive pressures generated by current economic difficulties, and *(b)* government policies, supported by unions, favouring more workers' participation in local decision-making through works councils or an enhanced union presence at the workplace, or even both.

20. The extent to which governments make use of their sovereign powers to establish and monitor the basic "rules of the game" for collective bargaining ranges from minimal involvement to extensive and detailed regulation. On the whole, government intervention is more pervasive in countries where the prevailing level of bargaining is relatively close to the workplace than in countries where negotiations take place at some remove, such as the regional or national level of an industry. The reason is probably that employers' resistance to trade unions and collective bargaining tends to vary directly with the degree of union penetration into the enterprise and the degree to which union demands represent a threat to the unrestricted exercise of management rights. Since local-level bargaining is considerably more likely than national or regional bargaining to impinge on management's discretionary authority, it is more likely to generate conflicts and to induce more government intervention to prevent or settle them. This may mean that an expansion of local-level bargaining in countries where industry-wide bargaining has been the rule will result in an increase in government regulation. Indeed this has already occurred, as for instance in legislation regulating in considerable detail the rights of works councils and unions at workplace level.

21. Most of the time governments prefer to let the parties themselves determine which subjects are to be covered in their negotiations. There are, however, several exceptions. One is the pre-emption of certain issues which occurs when governments adopt legislation covering areas that could have been subject to resolution through collective bargaining. While such legislation does not necessarily prevent the parties from negotiating supplemental arrangements, they are not likely to do so in countries where the bargaining power of unions is greatly inferior to that of employers or where collective bargaining is not yet

strongly developed. Declaring certain items to be mandatory subjects for collective bargaining or, on the contrary, prohibiting their consideration is a more usual form of government intervention in the subject-matter of collective bargaining. Prohibited subjects may be part of standing government policy, as in the case of restrictions on the right of the parties to agree to certain forms of compulsory union membership for employees in the bargaining unit, or may be intended to have a merely temporary character, as in instances when a declared national incomes policy establishes limits for wage bargaining for a given period of time.

22. Although the primary responsibility for implementing an agreement belongs to the parties, it is generally recognised that governments also have a role in ensuring its observance and under certain circumstances even in extending its application to employers and employees not represented in the negotiations from which the agreement emerged. The power of government to extend the application of an agreement to non-signing enterprises and their employees has its basis in the idea that collective bargaining is a desirable institution and that the parties to the process are entitled to protection against lower-cost competition from employers not bound by the terms of the agreement. Extension transforms a private agreement into a kind of industrial common law, and the enforcement of the terms of the extended agreement by the courts or administrative agencies constitutes a significant degree of government endorsement of the bargaining process itself, as of course does the enforcement of non-extended agreements.

23. There are many other ways by which governments may express support for collective bargaining, including making available the services of skilled professionals to operate a disputes settlement machinery (not covered here but consisting of, among other things, mediation and conciliation services, labour courts and industrial tribunals) as well as advisory, informational and educational services. On the whole, however, the latter activities do not appear to have a high priority and remain generally underdeveloped and underfinanced.

24. Of substantially greater importance in bringing about more government intervention in collective bargaining have been the extraordinarily severe economic difficulties — seen in high levels of unemployment, strong inflationary pressures, declining growth rates, rising budget shortfalls, trade balance deficits, and so on — that have in varying degrees beset virtually all industrialised countries. Government efforts to master the problems have had a distinct impact on collective bargaining, though they have of course also ranged far beyond it to include monetary and fiscal controls, as well as other measures. In the domain of collective bargaining governments have made use of an arsenal of instruments to achieve wage restraint, including appeals to the parties (with or without explicit guide-lines), direct or indirect government participation in wage bargaining and the outright imposition of various kinds of controls. Where exhortation and persuasion have not achieved the desired result, some

governments have made use of tripartite institutions to conclude central agreements or at least to enlist the support of the confederal organisations of employers and trade unions for their economic policies. But since reliance on voluntary measures has not always been sufficiently corrective, several governments have also resorted to direct wage controls in various forms. Whatever the measure or measures taken, the consequence in most countries, even if not everywhere, has been a substantial increase in government involvement in collective bargaining. That is likely to remain the case until the circumstances which brought it about have materially changed.

Notes

[1] AFL-CIO Committee on the Evolution of Work: *The changing situation of workers and their unions* (Washington, DC, 1985).

[2] This is also the principal argument advanced by Hugh Clegg in *Trade unionism under collective bargaining: A theory based on comparisons of six countries* (Oxford, Basil Blackwell, 1976).

PART II

RECENT TRENDS IN SELECTED COUNTRIES

RECENT TRENDS IN COLLECTIVE BARGAINING IN AUSTRALIA

Braham Dabscheck and John Niland [1]

Australia, like most Western market economies in the past decade, has had to face the joint problems of rising levels of unemployment and inflation. The search for an appropriate policy package to handle the post-1974 stagflation still dominates public policy debates. The formula most favoured has involved strengthening the centralised system of industrial relations regulation, with emphasis on wage determination at the national rather than at industry or enterprise level. There have, to be sure, been other aspects of industrial relations that have attracted increasing attention during the past few years — attempts to develop a legislative base for redundancy protection; concern about occupational health and safety issues; anti-discrimination legislation; legislation designed to place greater controls on certain forms of trade union action, such as secondary boycotts; and the emergence of a second peak-level body among employers to represent especially the interests of the larger firms. But the prime theme has been centralism and the development of a national wages policy. This has featured unions, tribunals and, more recently, a newly elected Labor Government searching for industrial relations stability while still preserving real wages in most, though not all, cases. There has been, ironically, less emphasis on redundancy. Equally intriguing in an era of unemployment is the waning influence and power of employers. In these respects recent trends in Australian collective bargaining — if that term can be applied to a system dominated by industrial tribunals — may run counter to the typical experience of other Western market economies.

The following discussion is organised in four sections. In the first we outline Australia's special framework of industrial relations regulation and identify several areas of significant change.[2] The second section examines the economic record in the post-1973/74 period of inflation, recession and unemployment. Our attention in the third section is focused on the industrial relations context and the search for an appropriate wages policy. We conclude with an assessment, and a brief look towards the future.

THE INSTITUTIONAL SETTING

Most national systems of industrial relations can claim some feature not commonly found elsewhere. With Australia this applies to the very foundation of the system, which emphasises conciliation and arbitration. The great difference from other industrialised countries lies in the key role played by industrial tribunals. While most countries have established public agencies that intervene in various ways in labour-management disputes, the profusion of such bodies in Australia, and their pervasive influence over day-to-day industrial relations, sets the Australian model apart. Their large number owes something to the readiness with which governments look to the tribunals for solutions to economic and industrial problems, and also to the federal system of government, under which the national parliament shares the power to create tribunals with the parliaments in each of the six states and the two main territories. The result of all this is that the industrial partners are required to conduct their relations under the watchful eyes of a plethora of industrial tribunals. By counting only bodies whose prime effect is to regulate aspects of employment relationships, we are able to list 18 Commonwealth tribunals, 33 in New South Wales, 20 in Victoria, six in Queensland, six in South Australia, ten in Western Australia, four in Tasmania, three in the Australian Capital Territory and seven in the Northern Territory — a total of 107 tribunals for an employed labour force of some 6 million workers.

Three significant aspects of the federal system should be noted. First, except for its own employees and territories, the Federal Government cannot become directly involved in industrial relations. Its major industrial relations power derives from section 51(xxxv) of the Australian Constitution, which empowers it "to make laws for the peace, order and good government of the Commonwealth with respect to . . . conciliation and arbitration for the prevention and settlement of industrial disputes extending beyond the limits of any one state".[3] This wording means that the Federal Government cannot regulate industrial relations directly, but must delegate this function to industrial tribunals, which exercise powers of "conciliation and arbitration". While most tribunals are independent of one another, the Australian Conciliation and Arbitration Commission (ACAC or Arbitration Commission for short) has assumed a leadership role. Tribunals, particularly the Arbitration Commission, have also developed considerable independence from governments, so much so that a leading Arbitration Judge once referred to himself and his colleagues as the "economic dictators of Australia".[4] The Arbitration Commission members hold their appointments till retirement, and they have never interpreted their role as meekly responding to the wishes of the Federal Government. An important consequence is the key role played by the Commission in national wages policy developments. A Federal Government wishing to implement a wages (and incomes) policy could not do so through direct legislation; it must secure the co-operation of the leading tribunals. But in turn, the Arbitration Commission could hardly implement and maintain a wages policy in the face of hostility and opposition from the Federal Government, which, after all, has control over fiscal and monetary policy. The result is a process of checks and balances in which the Federal Government and the Arbitration Commission are themselves in a bargaining relationship.

Second, state governments are not constrained in the same way that section 51(xxxv) of the Constitution limits the power of the Federal Government. Because state governments can legislate directly on wages and working conditions, political methods of achieving industrial relations objectives are more prevalent here than at the federal level. Hence, although state governments have created numerous industrial tribunals, they have not surrendered their legislative role to these bodies. For example, state governments over the years have legislated to introduce a 40-hour standard week, occupational health and safety standards and, more recently, the requirement that tribunals under their jurisdiction follow national wage case standards set by the Arbitration Commission. Approximately 40 per cent of workers are covered by federal awards and 50 per cent by state awards, while 10 per cent are covered by neither.

The third significant aspect of the federal system is the pivotal role of the High Court in interpreting the Australian Constitution. This body's decisions in effect determine the allocation of powers between the state and federal systems and also serve to define and limit the powers of the Arbitration Commission vis-à-vis other tribunals and the state and federal governments. Two recent decisions illustrate the Court's importance.

Until very recently the High Court adopted a narrow definition of the term "industrial disputes" used in section 51(xxxv); this served to deny access to the Arbitration Commission by certain groups, primarily workers in some white-collar areas which are not technically "industrial" in nature. Equally significant was the High Court's view that the Commission also lacked the constitutional authority to adjudicate in disputes involving questions of managerial rights. Such disputes were none the less regulated through a combination of conciliation and voluntary or private arbitration in which the parties waived any legal objections to the tribunal's involvement. In a case heard in 1983, however, the High Court revised its interpretation of the meaning of the term "industrial disputes", declaring:

The words . . . have to be given their popular meaning — what they convey to the man in the street. . . . It is, we think, beyond question that the popular meaning of "industrial disputes" includes disputes between employees and employers about the terms of employment and the conditions of work. Experience shows that disputes of this kind may lead to industrial action involving disruption or reduction in the supply of goods or services to the community. We reject any notion that the adjective "industrial" imports some restriction which confines the constitutional conception of "industrial disputes" to disputes in productive industry and organised business carried on for the purpose of making profits.[5]

The importance of this decision is that those groups of workers which have hitherto been denied access can now, if they wish, have their wages and conditions determined by the Arbitration Commission (assuming they satisfy the test of interstateness). The Commission will also have constitutional authority to hear disputes involving managerial rights, which will widen its jurisdiction in respect of such issues as dismissal and redundancy.

The *Tasmanian Dams* case,[6] also heard by the High Court in 1983, involved an environmental dispute between the Federal and Tasmanian Governments over whether or not the latter could build a dam in the Tasmanian wilderness. The High Court ruled in favour of the Federal Government on the basis of the external affairs power granted it under section 51(xxix) of the Constitution: being a signatory to an international treaty, the Federal Government was empowered to legislate to achieve the objectives of that treaty. The significance for industrial relations is that Australia has ratified many ILO Conventions [7] and it is conceivable that the Federal Government could now legislate to further the aims of those Conventions. One obvious example is in the area of occupational health and safety, an issue of growing interest in Australia.

These two High Court cases pave the way for a significant reassignment of power and responsibility between the various legislatures and industrial jurisdictions. The decisions favour the Federal Government first and the Arbitration Commission second, to the detriment of the influence of state-based bodies — both legislatures and tribunals. The effect of these cases is to make centralism easier to sustain.

Another factor in the shift to centralism is Australia's unique system of wage determination. In the federal jurisdiction a three-tier structure has evolved. This comprises national wage cases, industry cases and "over-award" negotiations, with the importance of each tier varying over time and between sectors. In national wage cases a bench of senior members of the Arbitration Commission determines or adjusts wages for all workers covered by federal awards. These set minimum levels which the Commission adjusts in line with broad industrial, social and economic changes. A major consideration in national wage cases since the 1950s has been the health of the economy and how to distribute the fruits of economic growth on an equitable basis, paying regard to such macro-economic variables as the level of inflation, productivity, investment, employment and the balance of payments. Usually, though not invariably, the state tribunals rubber-stamp national wage case decisions, allowing the increases to flow on to workers in their jurisdiction.

In industry cases the Arbitration Commission (or the appropriate state commission) deals with the wages of workers covered by a particular award. These are usually handled by individual tribunal members who have some latitude to take account of peculiar and relevant circumstances that affect the industry or the workers covered by the award in question. Wages gained at this level are added to those determined in national wage cases.

Beyond the ambit of the tribunals, and depending upon economic and political circumstances, unions may be able to negotiate "over-award" wages and benefits at the enterprise level. Although the tribunals are not initially involved in this process, unions and employers often seek to register their new agreement with a commission to give it greater legal and economic standing.

Such registration may be denied if the tribunal considers the settlement is too generous and breaches its (current) principles of wage determination. While cases of such over-award negotiation have been widespread, particularly prior to the mid-1970s and again during an 18-month period in the early 1980s, bargaining of the total package in the conventional overseas sense occurs only in isolated instances (e.g. metal trades in 1982, coal in 1982/83, oil in 1983 and, to a lesser extent, building in 1983/84). A key strategy for the Federal Government and the Arbitration Commission in enhancing centralism is to promote the first tier — national wage cases — and to downgrade the other two, particularly over-award negotiation.

A more common focus for direct negotiation between unions and employers has been redundancy arrangements. Here the Arbitration Commission, hampered by constitutional complications, has had a back-seat role, although the decision reached in August 1984 after a protracted test case has established uniform standards governing advance notice and compensation linked to the length of service. State tribunals have faced fewer technical impediments, but even in these jurisdictions the main moves to set redundancy criteria have been through direct negotiation. This perhaps reflects the unions' desire to try to win better settlements than the standard package expected from a tribunal.

THE ECONOMY

Over the past decade the performance of the Australian economy has substantially deteriorated, although some signs of improvement were evident in mid-1984. In the early 1970s the unemployment rate was relatively low, and whilst inflation was high by the standards of the 1950s and 1960s, it was not a cause of alarm. This all changed dramatically in 1973 and 1974. Australia found itself caught up in the world-wide inflation and experienced substantial increases in both prices and average weekly earnings. The Federal Government's attempt to use Keynesian tools of fiscal and monetary policy to control inflation resulted in a sharp rise in unemployment. Australia then experienced the worst of both worlds — increasing inflation and increasing unemployment. As table 1 shows, the unemployment rate, with the exception of 1979 and 1981, rose steadily after 1974.

Table 2 provides information on movements in the consumer price index (CPI) and average weekly earnings for the period 1971/72 to 1982/83. Since 1973/74 the rise in the CPI each year has hovered around the 10 per cent level. Only in 1977/78, 1978/79 and 1980/81 did it fall below this figure. Also, throughout most of this period real wages have been maintained or increased — average weekly earnings for most years increased at a faster rate than the CPI. The major exception was during the nine-month wages pause introduced in December 1982.

Table 3, which provides information on working days lost in industrial disputes, shows a peak in 1974, when more than 6 million working days were lost. This was also the year of particularly large increases in inflation and average

Collective bargaining: A reappraisal

Table 1. Unemployment rate, 1971-83 (as at August of each year)

Year	Unemployment rate (%)	Year	Unemployment rate (%)	Year	Unemployment rate (%)
1971	1.7	1976	4.7	1980	5.9
1972	2.5	1977	5.7	1981	5.6
1973	1.8	1978	6.2 [1]	1982	6.7
1974	2.4	1979	5.8	1983	9.9
1975	4.6				

[1] Break in continuity of series.

Source: Reserve Bank of Australia: *Australian economic statistics 1949/50 to 1982/83: I. Tables*, Occasional paper No. 8A (Sydney, 1984).

Table 2. Annual movements in the consumer price index (CPI) and average weekly earnings (AWE), 1971/72 to 1982/83

Year	% change in CPI	% change in AWE	Year	% change in CPI	% change in AWE
1971/72	6.8	10.1	1977/78	9.4	9.9
1972/73	5.9	9.0	1978/79	8.2	7.7
1973/74	13.1	16.2	1979/80	10.1	9.9
1974/75	16.7	25.4	1980/81	9.4	13.5
1975/76	12.8	14.5	1981/82	10.4	n.a.
1976/77	14.0	12.4	1982/83	11.5	11.4 [1]

n.a. = Not available
[1] Break in continuity of series.
Source: As for table 1.

Table 3. Working days lost in industrial disputes, 1971-83

Year	Working days lost ('000)	Year	Working days lost ('000)	Year	Working days lost ('000)
1971	3 068.6	1976	3 799.2	1980	3 320.2
1972	2 010.3	1977	1 654.8	1981	4 192.2
1973	2 634.7	1978	2 130.8	1982	2 158.0
1974	6 292.5	1979	3 964.4	1983	1 641.4
1975	3 509.9				

Source: Australian Bureau of Statistics: *Quarterly summaries of industrial disputes*, Cat. No. 6322.0 (Canberra).

weekly earnings. As the economy deteriorated, and with the stabilising effect of wage indexation, the level of industrial action declined. The short-lived economic recovery of the early 1980s saw a temporary burst of industrial disputation, but as the condition of the economy once more declined, so too did the level of industrial disputes. In interpreting these figures it should be noted that Australia's employed workforce throughout this period rose by about 30 per cent, to some 6 million workers. In other words, except for 1974, each Australian worker, on average, spent less than one day per year (often less than half a day) on strike. Unlike other market economies where conventional collective bargaining operates, most Australian strikes are of short duration — over 70 per cent are resolved (or terminate) within three days.

WAGES POLICY

The pre-indexation period

Yerbury and Isaac's 1971 survey of Australian industrial relations [8] documents the growth of direct negotiations between labour and management. Throughout the 1950s and 1960s industrial disputes were regulated by a combination of bargaining and conciliation and arbitration, with arbitration having the less significant role. This was the period of consent determinations, when tribunals readily registered agreements between the parties, and of conciliation in which they sought to accommodate their decisions to the needs or wishes of the parties. When tribunals became involved in disputes, they devised solutions to satisfy the *particular* needs of the parties before them rather than seeking a *uniform* solution to be applied in all situations. Flexibility and adaptability were their guide-posts.[9] The parties desired, and industrial tribunals permitted, if not encouraged, the resolution of disputes at the industry or firm level, rather than at the national level. Industry-wide determinations and over-award negotiations were accordingly a prominent feature of Australian industrial relations. Yerbury and Isaac describe a period in which Australia pursued a decentralised approach to industrial relations regulation — a period unique in Australian history and one that may never be repeated.

The corollary of this, of course, was that national wage cases declined in importance. Between 1969/70 and 1974/75 their contribution to the total increase in the weighted average minimum wage for males fell from 52.6 to only 21.2 per cent.[10]

The centralised indexation approach

In the second half of 1974 the Australian economy began to experience problems common elsewhere in the world. Against the background of a worsening economy the Australian Council of Trade Unions (ACTU) mounted a national claim before the Arbitration Commission, seeking increases in wages and the reintroduction of automatic quarterly cost-of-living adjustments. An earlier indexation scheme, but applying only to the basic (or minimum) component of wages, had been abandoned after 30 years in 1953 because of its suspected effects in helping to generate inflation.[11] The 1975 case turned on an assessment of whether automatic (or near automatic) indexation would aid or worsen the condition of the Australian economy. Relevant was the fact that in 1974 wages had risen on average by 24 per cent, largely through direct negotiations. Consequently, the Arbitration Commission was not prepared to countenance wage indexation unless the ACTU gave an undertaking that increases outside national wage case adjustments (i.e. wage indexation) would be kept to a minimum. Eventually, near the conclusion of the case, the ACTU gave the desired undertaking.[12]

The Commission's decision of 30 April 1975 effectively linking wage adjustments with CPI movements became the key element in Australia's strategy for resolving wages and other industrial relations issues in the subsequent decade of inflation, recession and unemployment. In announcing its decision, the Commission claimed that a central and orderly system of wage determination would help to solve Australia's economic, industrial and social problems. It said alterations to award wages would be considered after the publication of the CPI, but only if wage rises from other sources were negligible. The Arbitration Commission declared that "violation [of this condition] even by a small section of industry whether in the award or non-award would put at risk the future of indexation for all".[13] The Commission's guide-lines allowed exceptional wage increases for changes in work value ("a significant net addition to work requirements"); for the catch-up of general wage levels (for those who had missed out on the wage round before indexation's introduction); for anomalies (added in May 1976) and inequities (added in September 1978).[14]

Wage indexation lasted six years, from April 1975 to July 1981, during which period seven of the 19 decisions provided full indexation to CPI movements. As is evident from table 4, others provided either partial indexation, where a figure less than full indexation was granted (e.g. June 1977), or plateau indexation, where the Commission awarded a percentage increase up to a certain wage level, and a flat amount beyond that level (e.g. March 1976). The only other significant wage adjustment in this period followed a "work value" hearing for waterside workers, which resulted in an $8.00 per week increase in mid-1978. With a centralised system, however, the irresistible pressure for "parity" saw this flow to other workers, and by April 1981 the Arbitration Commission estimated that the waterside workers' $8.00 had been extended to 80 per cent of the workforce.

The success of the Commission in limiting wage increases to its own regulatory adjustments can be measured in table 5. Between August 1975 and June 1978 well over 90 per cent of the increases in total wages came from indexation decisions. After June 1978 the figure declined to less than 90 per cent for males and since July 1980 to less than 80 per cent for females, reflecting the work value round described in the previous paragraph. The key to the apparent success of wage indexation — the Commission's ability to maintain its grip on wage movements — was the state of the economy, which remained depressed

Table 4. Alterations to total wages under wage indexation, 1975-81

Date			CPI variation (%)	Wage variation
1975	March		3.6	3.6%
	June		3.5	3.5%
	September		0.8	nil
	December		5.6	(5.6% + 0.8%) 6.4%
1976	March		3.0	3.0% up to $125 per week $3.80 thereafter
	June		2.5	2.5% up to $98 per week Then $2.50 up to $166 per week 1.5% thereafter
	September		2.2	2.2%
	December		6.0	$5.70
1977	March		2.3	1.9% up to $200 per week $3.80 thereafter
	June		2.4	2.0%
	September		2.0	1.5%
	December		2.3	1.5% up to $170 per week $2.60 thereafter
1978	March		1.3	1.3%
	June/Sep.		4.0	4.0%
	Dec./Mar. '79		4.0	3.2%
1979	June/Sep.		5.0	4.5%
	Dec./Mar. '80		5.3	4.2%
1980	June/Sep.		4.7	3.7%
	Dec./Mar. '81		4.5	3.6%

Source: National wage case decisions. From September 1978 the hearings were changed from four a year to two a year.

Table 5. Wage indexation increases as a percentage of change in total wages, 1975-81

Year ended		Male wages	Female wages	Year ended		Male wages	Female wages
August	1976	92	94	January	1980	86	96
August	1977	94	96	July	1980	81	86
June	1978	98	99	January	1981	83	70
December	1978	89	97	May	1981	91	79
June	1979	86	95				

Source: Australian Bureau of Statistics: *Wage rate indexes (preliminary)*, Cat. No. 6311.0 (Canberra).

throughout the indexation era, thereby reducing the ability of trade unions to gain concessions through direct negotiation outside the tribunals' jurisdiction.

Strains of centralism

A centralised system of industrial relations regulation and wage determination produces a number of stresses and strains.[15] Not all participants saw the need for such an approach or accepted the wisdom of following the Arbitration Commission in its self-appointed task of national salvation. The Fraser Coalition Government initially saw some virtue in indexation, for even the full CPI adjustment in 1975 represented restraint in comparison with the dramatic wage movements the year before. But with rising unemployment in the latter part of the 1970s, the Federal Government felt that wage increases should be held much lower, even to zero adjustment.

The Arbitration Commission, for its part, encouraged the Federal Government to tailor its economic policies to maintaining the credibility of wage indexation by keeping prices under control.[16] Thus it urged the Fraser Government not to increase indirect taxes because of the flow-on effects to prices. However, throughout most of the later 1970s the Commission and the Government had difficulty seeing eye to eye on matters of economic policy: Plowman has estimated that, in the period December 1975 to September 1979, policy-induced price increases of the Fraser Government added 2.25 per cent each year to the inflation rate.[17]

Some state tribunals found the wage indexation guide-lines too restrictive. On a few occasions the major tribunals of Western Australia and South Australia handed down decisions which conflicted with those of the Arbitration Commission.[18] Tensions also developed among members of the Arbitration Commission itself. Mr. Justice Staples clashed with the Commission's President, Sir John Moore,[19] and a number of Conciliation Commissioners also expressed misgivings about the rigidity of wage indexation.

Peak employer spokesmen at the national level, while supporting a centralised system of wage determination, objected to wage indexation — they wished to link wages to national productivity increases rather than to prices. Employers in sectors experiencing growth and/or wishing to innovate following technological change objected to indexation because it restricted their ability to alter wages to attract labour; while those employers in declining sectors maintained that wage indexation resulted in cost increases which forced them to lay off workers. The unions, for their part, objected to those decisions of the Arbitration Commission which granted less than full indexation. Generally speaking, however, most unions supported wage indexation because it guaranteed wage increases in a period of economic decline. With wages centrally determined under indexation, some unions used the resources and energy they would have otherwise employed in wage campaigns to pursue other objectives. The most important of these was the 35-hour working week campaign conducted by metal trades unions during 1980 and 1981. In many ways the eventual adoption of the 38-hour working week as an Australia-wide standard can be attributed to wage indexation.[20]

In the latter part of 1980 and during 1981, the Australian economy began to recover. In the federal election campaign towards the end of 1980, the Fraser Government pointed to an incipient mining and resources boom. The demand for skilled workers increased and employers offered higher wages in an effort to attract and/or hold their labour. A number of employers and unions in both the private and public sectors negotiated outside the Arbitration Commission to win increases in the vicinity of $20.00 per week. Besides the mining/resources sector, the most conspicuous of these agreements were concluded in road transport, telecommunications, New South Wales railways, the Melbourne waterfront and sections of the Australian public service. A new wages round was unleashed, which the Arbitration Commission saw would be difficult to contain. In July 1981 it faced the inevitable and brought wage indexation to an end.

Towards a social contract approach

By Australian standards, the system of industrial relations and wage determination that now operated was decentralised: rather than being fixed by the Arbitration Commission in a national wage case, wages were being adjusted on an award-by-award basis with different sets of unions and employers negotiating changes to wages and working conditions, sometimes with the aid of tribunals. Undoubtedly the most significant agreement entered into in this period was that negotiated in the metal trades industry near the end of 1981.

Following the abandonment of wage indexation the metal trades employers (the Metal Trades Industry Association) found they had little choice but to enter into negotiations with the metal unions pushing for the 35-hour week. In December 1981 an agreement was reached which contained four key elements. These were an increase of $25.00 per week in the wages of a fitter (lesser amounts for workers in lower classifications); a mid-term adjustment of $14.00 per week for a fitter (again with lesser amounts for workers in lower classifications) to be paid from June 1982 unless "there is an unforeseen change of an extraordinary nature in the economic circumstances"; a 38-hour working week to be introduced from mid-March 1982; and an agreement by the unions not to make any further wage claims during the 12-month life of the agreement. The "no extra claims" clause constituted a major innovation in Australian industrial relations and helped to make the metal trades one of the few industries in Australia using conventional collective bargaining. The effects of the agreement soon extended well beyond the metal trades themselves, facilitated by the fact that trade unions are structured along occupational rather than industry or enterprise lines. In May 1982 the Arbitration Commission estimated that 75 per cent of employees had received wage increases since wage indexation's abandonment in July 1981.

In the second half of 1982 the condition of the Australian economy substantially deteriorated. Both the level of unemployment and the rate of inflation increased (see tables 1 and 2), and there were many rumours of workers

171

who, often over the strenuous objections of their union officials, had agreed to less than award rates or who were on short time: this despite the fact that, because awards set minima from which the industrial parties cannot themselves contract out, short-time working arrangements can only be approved through a tribunal hearing, which seldom happens. As the end of 1982 approached, the federal, state and territory governments initiated moves to freeze wages in both private and public sectors,[21] and following a state premiers' conference in December, the federal Minister for Employment and Industrial Relations made an application before the Arbitration Commission to freeze the wages of workers covered by federal awards.

In its December 1982 decision the Arbitration Commission expressed concern about the deteriorating condition of the economy and noted approvingly the united position of the various governments on the need for a wages pause. It decided to introduce a six-month pause (which in fact lasted a total of nine months), during which time the Commission itself would refuse to grant increases and it expected others to do likewise. The major exception was to allow workers who had not received an increase of the 1981 metal trades type to have their wages adjusted. This, once again, reflects the strong pressures towards wage uniformity in the Australian system. In handing down its decision, the Commission noted that "the pause is the beginning of a process of re-establishing a centralised wage fixing system;" [22] it was indeed the Commission's first step toward regaining authority in national wage setting.

In March 1983 the Australian Labor Party (ALP), under the leadership of former ACTU President Bob Hawke, was elected to government on a platform of national reconciliation and consensus. An important feature of the election campaign was the announcement of an Accord, following four years of negotiation, between the ALP and the ACTU. The Accord committed a federal Labor government and the ACTU to a centralised system of wage determination in which "the maintenance of real wages [was] a key objective".[23] The Accord also detailed a wide range of social and industrial reforms that would be pursued by a federal Labor government. The new Government's first act, as promised, was to call a National Economic Summit Conference of representatives of unions, employers, government and community groups to devise a programme of national reconstruction.[24] This was held in April 1983 against the background of Australia's worst economic crisis since the 1930s: inflation was running at over 11 per cent, and unemployment exceeded 10 per cent.

The most important function of the National Economic Summit was to set a negotiated framework for a social contract approach to wages policy. The employers present eventually formulated a united (though fragile) front, and even sought to join the Accord: Sir Peter Abeles, a prominent Australian businessman, lamented to Prime Minister Hawke that:

... it would be only an extension of the spirit of this Summit if business were incorporated as the third party of this Accord, as an equal partner. ... Most of us felt during the early days of this Conference as though we had been invited to play singles tennis against a championship doubles combination.[25]

The final communiqué of the Summit stressed the need for sustained economic growth and argued that this could be best achieved through a centralised system of wage determination, the mechanics of which would be laid down by the Arbitration Commission in a subsequent national wage case. In September 1983 the Commission took the appointed step and reintroduced a centralised system of wage determination based on six-monthly indexation for a period of two years, declaring that:

... it would be in the public interest for the Commission to try once again to operate a centralised system based on *prima facie* full indexation. We do so in the expectation that it would lead to a more stable environment and that it would provide the basis for a more rapid economic recovery than would occur in any alternative system.[26]

As before, national wage case increases were to be the major source of wage movements. The new guide-lines reflected the lessons of the old: fewer loopholes were allowed and strong emphasis was placed on self-enforcement to ensure the principles were observed in practice. In an unprecedented move the Arbitration Commission required each union to come forward and give a formal undertaking to comply with the Commission's wage-fixing principles before granting a 4.3 per cent wage increase. Six months later, in April 1984, wages were again increased in line with CPI movements, this time by 4.1 per cent.

CONCLUSION

In common with many other countries, Australia has experienced serious problems of unemployment and inflation in the past decade. But there have been major differences in its public policy responses and in the impact on its main industrial parties. Had this been a review of collective bargaining developments in virtually any other Western market economy, there would be little surprise in reading about decreases in the rate of unionisation, cuts in real wages, concession bargaining, and a general decline in the power and influence of unions. Australian unions, however, have been able to maintain, if not improve, their position notwithstanding the general decline of the economy in the post-1973/74 context of inflation, recession and unemployment. The rate of unionisation of Australian workers has remained fairly constant at 55 per cent throughout this period, real wages have been maintained in most cases, the length of the standard working week has been reduced to 38 hours, and a universal health care system (Medicare) has been introduced. With Labor parties in office federally and in four states (New South Wales, Victoria, South Australia and Western Australia), the political influence of unions, both individually and collectively, has probably never been greater since the period before the First World War. Instructive is a comment by a junior minister in the Hawke Government who complained that he would like to have as much access to the Cabinet as Mr. Bill Kelty, the Secretary of the ACTU.

What might be surprising about this analysis is the limited role apparently played by employers. Virtually every major employer or business group has voiced strong and continuing criticisms of the Arbitration Commission's second attempt at wage indexation. They are most critical of having cost-of-living wage adjustments forced upon them during a period of economic decline. However, as Isaac has observed, employers are more likely to accept arbitrated wage increases "not because employers generally are more law-abiding than unions, but because they have an easier escape route from unfavourable awards by raising prices or transferring capital".[27] In addition, employers have used their influence to obtain aid from both state and federal governments in the form of tariff protection, subsidies and tax concessions. Employers have also opposed the Accord-based wages policy on the grounds that the formal system is an alliance of self-interests which protects the wages of those who already have a job: in 1982 the unemployment rate of teenage girls was 21.5 per cent, up nearly 300 per cent on the previous decade.[28]

The unique feature of Australian industrial relations is the system of well-developed and influential industrial tribunals. Workers whose wages and working conditions are determined in the market will ultimately be forced to make concessions to employers in periods of economic decline. This does not necessarily happen when they are determined by industrial tribunals, since these often exert a ratchet effect on wages and act as a buffer between unions (or groups of workers) and employers. A constant of the past decade has been the preparedness of the Arbitration Commission to protect workers' real wages in exchange for acceptance of a centralised system of wage determination and industrial regulation. So long as unemployment is high, unions accept the Arbitration Commission's wage indexation packages, primarily because they probably would not do as well if left to their own devices in an open market. This is illustrated, for example, by the following extract from the ACTU's Wages and Salaries Policy adopted at its September 1983 Congress:

Congress declares that the maintenance of the real value of wage standards won over many years of struggle is essential, particularly in this period of serious economic decline. . . . The ... Accord ... is the labour movement's direct response to those which have attempted to force wage negotiations into the market place where wages would be determined on the basis of the so-called free labour market criteria.[29]

What will happen in the wake of a sustained economic upturn is problematic. On past performance the stronger unions will embark on a campaign for over-award increases, and eventually the Arbitration Commission will once again withdraw into the wings — at least until it can put together a package or proposal that returns it to centre stage. Thus Australia has developed a somewhat unusual system of national-level bargaining in which the Arbitration Commission is as much a stake-holder as it is a mediator in the process of fashioning the social contract. But while the tribunal's fortunes will ebb and flow along with economic fluctuations, a growing role for the Federal Government in industrial relations seems assured. Important here are the mounting effects of High Court decisions and the outcome of the forthcoming Hancock Committee of Review into Australian Industrial Relations Law and

Systems, the first wide-ranging review of the formal system since its inception some 80 years ago.

Notes

[1] Senior Lecturer and Professor of Industrial Relations, respectively, University of New South Wales.

[2] For a more detailed examination of the intricacies and nuances of Australian industrial relations, see B. Dabscheck and J. Niland: *Industrial relations in Australia* (Sydney, George Allen and Unwin, 1981); and D. Plowman et al.: *Australian industrial relations* (Sydney, McGraw-Hill, 1980).

[3] For an examination of other constitutional powers available to the Federal Government, see Dabscheck and Niland, op. cit., pp. 187-190.

[4] Quoted in M. Perlman: *Judges in industry: A study of labour arbitration in Australia* (Melbourne, Melbourne University Press, 1954), p. 32.

[5] *Social Welfare Union* case (mimeographed), pp. 13-14.

[6] 46 *Australian Law Reports* 625.

[7] For a list of these, see Dabscheck and Niland, op. cit., pp. 206-209.

[8] D. Yerbury and J. E. Isaac: "Recent trends in collective bargaining in Australia", in *International Labour Review* (Geneva, ILO), May 1971, pp. 421-452. Other articles to have appeared in the *Review* on various aspects of Australian industrial relations include O. de R. Foenander: "The achievement and significance of industrial regulation in Australia", Feb. 1957, pp. 104-118; idem: "Aspects of Australian trade unionism", Apr. 1961, pp. 322-348; K. Laffer: "Problems of Australian compulsory arbitration", May 1958, pp. 417-433; and R. D. Lansbury: "The return to arbitration: Recent trends in dispute settlement and wages policy in Australia", Sep.-Oct. 1978, pp. 611-624.

[9] For a succinct summary of how Sir Richard Kirby, the Arbitration Commission's President from 1956 to 1973, approached industrial relations regulation in this period, see R. Kirby: "Conciliation and arbitration in Australia — Where the emphasis?", in *Federal Law Review* (Canberra), Sep. 1970.

[10] W. A. Howard: "Australian trade unions in the context of union theory", in *Journal of Industrial Relations* (Sydney), Sep. 1977, p. 271.

[11] 77 *Commonwealth Arbitration Reports* 477.

[12] For the background to this original indexation undertaking by the ACTU, see B. Dabscheck: "The 1975 national wage case: Now we have an incomes policy", in *Journal of Industrial Relations*, Sep. 1975, pp. 298-303.

[13] 167 *Commonwealth Arbitration Reports* 18, p. 39.

[14] The original indexation decision implied that productivity cases would be heard annually, but the ACTU never mounted a productivity case in the six years of wage indexation's operation. In July 1984, however, it indicated that such a case would be a major part of its wages push in 1985.

[15] For a more detailed critique of the problems associated with Australia's system of compulsory arbitration, see J. Niland: *Collective bargaining and compulsory arbitration in Australia* (Sydney, University of New South Wales Press, 1978).

[16] For an analysis of the support offered to wage indexation by the Fraser Government, see D. H. Plowman: *Wage indexation: A study of Australian wage issues 1975-1980* (Sydney, George Allen and Unwin, 1981), pp. 126-138 and 157-160. Regarding the support offered by the Whitlam Labor Government, see D. Yerbury: "The government, the Arbitration Commission and wages policy: The role of the 'supporting mechanisms' under the Whitlam government", in K. Hancock (ed.): *Incomes policy in Australia* (Sydney, Harcourt Brace Jovanovich, 1981).

[17] Plowman, op. cit., p. 159.

[18] For example, see J. Nieuwenhuysen: "The South Australian Industrial Commission and the demise of wage indexation", in *Journal of Industrial Relations*, Dec. 1981, pp. 508-515.

[19] See J. F. Staples: "Conciliation and Arbitration Amendment Bill, 1979", in *Australian Quarterly* (Sydney), Dec. 1979; and idem: "Uniformity and diversity in industrial relations", in *Journal of Industrial Relations*, Sep. 1980, pp. 353-362.

[20] It should be noted that the 40-hour working week was introduced during a period when wartime and post-war regulations placed restrictions on wages. See T. Sheridan: "Labour v. Labor: The Victorian metal trades dispute of 1946-47", in J. Iremonger et al. (eds.): *Strikes: Studies in twentieth century Australian social history* (Sydney, Angus and Robertson, 1973).

[21] For details of the legislative initiatives of the various governments, see the December 1982 national wage case decision (Mis. 550/82 MD Print F1600), pp. 22-29.

[22] ibid., p. 10.

[23] *Statement of Accord by the Australian Labor Party and the Australian Council of Trade Unions regarding Economic Policy* (mimeographed), p. 5.

[24] For a stimulating analysis of the Summit, see D. A. Kemp: "The National Economic Summit: Authority, persuasion and exchange", in *Economic Record* (Burwood, Victoria), Sep. 1983, pp. 209-219.

[25] *National Economic Summit Conference*, 11-14 April 1983, Documents and proceedings. Vol. 2: *Record of proceedings* (Canberra, Australian Government Publishing Service, 1983), p. 194. The final communiqué appears on pp. 196-200.

[26] September 1983 national wage case decision (Mis. 300/83 MD Print F2900), p. 16.

[27] J. E. Isaac: "Australian compulsory arbitration and incomes policy", in J. R. Niland and J. E. Isaac (eds.): *Australian labour economics: Readings* (Melbourne, Sun Books, 2nd ed., 1975), p. 409.

[28] Data on the Australian labour market are given in B. J. Chapman et al. (eds.): *Australian labour economics: Readings* (Melbourne, Macmillan, 3rd ed., 1984), pp. 656-690.

[29] Minutes of the ACTU 1983 Congress, 12-16 September 1983, p. 152.

RECENT TRENDS IN COLLECTIVE BARGAINING IN BELGIUM

R. Blanpain [1]

In Belgium, as in many other countries, 1974 marked the beginning of an economic crisis triggered by the first oil shock, which has had a dramatic impact on labour relations in general and collective bargaining in particular. Labour relations are now conducted in the shadow of ever-increasing unemployment, which has reached record levels in recent years; between 1980 and 1981, for example, the number of unemployed rose by 22.7 per cent, between 1981 and 1982 by 14.6 per cent and between 1982 and 1983 by 11.2 per cent. By September 1983, 12.3 per cent of the active population, or 511,269 people, were out of work; moreover, the number of those unemployed for more than a year was increasing, and 30.8 per cent of the unemployed were less than 25 years old. In order to revert to the employment situation prevailing in 1973, 70,000 to 80,000 new jobs would have to be created each year until 1993.

Since 1975 collective bargaining over major issues has been virtually in an impasse, mainly because employers are no longer prepared to make concessions which they claim would further worsen the competitive position of Belgian enterprises; on the contrary, they are actually trying to reduce labour costs, for instance through staff cutbacks. Until 1981 the Government tried very hard to induce unions and employers to conclude inter-industry agreements, but when it became clear that these efforts were doomed to failure it took more drastic measures, imposing a far-reaching incomes policy, freezing wages and limiting the effects of negotiated cost-of-living clauses. The autonomy of the social partners, once one of the main characteristics of Belgian labour relations — especially where wage negotiations were concerned — has thus been considerably diminished.

Although both parties to the collective bargaining process have been affected by the situation just described, the unions, in particular, are baffled as to how to cope with their straitened circumstances. Lately, at least in the private sector, they seem to have lost much of their former power, and are having greater difficulty than before in mobilising workers and arousing their members' sense of solidarity.

177

PARTIES TO THE COLLECTIVE BARGAINING PROCESS

The workers' side

Representative trade unions

Strictly speaking, only *representative trade unions* have the right to conclude legally enforceable collective agreements. According to the criteria for representativeness laid down by the 1968 Act respecting collective industrial agreements and joint committees,[2] unions must be inter-occupational, be established at national level, be represented on the Central Economic Council and the National Labour Council and have at least 50,000 members. There are thus three representative organisations: the Confederation of Christian Trade Unions (ACV-CSC), the Belgian General Federation of Labour (ABVV-FGTB) and the Federation of Liberal Unions of Belgium (ACLVB-CGLSB); trade unions affiliated to these central organisations are also considered representative.

Roughly 70 per cent of Belgian employees (private and public) belong to trade unions, mostly those affiliated to the ACV-CSC and the ABVV-FGTB. In the major sectors of industry almost 90 per cent of blue-collar workers are organised; white-collar workers tend to organise less (approximately 40 per cent) while supervisory personnel are rarely unionised.

The ACV-CSC and the ABVV-FGTB have essentially the same structure; both are federations of national trade unions, the latter — with the exception of white-collar and the public-sector unions — usually being organised by sector of industry. The ACLVB-CGLSB has a unified structure. The national trade unions have autonomy in defending the interests of their members and in concluding collective agreements.

Recently, both major trade unions started to adapt their unitary structures to the new political and economic realities arising out of federalisation, and regional organisations have been set up. White-collar workers in the Christian trade unions have separate organisations along linguistic lines, and these bargain independently. This tendency is bound to gain momentum and spread to other unions in the near future. The metalworkers, for instance, although still organised nationally, already have two separate (linguistic) wings, which are empowered to deal with the regional political authorities and to formulate their own policies; collective agreements are, however, still concluded by the national union.

Other forms of workers' representation

Other forms of workers' representation exist mainly at the level of the plant. To that end three different bodies may operate, namely the union delegation (roughly the equivalent of the shop stewards' committee), the works council and the committee for safety, health and improvement of the workplace.

The composition, competence and functions of these bodies often overlap, and there are close links between them and the representative trade unions: as a general rule the latter control their membership either by direct appointment (e.g. of union delegates in the building sector) or by having the exclusive right to nominate candidates for elections (in the case of the works councils and most union delegates).

The function of the union delegation is to present demands and complaints with regard to wages and working conditions (in the broadest sense). Delegates can also discuss individual grievances. The 1971 Act respecting working time requires their agreement if the employer wants to exceed the limits on working hours in the event of an abnormal increase in work. It is a moot point — not without its importance — whether union delegates can conclude legally binding collective agreements, since some employers want to negotiate inferior wages and working conditions at plant level, which the unions at higher levels might well refuse. In practice union delegates do bargain informally and conclude agreements on quite a number of issues, especially in the larger plants.

A works council, comprising employers' and employees' representatives, has to be established in every plant usually employing a minimum of 100 employees. Workers' representatives in the council are elected by secret ballot every four years by all employees except managers from lists of candidates submitted by the representative unions. The council is entitled to receive information from the employer, but its competence is largely of an advisory nature, although it has decision-making powers regarding the establishment of works rules, the fixing of the date for the annual vacation, social welfare and the like. Works councils occasionally engage in informal bargaining on wages and working conditions.

The committee for safety, health and improvement of the workplace is established and composed in the same way as the works council and its competence is of a similar nature.

The employers' side

Both individual employers and employers' associations can be parties to a collective agreement. The principal employers' association is the Federation of Belgian Enterprises (VBO-FEB), which is composed of 48 sectoral associations, covering some 35,000 affiliated enterprises and most branches of economic life, excluding agriculture, retail trade, handicrafts and state-controlled enterprises. It represents about 75 per cent of enterprises employing ten workers or more. There are also a Federation of Smaller Enterprises and a number of agricultural organisations. Regional employers' organisations are becoming more important, although they do not yet effectively engage in collective bargaining.

ROLE OF THE PUBLIC AUTHORITIES

The national Government has recently intervened very actively in collective bargaining, mainly by trying to induce the national bargaining partners to conclude an overall agreement in line with its anti-inflationary policy and by imposing a wage freeze through legislation.

As already mentioned, no inter-industry agreements of the traditional type have been voluntarily concluded on major issues since 1975. The Government has repeatedly — and unsuccessfully — tried to bring trade unions and employers' associations together in order to conclude an overall collective agreement, its latest attempt being in 1980, on the occasion of a National Labour Conference. After this the Government had Parliament adopt an Act in February 1981 providing for mandatory wage restraint measures if labour and management could not conclude an agreement to this effect at national level. Such an agreement was, however, signed on 13 February 1981 and rendered binding by a Royal Order of 14 February 1981. It ran from 1 January 1981 until 31 December 1982.

This central agreement provided for existing agreements at industry level and below to be extended for 12 months from the date of their expiry under the same conditions. Should such agreements come to an end before 31 December 1982, new ones might be concluded subject to certain limitations: where the working week averaged 40 or 39 hours, negotiations might take place with a view to reducing this figure to 38 hours. Where an average 38-hour week or less had already been achieved, negotiations might concentrate on a pay increase of up to 1 per cent a year, or a reduction in working time of up to one hour a week, to be phased in over a two-year period. The agreement further provided for the continued operation of all incremental pay scales which grant annual or two-yearly increases to employees on the basis of length of service, age or merit.

The minimum wage was increased from 1 January 1982. Also important was the fact that industrial peace was guaranteed for the duration of the agreement and that the parties were to submit difficulties concerning the application of the central agreement to an interpretation committee. Although the committee had only advisory powers, its advice has been followed in practice.

In February 1982, in a further move to tackle the crisis, and with the explicit goal of making Belgian enterprises more competitive on international markets, the Government devalued the Belgian franc by 8.5 per cent, imposed a selective wage freeze and set drastic limitations on cost-of-living increases which had hitherto been the subject of clauses in collective agreements considered sacrosanct by all the parties involved in industrial relations.

Under an Act of 2 February 1982 giving the Government special powers to legislate in place of Parliament, an Order (No. 11) was issued on 15 February 1982 which provided for:

— no wage indexation from 1 March 1982 to 31 May 1982 for any employees except those on or below the standard minimum wage;

— from 1 June 1982 to 31 December 1982 partial wage indexation in the form of a lump sum for all employees.

Order No. 11 was extended by an Order (No. 180) of 30 December 1982 which provided that no wage increase, in cash or in kind, was to be granted before 31 December 1984 under an individual or a collective agreement or by way of a unilateral decision by an employer. The only increase allowed was in the form of a cost-of-living adjustment determined as follows:

— continuance of the lump-sum adjustment system in 1983;
— thereafter, a return to the traditional systems of negotiated adjustments with the difference that wage adjustments would be made less frequently than in the past.

The income forgone by workers as a result of wage restraint amounted to about 3 per cent in 1982; the figure for 1983 and 1984 is around 2.5 per cent. It was stipulated that the resulting savings for employers were to be used to increase employment, and works councils would be entitled to information about how they were spent.

Even though the Government has severely limited freedom to negotiate on wages, in another sense it has given a fillip to collective bargaining by obliging management and labour to negotiate on the reduction of working time and the hiring of new employees in an attempt to increase employment. The parties have had to agree on ways and means of reducing working time by 5 per cent and hiring a number of new workers equivalent to 3 per cent of the staff employed at 31 December 1982. If no agreement can be reached, a sum equal to the income forgone by workers as a result of wage restraint has to be paid to a Central Employment Fund. Exceptions are made for enterprises in difficulties or working in adverse economic circumstances.

As a result of these provisions, active bargaining has taken place in most sectors and has led to an impressive number of collective agreements: 78 have been concluded in the joint committees (see below) and more than 1,000 at enterprise level, covering almost 90 per cent of employees; it has been estimated that this will save or create between 25,000 and 40,000 jobs, thus stabilising employment in 1984 at the 1983 level. These negotiations have taken place in a relatively peaceful climate, although the public sector has contested the measures imposed by the Government. New measures (10 October 1983) entitle the works councils to monitor the implementation of the collective agreements on job creation and working time. In the building sector, where no agreement could be reached, the Government has imposed a reduction of working time by an Order.

The Government has indicated that the wage restraint measures may be continued even after 1984. The aim is to ensure that the rise of wage costs in Belgium is not higher than the overall average of rises in its seven most important trading partners. If no inter-industry agreement can be reached for 1985-86, the Government will introduce further legislation.

In addition to the above, an Act of 3 July 1983 gave the Government extraordinary powers to enact legislation concerning the introduction of new technologies if the social partners were unable to conclude a framework agreement by 1 October 1983. Such an agreement was practically dictated by the Government, since the social partners accepted its proposals — under heavy political pressure — and the agreement was signed on 13 December 1983.

The same strategy was used to impose wage restraint on the steelworkers of Cockerill-Sambre as part of the overall package of structural adjustment measures the Government envisages for the steel industry. On 24 December the Government decided to impose the following measures if no equivalent collective agreement could be reached by 15 February 1984: no wage increases until 1 January 1988 except for cost-of-living adjustments and increases due under existing seniority rules; a cumulative reduction of wages by 1.25 per cent each quarter from 1 March 1984 until 1 December 1985, amounting to a loss of about 10 per cent over a period of two years. The Government can adjust these measures in the light of circumstances, and extend the period of their application. They will be used to finance a reduction in working time to 36 hours starting on 1 January 1985 or thereafter and to 35 hours starting on 1 January 1986 or thereafter, the establishment of early retirement schemes and the reduction of overall costs. The works council will supervise the whole operation.

The Government has also made the granting of subsidies to enterprises or industries conditional upon the conclusion of collective agreements, as was the case with the textile industry in 1977.

Mention should finally be made of Royal Order No. 179 of 30 December 1982 permitting collective agreements to depart from binding labour standards [3] under certain circumstances and providing for experimental flexible working time arrangements designed to create additional employment. Such departures, to be agreed between an employer and the union delegation or, in the absence of the latter, other plant-level representatives of the employees, have to be approved by the Minister of Labour, who co-signs the agreement. As of December 1983, some nine agreements concerning the adjustment of working time had been concluded.

BARGAINING BODIES AND PROCEDURES

Bodies with specific bargaining functions have been set up at industrial sector level (joint committees) and at national inter-industry level (National Labour Council). Joint committees were first established in 1919; the National Labour Council, created by an Act of 29 May 1952, was granted bargaining powers by the Act of 1968.

Joint committees are established by Royal Order and are composed of an independent chairman and an equal number of representatives of the employers' associations and the representative trade unions. In 1983 they numbered 98, together covering most of the workers in private industry. In November 1983, 51 committees were competent for blue-collar workers, 23 for white-collar workers and 24 (mainly in the tertiary sector) for both. The joint committees held 1,040 meetings in 1981 and 999 in 1982, and concluded 243 collective agreements in 1981 and 187 in 1982.

The National Labour Council is composed of 22 members, representing employers' associations and representative trade unions and presided over by an independent chairman. Bargaining does not, however, invariably take place in these official bodies. Tripartite national inter-industry negotiations may also be conducted by a *de facto* working group (the "Group of Ten"), or occasionally in ad hoc round-table conferences. Bargaining is, as we have seen, frequent at enterprise level as well.

Hardly any research has been done in Belgium on the actual procedure of collective bargaining, but as far as the sectoral level is concerned the crisis does not seem to have had an important impact on procedures. Trade union claims are usually first formulated at local or regional level by union delegates. These claims are then forwarded to national committees of the respective federations, which decide whether to proceed further with them. In most cases the different national federations meet to work out a common programme, and often succeed in presenting one to the employers' association(s). The latter are represented by staff members and representatives of employers who are members of the associations (usually managers responsible for personnel or labour relations matters in the larger enterprises). Actual negotiations may take place inside or outside the official joint committee.

In the event of a disagreement the chairman of the joint committee may act as a conciliator, and if conciliation fails a political figure may be called in to mediate. Once a draft agreement has been drawn up, the national committees of the different unions have to state whether they accept or reject it. When a draft has been accepted, the agreement will be formally concluded in the national joint committee. Rarely are drafts submitted for ratification to the membership as a whole.

STRUCTURE OF BARGAINING

Levels

It can be seen from the above that bargaining takes place at different levels, namely national inter-industry level, national industry level, regional industry level and enterprise level. As a first round of high-level bargaining sets only minimum standards, these can always be improved and built upon during further negotiation at lower levels.

Between 1960 and 1975 inter-industry agreements were concluded at regular intervals, usually of two years. Since then, however, no more have been concluded — on major issues at least — for a number of reasons. First, as a consequence of the crisis, the difference between the stronger and the weaker sectors of the economy has become more pronounced, so that an overall agreement under which the trade unionists in the stronger sectors risk losing their comparative advantages has become a less realistic proposition. Second, inter-industry agreements have increasingly dealt with issues [4] leaving less room for bargaining at lower levels which would match the needs and aspirations of each sector or enterprise. A third reason seems to be a hardening of the respective attitudes of employers and trade unions to such issues as the role of free

183

enterprise, managerial prerogative, taxes, social security, the cost of living and industrial democracy. A fourth factor seems to be the diminishing control exerted by the central employers' and union organisations over their constituents as a consequence of the latter's more critical attitude and their demands that agreements should be ratified by them before conclusion. The linguistic problem, with its ever more marked social and economic overtones, is yet another reason. Despite this unfavourable climate, however, master agreements covering more technical and less dramatic issues continue to be concluded in the National Labour Council, as indicated above.

This lack of consensus has also been evident at the sectoral level, for similar reasons.[5] Thus, in the metalworking industries, no national wage agreements for blue-collar workers have been reached since 1974 and virtually no consensus of any kind has been achieved since 1977. Regional, provincial and enterprise agreements have, however, been concluded on a large scale. In 1978, 77 per cent of blue-collar workers were covered by regional agreements and 59 per cent by enterprise agreements.

In other sectors, such as textiles (blue-collar workers), insurance (white-collar workers) and retailing (white-collar workers) national agreements continued to be the rule, although they proved in some cases to be difficult to conclude, with more frequent intervention by official conciliators, strike threats and a longer time lapse before they could be reached.

Many of the national agreements include industrial peace obligations providing, for instance, that no additional claims whatsoever may be raised at national, regional or enterprise level (textiles, blue-collar workers) or that no additional claims may be raised concerning points covered at national level (metalworking, blue-collar workers).

Coverage

Bargaining is usually conducted separately for blue-collar and white-collar workers, and co-ordination between the two is rare. Since collective agreements reached in the joint committees may be extended by Royal Order to enterprises not affiliated to signatory employers' organisations, most workers are covered by collective agreements, especially national agreements.[6] Rarely do agreements contain provisions that relate specifically to managerial staff.

EXTENT, CONTENT AND OUTCOME OF COLLECTIVE BARGAINING

Extent

The number of collective agreements concluded in joint committees increased steadily in the early 1970s (from 396 in 1970 to 731 in 1974); in 1975, however, with the onset of the economic crisis, the process was reversed, and by 1982 the number had fallen to 187.[7]

Despite these developments and the degree of government regulation in many areas, collective bargaining in the joint committees continues to play an important role in the setting of labour standards, where emphasis has recently been placed on certain issues such as the employment of temporary workers, part-time work and the introduction of new technologies.

The National Labour Council, too, has concluded a large number of agreements which are binding on private industry as a whole. The number of items dealt with in such agreements is exceptionally high in Belgium, and their collective impact is so important that it would not be an exaggeration to describe the National Labour Council as a kind of social parliament.

The political pressure exerted by trade unions during negotiations with the Government has also profoundly influenced labour legislation, which is very extensive, covering individual labour contracts for both blue-collar and white-collar workers and regulating matters such as different forms of contract, damages for breach thereof, lay-offs, notice of dismissal, working time, overtime, female and child labour, safety and working conditions and paid leave. There are also very detailed social security regulations dealing with unemployment, sickness and health insurance, pensions, occupational diseases and family allowances. Many Acts contain only general principles, thus giving the executive broad powers to implement them by means of Royal or Ministerial Orders.

Content and outcome [8]

As we have seen, fewer major topics are dealt with in most sectors than during the pre-crisis period, so that new gains by the unions, if any, are usually insignificant and there has been a loss in real income due mainly to the Government's incomes policy. This was, for instance, the case in the textile industry (blue-collar workers) and has partly to do with the fact that inter-industry wage agreements are no longer concluded. Wages nevertheless remain a central preoccupation. Such increases as were still granted prior to the 1982 legislation (e.g. in enterprise agreements) were expressed in Belgian francs rather than in percentages as formerly and were sometimes granted in the form of a lump sum reserved to trade union members. Dates of increases were postponed and did not always coincide with the date stipulated in the agreement. Whereas the increase in real wages was as high as 10.76 per cent in 1972, it was nil in 1977 and only 2.42 per cent in 1980. In quite a number of enterprises a substantial reduction of wages has been negotiated, usually as a *quid pro quo* for maintaining the employment level.

In the metalworking industry (blue-collar workers), too, changes can be noticed. Bargaining is now centred less on individual concerns and more on overall employment, supplementary social security benefits (unemployment, sickness and invalidity, with a premium reserved for trade union members) and working time.

Employment security has obviously been one of the main objectives of the trade unions. In 1975 a recommendation by Fabrimetal, the metalworking employers' association, was addressed to all enterprises of the sector. This recommendation can be summarised as follows:

— no collective redundancies before all other solutions are exhausted;
— workers' representatives to be given adequate information;
— preference to be given to short-time working or temporary unemployment;
— transfers of employees between enterprises if necessary;
— no overtime unless absolutely necessary;
— temporary work to be strictly limited.

These points are now incorporated in some regional agreements of the sector and have been reinforced in a few of them. One agreement, for instance, imposes short-time working in the event of employment difficulties; if redundancies are necessary the union delegation and the trade unions are to be informed and negotiations can take place at the request of the unions. If necessary, a conciliation procedure — in the framework of the joint committee — can be called for, during which all projected dismissals must be suspended. If the procedure is not followed the workers affected are to receive compensation equal to the amount of wages due during the term of notice normally required in the event of dismissal.

In other sectors, too, employment guarantees have been considered or reconsidered; for instance, in retailing (white-collar workers) and insurance. In the latter, a system of job security was introduced in 1975. In the event of individual dismissals a procedure for informing the employees concerned and the union delegation has been set up, with the possibility of an appeal to a conciliation committee established in the framework of the joint committee; the conciliation committee must reach its conclusions within a month. In the event of dismissals for economic or technical reasons, the enterprise concerned must halt recruitment, transfer workers, training or retraining them if necessary, and negotiate arrangements for early retirement. If problems cannot be solved at enterprise level, the chairman of the joint committee is informed, who then places the question before a joint employment working party on relocation of employees. Where dismissals are unavoidable, certain criteria such as competence, merit, age, seniority and family responsibilities have to be taken into account. If these procedures are not followed, the employer concerned is liable to pay compensation equal to six months' wages to each of the employees affected. In 1977-78 agreements were also concluded to maintain the level of employment in enterprises which are members of the employers' association, to limit recourse to temporary workers and the like. An agreement of 1983 provides that no dismissal may take place for reasons of reorganisation and requires preferential re-engagement of employees dismissed for economic reasons.

In the petroleum sector (blue-collar workers), however, the coverage of the far-reaching employment protection agreements of 1959 and 1970 [9] was restricted in 1980. The unions were forced to accept a new agreement which maintains the former employment security system only for those already in service; employment security for those newly engaged is guaranteed for only five years, after which the worker can be dismissed on the sole condition that appropriate notice is given.[10]

COLLECTIVE BARGAINING AND WORKERS' PARTICIPATION

Collective bargaining remains one of the major channels for participation in managerial decision-making, and in this connection works councils and union delegations play an important role. Informal bargaining takes place in the works council on matters such as the establishment of works rules, the fixing of dates for annual vacations and the like. Union delegations play a more prominent part in bargaining than the works council, not only in the drafting and adoption of national or regional agreements, but also in informal bargaining on wages and working conditions at the level of the enterprise. Formerly, union delegates — sometimes assisted by trade union officers — attempted to bargain for better conditions than those laid down in national or regional agreements, but now they may in some cases be obliged to tone down their demands. This bargaining role is especially important in the bigger enterprises, since conditions negotiated there may be a good deal better than those stipulated in national agreements; this was also the case with wages before 1982. It is still rare in Belgium for employees to be represented on the boards of companies. Discussions to that end have lately been initiated by the Government, but no easy agreement on this is to be expected in the near future.

LABOUR DISPUTES

Available statistics indicate no clear long-term trend concerning the impact of the crisis on industrial disputes, although one has the impression that there has lately been less industrial strife than before.

The fact that any dispute of rights or of interests, whether individual or collective, may be settled by means of a strike and that there are few if any legal limitations on the right to strike, makes some authors call Belgium a strikers' paradise. However, Belgium is not a particularly strike-prone country, as table 1 shows.

Although no clear-cut trends can be drawn from these figures, they seem to indicate that strikes concentrate relatively more than before on issues like employment and job security and less on wages and benefits. Strikes occurring in 1982 [11] seem to confirm this (see table 2).

Statistics for 1982 show a decrease in the number of strikes at the enterprise level, but a rise in that of regional sectoral strikes in the private sector and of regional and national sectoral strikes in the public sector.

The regional and national strikes were mostly aimed at persuading the Government to safeguard employment, social security and the cost-of-living

Collective bargaining: A reappraisal

Table 1.   Strike trends in Belgium, 1976-81

Indicator	1976	1977	1978	1979	1980	1981 (Jan. to June)
No. of strikes	281	220	195	215	132	81
No. of enterprises	319	220	225	228	141	82
No. of strikers	106 654	65 761	90 813	55 722	26 727	42 054
No. of involuntary strikers	11 146	8 456	10 890	6 122	3 705	534
No. of working days lost by issue:						
Wages	287 263	454 603	121 867	113 313	60 035	12 438
Social benefits	326 919	30 155	22 671	13 607	1 100	1 675
Working conditions	11 675	10 301	101 991	19 000	18 885	7 938
Employment	141 006	93 263	38 360	76 622	44 951	181 540
Other	129 583	70 435	717 240	399 866	96 809	37 661
Total days lost	896 446	658 757	1 002 129	622 408	221 780	241 452

Source: "Statistiek der werkstakingen in België", in *Arbeidsblad* (Brussels), Jan. 1983, p. 46.

Table 2.   Strikes occurring in 1982, by region and issue

Issue	Flanders	Wallonia	Brussels	Total No.	%
Wages	15	34	4	53	32
Employment	18	40	6	64	38
Grievances	9	20	1	30	18
Conditions of work	6	12	2	20	12
Total	48	106	13	167	100

adjustment system. Some were intended to force the employers' associations to conclude an inter-industry agreement concerning the reduction of working time combined with the hiring of new workers.

In 1982 about ten large-scale occupations of enterprises were staged in an attempt to safeguard employment and prevent closures or collective dismissals. Practically all of them failed.

Official strikes, as opposed to spontaneous strikes, seem to be in a minority; [12] while Wallonia seems to be more strike-prone than Flanders and Brussels, as the 1982 figures indicate.

OUTLOOK

The crisis will undoubtedly continue to have a dramatic impact on collective bargaining. The Government is likely to maintain its dominant role given the lack of consensus between the social partners on ways of tackling the issues involved. That there are limits to government intervention in imposing restraint was shown by a largely spontaneous strike of public employees in September 1983, which lasted for more than a week. Given the problems of sharing out a cake that is smaller than before, bargaining will become an increasingly difficult process. Control of labour costs and the creation of employment will continue to be the key issues, the former implying wage restraint and social security reform and the latter requiring reduction of working time, recourse to part-time work and the like. The introduction of new technologies will undoubtedly become a more important concern.

Although bargaining will continue to take place at different levels, it will be more decentralised than before, since the crisis has highlighted differences between sectors, subsectors, regions and enterprises. It is likely to be some time before major inter-industry agreements regain their former prominence.

Notes

[1] Professor; Director of the Institute for Labour Relations, Catholic University of Leuven.

[2] For an English translation of this Act, see *Legislative Series* (Geneva, ILO), 1968 — Bel. 1.

[3] Statutory provisions and those of collective agreements rendered binding by Royal Order. The Council of State has indicated that it considers Order No. 179 to be unconstitutional. For an English version of the text of the Order, see *Legislative Series*, 1982 — Bel. 1.

[4] Yearly vacation, working time, maternity leave, collective dismissals, pensions and the like. M. Vranken: *De collectieve arbeidsovereenkomsten in België van 1974 tot 1980*, Evolutie en juridische evaluatie (Leuven, unpublished Ph.D. thesis, 1983), pp. 19-20.

[5] ibid., pp. 347-352.

[6] For the legal intricacies, see R. Blanpain: "Belgium", in *International encyclopaedia for labour law and industrial relations* (Deventer, Kluwer, 1977 onwards), Vol. 2, pp. 345-380. In 1982, 157 out of 187 collective agreements concluded in joint committees were rendered binding by Royal Order.

[7] No exact figures are yet known for 1983, but a record number may be expected, mainly accounted for by the agreements on working time.

[8] For a fuller treatment, see Vranken, op. cit., pp. 349-356.

[9] These imposed, among other things, negotiated dismissals deferred for a period of three months, investigation of the possibility of introducing shift work, transfer to other enterprises and the creation of a labour reserve from which new openings had to be filled.

[10] A. de Koster: *Multinationale ondernemingen en arbeidsverhoudingen in België: De petroleumsector* (unpublished Ph.D. thesis, 1982), Vol. III, pp. 541-546.

[11] C. Serroyen and C. Piret: *De stakingen in 1982* (Brussels, Research Department of the ACV-CSC, 1983).

[12] Kim Dai Won: *Au-delà de l'institutionalisation des rapports professionnels. Analyse du mouvement spontané ouvrier belge*, Ph.D. thesis (Catholic University of Leuven, Institute for Labour Relations, 1977).

RECENT TRENDS IN COLLECTIVE BARGAINING IN FRANCE

Guy Caire [1]

At the start of the 1970s it could well be argued that "collective bargaining has never bulked as large in France as it has in other countries" and that it was "an erratic phenomenon".[2]

Since then, however, new legislation has been introduced amending 358 sections of the Labour Code and a new Act, No. 82-957 of 13 November 1982,[3] has been promulgated on the subject of collective agreements. For their part, the authors of these changes have not hesitated to speak of a radical break with the past and a new approach to industrial relations: "The sensible revolution! That is the label I should like to see attached to the new workers' rights I am advocating." That comment by Jean Auroux, Minister of Labour from 1981 to 1983, well sums up, I think, the spirit that has imbued the social reforms undertaken by the Left since its accession to power: a peaceful revolution aimed at modernising the French system of industrial relations and attempting to make collective bargaining the favoured medium for dealings between the social partners.

In order to place these changes and developments in the French system of industrial relations in proper perspective we shall examine them from three angles:

(1) Looking at them from an essentially legal standpoint, we shall review the debate on the state of industrial relations that led, with the change of Administration in May 1981, to a rethinking of the collective bargaining system. This should enable us to judge the relevance of the framework within which the legislature intends that industrial relations should be conducted from now on.

(2) From a more factual angle, we shall attempt to describe what has been achieved through collective bargaining and also, inasmuch as the changes are still too recent to have fully borne fruit, what benefits the future is likely to bring.

(3) Adopting a more sociological approach, we shall try to pinpoint the problems that have to be overcome if the full potential offered by the new legislation is to be realised.

THE NEW LEGAL FRAMEWORK

To appreciate fully the importance of the innovations introduced in the Labour Code by the Act of 13 November 1982, it may be useful to take a brief look backwards. Collective bargaining was first regulated by labour law in the Act of 23 March 1919. However, this legislation had little effect and it was not until the adoption of the Act of 11 February 1950 (amended in 1967, 1971 and 1978) that free bargaining really began to take root. This Act, which placed plant and industry-wide agreements on roughly the same footing and introduced the notion of nation-wide agreements applicable either to one industry or to all industries, granted workers the real right to bargain collectively. Bearing in mind this legislative framework we can now attempt to take stock first of the developments during the seven years of the previous Administration (a French President is elected for a seven-year term) and then of the reforms launched under the new Presidency.

Developments during the 1974-81 Presidency

While evolution without revolution was one of the leitmotifs of the 1970s, it was nevertheless felt that the negotiating machinery needed a complete overhaul. Consequently, immediately following the elections of 27 April 1978, the Government announced in a letter addressed to employers' and workers' organisations that it intended to look into possible changes in the law with a view to "strengthening the role of collective agreements as an expression of the social dialogue". A number of studies on the subject were then published.

The first was carried out by Professor J. D. Reynaud at the request of the Commission of the European Communities as part of a wider programme of research on collective bargaining trends in the member States. According to this study,[4] there were three main types of problem. The most important perhaps was the grey area existing between what is negotiable and what is properly a matter of employers' prerogative. Second, there had never been a clear distinction in France between the issues that are subject to negotiation and those on which the employer has only an obligation to inform or consult the workforce. Finally, the French collective agreement was particularly remote from the spirit of a contract, with all that it entails in the way of reciprocal obligations.

The Adam Report, for its part, was commissioned by the Minister of Labour, who wanted to see what effect the 1950 Act had had and to discuss with the employers and the trade unions what amendments might be appropriate.[5] Professor Adam noted four respects in which bargaining structures had failed to keep pace with developments:

(a) the lack of uniform criteria for defining an "industry";

(b) the absence of any clear demarcation of negotiating levels, with the conflicts to which this was bound to lead;

(c) the fact that a considerable number of occupations or trades were not organised and, besides, were based on differing criteria such as technology (smelting), raw materials (wood), the market (hardware) or structure (department stores);

(d) the fact that the statutory provisions governing staff representation were designed for small, single-establishment enterprises and were ill-suited to more complex organisations.

Passing on to the recommendations, the study group chaired by Professor Adam suggested a policy designed to promote collective bargaining in three main ways:

(1) Representative employers' and trade union organisations (defined not according to the narrow statutory criteria but on the basis of a minimum number of members) should be made responsible for developing collective bargaining, especially at the industry level. This would entail strengthening their powers, particularly within the Central Collective Agreements Committee (a tripartite advisory body invited to state its opinion on the extension of collective agreements to other non-signatory enterprises or to other industries).

(2) The scope of collective bargaining should be broadened and its influence strengthened so as to allow it to play a fuller role in standard setting.

(3) Finally, legislation should be rid of provisions governing conciliation, mediation and arbitration that had fallen into disuse, and a system of supportive measures for bargaining should be set up, including public financing to make expert advice equally accessible to both sides and thus improve the bargaining process.

A third study that merits attention (not least because its instigator was Jacques Delors, who was then social adviser to the Prime Minister, Jacques Chaban-Delmas, and was to become Minister of Finance under the Government of the Left) was the one carried out by the *Echange et Projets* study group.[6] According to its authors, an attempt to bring about radical changes in industrial relations could take three complementary forms. The first would be to stimulate bargaining by reforming the context in which it operates (replacing the present, somewhat disorganised bargaining jurisdictions with a clear definition of branches of industry based on technical criteria; drawing up a timetable for the renegotiation of agreements, which might involve a review of the grading scales every five years and annual wage negotiations; the requirement, at least when an agreement was to be the subject of a ministerial extension order, that it be signed by trade unions representing at least 20 per cent of the workers in the industry concerned; and more far-reaching penal sanctions). *Echange et Projets* did not propose the abolition of existing procedures — even though they were seldom used — for conciliation, mediation and arbitration, but called for the setting up of an active industrial mediation council composed of specialists and the establishment of a social data bank for the use of the bargaining parties. The second suggestion was aimed at giving real substance to ongoing negotiations, which should serve two main objectives: reducing inequalities and promoting employment. The third series of proposals — which would have profound repercussions, since they were to be incorporated into a number of provisions in the Auroux legislation — were aimed at making the enterprise the main locus of bargaining: all enterprises employing more than 500 workers should be required to enter into annual negotiations and agreements on wages, grading, hours of work, works rules and arduous jobs. Finally, the ways and means for workers to voice their views directly and personally should be spelt out in detail at the plant level.

These limited critical appraisals were soon to be followed by a more ambitious assessment. Indeed, the Left, which had not had a part in government since the creation of the Fifth Republic, felt the quite legitimate need on coming to power of making an "inventory" of what it was inheriting. A stock-taking commission, chaired by François Bloch-Lainé, was therefore set up to make a wide-ranging assessment of the strengths and weaknesses of the French economy in 1981.[7] It found that in French industry the recession had led to new personnel management policies that had seriously disrupted the labour relations system.

A number of features of individual employment relationships were singled out. Considerable advances had been made in reducing working time, but the statistical averages concealed the marked contrasts between one enterprise or one sector and another. There were also great disparities in working conditions, with manual workers and women being particularly disadvantaged. While the purchasing power of wages had doubled between 1950 and 1980, after the onset of the recession the trend had slowed down and, in 1979, had even been reversed. Up to 1976 the (indexed) minimum wage (known in France as the SMIC), which is fixed by the Government on the basis of a model household budget following consultations with both sides of industry, had been the preferred lever for raising low wages; subsequently, the public authorities had put greater trust in collective bargaining by branch of industry, but this change of direction did not seem to have produced the expected results. Supplementary benefits had been appreciably improved by both legislation and bargaining. Profit-sharing had given the workers concerned an additional financial incentive, but otherwise had not affected social life in the enterprise. A reform of management's power to make regulations in the enterprise had long been felt necessary. The safeguards provided to workers against dismissal under existing legislation were not proving adequate in the present circumstances. The rapid expansion, with the recession, of increasingly precarious types of employment and reliance on temporary work agencies, subcontracting, fixed-term contracts, and so on, had also enabled management in many instances to side-step the statutory provisions governing dismissals, certain obligations laid down in collective agreements and the legislation on staff representation — all developments that were weakening the cohesion of the work community.

These management strategies, according to the commission, also had repercussions on collective labour relations by upsetting stable employment relationships and the very notion of the enterprise and hence undermining the representative institutions concerned. Three traits characterised these collective relations. The first, paradoxically, was a certain expansion in the representative institutions, which nevertheless represented only part of the workforce. The proportion of enterprises with works committees rose from 29 per cent in 1967 to 80 per cent in 1980; the number of trade union representations within the enterprise increased during the same period from 14,000 to 37,000. However, in enterprises with fewer than 50 employees, works committees and trade union representations were disappearing, leaving only the oldest representative institution, the staff delegates; and even this did not exist in more than 80 per cent of establishments with 11 to 49 employees. Despite the special protection enjoyed by staff representatives against dismissal, the number of authorisations for dismissing them had greatly increased, giving rise to numerous, complex disputes. The second characteristic, then, was a disputed and — with the blocking of the proposed reforms of 1978-79 — unchanged bargaining system marked by —

... serious inconsistencies that impair its efficiency and weaken its credibility:

— inconsistency first of all in the definition of the scope of collective agreements. . . . This results in a bargaining coverage "of variable geometry" with gaps that have not all been filled yet;

— inconsistency in levels of bargaining, with negotiations still being carried on largely at the national, industry or multi-industry level as a result of the failure to bargain at the plant or local level . . .;

— inconsistency finally, and above all, in a system in which collective agreements can be signed by trade union organisations that are not very representative of the branch of activity concerned but that happen to belong to a confederation recognised as representative at the industry and multi-industry level, and in which — since the reform of January 1978 [on this matter] — agreements can be extended to non-signatories despite the opposition, within the Central Collective Agreements Committee, of the most representative trade unions.[8]

Reforms under the new Presidency

The Presidential campaign of 1981 provided an opportunity for each of the trade union confederations to present its programme, in which industrial relations were of course accorded great importance.

The incumbent Administration was not without its own ideas: it had promulgated an Act requiring companies to submit an annual "social progress" report to the works committee and an Act respecting consultation with managerial staff; in a letter to the National Council of French Employers (CNPF) it had recalled the importance and urgency of respecting the workers' right to direct expression of their views and it was preparing draft legislation to establish this right and provide the necessary funds for its effective exercise.

The Opposition, for its part, was not to be left behind, and proclaimed its determination to undertake "a far-reaching reform of the labour legislation" based on two guiding principles developed in the "common programme" of the Socialist and Communist parties: on the one hand, the participation of workers and their organisations in the enterprise should be strengthened through collective agreements and plant agreements, compulsory consultation with the works committees and staff delegates, and increased material, financial and personnel resources for the representative institutions; on the other hand, democratic management of the public and nationalised sectors should be guaranteed through the rehabilitation of tripartism (introduced in 1945) and increased workers' rights.

The Auroux Report [9] spelt out this policy. It revolved around two key ideas and advocated four sets of measures.

The first key idea was that workers should retain their civil rights within the enterprise: this would require two kinds of measures. First, it was necessary to restore and enlarge workers' rights by reaffirming a number of fundamental rights and by creating new ones as well: the right to exercise civil liberties within the enterprise (right of assembly, right of access to company premises for trade union or political leaders) and the right of workers to express their views about their working conditions, which in turn would require strengthening the representative institutions specialised in such matters, namely the health and safety committees (CHS) and the committees for the improvement of working conditions (CACT). Secondly, it was necessary to reconstitute the work community as a meaningful entity. Since the onset of the recession, companies had devised new forms of manpower management: strict and precise regulations were needed for controlling new forms of employment and for assuring all workers of treatment similar to that accorded to permanent workers.

The second key idea was that workers should become agents for change in the enterprise by enabling them to influence decisions affecting them directly. Two types of action would be necessary to that end: strengthening existing representative institutions and enhancing collective bargaining. The main innovation, however, was the obligation for the employer and the organisations represented in the enterprise to enter into annual bargaining, principally on wages, hours of work and working conditions.

The Auroux Report was published on 8 September 1981 and its recommendations were implemented in three Ordinances and four Acts.

The first objective of the reforms was to restore and enlarge workers' rights. Act No. 82-689 of 4 August 1982 [10] amended the provisions on works rules and set out the main rules governing disciplinary penalties; it also dealt with the employees' right to express their views. The practical arrangements for the exercise of this right were left to the discretion of the employers and the trade unions but negotiations on the subject had to begin within six months of the promulgation of the Act in enterprises with more than 200 employees and the works committee had to draw up a report on the results obtained within two years. By 15 May 1983, 1,043 agreements covering 12.1 per cent of the enterprises concerned and showing great diversity in form and content were already known to have been negotiated.

The second objective was to restore the identity of the work community, which had been seriously diluted by the institution of many different types of employment contract. Three major pieces of legislation were issued concerning temporary work agencies (an Ordinance of 5 February 1982),[11] fixed-term contracts (another Ordinance of 5 February 1982) [12] and part-time work (an Ordinance of 26 March 1982).[13]

The third objective was to expand the role of the representative institutions. Some of these are covered by Act No. 82-915 of 28 October 1982,[14] under which the trade union presence on the shop-floor has been strengthened and the trade union representations within the enterprise have been given broader powers. As regards staff delegates, the most striking innovation is the introduction of "site delegates", which should enable the employees of small undertakings in an industrial estate or shopping centre to benefit from representation previously denied them. Moreover, in enterprises employing at least 50 persons where there is no works committee, the staff delegates are to be granted powers normally exercised by the works committee, together with the corresponding means. As regards works committees, the new Act gives them a whole range of rights they had not enjoyed before (increased information; possibility of calling on the services of various types of experts, particularly as regards technological changes; economic training for their members; establishment of an economic committee in large enterprises; right to call internal staff meetings and invite outside personalities; provision of operating subsidies equal to 0.2 per cent of the gross payroll, etc.). A final type of staff representation in the enterprise was the subject of a specific piece of legislation, Act No. 82-1097 of 23 December 1982.[15] Under this Act the health and safety committee and the committee for the improvement of working conditions were amalgamated into a single body, the health, safety and working conditions committee (CHSCT), a representative institution enjoying an overall allocation of time off from work, the possibility of calling in experts at the employer's expense and training facilities for its members.

The fourth and final objective of the Auroux policy was the reinvigoration of collective bargaining. Act No. 82-957 of 13 November 1982 [16] respecting collective bargaining and the settlement of collective labour disputes is aimed at making collective bargaining the mainspring of social progress in France. Some provisions, in our opinion, are of secondary importance, but the Act contains three essential innovations. Of secondary importance are the provisions for the establishment of joint bargaining committees in enterprises with fewer than 11 employees, the procedures for extending agreements, and recourse to mediation for settling disputes. The essential innovations lie in the obligation for all organisations bound by an industry-wide agreement to meet at least once a year to negotiate wages and at least once every five years to review the grading system; the obligation for the employer to enter into annual negotiations with the representative trade union organisation on wages, hours of work and the organisation of working time; and the right of trade union organisations obtaining more than 50 per cent of the votes at the last works committee elections to veto the application in the enterprise of agreements providing for exceptions to ordinary law.

THE IMPACT ON COLLECTIVE BARGAINING

Having reviewed the background and general scope of the changes that have taken place, let us now try to evaluate them to see what effect they have had on collective bargaining in practice. Two aspects need to be highlighted: the volume of bargaining has grown and will continue to grow — as have also the levels at which it is conducted — and new areas for negotiation have been opened up.

The growth of bargaining

Looking at collective agreements from a purely quantitative standpoint, we find that in 1983 the number of agreements in force that were negotiated at a level higher than the enterprise was over a third more than eight years before, in 1975 (see table 1). Looking at the pattern as it evolved over the years (see table 2), we find a marked break after 1968, subsequent variations being attributable to political and economic influences (the decline in 1977 and 1978, for example, being no doubt due to the anti-inflation programme of September 1976, known as the Barre Plan).

We can see from the survey carried out in April 1981 by the statistics department of the Ministry of Labour how many agreements were in force just before the change of administration and, by comparing its findings with those of the survey conducted in 1972 by the National Institute of Statistics and Economic Studies (INSEE), we can gain a clearer picture of the advances that had been made in collective bargaining and the shortcomings that still existed. In 1981, when there were 1,093 agreements in force (295 of them extended agreements), the proportion of industrial establishments covered by at least one collective agreement was 86.2 per cent (as against 62.1 per cent in 1972) and the proportion of workers covered was 90.4 per cent (as against 74.6 per cent in 1972). During this period there was a great increase in the number of collective agreements in establishments with fewer than 50 employees. Many of the agreements now in force are of very limited scope, covering only a few hundred workers, while conversely more than half of the labour force is covered by a mere 40 agreements. Plant bargaining is only of real importance in establishments with more than 200 employees (29.5 per cent of establishments with between 200 and 499 employees have plant agreements, and 45 per cent of those with 500 or over). Workers who are not covered by any collective agreement are to be found mainly in commerce, the services and construction as well as in the less industrial regions of the country.

Because the new agreements are of such recent date there is little information on which to base an assessment of their impact on the bargaining scene. A few points can nevertheless be made. As regards national agreements (746), the increase in 1982 was relatively greater than in 1981 and occurred mainly in two types of agreements — extended collective agreements, and national industry and multi-industry agreements (negotiated at the confederation level) extended mainly as a result of negotiations on the reduction of working time. The biggest increase was in subnational industry agreements,

Table 1. Agreements in force

	On 31 March 1975	On 31 December 1983
National and multi-industry		
agreements		
Extended	112	198
Not extended	141	220
Total	253	418
Regional agreements		
Extended	41	77
Not extended	88	223
Total	129	300
Departmental and local agreements		
Extended	100	135
Not extended	370	340
Total	470	475
Total agreements	**852**	**1 193**

Source: Ministry of Labour.

Table 2. Agreements signed and registered with the Ministry of Labour (including codicils)

Year	No.	Year	No.	Year	No.
1951	156	1969	1 445	1975	1 659
1955	578	1970	1 413	1977	1 295
1960	829	1971	1 393	1978	1 284
1966	1 054	1972	1 693	1979	1 487
1967	1 162	1973	1 647	1980	2 177
1968	1 626	1974	1 621		

Source: C. Jézéquel: "Aperçus statistiques sur la vie conventionnelle, en France", in *Droit social*, June 1981, p. 462.

with commerce starting to fill the negotiating vacuum from which it had previously suffered. Although the pace slackened somewhat in 1983 (as a result of the eclipse of hours of work and organisation of working time as bargaining topics), that year saw the conclusion of 1,003 codicils to previous agreements and 45 agreements in industrial sectors, of which 620 dealt with wages (a consequence of the obligation imposed by the Act of 13 November 1982) affecting 2.5 million workers. At the plant level, 4,850 agreements were concluded, 2,895 of them dealing with the workers' right of expression and 1,955 with wages and hours of work. The negotiating gap was further reduced: of the

3.5 million wage earners who were not covered by a collective agreement at the end of 1982, half a million have since been brought into the fold, and for 1.2 million others negotiations are under way.

Following this quantitative appraisal we can now adopt a more qualitative approach by examining the different levels at which bargaining is possible. Actually there are only a few cases in which the choice of bargaining level is dictated by the nature of the problem to be dealt with and where one can imagine a "rational" breakdown of bargaining topics; more often than not, it is strategic reasons that determine the choice of one level rather than another. During the period under review agreements have mainly innovated at the levels where legislation least envisaged it: the multi-industry and plant levels.

Action at the multi-industry level, which embraces all occupations, may be said to have had three main foci: co-ordinating results achieved at other levels (as was the case, for example, with paid leave and salaried status), though this can be done just as well by legislation; promoting bargaining in order to set wheels in motion (which was the case with declarations of intent or framework agreements such as the one dealing with working conditions); direct negotiation on a particular topic (as was the case with continuous training, a guaranteed income for the over-60s, compensation for partial unemployment, supplementary pensions and the reduction of working hours).

At the level of industry-wide negotiation, which was the rule up to 1971, complete disorder reigns. Some industries negotiate at the national level (chemicals and textiles, for example) but others prefer the local level and rule out any national agreement (e.g. metalworking). Sometimes (as in the construction industry) the national agreement explicitly relegates some matters — including wages — to supplementary local agreements. At other times, wage scales are determined at the national level with perhaps some local codicils being added later. Furthermore, the gap between the average number of workers covered by a national agreement (18,100 in 1981), a regional agreement (9,000) or a departmental or local agreement (5,600) is without any great significance in view of the enormous differences in the number of workers covered by particular agreements: the national agreement for the chemicals industry covers 350,000 workers and the one for the button industry only 1,500; regional agreements may cover a few hundred workers or as many as 650,000 (in the metalworking industry in the Paris area). Finally, the scope of the agreements leads us into a very complex field, as can be illustrated by the case of metalworking. In this industry manual and clerical workers, technicians, draughtsmen and supervisors are covered primarily by territorial agreements, which are supplemented by national agreements containing provisions on specific matters such as job security and supplementary pensions for foremen. Agreements for managerial staff are always concluded at the national level. The obligations arising out of the Auroux legislation should help to give a fresh impetus to industry-wide bargaining.

They should also give a new lease of life to bargaining at the plant level, where there has already been a proliferation of small and informal bargaining sessions (simple talks, oral agreements, negotiations culminating in a protocol or unsigned agreement); these often give rise to disputes over such issues as formal requirements not being observed or the signatories not having legal authority to conclude agreements. While some plant agreements have acted as a stimulus (in the areas of paid leave and supplementary pensions, for example), plant bargaining is not yet common practice; it is still mainly limited to large enterprises that can "afford" a social policy. It is undoubtedly at this level that the new section L. 132-27 of the Labour Code innovates most, with plant bargaining making it possible to deal with specific problems where they actually arise and giving workers the possibility of intervening effectively in the life of the enterprise.

New bargaining areas

Corresponding to the profusion of levels and forms of bargaining and the vagueness of the legal framework is the unevenness of the content of collective agreements. In March 1981, 11 per cent of national agreements were silent on the free exercise of trade union rights, 13 per cent on conditions of hiring and firing, 45 per cent on the industry-wide minimum wage, 62 per cent on the qualifications required for the various categories of jobs, and 87 per cent on ways of implementing the principle of "equal pay for equal work" for women and young persons. In addition, many of them need to be updated: on 1 January 1984, out of the 1,193 agreements in force, 53 had not been reviewed for five years. For their part, plant agreements on wages and hours of work cover only 7.5 per cent of workers in the private sector, the proportion varying considerably according to the size of the enterprise (20 per cent in those with more than 500 employees and 1.5 per cent in those with 50 to 149) and the sector concerned (57 per cent in the automobile industry and 16 per cent in chemical by-products and pharmaceuticals, and even less in commerce and services).

The oldest area is that of wages, for which collective bargaining — often circumscribed by the public authorities (Barre Plan of 1976, freezing of prices and wages by the Mauroy Government in June 1982) — is conducted at the industry level, the general practice being to negotiate only minima which enterprises, by unilateral decision, may exceed. The result is a gap between the negotiated and actual wage levels: in clothing or department stores actual wages tend to be close to the SMIC and hence it is the labour legislation rather than collective bargaining that determines wages here; in metalworking and the more sophisticated services, however, actual wages are well above the negotiated minima and it is plant-level negotiations that play the main role. The employers uphold this policy on two grounds: the need to take into account the diversity of enterprises and the need to retain room for manoeuvre if bargaining is continued at the plant level. The obligation laid down by the Auroux legislation to conduct annual bargaining on actual wage rates will doubtless alter this situation. In the field of wages there were only three innovations to speak of during the period under review. The multi-industry agreement of 10 December 1977 stipulated the minimum extent to which salaried status was to be granted to manual workers; the agreement of 19 July 1978, aimed at improving wage adjustments for the lowest-paid workers, especially manual workers, can be regarded as a continuation of the SMIC policy; and finally, following up the decision taken at the "Grenelle" talks in 1968 and the determination displayed in 1974 to work out a uniform scale, the agreement of 23 July 1975 replaced the old job classification system of 1945.

A second area, which at the start of the 1970s had constituted a notable innovation owing both to its subject-matter and to the new links it established between legislation and agreements, is that of continuous training. The agreement of 9 July 1970, whose provisions had been incorporated into the Act of 16 July 1971, was the subject of a codicil on 9 July 1976, but the new provisions do not so much define new individual rights as specify the means and principles of a joint policy.

A new area which has been opened up for bargaining and which the Auroux legislation also seeks to promote is that of working conditions. This is an area in which no clear boundaries have yet been set, but to which the Government attaches great importance and which the employers would like to turn into a showcase. The multi-industry agreement of 17 March 1975 contains few precise obligations but it sets forth general principles and guide-lines for industry-wide bargaining. The industry agreements concluded since then have sometimes had an innovative content (chemicals agreement of 26 March 1976, petroleum agreement of 4 June 1976). A particular aspect that has aroused much interest recently, and following the promulgation of the Auroux Acts is destined to become a compulsory subject for bargaining, is hours of work. Regarded up to 1974 as essentially a social issue, with the recession it has become an economic issue under the slogan of "work-sharing". The Act of 16 July 1976 introducing compensatory rest for overtime was followed up by the agreement of 26 March 1980 on reducing the number of hours of work for workers without a regular schedule, a leap-frogging process that has continued since with Ordinance No. 82-41 of 16 January 1982 on hours of work and leave with pay [17] being followed up by bargaining; between 1981 and 1 May 1984, 88 industry-wide agreements covering 5.5 million workers have reduced the average working week from 40.8 to 39.1 hours with arrangements for rescheduling timetables being the commonest form of reorganising working time. Furthermore, the Government has introduced a scheme to assist enterprises planning a reduction of the working week by at least two hours under "solidarity contracts", which the enterprises sign with the State and which often contain provisions concerning voluntary early retirement. The forecasting office of the Ministry of Finance estimates that these measures will create or preserve 70,000 jobs, or 0.5 per cent of total employment.

An important area for bargaining in the current economic situation is that of job security. While in the initial stages of the recession efforts were concentrated mainly on protecting employment, they are now focused on organising the inevitable restructuring of industries in the best possible manner. In the past the agreements, mostly multi-industry ones, dealt with compensation for full-time unemployment for economic reasons (multi-industry agreements of 1958 and 1974), compensation for partial unemployment (multi-industry agreement of 1968 and its subsequent codicils), and protection of employment through the establishment of joint employment committees (multi-industry agreement of 1969 and its codicil). Lack of space does not allow us to describe in detail the package of employment policy instruments which have given rise to increasingly complex labour-management relations. But it may be said that the iron and steel agreements (1977 and 1979) foreshadowed a number of provisions in the plan for modernising that industry adopted by the Government in February 1984. In this attempt to reconcile economic and social needs through a "social approach to unemployment" — a package combining training for youth under 25 (training contracts), shorter hours of work, a lower age of retirement and compulsory early retirement (solidarity contracts) — the traditional distinction between what are matters for legislation and what are subjects for collective bargaining tends to become blurred, leading us towards what some do not hesitate to call "neo-corporatism".

THE PROBLEMS

The numerous problems facing the social partners at present may be said to fall into three main categories: legal and jurisdictional; tactical; and economic.

Legal and jurisdictional problems

The relationship between the law and collective agreements in France has always been highly complex, fluctuating with historical events. Sometimes the law has been inspired by agreements, sometimes bargaining has followed the law. In fact the State influences collective bargaining in a number of ways: by setting an example in the labour field through its role as an employer in the public sector; by maintaining the major economic balances through its policy decisions — arbitrating, encouraging, discouraging or providing guidance, as the case may be; setting specific social policy guide-lines by suggesting subjects for negotiation, as was the case in 1978.

A number of interactions between the law and collective agreements can be identified. Legislation can extend agreements; and an agreement can implement legislative provisions (e.g. agreements cushioning the social effects of industrial restructuring). Agreements can lead to the law being amended (this was the case with salaried status for manual workers, maternity leave and vocational training; it could be the case in the future for hours of work). The law can reproduce the provisions of an agreement (for example the Act of 19 January 1978 gave legal force to the multi-industry agreement of 10 December 1977 on the salaried status of manual workers). There can be genuinely negotiated laws (the Act of 27 December 1968 on trade union branches, the Act of 13 July 1971 on collective bargaining). These complex legal relationships between the law and collective bargaining have not disappeared today, quite the contrary. In this respect the Act of 4 August 1982 on the workers' right to express their views in the enterprise may be said to be a truly experimental piece of legislation. Its practical implementation is to be determined through bargaining in enterprises with more than 200 employees (below that figure negotiations are not compulsory) and, in the light of the results, a new law will be adopted before 31 December 1985 whereupon the enterprises will have to bring their agreements into line with the legal provisions.

It has been noted that "bargaining is becoming harder and harder to distinguish from consultation; a composite of the two has gradually emerged. The parties do more than consult but less than bargain in the Anglo-Saxon sense of the term".[18] This is particularly the case in enterprises where the representative institutions do not always confine themselves to their appointed role: taking up grievances (in the case of staff delegates), consultation and participation (for the works committees) and bargaining (for the trade union representations). The frequent overlapping of terms of reference blurs the distinctions between representative institutions in almost 50 per cent of cases. The new legislation is not likely to untangle this situation as can be seen from the following example. The subject of working conditions is covered by the workers' individual right of expression (section L. 461-1 of the Labour Code), but the health, safety and working conditions committee (CHSCT) deals with the matter too (section L. 236-2) as does the works committee (section L. 432-2) and, in enterprises where there are one or more trade union representations, there is an obligation to negotiate on the matter each year, at least as regards the organisation of working time (section L. 132-27). In addition, where there is no works committee (section L. 432-3) or CHSCT (section L. 422-4), staff delegates can intervene in place of these committees to carry out all or part of their functions. Finally, the site delegate can also have his say on the subject.

Tactical problems

Except in nationalised enterprises where the total wage bill is a subject for collective bargaining, the employers' negotiators never commit themselves on actual wages, leaving these to be settled at the enterprise level. The workers' organisations, for their part, reject any industrial peace clause. It is clear, then, that in practice the collective agreement is closer to a simple "record" than to a contract or a standard-setting instrument, and the fact that its duration is unspecified reinforces this characteristic. It may be worth while therefore to look into the factors which make it so difficult for the partners to commit themselves and lead to so much importance being attached to terminology that the word "nominalism" has been used to describe the situation in France.

Collective agreements are based on the legal fiction that the signatories commit those they represent. In fact there is a gulf between law and fact since, in practice, the capacity to enter into commitments depends on the structures, the by-laws and the attitudes of the negotiating organisations. We have already spoken of the inconsistency of the employers' and trade union *structures* at the industry level, which hardly facilitates bargaining. A more rational demarcation of responsibilities should take into account two factors: the definition of the bargaining levels and the organising capacity of the bargaining parties. As far as the workers' organisations are concerned, perhaps only the French Democratic Confederation of Labour (CFDT) has tried, for strategic reasons, to rationalise its structures. The *by-laws* should, for their part, permit negotiations; the reform of the CNPF in October 1969 was aimed precisely at enabling it to enter into commitments at the national level (except as regards wages, which are the concern of the individual enterprises and occupational organisations), but the influence it exercises over different industries and enterprises has varied and the extension procedure has sometimes been the only way of getting the agreements applied in practice. As for the *attitudes* of the bargaining parties, they have usually concurred in a common refusal to assume obligations. Until the end of the 1960s it could be said that neither the employers nor the trade unions had any intention of committing themselves. For the employers, a collective agreement was a means of "stabilising" labour relations; for the trade unions, it was a source of protection. The upsurge in multi-industry agreements in the early 1970s suggested that employers might be expected to take the initiative in breaking the deadlock, but the situation was completely altered by the recession, when management returned to its shell determined not to surrender its freedom of action. Since the obligation to negotiate laid down by the Auroux legislation is not an obligation to conclude agreements, the chances of establishing the new labour relations which the legislature had in mind can only be judged at present from the reactions of the social partners to these legislative innovations.

Among the employers there are certainly some who consider that the Auroux legislation could generate real social progress, but on the whole the employers reject the principle of compulsory negotiations in the enterprise. They also oppose the right of majority trade union organisations to veto the entry into force of a works agreement providing for exceptions either to laws and regulations or to the wage provisions agreed upon at the industry or multi-industry level. Now that the laws have been promulgated the employers will have to decide what tactics to adopt. There are two possible attitudes.[19] The first would be to try as far as possible to maintain the status quo. The second would be to take a more dynamic approach and try to convert a constraint into an asset: they could take advantage of the annual negotiations, for example, to persuade the workers to give up certain acquired rights in return for other benefits, along the lines of the productivity bargaining initiated by ESSO at Fawley. When handled intelligently, the workers' right to direct expression can, for its part, constitute a real counterweight to the strengthening of trade unionism in the enterprise; but for this to happen, the executives will have to take the lead and gain the backing of the supervisory staff.

For the workers' organisations it is mainly the right to veto and the right of expression that have created dissension. The General Confederation of Labour

(CGT) takes a generally favourable view of the Auroux legislation but sees a number of shortcomings in such matters as the right to strike and the right to lay off workers, and has reservations about workers becoming involved in employers' decisions on economic matters. In the field of trade union rights, while acknowledging that some advances have been achieved, the CGT deplores the gaps still remaining and considers that workers are not guaranteed the indispensable means for exercising their right of expression. The CFDT, for its part, does not think the new provisions concerning trade union rights are strong enough, though there are two basic provisions that it regards as a significant breakthrough helping to make economic life more democratic: the obligation to negotiate and the workers' right to express their views. In reply to those who are sceptical about the effectiveness of this right, the CFDT points to the impact its exercise may have on productivity in the enterprise and on trade unionism itself, since the movement will be compelled to make adjustments in response to the views expressed by groups of workers. The General Confederation of Labour-*Force Ouvrière* (FO) naturally supported the objective of enhancing collective bargaining. On the other hand, there are three aspects that it considers particularly dangerous and in some instances legally questionable: the obligation to negotiate in the enterprise and the precedence that plant agreements take over the industry-wide agreements, with the risk that the latter may end up carrying no weight at all; the possibility for majority trade union organisations to oppose the entry into force of plant agreements; and the right of two representative organisations of employers and trade unions to veto the extension of collective agreements. The FO had no choice but to declare its hostility to the workers' right of direct expression since it believes that it is for trade unions alone to make collective commitments and to speak and act on behalf of the working class. The point of view of the French Confederation of Christian Workers (CFTC) differs yet again. Its conception of trade unionism necessarily led it to support the workers' right of expression; on the other hand, like the FO, it has strong reservations about two measures which it feels might constitute a challenge to established bargaining policy: the 50 per cent minimum representation of trade union organisations required to give effect to a negotiated agreement and the right of two organisations to veto the extension of collective agreements. The General Confederation of Executive Staffs (CGC) holds similar views.

Economic problems

Collective bargaining cannot be divorced from the economic situation, as events have shown. First of all, the recession, by jeopardising employment, has reduced the pressure exerted by workers as measured, for example, in terms of industrial disputes (see table 3). Next, it has narrowed down the scope of what is negotiable. Furthermore, although plant bargaining gained momentum in the early 1970s in the wake of the events of 1968 and the extension of salaried status to manual workers, and in turn gave a boost to industry-wide bargaining, from the mid-1970s on industry-wide bargaining grew rarer and weaker while plant

Table 3. Labour disputes from 1969 to 1976 and from 1977 to 1983 (annual average)

Indicator	1969-76	1977-83
No. of strikes	3 663	2 965
No. of strikers	1 986 000	690 000
No. of days lost	3 533 000	2 310 000

Source: Ministry of Labour.

bargaining also lost some of its substance. This, too, was a logical development. In a country like France, where demand-led recovery policies very rapidly run into balance-of-payment problems (as happened in 1976 and 1981), the first requirement is to curb inflation. Moreover, if the effects of external factors are to be held in check, a modernisation programme will be indispensable, and this can only be successful if the short-term macro-economic constraints are observed. All this presupposes the implementation of an incomes and prices policy involving tight controls on collective bargaining. This is particularly the case in the public sector and civil service where, at the start of the 1970s, the policy of "progress agreements" (which provided for the double indexing of wages — to the GNP and the productivity of the undertaking) had given bargaining an innovative character and where, since the introduction of an austerity programme on 13 June 1982, bargaining policy has been more or less frozen. Paradoxically, this first austerity programme (which was to be followed by another on 25 March 1983) was launched at the very time that Parliament was debating the Bill to introduce the annual obligation to negotiate actual wages. Reviving a planned economy policy and going well beyond the 1976 stabilisation plan, Prime Minister Mauroy suspended the Act of 11 February 1950 and imposed a freeze on wages for four-and-a-half months followed by a period of 18 months of controls — which left little room for manoeuvre in wage bargaining — and at the same time prohibited wage indexing (a prohibition already set forth in the Ordinance of 4 February 1959, but little observed in practice). One could doubtless argue that, while wages were the general focus of workers' bargaining demands during the period of economic growth, since the recession another general focus is increasingly being sought which may well turn out to be employment and working conditions under the slogan of "work-sharing".

Apart from the technical provisions which have attracted the attention of specialists, the new legislation poses two basic problems: that of the future of the industrial relations system and that of the ability of the work community to express the diverse and changing aspirations of the workforce. By endeavouring to stimulate bargaining at the industry level and consolidate it at the plant level, the law is attempting to establish a framework rather than regulations for industrial relations and a system that relies heavily on the social partners for defining the rules governing their relations. In introducing provisions to enable the workers to express themselves on everyday matters and suggest ways and means of adapting working conditions and work organisation, the lawmakers have put their faith in the workers' sense of initiative. Reuniting the work community and enabling each to exercise his own responsibilities — these, in short, seem to be the underlying orientations of the new body of law which is emerging and which is based on a clear and comprehensive concept of labour policy. However, leaving aside the economic difficulties arising out of the present recession, it may be asked whether this will suffice to overcome the weight of tradition and the social inertia that are still so strong.

Notes

[1] Professor of Economics, University of Paris X-Nanterre.

[2] Yves Delamotte: "Recent collective bargaining trends in France", in *International Labour Review* (Geneva, ILO), Apr. 1971, pp. 351-377.

[3] For an English translation of this Act, see *Legislative Series* (Geneva, ILO), 1982 — Fr. 2D.

[4] Jean-Daniel Reynaud: *Les syndicats, les patrons de l'Etat. Tendances de la négociation collective en France* (Paris, Les Editions ouvrières, 1978).

[5] Gérard Adam: "La négociation collective en France. Eléments de diagnostic", in *Droit social* (Paris), Dec. 1978, pp. 420-451.

[6] Echange et Projets: "La négociation salariale. Pourquoi? Comment?", ibid., Nov. 1978, pp. 392-398.

[7] *La France en mai 1981, forces et faiblesses* (Paris, La Documentation française, 1982).

[8] ibid.

[9] Jean Auroux: *Les droits des travailleurs.* Rapport au Président de la République et au Premier ministre (Paris, 1981).

[10] See *Legislative Series*, 1982 — Fr. 2B.

[11] ibid., 1982 — Fr. 1D.

[12] ibid., 1982 — Fr. 1C.

[13] ibid., 1982 — Fr. 1E.

[14] ibid., 1982 — Fr. 2C.

[15] ibid., 1982 — Fr. 2E.

[16] ibid., 1982 — Fr. 2D.

[17] ibid., 1982 — Fr. 1B.

[18] Adam, op. cit., p. 442.

[19] Michèle Millot and Jean-Pol Roulleau: *L'entreprise face aux lois Auroux* (Paris, Les Editions d'organisation, 1983).

RECENT TRENDS IN COLLECTIVE BARGAINING IN THE FEDERAL REPUBLIC OF GERMANY

Friedrich Fürstenberg [1]

BACKGROUND

The changing picture of collective bargaining in the Federal Republic of Germany has to be seen against the backdrop of several fundamental aspects of industrial relations — the principles of "conflictual co-operation" and bargaining autonomy, the dual system of negotiation, and the general legal framework.

Conflictual co-operation and bargaining autonomy. Collective bargaining is intended to establish and maintain a balance of interests between the parties or, to put it another way, to transform conflicting interests into limited co-operation. For organised labour it is a means of securing acceptable conditions of work, an equitable share of the benefits of economic growth, and a voice in establishing the basic rules and procedures governing work. For employers it is a means of arriving at uniform standards on pay and working hours and stable structures for working conditions, as well as generating a co-operative climate. While the two parties are not expected to renounce their differing interests — which would be tantamount to losing their identity — they are bound to refrain, while the agreement they have concluded remains in force, from any conflictual action with respect to the issues dealt with in the agreement. At the same time, the large degree of bargaining autonomy enjoyed by labour and management under the system of industrial relations in the Federal Republic of Germany relieves the public authorities of having constantly to intervene for the purpose of settling labour disputes.[2]

The dual system of negotiation. Bargaining takes place at two levels. The negotiation of collective agreements properly so called normally takes place at the industry level (region by region), and exceptionally at the enterprise level. The workers' side is always represented by the trade union. At the workplace or intra-plant level, the works council — which represents all the workers of the enterprise, whether unionised or not — may negotiate with the employer on certain issues that are subject to co-determination and are enumerated in the

209

Works Constitution Act of 1972,[3] but these negotiations do not lead to collective agreements in the legal sense of the term.

The legal framework. The legislation laying down the fundamental principles of collective bargaining in the Federal Republic of Germany has not been challenged or amended in recent years. Provisions establishing freedom of association and bargaining autonomy are contained in the Constitution. The basic rights and obligations of the parties to negotiation are governed by the Collective Agreements Act, as consolidated on 25 August 1969.[4]

* * *

While these fundamental aspects of the industrial relations system have weathered the two crises of the 1970s remarkably well, a number of developments have occurred, especially since 1979, in response to changes in the economic and social climate. We shall first look at the organisation and role of the parties to negotiation before going on to discuss the changes that have occurred in legislation, collective agreements and bargaining procedures and to see what results have been produced by evolving strategies. Finally, a few words will be said about the co-determination system as it affects collective bargaining, recent trends in labour disputes, and the outlook for the future.

THE PARTIES TO COLLECTIVE BARGAINING

The workers' side

Collective bargaining is conducted by four workers' organisations: the German Confederation of Trade Unions (DGB), which in 1981 had a total membership of 7,957,512 spread over 17 affiliated unions; the Confederation of German Civil Servants (DBB), with 820,262 members (1981); the German Union of Salaried Employees (DAG), with 499,439 members (1981); and the Confederation of Christian Trade Unions (CGB), with 294,916 members (1981). The distribution of the main categories of employees among these four organisations is shown in table 1.

Membership of DGB-affiliated unions grew appreciably during the 1970s, rising from 30 per cent of the labour force in 1970 to 35.1 per cent in 1979 (33.5 per cent in 1981). An increase occurred in all employee categories: from 32.8 to 40 per cent among civil servants (37.1 per cent in 1981), from 12.6 to 17.2 per cent among white-collar workers (16.8 per cent in 1981), and from 40.9 to 49.4 per cent among blue-collar workers (47.6 per cent in 1981). However, since students and pensioners are included in the trade union statistics these categories would have to be deducted in order to obtain a wholly accurate picture of the level of unionisation. It will also be noted from the above figures in parentheses for 1981 that a downward trend has occurred since the late 1970s, reflecting a deterioration in the general economic situation.

Table 1. Distribution of trade union membership, 1981 (%)

Employees	Civil servants	White collar	Blue collar	Total	Women
Organised employees					
DGB	50.23	72.47	97.62	83.13	77.49
DBB	44.22	2.58	0.31	8.57	9.87
DAG	–	21.25	–	5.22	9.11
CGB	5.55	3.70	2.07	3.08	3.53
Organised employees as % of all employees					
Total	73.92	23.14	48.78	40.24	23.88
DGB	37.13	16.77	47.62	33.45	18.50
DBB	32.69	0.59	0.15	3.45	2.36
DAG	–	4.92	–	2.10	2.18
CGB	4.10	0.86	1.01	1.24	0.84

Note: Civil servants made up 9.55 per cent of the labour force, white-collar workers 42.69 per cent and blue-collar workers 47.76 per cent. Women accounted for 37.5 per cent.

Source: Institut der deutschen Wirtschaft: *Zahlen zur wirtschaftlichen Entwicklung der Bundesrepublik Deutschland* (Cologne, 1982), table 85.

Under the dual system of negotiation described earlier the works councils play an active part in workplace and intra-plant bargaining. Such bargaining, however, is conducted on a statutory basis and excludes recourse to strikes. Some of the changes that have occurred in recent years as a result of works council elections are shown in table 2.

While the total number of non-union candidates elected to works councils increased, the proportion of non-union council members in the white-collar sector decreased sharply. It may be mentioned in passing that non-union candidates frequently become union members after their election.

In line with its federal structure, the real strength of the DGB lies in industry-wide unions. The biggest three are the Metalworkers' Union (IG Metall), with 2,622,069 members (1981), the Public Service, Transport and Communications Workers' Union, with 1,181,460 members (1981), and the Chemical, Paper and Ceramics Workers' Union, with 654,633 members (1981). These unions also dominate the four-yearly congress of the DGB. The DGB itself does not conclude collective agreements but mainly performs co-ordinating and representative functions for its member organisations.

Six DGB-affiliated unions also represent public employees. A high percentage of civil servants, however,[5] are organised in separate occupational associations. The DBB is the largest single organisation representing civil servants.

Except for the CGB, trade unions in the Federal Republic do not have any religious or ideological affiliation, so that there is ample room for internal

Table 2. Representation achieved in works council elections, 1975, 1978 and 1981 (%)

Works council members	Year of election	DGB	DAG	CGB	ULA [1]	Other	Non-union
Total	1975	67.9	10.4	2.6	← 1.6 →		17.5
	1978	58.6	14.6	0.8	← 2.8 →		23.3
	1981	63.2	8.5	3.7	0.4	0.9	23.3
Blue collar [2]	1975	87.1	—	3.1	← 1.3 →		8.5
	1978	78.3	5.6	0.8	← 3.8 →		11.6
	1981	88.2	0.9	2.4	0.0	1.9	6.6
White collar [2]	1975	43.9	22.2	2.2	← 2.8 →		28.9
	1978	43.3	21.6	0.8	← 2.1 →		32.3
	1981	62.5	22.3	1.6	0.5	1.1	12.0
Chairmen	1975 [3]	78.8	2.6	0.0	← 0.0 →		1.5
	1978	71.8	14.4	0.1	← 0.7 →		13.1
	1981	79.9	5.2	0.5	0.5	3.4	10.5

[1] Union of Executive Staffs. No separate breakdown for the ULA was available for 1975 and 1978. [2] The figures for blue- and white-collar workers not affiliated to the DGB or the DAG are incomplete owing to lack of data from some organisational sub-units. [3] No response from 17.1 per cent of the chairmen for this year.

Source: Institut der deutschen Wirtschaft: *Zahlen zur wirtschaftlichen Entwicklung der Bundesrepublik Deutschland* (Cologne, 1982), table 87.

competition among the various political persuasions, of which the Social Democrats are the most influential. Although the trade union movement operates on the principles of representative democracy, there is an important element of direct member participation. Except in the case of the Printing Workers' Union, a ballot among all the members resulting in a 75 per cent majority in favour is required before a strike may be called. By and large, however, trade union policy tends to be highly centralised for three reasons: collective bargaining takes place mainly at the industry and the regional level; the policy pursued by most unions includes societal issues and it is thought that these are best handled by higher trade union bodies able to take a more general view; and the trend is towards an increasingly bureaucratic and legalistic approach to labour problems, which implies the need for experts.

The employers' side

Employers' organisations are similarly centralised. The Confederation of German Employers' Associations (BDA) represents 47 national employers' federations and 365 regional groups, which in 1977 covered 80 per cent of all the enterprises in the country. Like the DGB, the BDA does not participate directly in collective bargaining but provides support as a co-ordinating body. It also serves as a brain trust, running a research institute and special research units.

The real centres of employers' power, however, are the member organisations. With the exception of enterprise-level bargaining (e.g. at the *Volkswagenwerk*), which covers only a small proportion of employees, it is they who are the unions' bargaining partners. The numerous committees and subcommittees set up by the employers' federations play an important role in this respect by providing expert opinions and preparing policy guide-lines.

In the public sector local, Land and federal government employers have established special associations for centralised negotiations with their employees. The Federation of Local Government Employers' Associations (VKA) at the municipal level and the German Länder Government Employers' Association (TDL) at the Land level have been in existence since 1949. At the national level the Federal Minister of the Interior has been a partner in the negotiations since 1960.

The public authorities

Intervention by the Government in collective bargaining is rare. There is no government mediation since labour and management have their own voluntary conciliation system. On major issues, however, and especially in the event of a dispute, considerable informal consultation and exchange of information with the Government may take place. The experiment launched in 1967 with a view to promoting "concerted action" aimed at some sort of national incomes policy ultimately failed in 1977 and was not renewed. The fact remains, however, that if their main strategies are to be successful both employers and trade unions must take government action into account, e.g. policy decisions on whether or not to use public money to generate additional employment. The general orientation of government policy in the field of industrial relations is nevertheless that of fairly strict non-interference, thus respecting the principle of bargaining autonomy, limiting state influence to the establishment of a legal framework and providing statistical data to the parties on which they can base their decisions.

LEGISLATIVE DEVELOPMENTS

Recent structural changes in both the economy and society in general have led to some rethinking about what bargaining autonomy should actually mean under the Constitution. In its so-called co-determination ruling of 1 March 1979, the Federal Constitutional Court stressed that the measures needed to safeguard bargaining autonomy and the contents of collective bargaining should be spelt out by legislation in the light of present economic and social realities. It pointed out that industrial peace can be achieved by different means: not only through the adversarial bargaining system but also through arrangements that emphasise agreement and co-operation.[6] Legislation on co-determination should therefore not be regarded as undermining bargaining autonomy, which should be considered in the context of the industrial relations system as a whole.

Two main tendencies need to be singled out. First, government policy has an increasing impact on issues related to the working and living conditions of the

213

labour force, and government agencies are indirectly influencing decisions in the sphere of bargaining, thus taking out of the hands of the trade unions some of the issues that would normally be decided through the autonomous bargaining procedure. An example is the Government's introduction of general economic measures such as those aimed at stimulating investment. These obviously limit the scope for collective bargaining on wages.[7]

Second, the boundaries between the statutory activities of the works councils and the bargaining activities of the unions have shifted with the establishment of new areas of co-determination and new co-determination rights. The competence to deal with such questions as partial lay-offs and intra-plant wage fixing through the application of payment-by-results schemes, especially for piece rates, has been transferred to the works councils. It will easily be appreciated that under these circumstances the statutory activities of a works council may overlap with the traditional function of trade unions. Unions are therefore trying to strengthen their presence within the enterprises, especially by extending the shop-floor communications network of the union *(Vertrauensleute)*.

Moreover, a number of laws and regulations have been enacted recently that affect major aspects of collective bargaining, including minimum work environment standards (noise, lighting, ventilation, etc.) and the humanisation of work, protection against "socially unjustified" dismissals, protection for severely handicapped persons, guarantees for members of works councils, compensation negotiable between the works council and the employer in the event of dismissals due to organisational changes, tax-free capital accumulation by employees [8] under collective agreements, and improved pension plans. In other words, expanding labour legislation is tending indirectly to limit the scope for collective bargaining, including the possibility of fixing lower standards in collective agreements. There is thus a tendency for the contents and the legal boundaries of collective bargaining to shift according to societal change.

TRENDS IN COLLECTIVE AGREEMENTS AND BARGAINING PROCEDURES

Although collective agreements are legally binding, on the workers' side, only on union members, in practice their provisions are usually applied to all workers in the branch concerned. Any distinction in collective agreements between unionised and non-unionised workers was declared to be incompatible with the Constitution by a ruling of the Federal Labour Court in 1967.

Of the 38,537 collective agreements registered with the Federal Ministry of Labour and Social Affairs in 1979, 64 per cent were industry-wide agreements (covering the majority of employees) and 36 per cent were enterprise agreements (covering special cases). A distinction must also be made between master agreements and ordinary agreements. The latter regulate major conditions of work — wages, working hours, leave, etc. — usually for a period of one year, while the former establish a basic regulatory framework of longer duration. Of

Table 3. Proportion of all collective agreements containing selected benefits, 1974 and 1978 (%)

Benefits	1974	1978
Fringe benefits		
Holiday pay	79	93
Yearly bonus	60	76
Capital accumulation	77	92
Social protection		
Job security	32	52
Wage guarantees	40	62
Protection in the event of rationalisation	45	48
Supplementary old-age pension	–	23
Additional unemployment compensation	–	21
Wage payment during illness	30	42

Source: *Bundesarbeitsblatt* (Stuttgart), 1979, No. 9.

the 3,685 master agreements registered in 1978, 49 per cent were enterprise agreements.

As will be seen from table 3, a large number of collective agreements increasingly provide for a wide range of special benefits in addition to regulating general conditions of work.

Before considering recent developments in bargaining strategies, it may be useful to take a brief look at the various steps normally involved in bargaining procedures. These procedures, which follow a highly formal pattern, are not fixed by law but are based on internal union rules, custom and practice and sometimes collective agreements themselves. Let us take the case of IG Metall as an example.

1. Presentation of demands. The demands put forward and discussed in rank-and-file meetings and officers' meetings are screened by an internal trade union negotiating committee, which recommends to the union executive that it should notify the employers' federation of its wish to open negotiations with a view to the conclusion of a new agreement. After the union executive has taken a decision on the matter, the employer is informed of the demands four weeks before the termination of the agreement.

2. Start of bargaining. A bargaining committee is set up. Bargaining starts two weeks before the agreement expires.

3. Conduct of negotiations. The parties are required to negotiate peacefully during the four weeks following the termination of the agreement. After this period recourse may be had to demonstrations and other means of exerting pressure.

4. Failure to reach a new agreement. If a new collective agreement is not concluded, one or both parties may declare a breakdown in negotiations. The trade union negotiating committee then proposes a strike vote among all the union members.

5. Conciliation. The two parties may agree to submit the matter to conciliation. They may appeal jointly to a conciliation board within two working days after the breakdown in negotiations has been declared. After another working day has elapsed the appeal may be lodged by one party alone. The other party is bound to join in the proceedings after two more working days have elapsed. An independent chairman of the board must then be appointed without delay. The board must meet within three working days and submit a proposal for breaking the deadlock within five working days. The parties then have six working days for deciding whether to accept or refuse the board's proposal.[9]

In the public sector the nature of collective bargaining varies according to whether the workers concerned are public employees governed by private law or civil servants governed by public law. Public employees have the right to strike, while civil servants do not.

Unlike workers in the private sector, public employees are represented by competing unions and associations. Collective bargaining for white-collar and manual workers is thus conducted in a twofold manner: the public employers negotiate separately with the DGB-affiliated Public Service, Transport and Communication Workers' Union and with the "bargaining community" embracing the DAG and nearly 30 other occupational associations. These "triangular" negotiations have led to rather complicated situations since isolated agreements are impossible and the negotiating parties have to arrive at identical pay increases.

Though the conditions of service of civil servants are governed by statutory provisions, they are also determined in part by lobbying and hearings conducted by the Federal Minister of the Interior. The principal means used by organisations representing civil servants may therefore be said to be political in nature. Salary increases for civil servants usually follow the pay increases granted to public employees.[10]

BARGAINING STRATEGIES AND RESULTS

On the whole, the past decade has been marked by growing pressures on the bargaining parties due to deteriorating economic conditions. Three different periods can be distinguished, the last of which is only just getting under way. First, from 1974 to 1979 the Federal Republic's economy, by comparison with that of many other countries, adjusted remarkably well to the steep rise in oil prices. Both price and wage increases gradually declined, a moderate growth of the GDP was re-established, and unemployment continued to be limited to a few problem areas. The real challenge, however, came with the second oil price increase in 1979: during the next period, from 1979 to 1983, GDP growth fell off steeply, the economy contracted, and the rate of unemployment rose sharply. Inflation was kept reasonably low but was offset by wage increases to a diminishing extent, so that real earnings eventually declined. Lastly, starting in the second half of 1983, there have been some signs of a slight improvement in economic performance. The GDP is expected to show a small positive rate of growth in 1984 and unemployment to level off or perhaps even turn down. No sharp rise in prices or wages is anticipated. Thus a period of moderate recovery might be ahead.

The various trends over the decade are shown in table 4.

These developments have had obvious repercussions on the results of collective bargaining. While prior to 1974 the trade unions had scored large gains both in organisational strength and in material benefits for their members through collective agreements, that trend came to an abrupt halt with the first oil crisis. As table 5 shows, there was a pronounced decline in the average increase of negotiated real wages for major industries in the years that followed.

A major shift in trade union bargaining strategies has in fact taken place. Quantitative demands focusing on monetary gains have increasingly given way to qualitative demands, reflecting the changes that have occurred in labour market structures and working conditions. The concern with compensating inflation has lost its edge as a result of fairly stable prices. The greatest pressure on real wages comes from the present taxation system and the increase in social security contributions (together rising from 22.7 per cent of gross incomes in 1970 to 30.1 per cent in 1980), resulting in decreasing net incomes.

The new qualitative approach is focusing on five major problem areas:

(a) protection against the consequences of rationalisation;

(b) job security;

(c) reduction of working time;

(d) improvement of working conditions;

(e) skill-based pay systems.

According to a survey carried out by the Federal Ministry of Labour and Social Affairs, in January 1979 about half of the employed labour force was already covered by negotiated safeguards against the consequences of rationalisation, including guarantees against dismissal for workers over 55 years of age and/or with at least ten years of service in the enterprise, severance payments in the event of redundancy and guaranteed pay rates in the case of intra-enterprise transfer. As a result, the employment impact of rationalisation measures now falls largely on older workers who take the option of early retirement and on young persons trying to enter the labour market.

Perhaps the most important single determinant of bargaining strategies at present is concern for job security. Between 1973 and 1982 the rate of unemployment rose from 0.8 to 7.5 per cent, and the prospects for the coming years are not reassuring. Between 1982 and 1990 the labour force is expected to increase by 1.5 million persons and this demographic growth will be accompanied by the widespread introduction of new, labour-saving

Table 4.   Trends in major economic variables, 1973-82 (%)

Variable	1973	1975	1979	1981	1982
Wage increases	10.7	8.2	5.5	5.2	4.4
Price increases	6.9	6.0	4.1	5.9	5.3
GDP growth	4.5	−1.6	4.1	0.2	−1.25
Unemployment rate	0.8	3.6	3.2	4.4	7.5

Source: OECD: *Main economic indicators — Historical statistics 1964-83* (Paris, 1984).

Table 5.   Average annual increase of negotiated real wages in selected industries, 1970-79 (%)

Industry	1970-74	1975-79	1970-79
Manufacturing	5.4	2.6	3.7
Automobiles	5.7	2.5	3.8
Electrical engineering	5.1	2.4	3.5
Chemicals	4.6	2.6	3.4

Source: *WSI-Mitteilungen* (Cologne), 1982, Vol. 35, p. 25.

technologies. Though basically in favour of maintaining the principle of bargaining autonomy, both unions and employers are calling for more governmental action — albeit for different reasons. According to Mettelsiefen,[11] five strategic concepts are serving as guide-lines:

(a) a concept of wage restraint aimed at offsetting the labour-saving advantages of technological innovations and thereby maintaining labour demand;

(b) a consumer-oriented concept of purchasing power growth based on the assumption that productivity increases brought about by technological advances should be offset by corresponding increases in consumer demand;

(c) a concept of general economic growth to compensate for productivity increases; however, the existence of constraints on growth, such as the scarcity of resources, has recently received widespread attention, especially among the younger generation;

(d) a concept of reduced working time aimed at distributing available manpower more evenly and affording workers more leisure time; and

(e) a concept of planned technological change geared to general social needs — though there is much controversy over what these really are.

In this context trade union strategies are directed towards the general introduction of a 35-hour week, if possible with no loss of pay. This is a highly controversial issue. In May 1984 the IG Metall, taking an uncompromising position, launched the longest strike in the Federal Republic's history, directly involving 57,500 union members in Hessen, North Württemberg and North Baden, as well as 147,000 locked-out employees. Financial support for the strikers cost the union some DM 500 million. The strike was finally settled by voluntary conciliation. The compromise reached provides in particular for a 38.5-hour week, while allowing works councils and managements discretion to fix the week anywhere between 37 and 40 hours. Another strike called by the IG Druck led to a similar outcome. Other unions, such as the IG Bau-Steine-Erden, prefer a reduction of total working life under the government-sponsored voluntary early retirement scheme. For their part, the employers, supported by the Government, advocate flexible arrangements, preferably at the enterprise and plant levels, backed by governmental measures for reducing the age of retirement.

During the 1970s bargaining strategies also focused on measures for improving working conditions, especially measures to prevent heavier workloads and to reduce job stress. The second master agreement concluded in 1973 for the metalworking industry in North Württemberg and North Baden was a pace-setter in this field. An overall wage guarantee for piece-rate workers (the main area of concern) was established, radically reducing fluctuations in individual pay. New regulations on time-rated work and work breaks (providing for a break of at least five minutes per working hour) were also introduced. For the first time a general standard governing repetitive work processes was established, prescribing a minimum work cycle of 1.5 minutes, which was to be achieved, for example, by making assembly operations more flexible. Attempts by the IG Metall to have these standards gradually extended to other regions, however, met with stiff opposition from the employers. Similar regulations were adopted only at the Volkswagen works. In April 1982 an attempt was made to extend the main guide-lines, under a master agreement, to South Württemberg/Hohenzollern and South Baden, but so far the unions have not been able to persuade the employers to bargain on this particular question.

A related issue in collective bargaining is the protection of workers against skill dilution. Trade unions in the Federal Republic are trying to achieve such protection by pushing for the adoption of overall performance as a basis for wage differentiation in which all the job requirements (including those not directly affected by rationalisation) are taken into account. Thus a lower evaluation of one aspect of the job may be offset by a higher evaluation of another factor, such as mental stress. Wage differentiation, it is argued, should not be based on a single function but on the worker's qualifications for a broader range of work with multiple components. A collective agreement, effective since 1 January 1983, was signed between Joseph Voegele AG in Mannheim and IG Metall under which the wage rates for the firm's 1,000 employees are no longer based on job evaluation in the narrow sense but on qualifications and individual performance. The employers' federation in this sector strongly objected to the provisions and has since excluded this company from its ranks.

Economic and technological developments have led to a thorough reconsideration of bargaining strategies in general. This has resulted both in major shifts of focus and in great flexibility in contractual provisions. Collective bargaining in the country is still quite capable of innovation. It is noteworthy in this respect that so-called concession bargaining so far has been out of the question. Indeed, great emphasis is given to the maintenance of acquired rights. When the big ARBED steelworks in the Saar were saved from bankruptcy only by substantial government aid, the aid was granted on condition that the employees would accept a reduction in their annual bonus payment. This proviso, however, was interpreted by the steelworkers' union as a breach of the collective agreement, and the case is now before the labour court.

In the public sector the situation is somewhat different. There have been general wage freezes since 1982, a sizeable reduction in starting salaries has been applied by the Government, and experiments with job-sharing, for example among teachers, are being attempted.

COLLECTIVE BARGAINING AND CO-DETERMINATION

Federal legislation, by granting co-determination rights to special bodies, provides for an elaborate system of workers' participation. As a result, collective bargaining and co-determination are highly complementary within the industrial relations structure. Bargaining at the intra-plant and workplace level is normally subject to co-determination procedures, but collective bargaining on key issues and in key areas is highly centralised at the branch and regional levels. Nevertheless, as noted earlier, there may be some areas of overlap, as we shall see from a brief glance at some of the works council's functions.

Under the Works Constitution Act the works council has the right of co-determination in such varied matters as working hours and work breaks, temporary short-time working and overtime, annual leave, principles and methods of remuneration, job and bonus rates, time and place of wage payment, personnel selection and vocational training, technical devices to monitor the workers' performance, occupational safety and health, and housing and welfare services. This right also obtains in the event of technological change affecting the workplace, the production process or the working environment. If major operational changes are introduced in the enterprise the employer and the works council must try to agree on ways of reconciling their interests and, where the changes entail the dismissal of at least 25 employees (in enterprises employing between 500 and 1,199) or 60 employees (in enterprises employing 1,200 or more), on the introduction of an appropriate social compensation plan. In its recent draft Employment Promotion Bill the Federal Government is seeking to limit the application of these plans. Under the new provisions they would be compulsory only when the dismissals affect 60 and 120 employees respectively and, in the case of newly created enterprises, only after a four-year period of exemption has elapsed. This reflects the Government's general strategy to make the application of statutory co-determination rights more flexible in order to lighten the burden on employers and thereby provide them with incentives for creating new jobs.

At the same time, however, it should be borne in mind that, owing to co-determination provisions (and social security payments), rationalisation measures involving dismissals and transfers have so far been applied without causing major social unrest. Of the total number of social compensation plans, for example, only 10 to 20 per cent have been set up under conciliation procedures.

Table 6 shows the nature and coverage of institutionalised co-determination rights in 1978.

LABOUR DISPUTES

Despite the lack of legislation on strikes and lock-outs in the Federal Republic, the incidence of strikes is rather low. Workers dispose of elaborate grievance machinery and systems of voluntary conciliation. Lawful strikes are strictly limited to cases of deadlock in collective bargaining — i.e. "interest" disputes as opposed to "rights" disputes, which are those caused by disagreement over the interpretation or application of existing standards, especially collective agreements. Disputes falling within the broad area of intra-plant negotiation seldom get to the stage where they become a lawful strike issue. Political strikes, too, are unlawful.

The patterns of industrial disputes have, however, changed significantly over the past decade. As a result of the traumatic experience of the large strike movement in September 1969, which got partly out of the unions' control, negotiations have been regionalised to a greater extent and the duration of most agreements has been shortened to 12 months. Unofficial work stoppages — though rare — are also tolerated more than before.

The new patterns which emerged during the major strike in 1973 in the North Württemberg and North Baden metalworking industry led to the second master agreement mentioned earlier. The strategy used by the IG Metall since then lies in flexible tactics of partial work stoppages prior to the strike, of "focal" strikes which, while directed against selected companies, disrupt production on a far larger scale, and of mobilising public opinion on the union side. In this way, the huge costs and risks of industry-wide strikes are avoided.

Focal strikes may nevertheless have a considerable "spill-over" effect that is difficult to control. Regional strikes in a key industry or in strategically important enterprises may eventually block production in plants throughout the country, resulting in short-time working and temporary lay-offs. There is then growing public pressure for settling the dispute. The workers indirectly affected by these strikes are not entitled to strike pay and their claims for unemployment compensation are still pending before the courts. Management may control the situation in specific enterprises for a time by moving forward the annual plant closure, but this is only a palliative and in instances where the strikes have continued, the employers have reacted by setting up a central strike fund and

221

Table 6.   Nature and coverage of institutionalised co-determination rights, 1978

Enterprises	Employee representation	Employee coverage
Coalmining, iron and steel	Full parity in supervisory boards; labour director on managing board; works councils	0.6 million
Large joint-stock companies with more than 2,000 employees	Quasi-parity in supervisory boards; works councils	4.1 million
Smaller joint-stock companies	One-third of supervisory board seats; works councils	0.9 million
Other private enterprises with 5 or more employees	Works councils	9.4 million
Public service	Staff councils	3.6 million
Private enterprises with fewer than 5 employees	No institutionalised employee representation	3.0 million

Source: *Süddeutsche Zeitung* (Munich), 27 Feb. 1979.

countering focal strikes with lock-outs.[12] These lock-outs are strongly opposed by the trade unions, which consider them to be illegal.

In order to give this "new flexibility" an institutional basis, IG Metall has called for a revision of the rules governing conciliation under which more leeway would be allowed for workers to press their case through mass demonstrations. The employers, for their part, hoped to win a lawsuit calling for a ban on any militant action before conciliation procedures have been exhausted, but the Federal Labour Court ruled on 12 September 1984 that token strikes *(Warnstreiks)* during negotiations are not unlawful. A basic consensus none the less exists between trade unions and employers' federations that full-scale strikes should be used only as a last resort, and with great caution. Because of their broad scale, strikes are likely to entail considerable social costs for all the groups affected. The recent strike in the metalworking industry has once again shown that major disputes are accompanied by a wave of lawsuits from both sides, hampering co-operation for some time.

OUTLOOK

There is little doubt that collective bargaining in the Federal Republic of Germany will continue to be based on the principle of bargaining autonomy. The dual symbiotic structure of centralised bargaining between trade unions and employers' federations and of statutory negotiations between works councils and management also shows signs of great stability despite union attempts to gain greater control over what happens within the enterprise. Perhaps the most significant change in collective bargaining has been in the type of issue negotiated, resulting in a more "qualitative" approach. Master agreements have consequently gained in strategic importance. Both unions and employers' federations are trying to improve their capacity to mobilise their troops and exert pressure on the other party. But there are no signs of a new, increased militancy going beyond the degree of engagement always shown in matters of vital concern. So far conflictual co-operation seems to stand a very good chance of remaining the dominant pattern notwithstanding a gradual weakening of the broad worker-employer consensus that was nourished by the Federal Republic's "economic miracle" and underpinned negotiations for the past two decades. Even so, and despite the considerable asset of their well-tried and efficient consultation and bargaining machinery, labour and management may well have to devise some more innovative approaches if they are to cope jointly with current economic and technological challenges.

There are three main challenges calling for such innovative approaches, and all of them imply the need for greater flexibility in centralised collective bargaining. First, general improvements may have to be adapted to specific local circumstances. A step in this direction is the new collective agreement for the metalworking industry in North Württemberg and North Baden in which some leeway is allowed for works-level agreements.

Second, there is the problem of adjusting levels of wages and benefits to deteriorating economic conditions. The trend towards taking vested interests for acquired rights has led to steadily rising expectations and constantly growing demands. Because of persistently high rates of unemployment, however, strategies have to be devised for providing greater access to the labour market, particularly for young people. This may entail a reduction in the labour costs that were acceptable in more prosperous times.

Third, account has to be taken of the diversity of workers' needs and interests arising from differences in status and life-style. Examples are the large numbers of women seeking part-time employment today and the evolving patterns of gradual retirement (as at Siemens). Accordingly, closer attention is required in collective bargaining to ways and means of ensuring greater flexibility in working time arrangements, methods of remuneration and other conditions of work.

If it can meet these challenges successfully, collective bargaining in the Federal Republic of Germany will have shown that it is not merely an efficient mechanism of industrial relations but also a major instrument of social change.

Notes

[1] Professor of Sociology, Ruhr University, Bochum.

[2] See Walther Müller-Jentsch: "Kollektive Interessenvertretung: Das System der 'industriellen Beziehungen'", in W. Littek et al. (eds.): *Einführung in die Arbeits- und Industriesoziologie* (Frankfurt on Main, Campus, 1981), p. 384.

[3] For an English translation of this Act, see *Legislative Series* (Geneva, ILO), 1972 — Ger.F.R. 1.

⁴ For an English version of the consolidated text, see ibid., 1969 — Ger.F.R. 4.

⁵ A distinction is made between public employees and civil servants. As will be seen later, in the section on collective agreements and bargaining procedures, there is no real collective bargaining for civil servants.

⁶ See Federal Constitution Court ruling of 1 March 1979, in *BVerfGE* (Karlsruhe), No. 50, footnote 5, p. 371.

⁷ See Otto Ernst Kempen: "Ansätze zu einer Neuorientierung des gegenwärtigen Tarifvertragsrechts", in *Arbeit und Recht* (Cologne), 1980, Vol. 28, pp. 196 ff.

⁸ The provisions governing capital accumulation benefits are contained in the Capital Accumulation Act (No. 3) of 27 June 1970. For an English version of this Act, see *Legislative Series*, 1970 — Ger.F.R. 1.

⁹ See IG Metall: *Daten-Fakten-Informationen* (Frankfurt on Main, 1983), and Ulrich Zachert: "Der Ablauf einer Tarifverhandlung", in *Gewerkschaftliche Monatshefte* (Cologne), 1979, Vol. 30, pp. 172-178.

¹⁰ See Berndt K. Keller: "Public sector labor relations in West Germany", in *Industrial Relations* (Berkeley), 1978, Vol. 17, pp. 18-31, and idem: "Determinants of the wage rate in the public sector: The case of civil servants in the Federal Republic of Germany", in *British Journal of Industrial Relations* (London), 1981, Vol. 119, pp. 345-360.

¹¹ See B. Mettelsiefen: *Technischer Wandel und Beschäftigung* (Frankfurt on Main, Campus, 1981).

¹² See Klaus Lang: "Arbeitskampfformen im Wandel der Tarifpolitik", in *WSI-Mitteilungen* (Cologne), 1982, Vol. 35, pp. 543-552.

RECENT TRENDS IN COLLECTIVE BARGAINING
IN ITALY

Gino Giugni [1]

INTRODUCTION

Over the past ten years Italy has witnessed sweeping changes in the structure and content of collective bargaining as well as in the parties that conduct it. Both collective bargaining and the industrial relations system as a whole have been marked by even greater instability than in the 1950s and 1960s.[2]

The chief reason for this has of course been the recession, which has had a devastating effect on the economic and social system, and not just in Italy. The rises in the price of oil and raw materials during the 1970s, inflation (21.2 per cent in 1980 and 14.7 per cent in 1983) and soaring unemployment (12.5 per cent in 1983) have had serious repercussions on industrial relations. Furthermore, the economic and social order has been upset by the rapid and continuing spread of new technologies (computers, telematics and robotisation of the production process), by the increase in the tertiary sector workforce (which now outnumbers that of industry), by continued rural-urban migration, and by the new distribution of wage earners among the various socio-occupational categories that has resulted from a significant drop in the number of manual workers and a marked increase in that of white-collar staff.

The deterioration in the economic situation could not fail to influence the behaviour of the parties involved in the industrial relations system.

The State, in its efforts to mitigate the effects of the recession, has pressed ahead with the adoption of "emergency" legislation and has also set out to exert more control over collective bargaining or limit its scope: in many cases it has permitted departures from the legal standards in force, even to the workers' detriment.

The trade unions have had to reappraise their demands and their bargaining policy; they have shifted the emphasis from wages to control over the strategic choices of management and subsequently, even though this has caused serious internal dissension, to the Government's economic policy.

The employers have had to launch restructuring or reconversion projects with generally limited resources, and consequently have stepped up their resistance to increases in labour costs (particularly those triggered off automatically by the indexing of wages to the cost of living) and have insistently called for the waiving of statutory and negotiated obligations that curb the productivity of their undertakings.

Finally, since 1982 the Government itself has entered the arena, calling upon labour and management to accept a policy of restraint aimed at reducing public expenditure and bringing down the rate of inflation.

During the period under review industrial disputes did not follow the same trend as between 1968 and 1972. The situation then was particularly critical owing to the frequency of strikes and the number of strikers involved; it was a time of bitter, widespread and protracted social strife.[3]

Since 1973 the tide seems to have turned; [4] the number of strikes and days lost as a result of industrial action has dropped steadily, with the exception of the years fixed for the renewal of the most important national collective agreements, i.e. 1973, 1975, 1979 and 1982.

THE PARTIES TO COLLECTIVE BARGAINING

Workers' organisations

Trade union confederations

The biggest trade union organisations are three in number: the Italian General Confederation of Labour (CGIL), the Italian Confederation of Workers' Unions (CISL) and the Italian Workers' Union (UIL). The membership of each, with some qualifications, covers workers in both the public and the private sector.[5] The CGIL, with more than 4 million members, is composed of a Communist majority, a sizeable Socialist minority and a movement made up of political groups on the extreme Left. In the CISL (approximately 3 million members) the vast majority of its members, and especially its leaders, have ties with the Christian Democrats; there is also a smaller proportion with Socialist views and a wing which, though small, is politically very diversified (again, with representatives of the extreme Left well in evidence). Finally, the UIL (over 1 million members) has a Socialist majority with the remainder more or less evenly split between Republicans and Social Democrats. Only the CISL prohibits in its by-laws the formation of political groupings and holds firmly to this principle.

Two important events have marked the period under review: the conclusion (in July 1972) and then the dissolution (in 1984) of the CGIL-CISL-UIL Pact establishing a Unitary Federation.

As regards the conclusion of the Pact, it is sufficient to recall that in Italy a structural unification of the trade union confederations would have been the logical outcome of the struggles of 1968-69 and the establishment — almost spontaneously — of a new form of representation in the undertaking by so-called delegates (in actual fact, shop stewards) grouped in works councils. However, mainly because of resistance encountered within the CISL and UIL this structural unification was not achieved but instead a compromise in the form of the "federative pact" whose ties gradually grew weaker and weaker. In the end it was planned to create common structures and bodies at several levels (territorial and by industry) with equal representation and endowed with powers of decision by a four-fifths majority. The powers delegated to the organs of the federative structures were defined fairly broadly (they covered bargaining, and economic and social policy). In the undertakings the works councils, which were elected by all the workers and not just by the members of a trade union, were adopted as the grass-roots unitary organisation.

The establishment of the Unitary Federation — requiring joint formulation of policies at the national level and hence detailed internal bargaining — set in motion a process of centralisation of trade union organisation,[6] a process further accentuated by the recession, which put paid to the developments of the period 1968-72. At that time the industrial unions and works councils had been strengthened at the expense of the horizontal (i.e. multi-industry) structures like the confederations and provincial chambers of labour; after 1978, on the other hand, the number of industrial unions dropped by almost half,[7] the system of trade union finances was modified in a way that favoured the horizontal structures and, above all, new powers and authority were conferred on the latter, particularly the confederations.

The federative pact ceased to be applied in 1984 following divergences that appeared during three-sided negotiations with the Government and the employers (see below). The causes, of recent origin, are to be found in political, structural and cultural factors.

On the political plane, it should be noted that once the flame of unity of the early 1970s had died out, the federative pact received indirect backing up to 1978 from governments of "national unity", supported by the Communist Party. With the collapse of political unity, the split between the Communist Party and the parties which had formed several coalition governments became inevitable and the federative pact ran into more and more serious problems.

The main structural factors that reinforced hostility to maintenance of the federative pact were the change in the composition of the workforce, increased unemployment, the breakdown of social structures and the decline in trade union membership.

Finally, there were the cultural causes, which are far from being the least important if culture is taken to mean the system of values to which the leaders of trade unions adhere. These leaders, particularly at the middle level, proved to be incapable of understanding the new needs arising out of the profound economic and social changes that were taking place. Shop stewards and junior trade union officials had acquired their basic outlook at a time marked by numerous disputes and they did not know how to adapt themselves to the incomes policy, the measures designed to increase productivity, and the commitment to industrial peace.

In the past few years, however, decisions adopted at the various levels have been the fruit principally of compromises aimed at avoiding a break between the often totally opposing theories upheld by the three confederations. The gulf has widened between trade union officials and the rank and file as well as between unionised and non-unionised workers.

Trade union membership passed through two phases. During the first (1973-78) it increased considerably and the unionisation rate climbed to almost 50 per cent.[8] The main reasons for this rise were the increased representativeness of the trade unions for bargaining purposes (especially in industry), the weakening of political, social and cultural resistance to the membership of certain social strata of the economically active population (salaried employees and technicians, public employees) and also, in certain branches of activity such as agriculture, the relationship between membership of a trade union and the benefits received.

The rise and then the fall in membership were spread fairly evenly over the three confederations. It should be noted that, especially in some branches of industry, it became established practice for workers to become members of the Unitary Federation rather than of one of the constituent confederations and to be issued with a Federation card. The almost universal recourse to the check-off system for collecting trade union dues also contributed to the stabilisation of the membership figures.

The second phase was marked by the reversal of this trend after 1978: in five years the unionisation rate dropped by almost 4 per cent.

The loss of representativeness is not measured, however, solely by the drop in the number of members. A dramatic turn of events occurred in 1980 in Turin on the occasion of a serious dispute caused by the announcement that 1,400 workers were to be laid off by FIAT. Almost all the middle management, followed by a good part of the skilled manual and non-manual personnel, then organised a demonstration against the confederations: this was the "march of the 40,000". The dispute ended in an honourable compromise, which for all that was basically a defeat for the trade unions, their first since 1968.

Besides the drop in the number of union members in FIAT, the march of the 40,000 marked the end of a decade of social and perhaps even political leadership by the three confederations. Public opinion, which had been mostly favourable to them, expressed its disenchantment by supporting this act of rebellion, and the trade unions found themselves increasingly isolated and reduced to the sole backing — not even always wholehearted or unconditional — of the Communist and Socialist Left.

Finally, a few words ought to be said about democracy within the trade unions. The structure established after 1969 is in theory one that relies most on rank-and-file participation: all the important decisions, particularly the formulation of demands and the ratification of agreements, are taken after the views of workers' meetings held in each undertaking have been heard; delegates are elected and can be removed from office at any time by the workers, whether they are members of a trade union or not. In reality, things are quite different: union structure has become increasingly oligarchical; attendance at meetings is small and proceedings undemocratic since voting by show of hands takes precedence over secret ballot; the referendum is almost non-existent; the works councils sometimes stay in office for years without being renewed; and union leaders are co-opted rather than elected. After the federative pact fell into disuse, separate trade union sections constituted by each confederation reappeared in some undertakings. This development could weaken the representativeness of the works councils or even lead to their disappearance.

Independent trade unions

The biggest independent trade union organisations are to be found almost exclusively in the tertiary sector, whether public (especially in the schools) or private (banks and credit institutions) as well as in the public services (urban, rail and air transport, health).[9]

There are so many of these organisations, which are often craft or occupational unions, that it is not possible to give exact data on their membership, structure and organisation. In the above-mentioned branches, they often join up with the confederations to sign national collective agreements, or endorse agreements already approved by the confederations.

The picture is just as disparate for the organisations of senior and middle managers.

For upper management there is a confederation organised on professional lines, which has a sizeable membership, concludes national collective agreements, and administers the social insurance affairs of this category.

The professional associations of middle management that have been active since the march of the 40,000 are different in character. Their membership is still quite small and their representativeness as trade unions not well defined. At the present time they have not yet concluded any collective agreements and are having difficulty in getting themselves recognised as representative associations by employer circles. Moreover, they are aimed at an imprecisely defined category of employees, oscillating between supervisory and managerial staff.

Employers' organisations

Italian enterprises belong to a variety of associations: in the industrial sector, private undertakings are for the most part members of the Confederation of Industry *(Confindustria),* whereas those that are under state control join either *Intersind* or ASAP (energy and chemicals). The Confederation of Commerce *(Confcommercio)* is the biggest organisation in commerce and tourism, while agricultural producers belong to the Confederation of Agriculture *(Confagricoltura).*

It should be noted that *Confindustria* and *Intersind* do not fulfil the same functions: the former defends and promotes the interests of its members as regards both industrial relations and general economic policy, whereas the latter's competence is limited to industrial relations.

Currently, *Confindustria* is composed of associations set up by industry and by province; the undertakings are free to join one or the other structure but for some time now it has been strongly recommended that they join both types.

An important development in connection with the organisation of *Confindustria* was the establishment in 1971 of *Federmeccanica,* made up of private metalworking undertakings belonging to provincial associations, reflecting a tendency on the Confederation's part to withdraw from direct involvement in disputes and to delegate negotiating responsibilities to these vertical organisations. From 1981 on, however, after the dispute broke out over the automatic indexing of wages, the opposite trend towards direct intervention and the formulation of bargaining policy reappeared.

Another significant development on the employers' side is the disappearance of a feature characteristic of the 1960s: the sometimes very wide gap between the industrial relations policies of *Intersind* and *Confindustria.* The former used to pursue a much more open policy vis-à-vis the organised labour movement and often went ahead and signed collective agreements before *Confindustria* was ready to do so, thus splitting the employers' front. This gap has almost totally disappeared since 1980.

The public authorities

State intervention in the industrial relations system has gradually increased at three levels: first, the State has come to play a more active role in settling national and local labour disputes; secondly, numerous laws have been adopted, for the most part in the form of "negotiated" legislation (i.e. drafted in consultation with the trade unions and employers' organisations or just with the trade unions); thirdly, since 1983 the Government has itself been a party to major tripartite agreements.

The mediating role of the State calls for some comments. During the period under review, government machinery continued to perform a mediating function — although no provision is made for this in law — when collective agreements came up for renewal or particularly tough disputes arose, such as those sparked off by dismissals or staff retrenchments. Generally speaking, it is the Minister of Labour or his external services that intervene,[10] though in the public sector it is the Minister of the Public Service or the Minister responsible for the branch concerned (for example, the Minister of Public Education in disputes involving teachers). There is, however, no single authority responsible for wage matters. The regional governments also seem to be called upon more and more frequently to help settle industrial disputes concerning employment problems.[11]

As for the so-called negotiated legislation, recent years have seen a trend towards adopting labour laws that reproduce *in toto* or in part the content of inter-confederation agreements (Wage Protection Act No. 164 of 1975 (see below), Legislative Decrees Nos. 17 of 1983 and 10 and 12 of 1984 respecting the implementation of tripartite agreements), or that are drawn up following in-depth consultation with labour and management (Act No. 675 of 1977 on industrial reconversion, Act No. 91 of 1977 on reducing the cost of labour, and Act No. 297 of 1982 on severance pay).

Finally, the conclusion of the three-sided agreements of 1983 and 1984 marked a qualitative change in state intervention. These two agreements ended disputes relating mainly to the deceleration of automatic wage indexing, provided for in post-war collective agreements, as one of the measures to combat inflation. These tripartite agreements nevertheless have a broader scope, extending as they do to the review of tax and family allowances to offset the fiscal drag; measures to promote employment, reduction of working time and flexibility of work schedules; regulation of the labour market, etc. Such intervention has led the public authorities to act as a negotiator: the State has undertaken to adopt legislative and administrative measures, sometimes occasioning the incomprehension of Parliament which has complained about being short-circuited. In 1984, however, a new situation arose: the national agreement was signed by only two of the confederations, the CISL and the UIL; in the CGIL it was approved only by the Socialist minority. To make the agreement operative, the Government reproduced the main points in a Legislative Decree. Under the Constitution Parliament must approve or reject legislative decrees within 60 days of their publication. Filibustering by the Opposition resulted in the rescinding of this Decree, which was immediately replaced by another, with the result that Parliament debated the question for four months before giving its approval. The social and political climate became very tense and, following the split that occurred in the Unitary Federation, Italy entered into a delicate phase of attempting to straighten out its industrial relations system.

COLLECTIVE BARGAINING IN INDUSTRY

The end of the 1960s had seen the weakening of the principles of "articulated" bargaining set forth in the national industry-wide agreements concluded in 1962 and 1963, which contained formal provisions referring some matters back to the plant agreements; all this was accompanied by an industrial peace clause.[12]

During the 1970s, and before the signing of the three-sided agreement of 1983, the collective bargaining system developed at two levels (national and enterprise) without any co-ordination between them, so that negotiations in the enterprise often dealt with questions already settled at the higher level. It was the 1983 agreement that first introduced a procedure governing the different negotiating levels. This agreement imposed a truce of 18 months in wage bargaining at enterprise level and embodied the principle of non-duplication of bargaining on any subject. It thus confirmed, and even in a sense made official, the trend towards centralising collective bargaining which had already begun to emerge in 1975 as the effects of the recession were making themselves felt, following a period of extreme decentralisation of bargaining.

Inter-confederation bargaining

Inter-confederation bargaining is very wide in scope since it covers all the manufacturing industries and, indirectly, the other branches which, following their example, take up the items that have been agreed upon. Agreements of this type are concluded at varying intervals between the workers' and employers' confederations.

One of the most significant changes that occurred during the period under review was the strong revival of inter-confederation bargaining. It was significant not only because of the large number of agreements signed but also because of the importance of the matters dealt with, which have left a sharp imprint on the whole bargaining system.

This centralisation results from a number of factors. It hardly needs to be said that centralised bargaining comes back into favour in times of crisis; and these past few years have been marked by such pressing general problems as employment and mobility, on the one hand, and the fight against inflation, on the other.

The agreements concluded over the past ten years cover three main areas. The first is wages, which were the subject of four agreements concluded in 1975, 1977, 1983 and 1984. The 1975 agreement revised the cost-of-living sliding scale applied uniformly to industry as a whole and, since it provided for equal adjustments for all, resulted in a levelling out of remuneration, which would have been even more marked if it had remained unmodified.[13] In 1977 labour costs were reduced owing in particular to the non-indexing of severance pay.

On the other hand, the two most recent tripartite agreements of 1983 and 1984 sought to link collective bargaining to the real possibilities of the economy; thus wage increases were to be kept within the limits fixed by the targeted rate of inflation. The means adopted for achieving this included a reduction in the scope of the sliding scale; the fixing of a ceiling for wage increases granted on the occasion of the renewal of national collective agreements in 1983; and in 1984 the linking, for a period of six months, of the proportion of the wage covered by the sliding scale to the targeted rate of inflation and not the actual rate. It should be noted that this move was only partially successful in 1983 when inflation was 14.8 per cent whereas the target had been 13 per cent, and labour costs increased by 16.2 per cent in the private sector and even more in the public sector. In 1984, however, it is expected that inflation will be 11 per cent or less, close to the targeted rate of 10 per cent.

The second field covered by inter-confederation bargaining — measures concerning the labour market — is relatively new, at least in relation to the preceding years.

In 1975 it became clear that undertakings were resorting more and more to lay-offs of workers with compensation of up to 80 or even 90 per cent of the previous wage; this compensation was paid by the State through an institution known as *"Cassa integrazione guadagni"* (this fund, which was originally intended to offset temporary loss of earnings, came to be used more and more to compensate workers who had lost their jobs as a result of permanent cut-backs but who were still formally on the books of undertakings that used to employ them). The social partners therefore agreed on new regulations that were taken up in part by the legislature when it passed Act No. 164 of 1975 mentioned above. But it was mainly the agreements of 1983 and 1984 that tackled anew the question of active employment policy. The measures adopted included negotiated provisions designed to ensure greater flexibility and effectiveness in the utilisation of manpower in the undertakings and on the market (increasing the possibilities of part-time work and fixed-term contracts; granting the employers greater freedom of choice in hiring less-skilled workers; undertaking to reform and partly regionalise the public employment service; adjustment of working hours and encouragement of inter-plant mobility in order to improve productivity and efficiency; staggering of holidays; solidarity contracts for reducing hours of work with reductions in pay partly compensated by the State; tightening up of controls to combat absenteeism, etc.). In addition, the agreements of 1983 and 1984 attacked the employment problem, providing in particular for the hiring of young persons by the public administration, the introduction of work-cum-training, the creation of an investment fund financed by workers' contributions and run by the trade unions,[14] and the development of a number of measures aimed at sustaining employment in the areas hardest hit by the recession.

National collective bargaining by industry

National industry-wide agreements have long played an important part in the Italian system of industrial relations. They cover a particular branch of industry and are normally concluded for three years. The bargaining parties are the national federations of trade unions and of employers' organisations.

During the 1960s, and especially in the early 1970s, these national agreements performed an essential role. The renewal of the pace-setting agreement — the one covering metalworkers — was (in 1969, 1973, 1976 and 1979) an event of great trade union and economic consequence which even had repercussions on the country's political equilibrium. While this national agreement still carries considerable weight since it fixes the general framework of minimum conditions (wages and rules governing working conditions) applicable to workers in this branch, it has in recent years gradually yielded in importance to the agreement concluded at the inter-confederation level.

This loss of influence is due of course to the effects of the economic recession but also to the impossibility of extending the social gains beyond the already considerable benefits that had been obtained during the 1970s in particular. Furthermore, the metalworkers' agreement is more and more difficult to apply in view of the wide variety of branches covered by it; frequent proposals have been made, moreover, for dividing this bargaining unit into separate sectors covering the automobile, electronics, iron and steel industries, and so on.

Remuneration retains pride of place in the list of points dealt with in national agreements. Nevertheless, after a period in which increases succeeded each other regularly and uniformly for all categories of workers — which, with the sliding scale, contributed to the levelling out of remuneration and raised appreciably the real wages of the lower categories — the problems that arise nowadays relate more to the structure than to the level of wages. After ten years of egalitarian policy, the two most recent rounds of negotiations, and particularly the last, have been marked by the reintroduction of differentiated increases favouring the most skilled workers (managers, technicians and white-collar staff), even though not to the extent that they would like. The crisis confronting national agreements is attributable mainly to the rigidity of the automatic mechanisms like cost-of-living indexation, seniority and promotion by seniority. On the occasion of the latest renewals (1982-83) it was found that, if one wished to keep within the bounds of targeted inflation, the possibilities of increasing the minimum wage were exhausted by the action of these mechanisms. As a result, the wage drift has resumed, especially for the higher categories whose salaries almost always exceed those in the agreements.

Grading has always been one of the most controversial subjects in national agreements. During the period under review two trends clearly emerged: in the initial phase, i.e. up to the end of 1977, bargaining policies were strongly inspired by egalitarianism and led to a sharp reduction in the number of grades after manual and non-manual workers had been placed (in 1973) in a single occupational hierarchy and conditions of employment made virtually the same for both categories (leave; sickness, injury and maternity compensation; salaried status). In recent years the trend has been reversed under the influence of the levelling out of remuneration and the decline in professional motivation; some agreements now define the term "middle managers" and contain provisions aimed at paying proper value for the professional skills of these workers. Nevertheless, these innovations still apparently fail to meet the needs or solve the problems. Middle managers are exerting pressure on the legislature to obtain recognition of their specific character and this demand has been well received by the moderate Centre parties.

National agreements are also losing much ground on the question of work organisation. In fact the employers have regained considerable freedom of action in this area. The trade unions are on the defensive here and they act almost solely at the level of the undertaking.[15]

The 1976 round of negotiations introduced the obligation for employers' organisations or the managements of undertakings employing more than 200-300 persons to provide the trade unions with periodic information on investment, restructuring, technological changes, reorganisation, decentralisation of production, and so on. Generally speaking, practice has fallen short of trade union wishes and even the negotiated standards.[16] The system has functioned correctly only in the big undertakings, especially the state-controlled concerns in which industrial relations are generally based on close consultations between management and the works councils.

In general the undertakings have sought to use the regulations on the right to information to propose that collective bargaining should also take into account the requirements of productivity and the undertaking's efficiency. The trade unions, for their part, have only rarely succeeded in using their right to information as a means of supervising the undertaking's decisions and strategy, especially since 1980, the year of their FIAT defeat.

The reduction in hours of work, which has always been a traditional demand, is linked in Italy as elsewhere to two completely different demands. Until the 1970s it was presented as a means of reducing the mental and physical fatigue of the workers; then it was put forward as a means of sharing work and increasing employment.[17] The results obtained are still limited, if only because the trade union confederations have no common strategy. It has to be stressed that such reductions as have been achieved are mainly in the form of extra leave and not of a shorter working day or working week, which remains fixed at 40 hours. The average working week has dropped to 39 hours in metalworking, chemicals, and so on, and to 36 hours for shift workers. Reduced hours are gaining ground in undertakings that conclude solidarity agreements.

Here and there, another trend is emerging alongside the demand for reduced working hours. Up to 1975 the trade unions sought to impose definite constraints on the use of manpower by limiting the duration of working time and, in particular, by exerting strict control over overtime through the establishment of ceilings and, especially, by requiring prior authorisation of the works council. This trend was subsequently reversed and provision is now made for flexible schedules taking into account variations in the activity of the undertaking; negotiated restrictions on overtime have been relaxed and the practice of part-time working has spread. In addition, although there is still a trend towards increasing the length of annual leave (at present almost one month for all workers), it should be recalled that under the inter-confederation agreement of 1977, whose terms have been reproduced in the legislation, seven of the 17 paid public holidays were abolished.

There have been no notable developments regarding the question of trade union rights. It should be remembered, however, that these were rapidly expanded within a brief span of time. These rights began to be regulated in the early 1960s and were considerably enlarged on the renewal of collective agreements in 1969, at the same time as the "Workers' Charter" contained in Act No. 300 of 1970 was approved.[18] In the following years, national collective agreements mainly served to define more clearly the rules for the exercise of certain rights, sometimes reproducing the statutory provisions textually. An innovation was the introduction with the 1983 agreement, on an experimental basis, of a direct procedure aimed at defusing minor disputes or grievances through preventive conciliation.

Collective bargaining in the enterprise

In the manufacturing industries, decentralised collective bargaining mainly takes place at the plant level. Agreements covering an entire company are common; there are others whose scope extends to a group of companies with activities in several branches or to a holding company. It is rare now for bargaining to occur at the shop level. It is only in construction (and agriculture) that decentralised bargaining takes place almost exclusively at the provincial level on subjects that are not covered by the national agreement.

The bargaining agents are the management of the enterprise and the works council.

Over the period examined bargaining in the enterprise changed somewhat compared with the period 1968-72. There was, in particular, a gradual decline of plant-level bargaining as a result of the recession, the trend towards centralisation, and the predominance of wages and employment questions over the quality of working life (environment, organisation, etc.). This explains why for some years now bargaining in the enterprise no longer fulfils the pace-setting function typical of the earlier period when, at this level, new formulas were launched (such as the unified grading system for manual and non-manual workers) which were then extended by collective agreements at the national level.

As regards the subjects of bargaining, we should say straight off that the lack of national information on plant-level bargaining does not allow us to give a clear-cut account of the situation.

The economic aspects in any event call for much the same comments as we have made about national bargaining. Following an initial phase — up to 1977 — when wage increases were fixed equally for all workers, a second phase saw a reversal of the trend. In the small and medium-sized enterprises, in particular, increasing recourse was had to provisions linking wage increases with attendance or productivity clauses.[19] Even the subjects of grading and work organisation, formerly the *leitmotiv* of plant-level bargaining, are now attracting less and less attention.

Particularly fertile ground for plant bargaining is afforded by the problems arising from changes in production, especially when the enterprise has surplus manpower. Agreements here usually attempt to reconcile the restructuring requirements with the need to avoid dismissals. Many means have been used to this end: lay-offs have taken the form of suspensions for indefinite periods (with access to the compensation fund for loss of earnings which, for some time now, has become the principal prop for plant bargaining), systems of rotation of the workers concerned, early retirement and voluntary redundancy with payment of compensation. Less common is the provision in trilateral agreements (between local authorities, employers' associations and trade unions) for measures to facilitate outside mobility, despite the existence of legislation enacted for that purpose. Moreover, even the right to information — which, for the reasons given above, has not gained much new ground — is invoked for the most part simply to monitor restructuring.

Finally, it is pertinent to recall the remarks made earlier about hours of work. The trade unions' power of control is gradually weakening and the trend is towards intensive use of equipment and more flexible utilisation of manpower (less rigid schedules, acceptance of overtime, reintroduction of the night shift, weekend working).

RELATIONSHIP BETWEEN COLLECTIVE AGREEMENTS AND BETWEEN COLLECTIVE BARGAINING AND THE LAW

Some years ago the relationship both between collective agreements and between collective bargaining and the law was governed by the following rule: no departure from the law was permitted unless it marked an improvement for the workers. In the event of a conflict between two standards (whether both originated in a negotiated agreement or one was negotiated and the other was laid down by legislation), it was the one most favourable to the workers that prevailed. In recent years, however, the recession, political developments and the content of the legislative standards or the negotiated provisions have encouraged even the courts to relax the principle guaranteeing the workers an improvement whatever the case; they have decided, for example, that a collective agreement could contain provisions that were less favourable to the workers than those that were founded solely on previous agreements. A similar principle then compelled recognition in the event of a possible conflict between agreements concluded at different levels.[20]

Finally, since 1977 Parliament has approved laws providing for two types of exceptions to the above-mentioned rule: in some cases they provide that collective agreements may lower the protective standards of the law;[21] in others they limit the possibility for collective agreements to improve the statutory conditions.[22]

COLLECTIVE BARGAINING IN THE PUBLIC SERVICE

By and large, the principle of collective bargaining in the public service was established only recently, by Act No. 93 of 1983, although it had been gradually gaining acceptance earlier, if only partially and discretely depending on the sector (hospital staff, employees of semi-public bodies and local administrations, civil servants).[23] Previously, the role of the trade unions in bargaining was limited to the conclusion of unofficial agreements without legal force and binding only from the political standpoint. In fact the provisions of these agreements were applicable to the workers only after they had been embodied in a law; Parliament was in the habit of heavily revising such agreements and their contents were subject to strong political pressure. The formal bargaining system established by Act No. 93 of 1983 is aimed primarily at ensuring that everything is open and above-board and at instilling a sense of responsibility in the persons concerned, who used to operate in the dark. The system of collective bargaining in the public service is now simplified since Act No. 93 prescribes the same basic elements for all sectors (bargaining structure and agents, fields of competence and points to be covered).

Bargaining must take place by sector (section 5); the number of sectors is limited and is fixed by Decree of the President of the Republic on the

Government's recommendation. Decentralised agreements may also be concluded (section 4) on condition that they are provided for at the higher level and deal exclusively with questions defined as unrelated to remuneration (e.g. vocational training, organisation).

The bargaining agents are designated by the law. For the workers, the agent is a delegation of representatives of the most representative national occupational organisations of the sector and of the most representative confederations at the national level. The reasoning behind this rule is easy to follow: the legislature wished to avoid claims of an excessively sectoral nature and required the presence of trade union confederations which are supposed to be more concerned about the general interest. The composition of the "employer" (public authority) delegation varies according to the administration concerned but it always includes a government representative (sections 6 to 9).

In the public service, unlike the private sector, there are matters (sections 2 and 3) that may not be the subject of collective bargaining inasmuch as they relate to the actual organisation of the administration.

Finally, the points to be covered by the agreements (section 11) are also specified by the law, and it is interesting to note another difference compared with the employment relationship in the private sector: it is stipulated that collective bargaining in the public sector shall lay down not only minimum standards but also model standards from which it is forbidden to deviate, whether to the workers' advantage or disadvantage.

CONCLUSIONS

While it is very difficult at the moment to put one's finger on the principal trends in the Italian system of collective bargaining, in the long run they will no doubt be similar to those in the other highly industrialised countries, with all the problems that go with the expansion of employment in the services sector, a process which in Italy is even being compressed in time. In the 1950s the economically active population of Italy was still mostly agricultural and trade unionism was firmly implanted in this sector; its influence was felt throughout the trade union movement both as an inspiration and as a cultural model (the prominent CGIL leader Giuseppe di Vittorio was an agricultural worker). Nowadays agriculture employs only 10 per cent of the country's manpower and the agricultural trade unions play a secondary role. But scarcely had industrial trade unionism become stabilised when the shift towards the tertiary sector began to gather momentum, especially from 1980 on, causing employment and retraining problems as well as a profound crisis in the trade union movement, based as it was on the cultural models of industrial trade unionism.

For the near future there seem to be two options open at present: bargaining dominated by a tripartite relationship and hence comparable to the models currently referred to as neo-corporatist or corporative democracy, or social dialogue,[24] or bargaining carried out mainly at the plant level. Each of these approaches, which do not rule each other out, is marked by a desire to retain control over changes in the production system. The first corresponds to the spirit of the 1983 and 1984 agreements, but the opposition of the Communist component of the CGIL, which is very representative, renders uncertain the possibility of pursuing a "social pact" policy. In this case, trade union control over changes will be exercised through bargaining at the industry level and especially at the plant level, with partial and occasional agreements with the government on specific questions.

The employers themselves seem to be hesitating between a policy of dialogue at various levels, which would broaden the scope of social consensus, and a policy of edging out the trade unions, which has seemingly been made possible by the new vulnerability of labour's position.

All these choices depend on a number of ideological, political and strategic factors that have emerged during this period and whose analysis would only confirm the uncertainty of predicting the future.

Notes

[1] Professor of Labour Law, University of Rome; Chairman of the Senate Labour Commission.

[2] See G. Giugni: "Recent developments in collective bargaining in Italy", in *International Labour Review* (Geneva, ILO), Apr. 1965, pp. 273-291, and idem: "Recent trends in collective bargaining in Italy", ibid., Oct. 1971, pp. 307-328.

[3] See A. Accornero: "Sindacato e rivoluzione sociale. Il caso italiano degli anni 70", in *Laboratorio Politico* (Turin), No. 4, 1981, pp. 5 ff., and, more generally, in G. P. Cella (ed.): *Il movimento degli scioperi nel XX secolo* (Bologna, Il Mulino, 1979).

[4] See L. Bordogna: "Conflittualità", in Centro di Studi Sociale e Sindacali (Cesos): *Le relazione sindacali. Rapporto 1982-83* (Rome, Edizioni Lavoro, 1984), pp. 56-57 and 60.

[5] Giugni: "Recent developments ...", op. cit.

[6] G. Romagnoli: "Il sindacato", in G. P. Cella and T. Treu (eds.): *Relazioni industriali* (Bologna, Il Mulino, 1982), pp. 84-85 and 105-107.

[7] For a confirmation of the emergence of this phenomenon at the international level, see J. P. Windmuller: "Concentration trends in union structure: An international comparison", in *Industrial and Labor Relations Review* (Ithaca, New York), Oct. 1981, pp. 43 ff.

[8] Romagnoli: "Sindacalizzazione e rappresentanza", in Cesos, op. cit., p. 213.

[9] The only study published on the subject is R. Stefanelli: *I sindacati autonomi* (Bari, De Donato, 1981).

[10] B. Veneziani: "Interventi dello Stato e relazioni industriali", in Cesos, op. cit., p. 48.

[11] M. Fidanza and T. Treu: *La mediazione della Regione nei conflitti di lavoro* (Bologna, Il Mulino, 1976).

[12] Giugni: "Recent trends ...", op. cit., pp. 314-315.

[13] See E. Ghera: "Retribuzione, professionalità e costo del lavoro", in *Giornale di Diritto del Lavoro e di Relazioni Industriali* (Milan), No. 11, 1981, pp. 406 ff.

[14] The solidarity funds provided for in the two three-sided agreements of 1983 and 1984 were to be financed from a voluntary deduction of 0.5 per cent from the workers' wages. This fund was to finance investment aimed at creating jobs, particularly in the South.

[15] G. Della Rocca and M. Rollier: "Azione sindacali e mutamenti dei processi produttivi", in Cesos, op. cit., p. 205.

[16] On this point, see the research conducted by G. Della Rocca and S. Negrelli: "Diritti di informazione ed evoluzione della contrattazione aziendale (1969-1981)", in *Giornale di Diritto del Lavoro e di Relazioni Industriali*, 1983, No. 19, pp. 549 ff.

[17] Commission of the European Communities: *Problems and prospects of collective bargaining in the EEC Member States* (Brussels, 1979), Collection Studies, Social Policy Series No. 40, Ch. 1, section 1.4.

[18] *Legislative Series*, 1970 — It. 2.

[19] G. P. Cella and T. Treu: "La contrattazione collettiva", in idem, op. cit., p. 209.

[20] For an analysis of the legal aspects, see M. Grandi: "Rapporto tra contratti collettivi di diverso livello", in *Giornale di Diritto del Lavoro e di Relazioni Industriali*, 1981, No. 11, pp. 355 ff.

[21] See Act No. 36 of 1978 and Act No. 215 of 1978 to facilitate worker mobility and the use of the compensation fund for loss of earnings; Act No. 18 of 1978 on fixed-term employment contracts in commerce and tourism; and Act No. 903 of 1977 respecting equality of treatment as between men and women in questions of employment (*Legislative Series*, 1977 — It. 1).

[22] See in particular Act No. 91 of 1977 to revise the sliding scale machinery and the seniority bonus and Act No. 297 of 1982 on termination of the employment relationship.

[23] See G. Giugni: "La contrattazione collettiva nell'impiego pubblico in Italia", in *In memoriam Sir Otto Kahn-Freund* (Munich, Verlag C. H. Beck, 1980), pp. 107 ff.

[24] For an examination of the possibility of applying this method to the Italian system, see G. Pirzio Ammassari: "Relazioni industriali e scienza politica. Recenti interpretazione teoriche e il caso italiano", in *Giornale di Diritto del Lavoro e di Relazioni Industriali*, 1979, No. 3, pp. 383 ff.; for more information on the system following the introduction of tripartite bargaining, see M. Regini et al., in *Stato e Mercato* (Bologna), 1983, No. 3.

RECENT TRENDS IN COLLECTIVE BARGAINING IN JAPAN

Taishiro Shirai [1]

In 1974 the Japanese economy entered a period of prolonged recession caused mainly by the oil crisis of 1973 and aggravated by that of 1979. This had serious effects on a number of major industries — steel, shipbuilding, engineering, chemicals, textiles, railways and shipping — where severe problems of redundancy arose. Yet Japan, unlike most other industrialised countries, has managed to weather the storm without suffering from persistent inflation, large-scale unemployment or major industrial action over dismissals. The rapid introduction of new technology in various industries has not, at least so far, caused difficulties in manpower training, adjustment or reallocation; an appropriate balance has been maintained between wage increases and productivity, thus obviating the need for an incomes policy; and the numbers of labour disputes, of workers involved in them and of working days lost have sharply decreased since 1974, as is shown in table 1. The industrial relations system in Japan can take the credit for facilitating the adjustment of the economy

Table 1. Numbers of disputes accompanied by industrial action, workers directly involved and working days lost, 1974-82

Year	Disputes	Workers involved ('000)	Working days lost ('000)
1974	9 581	5 325.1	9 662.9
1975	7 574	4 614.0	8 051.8
1976	7 240	3 400.4	3 253.7
1977	5 533	2 412.7	1 518.5
1978	4 852	2 082.7	1 357.5
1979	3 492	1 476.2	930.3
1980	3 737	1 768.0	1 001.2
1981	7 034	2 913.6	553.7
1982	6 779	2 385.7	538.1

Source: Ministry of Labour: *Rôdô sôgi tôkei chôsa* [Statistical survey of labour disputes] (Tokyo, various years).

to radically altered circumstances; in particular, collective bargaining, complemented by an effective joint consultation system, has worked not only as a mechanism for settling disputes but as a channel of communication between labour and management. Far from obstructing the Government's anti-inflationary policy, it has proved to be a powerful pillar of support for the national economy in the past critical decade.

The present article will begin by examining the main characteristics of the machinery that has made these achievements possible; next, it will discuss the way the machinery operates; and finally, it will attempt to assess the outlook for collective bargaining in Japan.

STRUCTURE OF COLLECTIVE BARGAINING

Enterprise-level bargaining

As in the past, most collective bargaining in Japan is still conducted at the level of each enterprise or plant between an enterprise union and the management.[2] Things appear to have changed little since the Basic Survey of Trade Unions conducted by the Ministry of Labour in 1975, when more than 80 per cent of all unions in Japan were enterprise unions and 90 per cent of all trade unionists belonged to them.

Membership of enterprise unions is limited to the regular employees of a particular firm. Other workers not regularly employed are not normally eligible. In general, both blue- and white-collar workers (the latter including junior supervisory and managerial staff) are organised in the same union. Union officers are generally elected from among the regular employees of the enterprise; during their tenure of office they usually retain their employee status but are paid by the union. About 72 per cent of the enterprise unions are affiliated with some type of federation; the role of these organisations, which was minimal in the past, has somewhat increased in importance during the past decade, as we shall presently see.

The role of union federations and employers' associations in collective bargaining

The role of national trade union centres such as *Sôhyô* (General Council of Trade Unions), *Dômei* (Japanese Confederation of Labour), *Shinsanbetsu* (National Federation of Industrial Organisations) and *Chûritsurôren* (Federation of Independent Unions) is to co-ordinate the action of their affiliates in support of wage increases or other demands, to establish overall policies and to serve as information centres for their affiliates and others. National employers' organisations have a similar role. The representatives of both types of bodies often meet government officials, including the Prime Minister and the Minister of Labour, in order to exchange views, to present the demands of their respective constituents and to speak out against economic and social policies which they feel may run counter to their members' interests. The national trade union centres and employers' organisations do not participate in collective bargaining; in this sense their role has not changed in the past ten years. They do, however, co-operate more closely with each other than before, the trade union federations, in particular, abandoning ideological strife and organisational rivalries in the search for a common strategy with which to face the drastic changes in the country's economic circumstances.

Industrial federations in Japan usually take the form of industry-wide federations of enterprise unions. They are in general loosely organised and are seldom authorised to participate directly in bargaining within the enterprise. The same can be said for industrial associations of employers. According to the Ministry of Labour survey of collective bargaining agreements, only 10 per cent of enterprise unions surveyed in 1967 and 13 per cent in 1977 allowed the participation of outside union officials in bargaining. Of these, 3 and 4 per cent respectively permitted only officials of the federations of unions at multi-plant corporations to participate. The corresponding figures for firms permitting officials of employers' organisations to participate were even lower — 3 and 2 per cent respectively.[3] The involvement of officials of industrial federations of unions mostly takes the shape of formulating union demands and policies for prosecution in enterprise bargaining, synchronising industrial action, checking the starting and expiry dates of agreements and co-ordinating agreed terms, and exchanging information with affiliated unions and unions in other industries.

Industry-wide bargaining has, however, to some extent developed both at national and at regional level. It has, for instance, long been the rule between the All-Japan Seamen's Union *(Kaiin-kumiai)* [4] and four associations of shipping corporations. It is also prevalent between employers or their associations and industrial federations in the textile industries, the private railways, the coal and metalliferous ore mines, the chemical industries and some breweries. Nevertheless, the role of industrial federations and employers' associations remains on the whole as restricted and ill-defined as before, firstly, because they cannot force their affiliates to relinquish their jealously guarded bargaining rights, and secondly, because the matters negotiated at industry level tend to be limited to general principles or standards whose application to a particular enterprise or plant is subsequently decided by agreement between the enterprise union and the firm concerned.

Of greater significance than formal industry-wide collective bargaining is the development since 1973 of *de facto* bargaining in some major exporting industries such as steel, shipbuilding, automobiles and electrical appliances. This has given a further impetus to the nation-wide annual spring wage offensives *(Shuntô)* first launched by *Sôhyô* in 1955, which now cover nearly 10 million organised workers and also exert a substantial influence on wage fixing in the unorganised sector. In *de facto* negotiations the representatives of industrial federations of unions do not act as bargaining agents for the affiliated enterprise unions, but negotiate annual wage increases informally and directly with the top management of leading corporations.

The most typical case is that of the centralised bargaining practised since 1959 in the steel industry between the leaders of the Japanese Federation of Iron and Steel Workers' Unions *(Tekkôrôren)* and the managements of the five major steel corporations. Here the parties first negotiate a provisional agreement on the wage increase for the year. Early in April the five major corporations then simultaneously announce their final wage offer. The Federation has nearly always accepted the employers' offer without taking a strike vote among its members. This has become the normal method of wage fixing in the iron and steel industry and has set the pattern for the wage settlement procedure followed in some other major industries. Because of the strategic position of the iron and steel industry in Japan this trend has become more marked over the years, particularly since the oil crises, with the shipbuilding, automobile and electrical appliances industries being the most concerned. With a view to strengthening their co-operation and co-ordinating their policies and action, the federations for the four industries mentioned formed the International Metalworkers' Federation — Japan Council (IMF — JC) which has now virtually taken over the leadership of *Shuntô* from the National Joint Committee for the Spring Offensive set up by *Sôhyô* and *Chûritsurôren.* Although such group bargaining remains informal, it has practically the same effect as more systematic procedures of industry-wide or multi-industry negotiation since the industries concerned are closely related and exert a decisive influence on wage settlements in other branches such as chemicals, metal engineering, private and national railways, telecommunication and postal services, and national and local civil services. In this sense *de facto* industry-wide bargaining in major metal industries may be said to have instituted a gradual trend towards centralisation of collective bargaining in Japan. It has also somewhat strengthened the cohesion, authority and prestige of national and industrial trade union federations and employers' associations.

The role of the Government in collective bargaining

The role of the Government in collective bargaining in Japan differs according to whether the private or the public sector is involved.

As far as the private sector is concerned, the Government's policy is to assist the development of voluntary collective bargaining between the two sides of industry. It intervenes only indirectly, when collective negotiations break down, through the tripartite labour relations commissions, independent administrative bodies which may, if necessary, be called upon to settle disputes by means of conciliation, mediation and arbitration. The number of labour disputes settled by the commissions and their percentage in the total number of disputes have decreased sharply during the past decade and no major dispute has come before a commission in the past five years. This is a sign that free and autonomous industrial relations are functioning far better than in the past.

As for the public sector, there are still problems between the unions and the Government. In Japan national and local civil servants, although they are highly organised, have no legal right to bargain over pay or other employment conditions or take concerted action such as strikes. In order to compensate for the restriction of these rights the National Personnel Authority (NPA) for national civil servants and the local personnel commissions for local civil servants play a crucial role in pay adjustments. If the NPA finds in its survey of wage conditions in private industry that pay levels in the private sector exceed those of civil servants by 5 per cent or more, it has to recommend adjustments to the Diet and the Cabinet. However, such recommendations become effective only when the law regulating pay for national civil servants is revised and the necessary budgetary provisions are authorised by the Diet; it is for the latter and the Government to decide whether the recommended adjustments should be put into effect. Although the system has been in operation since 1949, budgetary constraints made it impossible for the Government to give full effect to the NPA's recommendations before 1970. From then until 1981 it continued to do so, and it seemed that this system of pay adjustment for national civil servants was firmly established. In 1982, however, because of the substantial deficit in the national budget, the Government declared the outright freezing of national civil servants' pay for a year as an emergency arrangement, despite the protests of the unions. In 1983 the Government reduced the 6.47 per cent pay increase recommended by the NPA to 2 per cent. These developments again jeopardised the pay adjustment system for national civil servants and, moreover, had repercussions on the pay of employees of semi-public corporations for housing, construction and water supply, social welfare agencies, private hospitals and schools, and on the remuneration of local civil servants, which is adjusted by local personnel commissions with reference to national civil service rates.

Employees of public corporations and national enterprises (e.g. the National Railways Corporation, the Japan Monopoly Corporation, the Nippon Telegraph and Telephone Corporation, the Postal Service, the National Forestry Agency, the Mint) are not allowed to strike but have the right to bargain collectively. However, as far as their basic pay is concerned collective bargaining is practically meaningless, because they are under the strict financial control of the Treasury and their managements have no powers to negotiate pay increases with unions. Accordingly, in the annual spring offensive, after a series of purely formal, ineffective negotiations, the issue of pay increases is referred first to the National Enterprises and Public Corporations Labour Relations Commission (NEPCLRC) for mediation — another purely formal procedure — and then to the same body for compulsory arbitration. Only after the Commission makes its award does the Government take steps to implement it with the approval of the legislature.[5] The unions in these corporations and enterprises are dissatisfied with the whole procedure, which virtually denies their right to bargain collectively on the all-important issue of their members' pay. In order to change the system radically, and particularly to win the right to strike, the National Railway Workers' Union and the National Railway Locomotive Engineers' Union waged a seven-day general strike in 1975 in defiance of the law and of public opinion, which has been very critical of some locally agreed practices on the grounds that they result in overmanning and slack discipline. The strike was unsuccessful, and since then the situation has become more unfavourable for the unions because of the tremendous financial deficit of the National Railways. Accordingly, the vexed question of restricted and ineffective collective bargaining in public corporations and national enterprises seems to have no prospects of solution in the near future.

HOW THE INDUSTRIAL RELATIONS MACHINERY OPERATES

The scope of enterprise-level collective bargaining

Since there is no provision in the Trade Union Law that defines the scope of collective bargaining, the range of subjects dealt with at the bargaining table can be wide, covering practically every issue relating to conditions of work and employment. The general tendency in Japan has been for it to expand to take in issues that were formerly decided unilaterally by employers.

The monetary income of employees (wages and salaries, half-yearly bonuses and retirement allowances) is the major subject of collective bargaining. Although reduction of working hours, introduction of the five-day week and extension of paid vacations are increasingly being dealt with at the bargaining table, these matters are still of lesser concern to Japanese workers. Personnel issues, including hiring, transfer, retraining, reassignment of employees, staff cutbacks and dismissal, have become increasingly important subjects for collective bargaining in Japan during the past decade because of the prolonged recession and structural changes. It can be said that this is the most significant feature in the recent development of collective bargaining in Japan.

However, a number of personnel matters are still excluded from collective bargaining. These are regarded by Japanese employers as being the prerogative of management, along with matters related to organisation and production such as the introduction of new technology, changes in managerial organisation, relocation of plants, mergers of firms, closures of plants, subcontracting and production plans. Here disputes often arise over whether an issue is negotiable. In public corporations and national enterprises in particular, the scope of collective bargaining has been a bone of contention, especially at the shop level, ever since section 8 of the Public Corporation and National Enterprise Labour Relations Law of 1948 excluded from collective bargaining "matters affecting the management and operation of the business", a "catch-all" term susceptible of a variety of interpretations.

Information and joint consultation within the enterprise

Most of the sensitive problems mentioned above have, however, been successfully solved — at least in the private sector — by referring them to joint consultation instead of handling them directly by collective bargaining. Rather than bicker over "negotiability", most employers now appeal to the comprehension of unions and employees. Unions are also generally realistic in their reactions to managerial decisions which are vital to a company's survival and to its competitiveness in home and overseas markets. Instead of fighting a managerial decision a union will try to secure adequate information about it well before its enforcement, and if necessary will press the management to modify it to take account of the employees' views. This was the case as early as 1969, when 51 per cent of 1,203 enterprise unions surveyed by the Ministry of Labour reported that they participated in joint consultation bodies. The percentage was still the same at the time of the last survey in 1977, although more unions were surveyed (1,700). The proportion varied according to the size of the undertaking: 69 per cent in enterprises with 1,000 employees or more, but only 19 per cent in those with 29 employees or fewer. According to another survey by the Ministry of Labour in 1977, 70.8 per cent of all establishments surveyed — unionised and non-unionised — covering 82.3 per cent of workers included in the sample, had standing committees for joint consultation.

The employee representatives who participate in the joint consultation machinery are almost always officials of the enterprise union. For this reason the boundary between joint consultation and collective bargaining is generally indistinct; in most cases the same items are discussed in both systems, although the Japan Productivity Centre has strongly advocated making a clear-cut demarcation between the items dealt with by the two institutions. In most cases, however, there is a procedural continuity between the two; if an agreement is not reached in the process of joint consultation, the issue is referred to collective bargaining. It is a generally accepted practice for unions to refrain from calling a strike on an issue that is still being considered under the joint consultation procedure.

Joint consultation serves as an efficient channel of communication between the employer and the employees and helps to promote mutual understanding and co-operation at the enterprise and plant level. In recent years improvements have also been achieved in both the quality and the quantity of the information exchanged. Managements tend increasingly to provide employee representatives with detailed and often confidential information on management policies and objectives, investment programmes, production plans, the firm's financial position, manpower planning, manpower adjustments, training and retraining programmes, measures for dealing with redundancies, business prospects, and so on. Not only the employees' representatives but regular employees in general take a keen and responsible interest in such information because most of them expect to work for the company until retirement and so feel that it is in their direct interest to co-operate with the employer to ensure the survival and prosperity of the company. The cultural and ethnic homogeneity and relatively high level of education of Japanese workers, the simple structure of enterprise unions, which consist of manual and non-manual employees without distinction as to occupation, and close communication between union officers and rank-and-file members — all these are major factors ensuring that information is disseminated extensively.

Another factor which explains why employers in Japan are generally willing to share vital managerial information with employees is the process by which managerial élites are formed. With few exceptions, the top executives of big companies have risen from the ranks through internal promotion within their corporations and were thus once members of an enterprise union. Even where this is not so, top managers tend to regard lower-grade employees not as wage earners with conflicting interests, but as junior members of the community formed by the enterprise, with a common stake in its future. In such a context, the relations between the top executives and the employees, and between the management and the union, tend to be more co-operative and positive.

While in the past information concerning management and production was mostly provided at the discretion of the employer, unions are now taking the initiative — often with considerable firmness — in asking managements to provide them with details of plans for future investment, plant location or relocation, the introduction of new technology, changes in production, manpower adjustment and reallocation, particularly when such matters affect their members' job security. It is now an established practice for the management to provide such information well before any decision is taken, so that the union can examine the situation from a policy viewpoint and make some workable counterproposals. This practice has contributed greatly to reducing the number of disputes over staff cutbacks in large companies during the present recession, in marked contrast to the two immediate post-war decades with their train of prolonged and bitter strikes.

Another positive role of employees in information-sharing is at the workshop level, where voluntarily constituted groups of workers, as distinct from formal institutions like unions or joint consultation machinery, may make proposals to junior managers or supervisors for improving productivity, product quality, work organisation, and so on, and engage in research to this end. Such groups, which have been developing rapidly in Japan since the early 1960s, are known as quality control (QC) circles or zero defect (ZD) groups. According to a survey conducted by the Union of Japanese Scientists and Engineers, the number of QC circles grew from 23 in 1962 to 115,254 in 1980 and the number of participants from 70,920 in 1965 to 1,062,759 in 1980.[6] The contribution of QC circles and ZD groups to improving productivity and quality of output in Japanese industry is now widely recognised both at home and abroad.

There have been active discussions about workers' participation in management in Japan over the past decade. However, as far as the direct representation of employees in the board of directors is concerned there have been almost no significant developments in recent years. The main reason may be that Japanese workers find that the development of collective bargaining and joint consultation machinery within the enterprise, combined with the internal promotion system, already gives them enough say in how the enterprise should be run.[7] It is reasonable to assume that, if the workers and their representatives continue to influence management decisions in this way, there will not be a strong incentive for unions to demand other types of workers' participation.

Joint consultation at the industrial and national levels

Joint consultation machinery at the industrial level has been established in a growing number of industries in Japan, beginning with the textile industry in 1956. By the mid-1970s it had been set up by industrial federations of unions and employers' associations in 19 industries, including shipbuilding, automobiles, electrical power, shipping, metalliferous ore mining, coalmining, iron and steel, electrical machinery and cement, mostly during the 1960s after the liberalisation of international trade and capital investment in Japan. Although the parties refrain from discussing wages and other working conditions, both of them have found joint consultation increasingly useful in dealing with problems of common concern such as industrial reorganisation, technological change, industrial pollution, the labour market and employment situation, and international trade conflicts. The system has the great merit of enabling the parties to obtain a realistic picture of the situation and prospects of a given industry, the problems involved and the way in which they can be solved.

Dialogue has also developed at the national level. The year 1970 saw the establishment of the Industry-Labour Council *(Sangyô Rôdô Konwakai — Sanrô-kon)* consisting of leaders of national union centres, employers' associations and eminent authorities on labour questions. The council, whose purpose is to advise the Minister of Labour, holds monthly meetings which are attended by the Minister of Labour and often by other members of the Cabinet, including the Prime Minister himself. The council has no decision-making powers, but its discussions are wide-ranging, covering the current situation of the Japanese national economy and its future prospects, the Government's social and economic policies and the reactions of labour and management to them. Although there has been occasional and sometimes bitter confrontation between the parties, the council has on the whole been effective in working towards mutual understanding and a common recognition of the current problems facing the Japanese economy. It is united by the conviction that the employment security and living standards of the nation's workers will in the long run depend on the position of Japanese industry in changing world markets.

The outcome of collective bargaining

Except in the shipping industry, collective bargaining as a rule-making procedure has developed in Japan only since the end of the Second World War. Before then, the concept was quite alien to the traditional attitudes, values and customs that governed the labour relationship: employment conditions were decided for the most part unilaterally by the employer and were not negotiable. Even now, and particularly in small and medium-sized companies, collective bargaining is not necessarily a negotiation over the terms of a written agreement, since a formal labour contract does not always emerge; there is often merely a "gentleman's agreement", partly because some unions are not yet familiar with the practice of contract negotiation, and partly because many managers still strongly resist committing themselves in writing.[8] Nevertheless, the number of unions which conclude agreements and the number of union members covered have increased steadily. According to a survey conducted by the Ministry of Labour in 1980, 83.2 per cent of registered unions had written collective agreements and 90.1 per cent of their members were covered, although there was still a notable difference between large firms and smaller ones.[9]

The content of collective agreements has changed little in the past decade.[10] They usually have provisions on union recognition, categories of employees to which the agreement applies, union security clauses, check-off of union dues, union activities during working hours, use of company facilities for union purposes, labour disputes, industrial action and joint consultation machinery; wage increases, half-yearly bonuses, retirement allowances, working hours and provisions relating to staff cutbacks are the subject of separate agreements.[11] In recent years there have been differences of views between the parties regarding the employees to be covered by agreements. The unions would like to include higher-level supervisory or managerial employees as far as possible; managements are opposed to this. There is also a tendency among managements to be more restrictive in concluding or applying provisions concerning time off for union activities during working hours and the use of company facilities for this purpose; the unions look upon such moves as an infringement of their vested rights.

THE OUTLOOK FOR COLLECTIVE BARGAINING IN JAPAN

It can be fairly said that collective bargaining has become firmly established in Japan as a procedure for determining wages and other employment and working conditions as far as large companies in the private sector are concerned, and it is safe to assume that, as unions and managements mature, the pattern of collective bargaining will become more systematic. However, the overall prospects for the future seem less bright, for a number of reasons.

Firstly, the coverage of collective bargaining is unlikely to grow because of the difficulty of expanding union organisation in the future. The organisation rate has already been slowly but steadily decreasing in the past several years. This has been brought about not only by the prolonged recession and the drop in employment since the oil crises but by successive changes in technology, in the relative importance of different industries in the Japanese economy, in industrial location and relocation, and in the composition of the labour force by occupation, age, educational background and sex. This is not the place to analyse all the aspects of these structural changes, but their impact on organised labour and on the coverage of collective bargaining has been unfavourable in Japan as elsewhere. Non-organised or poorly organised sectors of the economy have continued to grow at the expense of the organised sector. The numbers of workers who are difficult to organise, such as housewives and temporary or part-time workers, have increased more rapidly than the numbers who are in steady full-time employment and who are hence potential union members. Because of its basic structure, in which enterprise unions are predominant, the

Japanese union movement is very weak in its efforts to organise non-unionised workers. If the situation remains as it is, the coverage of collective bargaining will be narrowed and organised labour enjoying the benefits of collective bargaining will decline as a percentage of the total employed labour force.

Secondly, the power of unions to strike in support of their demands will be increasingly circumscribed by the structural changes described above. As elsewhere, the most effective strikes in Japan have been conducted in such industries as mining, manufacturing, transport and communications, where unions have been strong and well organised. However, these union strongholds are being undermined, largely through the introduction of technological innovations and the decline of the industries concerned. The growing industries, such as the "information industries" or those in the tertiary sector, are as a rule poorly organised, and the power of unions in these industries to wage effective strikes is very restricted. Already industrial action in Japan is largely limited to protest strikes of short duration, and it is likely that this trend will be intensified.

Thirdly, the development of joint consultation machinery at various levels, and its increased sophistication, will doubtless relegate collective bargaining to a minor role. Management will continue to try to solve disputes through joint consultation as far as possible since unions refrain from strikes or other industrial action while it is in progress. Most unions go along with this management policy because it is an easier and less costly way of solving problems. However, it may lead to the frustration or dissatisfaction of the rank and file because decisions tend to be made without their direct participation or concerted action.

Fourthly, as long as the basic structure of collective bargaining (i.e. the predominance of enterprise bargaining) remains unchanged, it will not be effective in solving the wider problems arising out of structural change and the rapid ageing of the labour force. In the latter connection, problems concerning the employment and unemployment of older workers, their retraining and reallocation, the compulsory retirement age, pensions and other income security, welfare services and medical care are all becoming more pressing than in the past, particularly in the light of the Government's austerity policy. These problems are mostly beyond the reach of enterprise collective bargaining and can only be handled by industry-wide or nation-wide collective bargaining or by a united political stand on the part of the labour movement, the prospects for which do not appear favourable in view of the power structure, political divisions and ideological conflicts that still persist in the Japanese union movement.

Collective bargaining in the public sector is a final problem to be solved. However, the prospects for this do not appear promising for the unions concerned in view, among other things, of the lack of sympathy shown by public opinion over the years for the stand taken by the public-sector unions.

Collective bargaining: A reappraisal

Notes

[1] Professor of Personnel Management and Industrial Relations, Faculty of Business Administration, Hosei University, Tokyo.

[2] K. Koshiro: "Development of collective bargaining in postwar Japan", in T. Shirai (ed.): *Contemporary industrial relations in Japan* (Madison, University of Wisconsin Press, 1983).

[3] Ministry of Labour: *Rodo kyoyakutô jittai chôsa hôkokusho* [Survey of collective agreements] (Tokyo, 1979).

[4] This industrial union is a special case in that its members are individuals, not enterprise unions.

[5] For details of this somewhat unusual procedure, see K. Koshiro: "Labor relations in public enterprises", in Shirai, op. cit., pp. 272-273.

[6] For an analysis of the development of QC circles' activities in Japan, see T. Inagami: "Q.C. circle activities and the suggestion system", in *Japan Labor Bulletin* (Tokyo, Japan Institute of Labor), Jan. 1982.

[7] T. Shirai: "A theory of enterprise unionism", in Shirai, op. cit., pp. 120-121.

[8] idem: "Collective bargaining", in K. Okochi, B. Karsh and S. B. Leine (eds.): *Workers and employers in Japan* (Tokyo, University of Tokyo Press, 1973), pp. 284-291.

[9] Ministry of Labour: *Rodokumiai kihon chôsa* [Basic survey of trade unions] (Tokyo, 1980).

[10] For a description of the content of collective agreements in 1972, see T. Mitsufuji and K. Hagisawa: "Recent trends in collective bargaining in Japan", in *International Labour Review* (Geneva, ILO), Feb. 1972, pp. 137-140.

[11] For some basic characteristics of collective agreements in Japan, see Y. Suwa: "Recent trends in collective bargaining agreements in Japan: Based on results of the 1977 Labour Ministry Survey", in *Japan Labor Bulletin*, July 1979.

RECENT TRENDS IN COLLECTIVE BARGAINING IN THE NETHERLANDS

W. Albeda [1]

The labour scene in the Netherlands has undergone a number of profound changes over the past decade. For many years before this, labour relations had conformed to a fairly stable pattern, the main features of which were organisation of workers and employers along denominational lines, a high degree of centralisation, institutionalised co-operation between the Government, employers and trade unions, and industrial peace. This pattern, which had developed before the Second World War, proved strong enough to resist the stresses of the war and post-war recovery, and indeed was even reinforced by them; but it could not withstand the pressures of rapid economic growth and mass consumption.

This article attempts to describe and explain the changes that have occurred over the past ten years or so. It should be borne in mind, however, that many of these changes had their origin in previous developments and were already well under way by the early 1970s.

THE CHANGING INSTITUTIONAL SCENE

Since the end of the nineteenth century, employers, farmers and workers had tended to organise themselves according to their religious beliefs. In the trade union movement this led to the creation of three separate central organisations: the social democratic Netherlands Federation of Trade Unions (NVV), the Netherlands Catholic Federation of Trade Unions (NKV) and the Netherlands Federation of Protestant Christian Trade Unions (CNV).

Attempts were made in the early 1970s to create a single confederation in which the three tendencies of the movement would still be recognisable. The Catholic trade unions, following important changes in the Netherlands Catholic Church, had already expressed their readiness to amalgamate with the NVV during the 1960s. The Protestant federation, the CNV, however, wanted greater safeguards than did the NKV for retaining its identity within the new confederation. As a result, the NVV and NKV decided to form their own "Confederation of the Netherlands Trade Union Movement" (FNV) in 1976.

Since 1978 individual unions have affiliated directly with the FNV; this marked an important change in the pattern that had dominated labour relations since 1900. Today, however, as a consequence of the growth of (mainly white-collar) unions outside the traditional centres, the Netherlands once again has three trade union federations: the FNV, with about 920,000 members; the CNV (which gained 100,000 additional members when some unions — police, teachers — left the NKV), with 315,000 members; and the MHP, a federation of independent white-collar unions, with 110,000 members.

The employers, who are divided into three main groupings — farmers, small entrepreneurs and larger industrialists — had also been organised along denominational lines. Since the Second World War, however, while the farmers have retained the triple organisational structure ("general", Catholic and Protestant), among the small entrepreneurs the Catholic and general organisations have amalgamated, with the Protestants remaining apart, and among the industrialists the Catholics and Protestants have merged.

THE TRADE UNIONS AND WAGE POLICY

During the past decade full employment in the Netherlands has given way to mass unemployment. This has naturally had far-reaching consequences for wage bargaining.

Following the collapse in the 1960s of the centralised system of wage control based on consensus and co-operation between the Government and the social partners,[2] attempts were made to introduce a "freer" wage policy. Neither the trade unions nor the employers' organisations wanted to go back to the centralised wage policy through which, by helping to draw up government guide-lines for wages, they were brought into constant conflict with their members in labour markets where their bargaining power might have secured them a better deal. However, while this was ruled out, a return to the pre-war system of completely free wage bargaining within the different branches of the economy was equally impossible.

In the Netherlands system of labour relations a few large organisations covering several industries and many workers set the pattern of bargaining everywhere. Once the collective agreements for the metal industry, Philips and the building trades have been concluded, for example, other industries follow suit. The need is therefore felt, on both the workers' and the employers' side, to engage first in a round of central bargaining to ascertain whether there is already some consensus about current trends and possible areas of agreement. Naturally enough, the Government is interested in the outcome of such central bargaining; and following the breakdown of the centralised wage policy it tried every year to convince both sides of industry of the need to limit wage increases. Although central bargaining took place each year, only once (in 1972) was a "social contract" concluded between the Government, labour and management, covering the year 1973; in no other year was agreement at the central level reached. While such bargaining influenced negotiations in the individual industries and enterprises by setting the upper and lower limits for contract wages, it did not prevent a steady rise in real earnings or in inflation. The Government and the social partners failed during this period to repeat the successes achieved by the wage control system that had made the Netherlands model unique in the 1950s.

It might perhaps be said that the collapse of the centralised wage policy produced a kind of trauma in labour relations in the Netherlands. The Government was abruptly deprived of the political control over wages on which it had come to rely; and indeed, in the years that followed, it came in for considerable criticism for allowing wages to rise too fast. The trade union movement, which had supported the wage policy for so long, found that in tight labour markets its members did not hesitate to fend for themselves, with the result that a return to centralised wage fixing had become unacceptable in their eyes. The employers, for their part, had had their share of internal problems during the final years of the wage policy, but during the 1970s they sometimes looked back nostalgically to the period of government-set wages; it was only with the advent of mass unemployment that their belief in free bargaining revived.

The 1960s and early 1970s were marked by two contradictory developments. First, the tight labour market pushed up wages faster than the increase in productivity. Before 1960 the Netherlands had been a "cheap" country, with lower wages and substantially lower prices than the other EEC members. By the end of the 1960s this was no longer the case. Secondly, while the bargaining partners no longer accepted the discipline of the past, the Government had developed a fairly comprehensive system of social security in which every category of benefit (unemployment, sickness, disability) was linked to the wage level in two ways: *(a)* through "net linking" — the absolute minimum for all benefits was the net minimum wage, which was itself adjusted automatically in line with the weighted average of private industry wages; and *(b)* through "gross linking" — all benefits above the minimum were calculated as a percentage (generally 80 per cent) of the insured person's most recent wage; old-age benefits, for their part, were related (through net linking) only to the minimum wage.

Salaries and wages in the public sector (and in the growing semi-public and subsidised sectors) were automatically linked to the index of wages calculated by the Central Bureau of Statistics.

As a result, since the mid-1970s the wage level set by the social partners has determined (without any government intervention) all social security benefits and all salaries and wages paid by the Government. Furthermore, the Government sought to impose a ceiling on the incomes of the liberal professions (doctors, architects, accountants, etc.) by linking them to the incomes of persons performing comparable functions in the public service. Consequently, the incomes of virtually all groups were determined, directly or indirectly, by free collective bargaining in the private sector. It was of course not surprising that the Government found it difficult to wait passively for the results of the negotiations.

With two-thirds of its budget hanging on the bargaining process, should it not at least attempt to influence the wage level?

The Wage Determination Act, which had been adopted in 1970 over the strong protests of the trade union movement, empowered the Government not only to impose a general wage freeze in a national emergency but also to intervene in the collective bargaining process in the general social and economic interest.[3] It was to play an important role in the following years.

However, the Wage Determination Act did not really provide the Government with a handy instrument for regulating wages. Its existence intensified the struggle over incomes policy that had started in 1963 and had continued unabated until the depressed labour market of the early 1980s put a halt to the constant increase in real wages that had been worrying each successive government.

Every Minister of Social Affairs (who between 1967 and 1981 had always been a former trade union secretary with a CNV background) knew that a social contract would be politically more acceptable and at the same time more effective in the labour market. But given the failure to arrive at some form of social contract (with the single rather ineffective exception of 1972), the temptation to use the Act to limit the continuing wage increases proved to be irresistible.

In 1974 the oil crisis led the Government to ask for broad powers to control all incomes, including wages, dividends and profits under the Incomes Policy and Employment Opportunities Protection (Enabling Provisions) Act, adopted that year and effective for that year only. In 1975 and 1976 the Government felt compelled to use the Wage Determination Act to impose a limit on wage increases. It is interesting to note that in this respect the Centre-Left Government headed by the Social Democrat Mr. Den Uyl did not proceed so very differently from some earlier and subsequent Centre-Right governments.

The Van Agt Government (1977-81), for its part, tried to gain the confidence of the trade unions by not applying the Wage Determination Act in 1978 and 1979. But real wages continued to rise during those years, and in 1980, and again in 1981, wage freezes were imposed.

In both these years the wage controls contained an additional limitation on higher incomes by putting a ceiling on the compensation for cost-of-living increases. However, this failed to soften the resistance of the trade unions and it infuriated the employers. The employers and the trade unions accordingly found themselves united in their opposition to government wage controls at a time when mass unemployment had rendered them superfluous. After 1981 no further wage controls were imposed. Not only did growing unemployment achieve what no government had been able to do, namely convince the unions and the employers of the necessity for a pay standstill, but at the same time government and employer circles alike began to realise that wage controls were making the remuneration system more and more inflexible.

THE TRADE UNIONS AND EMPLOYERS DURING THE RECESSION

The onset of the recession found the Netherlands in a somewhat unfavourable position in several respects.

First of all, during the 1960s and early 1970s a number of rigidities had been built into the labour relations system. The automatic price indexation clause contained in all collective agreements precluded any downward flexibility of real wages, while the linking of private sector wages with public pay rates and the social security system reduced the Government's room for manoeuvre.

Secondly, relations between employers' organisations and trade unions were at a post-war low. (An abortive attempt by the employers to eliminate the price index clause from all collective agreements in 1977 did nothing to improve matters.)

Thirdly, the post-war consensus, already shaken by the collapse of the wage policy, was unable to survive the crisis that blew up in the social security system and in the Welfare State in general. Employers and trade unions developed their own strongly differing strategies. Moreover, the creation of the FNV and the refusal of the CNV to join the new Confederation led to permanent differences of opinion within the trade union movement.

The employers, who during the 1960s had strengthened their organisations by appointing professional officials and increasing their permanent staff, have now assumed an uncompromising "free enterprise" stance. They are calling for more freedom for private entrepreneurs, a contraction of the public sector, a large degree of deregulation, and the decentralisation of industrial relations. Moreover, they are conducting a very active public relations campaign, particularly through the media. Given the financial problems of the Government and the savings that a policy of deregulation could achieve, the employers stand a good chance of seeing their aims realised.

The trade unions are in a much less favourable position. They have opposed every proposal to implement restrictive financial policies of the sort favoured by so many governments today and every move to reduce social security benefits. Their counter-proposals, which have been difficult enough to put across to their members and offensive to some of them, have been consistently rejected by the Government and employers alike. In several cases the Christian trade union movement was close to agreement with the employers and the Government, but the FNV always found it impossible to join in the consensus. The instance that comes most readily to mind occurred in 1980 when the Foundation of Labour [4] almost reached agreement on a three-pronged policy combining wage controls with the reduction of hours of work and certain labour market reforms.

As the recession deepened it became increasingly clear that a declining economy with such close links between wages and social security and between private sector and public sector wages could not afford to let the system of automatic price-indexed increases continue unchecked. As we have seen, the employers tried to do away with the indexation clauses during the bargaining round of 1977, but this met with stiff trade union opposition. Selective strikes were organised in many industries and the employers gave in after only a couple of days. The problem was therefore left in the Government's lap.

Nevertheless the recession, which hit the Netherlands harder than most industrialised nations, eventually prompted the parties to come to terms. At the end of 1982 a basic agreement was reached between employers and trade unions on forms of work-sharing, mainly through the reduction of working hours.

In the two years that have passed since this basic agreement was concluded, provision for reduced working hours (with some reduction of pay) has been made in most collective agreements. It is interesting to note that proposals made by employers' organisations regarding flexible working time — for instance that the total number of annual working hours should be stipulated in the collective agreement and that it should be left to the enterprise to negotiate detailed arrangements with the unions — were agreed to by the unions subject to certain conditions (setting limits to the number of daily working hours, fixing those within which "normal" working time takes place, etc.).

Difficulties arose, however, when the employers sought to go even further — for example when they wanted to decide unilaterally what hours were to be worked, or to abolish overtime pay for work in the evening or on Saturdays, or both. A compromise had to be worked out between the almost total flexibility sought by the employers and the security of fixed working hours which the unions had won after years of struggle and were very reluctant to give up. In 1984, however, the 1982 agreement was not renewed. The employers seem increasingly resolved to resist any further reduction in working time. It is not yet clear how determined the trade unions are to pursue their demands for shorter hours; they might propose wage increases as an alternative.

Meanwhile the Government's decision in the autumn of 1983 to cut the gross pay of all public service workers and all social security benefits by 3.5 per cent (later reduced to 3 per cent) from 1 January 1984 led, as we shall see, to massive protests by the three trade union federations and to strikes and working to rule in the public sector; all that had been gained in 1982 seemed to have been lost again in the autumn of 1983. However, in the early spring of 1984 both the FNV and the CNV leaders made it clear that they wanted to resume centralised bargaining, not only with the employers but also with the Government.

Another important development was the agreement reached in May 1984 between employers and trade unions in the manufacturing sector regarding the employment and training of young workers. This agreement provides for the strengthening and extension of the apprenticeship system and the development of part-time jobs and "growth jobs", i.e. jobs that over a given period will evolve from part-time jobs (traineeships) into full-time jobs. As it now stands, however, it is only an agreement on principles, and will have to be implemented in practice through collective agreements and other means. The parties recognise that, to be effective, it will also require a measure of government support, and they have expressed the hope that it will be presented to the Foundation of Labour and be discussed with the Government with a view to expanding it into a national agreement. Resistance within the trade union movement (especially from organisations of young workers) has so far prevented the implementation of the agreement, even in manufacturing.

THE TRADE UNIONS AND SOCIAL SECURITY

Relations between the trade unions and the Government have been difficult during the past eight years, and not only because of the composition of the Government itself (a coalition of Christian Democrats and Liberals, whereas coalitions including the Socialists usually get on better with the unions). More serious irritants have been the Government's measures to control real wages, mentioned earlier, and, especially, its moves to cut back on social security benefits.

Action of this kind had already been threatened in 1974, when the Centre-Left Den Uyl Government proposed that the growth of public expenditure (including social security) be limited to 1 per cent annually, but this proposal had been withdrawn following trade union protests. In 1979 the Van Agt Centre-Right Government issued the "Bestek 1981" White Paper, in which the first modest cuts in social security benefits were announced. These were limited to adjustments in the operation of the mechanisms linking benefits and wages. "Bestek 1981" led to strong protests from the whole trade union movement and made consultations between trade unions and the Government even more difficult. In 1981-82 the short-lived second Van Agt Government (Centre-Left) in which the former Prime Minister, Mr. Den Uyl, was Minister of Social Affairs, clashed head-on with the trade union movement over sickness benefits.

The present Centre-Right Lubbers Government is pursuing a "no nonsense" policy of budgetary compression, which includes cuts in social security benefits. All public service gross wages and all social security benefits were frozen on 1 January 1983 and, as we have seen, were reduced by 3 per cent on 1 January 1984. Further cuts in benefits took effect from July 1984 and proposals for a restructuring of the whole social security system were laid before Parliament, though so far no decision has been taken owing to technical problems.

The question of solidarity between the employed and the unemployed has given rise to an uneasy debate within the trade union movement. Some unions (e.g. the FNV industrial workers' union) concede that certain aspects of the Welfare State need to be modified and that priority should be given to a policy of industrial recovery carried out in co-operation with employers and the Government. Other unions (especially those with many unemployed and other non-active members, such as the FNV food and agriculture union) contend on the contrary that all available means, including civil disobedience, should be used to dissuade the Government and Parliament from making cuts in social security benefits.

DEVELOPMENTS AT THE ENTERPRISE LEVEL

The "agonising reappraisal" of the structure of the trade union movement, its tactics and even its ideology that started in the 1960s [5] has resulted in two distinct developments: the presence of trade unions on the shop-floor has been strengthened, and the legislation on workers' representation within the enterprise (based on the Works Councils Act of 1950) has been substantially amended.

A union presence on the shop-floor

Since the idea of in-plant union activity *(bedrijvenwerk)* was first introduced in the late 1960s,[6] provisions regulating such activities have been incorporated into an increasing number of collective agreements: 44 (covering 833,000 workers) in 1974 and 67 (covering 1,117,500 workers) in 1977. Nowadays most agreements contain such provisions.

Generally speaking, the purpose of these activities is defined as being to improve communications between trade unions and their members. Some agreements specifically provide that they are intended to assist the works council. The plant-level union representatives are workers elected by the union members in the enterprise and enjoy protection against dismissal. The employer undertakes to grant the representatives a number of facilities, allowing them to devote a certain amount of their working time to trade union activities, the use of company rooms and access to company information, bulletin boards, and so on. Under some agreements employers are entitled to suspend the work of trade union groups within the enterprise during labour disputes.

When I was Minister of Social Affairs in 1981, I introduced a Bill under which employers would be bound to accept trade union activities on the shop-floor provided at least 3 per cent of the personnel or ten workers in the enterprise were members of the trade union in question. The employer and the trade union would negotiate the exact extent of the activities to be permitted. The union members engaged in such work would enjoy special protection against dismissal (similar to that enjoyed by members of works councils). The Lubbers Government withdrew this Bill in 1983.

The new Works Councils Act of 1979

In 1979 Parliament adopted a new Works Councils Act [7] recognising the dual role played by these bodies. Besides representing the workers and expressing their views, the works council is responsible for furthering the interests of the firm as a whole. Under the new Act the works council has the following rights:

(a) decisions on economic matters that have important social implications (e.g. new investment, closing down of the enterprise or expansion of its activities) may be taken by the employer only after the works council has been consulted and has had the opportunity of expressing its opinion on the

matter. The employer is required to take the council's opinion into account in his decision; if the council considers that he has failed to do so, it may appeal against the decision to the special Chamber for Undertakings of the Court of Justice in Amsterdam;

(b) other decisions — known as "social" decisions — may only be taken with the council's consent. In such cases, the council has the right of veto. One example is the appointment of any new member of the supervisory board of a company. A new element in the Act is the rule that the works council appoints its own chairman (previously the employer/manager acted as chairman). The council is, therefore, now complete even in the absence of the employer.

STRIKES

Strikes tend to be particularly costly to both parties in countries with centralised bargaining systems, and this has helped to keep strike figures on the low side in the Netherlands. Indeed, the number of days lost by strikes while the centralised wage policy was in force was extremely low, but the situation has not changed radically since it collapsed. The number of days per annum lost by strikes seldom exceeds a few hundred thousand: it was 300,000 in 1979, but only 56,000 in 1980 and 24,100 in 1981. A wave of labour unrest, however, swept the country in 1983.

In the annual budget drawn up that year the Government proposed, as mentioned earlier, that all public employees' gross wages should be reduced by 3.5 per cent from 1 January 1984. This proposal, which was accepted by Parliament, led to strikes and working to rule in some public service sectors — the railways, postal services, Customs and, initially, the police. The work-to-rule protest by the police was banned by court order. The railway workers engaged in "rolling" strikes (one region after another going on strike) and working to rule. In the postal services well-organised strikes lasting three weeks stopped the collection and distribution of mail. This was the first major outbreak of strikes in the public sector since 1903.

While the right to strike is not regulated by law, it had long been accepted by the courts where the private sector was concerned. When the Government ratified the European Social Charter in 1980 it was expected to introduce legislation granting the same right to public employees. Its failure to do so led the courts to decide that the Government had *de facto* recognised this right, which they upheld in a number of judgements. During the 1983 strikes, however, the courts ruled that the police did not have the right to strike and that there were limits to the amount of prejudice which a strike might cause to the public. When a court in The Hague was asked to end the railway workers' strike, it ruled that the Government and trade unions must return to the bargaining table.

The strikes did not cause the Government to backtrack, although it did decide, so as to avoid any actual fall in the take-home pay (including cost-of-living allowances) of most public servants on 1 January 1984, to reduce the cut in their gross wages from the intended 3.5 per cent to 3 per cent. The strikes that had begun at the end of October petered out after the first week of December. The dispute with the public service employees was attributable to the Government's decision to use its power as an employer to force through the policy it had adopted as custodian of the country's economic health. The trade union movement now solidly opposes the Government's economic policy, which is dictated more and more by the conviction that the budget deficit has to be reduced. Although the leaders of the private sector unions have from time to time expressed a lack of sympathy for the public service employees' position, their shared distaste for the economic model followed by the Government has united the three trade union federations with the public employees.

PROPOSALS FOR PROFIT-SHARING

Over the years a good deal of thought has been given to the establishment of machinery whereby workers could share in the profits and capital wealth of the firms they work for, but so far all efforts in this direction have proved abortive.

Following the publication in 1964 of a report by a joint study group set up by the three trade union federations to consider worker participation in the growing capital formation in the industry of the Netherlands, a plan was put forward to allow workers to share in companies' undistributed profits. A combination of profit-sharing and property ownership for employees was worked out. By participating in "social investment societies", workers would be able to share in the accumulation of capital in the economy. To make the scheme generally applicable, a system of investment wages was recommended for public employees and other workers in non-profit-making institutions. However, the plan was widely criticised on the grounds of its complexity and the threat it was said to pose to the future of private enterprise, with the result that it never got off the ground.

In 1974, during a parliamentary debate on the need for a wage freeze, the then Minister of Social Affairs, J. Boersma, proposed that legislation should be prepared to introduce a general system of "property-sharing through profit-sharing" *(Vermogensaanwasdeling)*. Following the collapse of the Centre-Left Den Uyl Government in 1977, it fell to the Centre-Right Van Agt Government to develop this legislation. However, the technical problems of the proposed system turned out to be insurmountable, political differences within the coalition led to a stalemate and in 1982 the Centre-Right Lubbers Government withdrew the proposal.

FUTURE OUTLOOK

The labour relations scene in the Netherlands is fraught with uncertainty, fluctuating between consensus and controversy. Although the trade unions clashed with the Government during the autumn of 1983, the central agreement on the reduction of working hours is being implemented through peaceful collective bargaining in all industries and in many undertakings. Moreover, the FNV, which had withdrawn from the consultative machinery (and most importantly from the Social and Economic Council) as a protest against government policy, returned to the bargaining table in January 1984. Its president is calling for new central agreements on such matters as further reductions in working hours and technological change. Within the FNV the debate continues over the stand taken by the industrial workers' union that the main priority is industrial recovery and that all other matters, including social security, should be subordinated to that need. The industrial workers' union is prepared to co-operate closely with the employers and the Government in trying to achieve an industrial upturn. Other unions have quite different ideas.

In short, the old controversy over the respective merits of confrontation and co-operation has been reopened within the largest trade union federation. It is not yet clear what the outcome will be. The Government has adopted a policy of economic austerity that does not appeal to any of the trade unions. Even the CNV, long known for its "reasonable" attitude, is bitterly critical of the Government and the parties comprising the present coalition (especially its political relative, the Christian Democratic Party).

Meanwhile the trade unions are losing members. The FNV membership dropped from 1,080,000 in 1979 to no more than 920,000 in 1984. Given the new affiliation of former Catholic unions, the CNV might have been expected to have about 350,000 members, but has in fact only 315,000. The white-collar unions are not faring much better. And the unions' power is declining not only in the labour market but also in the political arena.

The employers' organisations are much better off. They support the Government's policy and are reaping the fruits of their stronger position. They see the signs of an economic recovery that promises to mark the beginning of the end of the recession.

Meanwhile the principal consultative organ (the Social and Economic Council) is going through a difficult period. The Council complains that the Government does not heed — and often does not even ask for — its advice. A committee of independent experts (the Wagner Committee) has published four reports which have had much more influence on official policy than any report of the Social and Economic Council. It came as no surprise to anyone that the Council had great difficulties in finding a new president and had to fall back on a relative outsider to succeed Dr. de Pous in February 1985. The "neo-corporatist" tradition of labour-management and even tripartite co-operation in the Netherlands has certainly been seriously weakened. Whether it will be able to survive the problems created by the economic situation, the breakdown of the consensus achieved during the early 1970s and the blows dealt to the trade union movement by the recession, it is still too early to say.

Notes

[1] Professor, Faculty of Economics, Limburg University.

[2] See W. Albeda: "Recent trends in collective bargaining in the Netherlands", in *International Labour Review* (Geneva, ILO), Mar. 1971, in particular pp. 252-256.

[3] Wage Determination Act, 12 February 1970. For an English translation of this Act, see *Legislative Series* (Geneva, ILO), 1970 — Neth. 1.

[4] The Foundation of Labour is a private bipartite body set up by the three trade union federations and the employers' federations, in which the workers' and employers' representatives have equal voting rights.

[5] Albeda, op. cit., p. 260.

[6] ibid., p. 261.

[7] For an English translation of this Act, see *Legislative Series*, 1979 — Neth. 1.

RECENT TRENDS IN COLLECTIVE BARGAINING IN SWEDEN

An employer's view

Lars-Gunnar Albåge [1]

Ever since the noted American writer Marquis W. Childs published his book *This is democracy — Collective bargaining in Scandinavia* in September 1938, the Nordic countries in general, and Sweden in particular, have enjoyed a reputation for enlightened co-operation between employers and trade unions. In the 1950s and 1960s, in fact, Stockholm became a Mecca for students of stable and harmonious labour-management relations.

Some hopeful pilgrims still turn up in the Swedish capital from time to time and find, to their surprise, that things are in a state of flux nowadays. Most arrive unaware of the dramatic changes that have occurred on the Swedish economic and social scene over the past ten years as a result of a number of important developments. Our aim in this article will be to analyse these developments and describe the changes that have taken place, particularly in the pattern of collective bargaining.

ECONOMIC DEVELOPMENTS

Two developments in particular have radically affected Sweden's economic situation in recent years: the growth of the public sector, accompanied by an increasing burden of taxation, and the repercussions on the economy and on international trade of the oil price rises in the 1970s.

In 1960 public expenditure, i.e. on government and municipal services and social transfer payments, corresponded to 31 per cent of the gross domestic product (GDP), roughly the same proportion as in several other advanced industrial nations. By 1970 it had reached almost 44 per cent and Sweden was about to take the lead in public spending. Today, the figure is about 65 per cent — the highest in any free market economy. The corollary of course is higher taxes, which in Sweden's case now fall most heavily on the employer. In 1984 the total tax burden in Sweden was estimated to correspond to 51 per cent of GDP. The large budget deficit resulting from the difference is reduced somewhat by other sources of government revenue but it still amounted to approximately 10 per cent of GDP in 1984. At the end of that year the national debt came to some

540,000 million kronor (with a foreign debt of 135,000 million). Interest on the national debt amounts to 55,000 million kronor annually. (By late 1985 there were about 8 kronor to the US dollar.)

Part of the spending programme has been financed by higher payroll taxes or levies — charges for the national pension scheme, social security, labour exchanges, adult education, child care, etc. — paid in full by the employer. (The Swedish system differs from that in many other industrial nations, where part of these charges is paid by the employee.) These payroll or salary charges added 42 per cent in 1984 to the pre-tax basic wage cost of blue-collar workers and 46 per cent to the salary cost of white-collar personnel. Most of the charges — 36 percentage points — are statutory while the rest relate to benefits negotiated between the employers' organisations and the unions. The rapid increase in the statutory charges in the mid-1970s narrowed the scope for labour-management negotiations.

Of special interest to wage negotiators has been the marginal effect of the highly progressive state income tax on personal net earnings. In 1960 the average married industrial worker paid a marginal income tax of 29 per cent — i.e. of the last 100 kronor earned, 29 were paid in personal income tax. In 1974, when the marginal tax effect peaked, the figure was 64 kronor out of the last 100 earned. Local taxes are not progressive but the average tax rate levied by 285 local governments has doubled since 1960, from about 15 per cent to more than 30 per cent.

Furthermore, there are additional marginal effects for wage earners in the low- and middle-income brackets. For instance, many local authorities charge fees for children at day nurseries or kindergartens according to the parents' annual income and subsidise housing in the same manner. For some wage earners, a pay increase can mean a lower net income if kindergarten fees are increased and housing subsidies reduced.

This tax burden has of course caused problems for pay negotiations, not only because individual employees have derived little benefit from whatever pay increases have been granted but also because of the varying effects of taxes for different groups of employees. Political transactions on the subject of taxes were a recurrent feature of the 1970s. Key years were 1974 and 1975 when the Social Democratic minority Government of Olof Palme met with representatives of the non-socialist Opposition at the Haga Palace on the outskirts of Stockholm to work out a series of "sweeteners" for the forthcoming wage negotiations: essentially these had the aim of lightening (at the cost of increased employers' charges) what had become an oppressively heavy tax burden on the average industrial worker.

Again in the spring of 1981 the Centre-Liberal coalition Government of Thorbjörn Fälldin met with the Opposition to try to hammer out a similar set of agreements. As a result, the direct marginal tax effect for the average industrial worker declined from 64 per cent in the mid-1970s to 50 per cent in 1985. But even the current tax scale is a subject of considerable debate — a debate that centres on the role of government and parliament in wage setting.

It is now widely recognised in practically all political camps that the signatories of the Haga agreements seriously underestimated the demand-triggering effects of the legislative and political steps they took. Together with the effects of the oil shock these resulted in a home-made inflationary bomb which exploded in the years 1974-76, increasing overall labour costs (negotiated pay increases plus wage drift plus additional employers' charges) by some 55 per cent. At the same time productivity improvements slackened dramatically.

The international reader should bear in mind that no Swedish post-war government has attempted to fight inflation with unemployment. "Full employment" has been the motto for all governments, regardless of their political colour. The official visible unemployment rate has been kept down to between 2 and 3 per cent of the total workforce. However, this has been achieved in part by giving a great number of people employment in government-subsidised public works, state-run adult education and vocational training programmes, municipal youth centres, and so forth.

Sweden's reaction to the first oil-price rises in 1973-74 was somewhat different from that of many other industrial nations: rather than tighten their belts the Swedes attempted to eat their cake and have it too. The Government earnestly attempted to follow the recommendations of the OECD for bridging the gap in demand caused by the oil-price shock: in particular, it encouraged export industries to carry on manufacturing goods as normal, in spite of declining international demand, and to stockpile finished and semi-manufactured products. (As it turned out, international demand remained at a low level for years and most of the stocks eventually had to be sold at a loss.) Public spending and investment were also vastly increased.

Sweden's unsuccessful attempt to bridge the gap in international demand softened the immediate impact of the first oil shock, but made things worse in the long run. During much of the 1973-82 period the economy recorded little or no growth. The average annual increase in GDP during the 1970s was barely 2 per cent as against 4.6 per cent in the 1960s. In spite of the low growth rate and the rising national debt, however, the social welfare system continued to expand. And this, together with the so-called automatic cost increases in the public sector, absorbed a constantly growing share of the nation's total resources. The result was that there was not enough economic growth to allow any increase in real wages and salaries. On the contrary, workers' purchasing power actually decreased.

All in all, the years since the 1973 oil shock have been a time of trial for business and industry. Considerable structural changes have had to be made because of the country's altered competitive position in world markets. The Swedish shipyards that once ranked second in the world to those of Japan, the steel mills, the iron-ore mines, pulp and paper, and several other industries have carried out large-scale restructuring programmes, in many cases with the aid of massive government investment and accompanied by state take-overs.

During the late 1970s profitability in Swedish business and industry was catastrophically low. These developments forced rationalisation measures and mergers among private companies, when the Government was not begged for help. As a result, private industry has become more sensitive than ever to industrial relations conflicts.

Increased costs resulting in particular from collective agreements, wage drift, and higher payroll or salary charges have caused a gradual deterioration in the competitive position of Swedish export industries. Sweden has devalued its currency no fewer than five times since 1970, and twice within two years: in 1981 by 10 per cent and again in 1982 by 16 per cent.

Owing to improved economic conditions abroad and the 1981 and 1982 devaluations, Sweden's export industries experienced a boom in 1983-84. However, this must not be allowed to hide the fact that some of the individual agreements recently concluded between employers' associations and unions at the industry level (discussed below in connection with decentralised bargaining) have already led, and will continue to lead, to excessive cost increases that will eventually jeopardise the beneficial effects of the devaluations on Sweden's competitive capacity.

ORGANISATIONAL DEVELOPMENTS

As a corollary to the rapid increase in public spending, employment in the public sector has more than doubled, from less than 775,000 in 1965 to 1.6 million today. During the same period employment in the private sector decreased, from approximately 2.9 million to some 2.6 million.

In 1969 a political initiative by the Social Democrats resulted in the separation of state-owned companies from private sector employers for purposes of representation and bargaining. Sweden today has no fewer than six major employers' negotiating bodies besides the old-established Swedish Employers' Confederation (SAF).

This is a big change from the time of Childs's book when there were only two major central organisations sitting at the bargaining table in the Grand Hotel in Saltsjöbaden — the SAF and the Swedish Confederation of Trade Unions (LO). The basic agreement they signed in 1938 had far-reaching consequences for the entire labour market. During the post-war period the salaried employees' unions in the private sector grew in strength, but employees in the public sector did not really come into the collective bargaining picture until 28 years later. It was only in 1966 that they were granted a major extension of their right to negotiate and were allowed to go on strike. Public employees began to play a leading role in the annual wage bargaining process in the mid-1970s, a prominence that was confirmed in 1980 and again in 1984. Let us now see how the current situation on the organisational front compares with that described by Gunnar Högberg in these pages in 1973.[2]

Private sector organisations

Established in 1898, the LO is the central organisation for 24 branch unions with 2.1 million members. Approximately 90 per cent of all blue-collar workers in Sweden belong to unions affiliated to the LO. The Swedish Federation of Salaried Employees in Industry and Services (PTK) was formed in 1973 and negotiates on behalf of a score of unions belonging to the Swedish Central Organisation of Salaried Employees (TCO) and the Swedish Confederation of Professional Associations (SACO), which in 1975 merged with the National Federation of Civil Servants (SR) to form the Central Organisation of Swedish Professional Workers (SACO-SR). Unions negotiating through the PTK have a combined membership of almost 500,000. The TCO, covering about 70 per cent of all white-collar workers, has approximately 1 million active members, and the SACO-SR some 260,000.

The most important organisation on the employers' side is the SAF, which was founded in 1902. It is made up of 36 employers' associations, to which some 40,000 enterprises are affiliated. They have a total workforce of 1.3 million, of whom 60 per cent belong to unions affiliated to the LO and the remainder mainly to the white-collar unions.

Negotiating with the same counterparts are the Employers' Association (SFO) for state-owned and public companies, covering 108,000 employees, and the Swedish Co-operative Employers' Association (KFO) covering 100,000 employees.

Public sector organisations

Two LO unions negotiate on behalf of blue-collar workers in the public sector: the Swedish Municipal Workers' Union (SKAF), the biggest single union in the LO family with 567,000 members (but not all working full time), and the State Employees' Union, which has 202,000 members. As for white-collar workers, the Swedish Central Organisation of Salaried Employees-Federation of Civil Servants (TCO-S) comprises 12 unions with a membership of 260,000 civil servants. The Swedish Federation of Salaried Local Government Employees (KTK) is a negotiating cartel for eight TCO unions with some 215,000 members.

Organisations negotiating on behalf of employers in the public sector are the National Agency for Government Employers (SAV), covering 605,000 employees; the Swedish Association of Local Authorities, covering 520,000 employees; and the Federation of Swedish County Councils, covering 377,000 employees. These have their own co-ordinating committee called OASEN.

LEGISLATIVE DEVELOPMENTS

During the 1970s Sweden witnessed a veritable flood of new legislation in the field of labour-management relations. This, too, can be viewed as a break with the pattern described by Childs, who had made a point of the frequent informal talks between central union leaders and top spokesmen for the SAF. One of the hallmarks of what was later to become known as the "Swedish model" was precisely this readiness to reach an understanding through informal contacts and to have its terms confirmed by an agreement but not spelt out in any law.

It is difficult to say what caused this tide of legislation. For several years during the 1960s, the Liberal Party pressed for more active labour legislation in Parliament, a line that was taken up, rather reluctantly, by the Social Democrats. At the same time the LO adopted an increasingly radical stance and persuaded the Government to follow it on many issues. Some argue that one of the reasons for the growing body of legislation was that union leaders in the public sector had not really grasped the uniqueness of the "Swedish model". They demanded legislation where an agreement had sufficed before. Others claim that it was a wildcat strike in the winter of 1968-69 at the state-owned iron-ore mines (LKAB) that triggered the change. Wildcat strikes spread to other industries for a brief period.

An Australian, Doron Gunzburg, Assistant Secretary of the Human Relations Branch of the Commonwealth Department of Productivity, who in 1975-77 spent 15 months in Sweden as an exchange scholar, wrote:

The discussions and debates surrounding these strikes, which had as their basis the nature of working conditions and the lack of influence of workers, led to the expression and clarification of many issues which had been emerging for some time. These issues covered such matters as the isolation of the central unions from the feelings of their members, the extent and speed with which social reform had transformed workers' general living conditions outside their workplace, where changes had not occurred to the same degree, the adverse effect on workers of rationalisation and technology over which they had little control or influence, the shifting attitudes and priorities of young workers entering the workforce and growing disenchantment among trade unions with the role of works councils as an avenue of influence.[3]

It is generally agreed that the psychological effect of the LKAB strike was far greater than its practical consequences, and it may have led politicians and union leaders to overestimate the effectiveness of legislation. New laws were passed regulating a number of issues that had previously been dealt with in collective agreements, and the subject-matter for collective bargaining between the social partners was considerably reduced.

In 1971 the LO Congress (which meets every five years) adopted a comprehensive programme on co-determination and demanded extensive changes in the labour legislation. Since the LO has close links with the Social Democrats, a whole series of labour Bills were laid before Parliament by the Social Democratic Government. Suffice it here to mention only the most important of the laws adopted.

In 1972 an Act was passed on the representation of employees on company boards.[4] As revised in 1976, this law now provides that the local trade unions have the right to appoint two members and two deputy members to the boards of virtually all companies with at least 25 employees.

The 1974 Act on the status of trade union representatives at the workplace [5] regulates the right of shop stewards to time off for union activities. The trade unions can also decide, within certain limits, what activities they may engage in during company-paid hours at the workplace.

The 1974 Act respecting the right of employees to time off for training purposes [6] extended the prerogatives of employees and the trade unions substantially. There are today no real restrictions on the type or duration of training and studies that individual workers are entitled to request.

The 1976 Act respecting co-determination at work [7] has attracted some international attention. The law covers all firms employing one or more union members. The most important co-determination elements in the Act are the following. The employer has an obligation to negotiate before making any major change affecting the employees in general or any individual employee. If no agreement is reached at the plant level, the union can refer the matter to "central" negotiations. If the employer fails to negotiate or to observe the rules he can be ordered to pay damages to the union. The employer also has an obligation to disclose information. Unions are granted wide access to most company books. They are also granted a "priority" right to interpret agreements, which means that the union's view on "joint regulation" rights or the duties of an individual worker prevails unless it is overruled by the Labour Court or another legal authority. In certain circumstances, the unions have the right to veto the use of subcontractors.

The 1977 Working Environment Act [8] replaced an older law on occupational safety and health and extended the rights of unions to demand improvements.

The 1979 Act respecting equality between men and women at work [9] was passed when the non-socialist parties were in power. The majority of the unions and the Social Democratic Party — and of course the employers — would have preferred to go on developing the labour-management agreements that already existed.

Another important — and extremely controversial — piece of legislation came in 1983 with the Act establishing Sweden's five wage earner funds. These funds, which are financed by both a payroll tax of 0.2 per cent and a proportion of the profits of Swedish joint-stock companies, are used to buy shares in Swedish firms. If the local trade union in a company in which the wage earner fund owns shares so requests, the fund transfers to the union 50 per cent of the voting rights corresponding to its holdings.

In our view, the new laws have deprived the Swedish labour market of much of the "spirit of Saltsjöbaden" as evinced in the old agreements between the SAF and the LO — and in the direct telephone talks between the two chairmen described by Childs in 1938. This change of attitude, together with the other trends described in this article, has also presented a threat to labour peace. The new legislation did not prevent a major conflict from breaking out in 1980. Following a series of limited strikes aimed at paralysing key sectors of the economy, the SAF responded with a lock-out which lasted one week and affected some 600,000 LO members. Massive strikes and lock-outs also beset the public sector in 1980. In 1981 a strike by white-collar unions hit a few big companies affiliated to the SAF. In the spring of 1985 a full-scale strike in the public sector, with air-traffic controllers and Customs officers in the forefront, paralysed Sweden's airports and harbours and seriously hurt the country's export industries.

UNION RIVALRY AND PAY COMPARABILITY

One of the radical changes on the Swedish labour market scene attributable to the lack of economic growth is that which has taken place in the aspirations of trade unions. Instead of sitting down at the bargaining table as before to claim a share in the fruits of ever-increasing production, the unions have had to content themselves with redistributing existing — even shrinking — resources.

This has led to growing competition among various groups of employees. In the private sector blue- and white-collar workers have been pitched against each other, while public servants have found themselves involved in a wage battle against the private sector.

Although, as mentioned earlier, trade unions and their central organisations in the public sector have grown in size and strength and have at times even taken the lead in wage negotiations, the common pattern for concluding agreements has been for the LO and the SAF to set the "norm" and for the rest of the labour market to follow suit. One of the main reasons for this procedure, accepted by Government and Opposition alike, and agreed to with some grumblings by public sector spokesmen, has been the fact that the LO and the SAF negotiate the wage levels for most of the blue-collar workers in Sweden's key export industries. (The only major exceptions are some state-owned and co-operative manufacturing industries and the iron-ore mines.) It was thought that the ceiling for wage increases ought to be set at a level where Sweden's competitiveness in its main export markets is not jeopardised. Awareness of what is happening abroad should act as a moderating factor at the LO-SAF bargaining table.

Since the 1973-74 oil shock, however, the higher labour costs resulting from the excessive rise in payroll charges in 1974, 1975 and 1976, from the new legislation described above, from negotiated wage increases and from inflation-induced wage drift (Sweden has had a higher rate of inflation than its main competitors in recent years) have reduced the profitability of Swedish enterprises to the point where there would have been very little indeed to negotiate about had the export-competition criterion been applied. But it was not. With the LO unions demanding wage increases that could not be justified by Sweden's competitiveness abroad, and the non-LO unions determined not to fall behind in the wage race (many of them had succeeded in having pay comparability or "catch-up" clauses included in their collective agreements), the restraint that had hitherto characterised Swedish pay bargaining disappeared and even the reduced wage settlements dictated by the unfavourable economic situation had a snowball effect across the entire labour scene. As we have already seen, in 1980 a major labour market conflict could not be avoided, and the currency has been devalued twice since then.

These tendencies have intensified the employers' criticism of the centralised bargaining system that was already mentioned by Högberg in 1973.

CENTRALISED VERSUS DECENTRALISED BARGAINING

The main criticism from the employers' side has been that the industry-wide and sometimes nation-wide centralised negotiations have led to large cost increases and yet have not been able to prevent labour disputes. Central agreements have been too inflexible and detailed and have tended to exert an exaggerated influence over the local labour market, allowing the individual employers' associations and companies insufficient leeway to adapt wages to their own circumstances. They have tended to become an instrument for promoting the LO's policy of "wage solidarity", and the narrowing of differentials has gone too far. In this way, the centralised collective bargaining system, which was warmly supported by the employers in the 1950s as the best solution to the problems of the day, has in their view gradually developed into a stiff, inflexible framework which allows only negligible adjustments to the diverse requirements not only of the employers but also of individual employees and of the local labour market.

What lay behind the introduction of centralised bargaining in the mid-1950s was the employers' desire to avoid drawn-out negotiations and bring labour peace to the entire private sector. The LO, for its part, saw centralised bargaining as a means of putting into effect the policy of wage solidarity adopted by the Swedish labour movement in 1951 and followed ever since.

The first central agreements were fairly simple documents defining a "frame" for wage increases and leaving it to the parties in each contracting sector to distribute the benefits as they saw fit. Over the years, however, the central agreements have become ever more complex, reflecting the growing desire of the LO and its unions to decide most of the particulars at the bargaining table in Stockholm. In the name of solidarity the LO has increasingly concentrated its efforts on obtaining larger increases for the lower paid and for those deriving little or no benefit from wage drift. The resulting demands for equivalent pay rises by other groups, especially private sector salaried employees, have put an additional strain on the negotiating system and conflicts have occurred.

Since the mid-1970s the centralised bargaining system has been under attack, primarily from the employers' side, but also from blue-collar unions with a tradition of "sweating for a good buck" (high pay for hard work), such as the iron miners in the north, as well as from some white-collar groups. They feel that the levelling-down of incomes in Sweden has hit rock bottom and can go no further.

There are differences of opinion among the employers about how the situation should be corrected. Most of the associations belonging to the SAF consider that the system of centralised negotiations should be reformed within its existing framework. Overall co-ordination of negotiations would be retained but the results would take the form solely of recommendations and constitute a much looser "frame". Bargaining proper would be carried out at the industry level. Catch-up clauses and other detailed provisions would be eliminated from future agreements.

However, the desire has been expressed, especially in the engineering industry, to go further and reject the centralised bargaining system altogether. The Swedish Engineering Employers' Association (VF), a SAF member, did not give the parent organisation a mandate to represent it in the 1983 negotiations. Its wish to keep wage negotiations at the industry level turned out to be shared by its counterpart, the Swedish Metalworkers' Union, and a separate agreement was signed in 1983 for the engineering industry. Negotiations for the other industries were co-ordinated under the direction of the SAF and the LO. The same pattern was followed in the negotiations covering white-collar workers.

Prior to the 1984 round of negotiations, internal discussions were renewed within the main central organisations — the SAF, the LO and the PTK — on the appropriate formula for future talks. The mood was for a more decentralised approach: in 1984 separate negotiations were held between industry associations and the corresponding unions for all LO-affiliated blue-collar workers. They were not preceded by any centralised talks between the SAF and the LO, as had been the case in 1983 for industries outside the VF. As in 1983, white-collar workers in the engineering industry also signed a separate agreement with the VF; for the rest of industry the negotiations covering white-collar workers were co-ordinated by the SAF and the PTK.

In 1984 there was also less co-ordination than before in the public sector, where the unions and their employer counterparts representing municipal governments and county councils were the first to announce officially the conclusion of an agreement.

GROWING GOVERNMENT INTERVENTION

As part and parcel of the original "Swedish model" for harmonious labour-management relations, a tacit understanding existed that there should be no government interference before the talks between the social partners started, while they were under way, or after the agreement had been signed. The signatories were responsible for their acts and should bear the consequences. All that belongs to the past, and recent years provide several examples of government intervention in one form or another.

In the early 1970s the Government found itself forced to intervene in a civil servants' dispute and, as we saw earlier, judged it expedient to alter the tax rules before the annual round of wage talks took place. The widespread labour unrest in 1980 was termed "political" by some observers, implying that one of the aims of the unions was to topple the non-socialist Fälldin Government which, however, intervened during the course of negotiations with a package of economic policy measures that favoured the workers' side. The Government brought the dispute to an end by a direct appeal to the SAF to accept the mediation offer.

The introduction by the Social Democratic Government in 1983 of the extremely controversial employee investment fund scheme (the so-called wage earner funds, referred to above) is a measure that has also been interpreted as intervention in pay negotiations, as well as one with far-reaching political and ideological implications.[10]

In the same year the Government set itself the target of keeping inflation down to 4 per cent during 1984. When it realised early in 1984 that it would be unable to do so because of over-generous pay agreements, it fixed an even more ambitious inflation target for 1985: 3 per cent. The Social Democratic Government was thus led to intervene in the preliminary phase of the negotiating process in a number of ways.

The tactic employed in the 1985 wage round was to invite the heads of the various central organisations — in a blaze of publicity — to the Prime Minister's office in the Rosenbad House in Stockholm where the Prime Minister and the Minister of Finance urged the parties again and again to keep wage increases in line with the Government's anti-inflation policy. The Government announced a target of 5 per cent for the maximum increase in labour costs in 1985. In order to gain the unions' support for this it decided on further economic policy restrictions, including a freeze on the distribution of company profits.

As a result of the Government's intervention through the Rosenbad talks, the 1985 pay negotiations might be described as a combination of centralised and decentralised bargaining. In February the SAF and the LO agreed on a very loose recommendation endorsing the 5 per cent target. Negotiations covering salaried employees in the private sector followed the same pattern as in 1983 and 1984. Difficulties arose in the public sector when white-collar workers put forward pay demands based on promises contained in earlier agreements and, as we have seen, a damaging strike broke out. By breaching the 5 per cent limit the settlement finally arrived at is bound to store up trouble for the future.

From what has been said above it will be clear that the situation today bears little resemblance to what it was in 1938 when the "Swedish model" was born. SAF and LO leaders then met at a quiet seaside hotel in Saltsjöbaden away from the curious eyes of the Stockholm press, and the Prime Minister of the day, far from intervening in these talks, advised against even sending a messenger to hear how things were going.

CONCLUDING REMARKS

The historical course of events leading up to the present situation has been extremely complex and the various participants may view what has happened in different lights. Our selection of trends and our evaluation can of course be challenged, but the fact remains that Sweden is now a very different type of society both from the one Childs described in the 1930s and from what it was during the 1950s and 1960s when the "Swedish model" flourished.

In our own view these changed circumstances call for a searching reappraisal of the present policies, especially within and among the trade unions, but also within the employers' organisations. As we have seen, the mood of collective bargaining in Sweden has shifted from consensus to polarisation.

To put it in a nutshell, the challenge now confronting the parties on the Swedish labour market is to adapt their policies to a new economic climate where growth is difficult to achieve, where governments will be struggling with a large public sector deficit for years to come, and where Sweden's export industries face an entirely new competitive situation in world markets.

Such is the turbulent position in which we find ourselves at the present time. We definitely cannot say that there is a clear-cut model for collective bargaining in Sweden today. Whether the social partners will be able to act in concert in order to get the economy moving again is something we cannot yet tell. If they fail, then increased government intervention in the collective bargaining process may become an enduring characteristic of the Swedish labour market. We can only express the hope that out of the present labour pains a new Swedish model will be born, resembling its forerunner.

There are, in fact, good chances of this. Despite the adverse trends mentioned above, there are many sound elements of the Swedish economy and industrial relations system that have survived and can be built on. Sweden has a fundamentally strong business sector rooted in a well-structured and efficient manufacturing base. In their hearts the Swedes share a deep community of values. The representatives of labour and management can still mix with each other centrally and locally in a spirit of trust and are capable of working together on matters of common interest. Promising signs are the agreements that have been concluded in recent years on such collaboration and, above all, the fact that the debate on wage policy is now being conducted in the broader context of the nation's economic health. The LO is actively participating in this debate and has taken upon itself to tell its members that Sweden's standard of living in the future will depend on its ability to adjust costs in industry to levels comparable with those prevailing in its competitors.

A trade unionist's reply

Harry Fjällström [11]

Swedish collective bargaining today indeed presents a very different face from the one it assumed at Saltsjöbaden nearly 50 years ago, but not, I submit, for the reasons given by Albåge.

The Saltsjöbaden agreement had been preceded by many years of turbulent industrial relations during which the negotiation of separate agreements covering different groups of workers and employers and different periods of time was a never-ending process. The result was frequent work stoppages and poor economic performance — with a real danger that the authorities would be tempted to intervene.

It was to combat this risk, but above all because both sides of industry recognised that labour peace was the most important single factor for economic growth and the reduction of unemployment, that the 1938 agreement was concluded. The "Swedish model" of industrial relations that was to grow out of the Saltsjöbaden agreement worked well. The centralised bargaining system introduced during the 1950s further improved the model, inter alia by offering an opportunity to promote the fairer distribution of pay increases — what has come to be known as the policy of "wage solidarity".

In the mid-1970s the situation changed. There are a number of reasons for this. One of the most important was the increasing dissatisfaction felt by employers at the situation they found themselves in following the first oil shock.[12] In their view taxes and labour costs were too high, the return on capital was too low, and the labour legislation enacted in the 1970s was too restrictive. (It may be noted in passing that some of this legislation was adopted only when it proved impossible at the bargaining table to win some form of say for the workers in such vital matters as the representation of employees on company boards.) These factors, which combined to depress company profits, and the return to power after so many years of a non-Social Democratic Government in 1976, strengthened the employers' determination to make a stand. The result was to be seen in the lead-up to the 1977 bargaining round when they announced that pay increases must be conditional on a whole series of measures whose effect would be to impair workers' fringe benefits and legal rights.

A problem to which the employers were particularly sensitive was the alleged inadequacy of wage differentials, attributed to the LO's policy of wage solidarity. In fact, these differentials were (and still are) not all that small, for two main reasons. In the first place, the non-socialist Government introduced a policy of income redistribution which, through devaluation, tax changes and inflation, resulted in large transfers of resources from the lower paid to the more prosperous income groups. The second and probably more important reason was that the LO's efforts to improve the position of low-paid workers were resisted not only by the Government and the employers (who pinned much of the blame for their high labour costs and diminishing competitiveness on the policy of wage solidarity), but also by a number of the union groups outside the LO.

This trend had been noted as long ago as 1968 when the then LO President, Arne Geijer, observed that the relative position of the low paid could never be improved if the TCO and SACO unions (representing white-collar and graduate employees respectively) continued to insist on maintaining their members' differentials. The following year the SAF broke with tradition when, in the midst of negotiations with the LO, it suddenly concluded an agreement with the white-collar employees in the private sector. This five-year agreement was original in that it contained a clause which provided the possibility of adjusting white-collar pay to wage improvements secured by the LO unions. This had the important consequence that non-LO affiliates benefited from the efforts made by the LO on behalf of its low-paid members, thereby defeating the aim of greater wage equity.

By the mid-1970s a new union negotiating body, the Swedish Federation of Salaried Employees in Industry and Services (PTK), had appeared on the scene and was demanding substantial increases to offset wage drift favouring LO members. In the public sector, too, pay claims were being put forward to match the increases agreed for the LO. The result of all this — aggravated by uncertainty about how inflation might develop — was that everyone wanted to know what everyone else was going to get before they would sign an agreement. Those who had to settle first reserved the right to reopen the negotiations if other groups did better, and even those who settled later insisted on similar safeguards.

All this was a far cry from the traditional Swedish model of orderly bargaining and restraint. It was not long before the effect on labour peace made itself felt. The LO had always been extremely reluctant to resort to industrial action and invariably afforded the conciliation commission an opportunity to propose a compromise solution. By the second half of the 1970s, however, it seemed that this determination to uphold labour peace was no longer shared by either the employers or some of the other unions.

I have already referred to the tougher stand taken by the employers during this period. It seemed in fact that they increasingly meant to get their way even at the cost of open conflict. They also adopted a new tactic: when a dispute loomed, they omitted to reply to the conciliation commission's proposals within the stipulated time-limit and simply waited for the LO to give its answer before giving theirs. This undermined the trust between the two sides and made it harder for the conciliators to do their work.

When the 1980 pay talks between the LO and the SAF broke down, the employers dragged their feet on the appointment of a team of conciliators, with the result that the LO had to give notice of industrial action before the Government would name them. Technically, then, a strike had already started before the conciliators began their work, and the LO rejected their appeal to call off industrial action during the conciliation proceedings: things were not made easier by the fact that the chairman of the conciliation commission had already come down on the employers' side. The LO reacted to what it saw as the SAF's obstructionist tactics by itself taking a firm stand, and the upshot was a large-scale dispute that soon spread to the public sector.

The deterioration that had occurred in industrial relations from the mid-1970s onwards — symptomatic was the SAF chairman's description of the 1980 lock-out as "an investment in the future" — led some employers to conclude that it was the system of centralised bargaining that was at fault. In our view it could more accurately be attributed to the progressive *weakening* of centralised bargaining with the emergence of new trade union groups and the growing doubts among employers that the traditional system served their interests. These doubts were reinforced when the PTK unions called a series of selective strikes by key categories of employees, causing major disruption to the firms affected. If centralised bargaining cannot prevent such disputes, the employers argued, then better have decentralised bargaining. This was not entirely logical, since agreements reached centrally in no way preclude agreements covering specific branches — indeed, the PTK unions have their own wage scales — and in any case, while employers are not immune to industrial action under centralised bargaining, they are even more vulnerable under agreements concluded with individual unions.

Over the past few years bargaining has been in disarray and, in the last analysis, unprofitable to all parties. The unions have obtained high nominal pay increases but little or no improvement in real earnings (these would have fallen sharply in 1983-85 but for certain tax adjustments). The international competitiveness of Swedish business improved thanks to the devaluations and rises in productivity. But it was *not* helped by the employers' unsuccessful efforts to reduce pay increases through negotiating with individual unions — indeed, by sparking off a free-for-all, this had the contrary effect.

Many people in Sweden see this unsatisfactory experience and the frequent breaches of labour peace as linked to the departure from the centralised bargaining system. At the same time there is widespread agreement that prosperity must be safeguarded and equitably shared. This is why I believe that the pressures favouring the return to co-ordinated central negotiations will prevail, even if slight changes may be expected in the unions' distribution policy. The bargaining system that has come to be known as the Swedish model of industrial relations has stood the test of time and I am confident that, provided it is given the opportunity, it will continue to serve both sides of industry well for many years yet.

Notes

[1] Deputy Director-General, Swedish Employers' Confederation (SAF).

[2] G. Högberg: "Recent trends in collective bargaining in Sweden", in *International Labour Review* (Geneva, ILO), Mar. 1973, pp. 223-228.

[3] D. Gunzburg: *Industrial democracy approaches in Sweden. An Australian view* (Melbourne, Productivity Promotion Council of Australia, 1978).

[4] For an English translation of this Act, see *Legislative Series* (Geneva, ILO), 1972 — Swe. 1.

[5] ibid., 1974 — Swe. 3.

[6] ibid., 1974 — Swe. 6.

[7] ibid., 1976 — Swe. 1. See also A. Bouvin: "New Swedish legislation on democracy at the workplace", in *International Labour Review*, Mar.-Apr. 1977, pp. 131-143.

[8] *Legislative Series*, 1977 — Swe. 4.

[9] ibid., 1979 — Swe. 2.

[10] On this point, see R. Meidner: "Collective asset formation through wage-earner funds" and H.-G. Myrdal: "Collective wage-earner funds in Sweden: A road to socialism and the end of freedom of association", in *International Labour Review*, May-June 1981.

[11] Head of Department, Swedish Trade Union Confederation (LO), and member of the LO Presidium.

[12] Not all the problems confronting employers at this time were new. Thus high taxes and labour costs had long been a feature of the Swedish scene, but they were perceived as particularly burdensome once the recession began to bite.

RECENT TRENDS IN COLLECTIVE BARGAINING
IN THE UNITED KINGDOM [1]

B. C. Roberts [2]

INTRODUCTION

The decade which has passed since the publication in the *International Labour Review* of the previous study of trends in collective bargaining in the United Kingdom [3] has seen fundamental changes in the level and structure of employment, the membership and power of unions and the legal framework of industrial relations. In spite of these changes industrial relations are still primarily based upon collective bargaining arrangements voluntarily accepted by employers and trade unions without the intervention of the State. But voluntarism no longer means that the law is virtually absent from industrial relations. In the collective bargaining process unions must now exercise their power within legal boundaries which set limits to their freedom to strike and to picket that are much closer to those existing in many other countries. Individual employment rights have been extended by law to provide remedies for unfair dismissal, redundancy, and sex and race discrimination. The Government intends that the rights of union members to run for office, to vote for their leaders in a secret ballot and to have an opportunity to express their support or opposition when asked to come out on strike are no longer to be dependent on the union rule book alone, and introduced a Bill in 1983 to establish these rights in law.

The past decade was extremely volatile. It began with a bitter conflict between the unions and the Government over the comprehensive reforms introduced by the 1971 Industrial Relations Act. On the election of a Labour Government in 1974 the 1971 Act was swept away to restore the total immunity which the unions had enjoyed from legal action against them by employers. At the same time they were given the support of the law in gaining recognition and securing improvements in minimum pay, and individual employee rights were further extended. As public policy leaned in support of the unions the balance of power was tipped against the employers.

Faced, however, by the failure of the British economy to reach the growth targets that could sustain the pay levels achieved by the unions through collective bargaining and the improvements which they demanded in social welfare and public services, the Labour Government was compelled to try to secure a social contract that would restrain union demands and lower the high levels of inflation that were undermining the stability of the economy. These efforts, which had some success for a period, led eventually to great tension between the unions and the Government and, after a "winter of discontent", contributed to a mood of disillusion which brought the Conservatives back into office in 1979.

Between 1979 and 1983 the new Government, against a background of general recession, rapidly rising unemployment and a collapse of manufacturing capacity in the steel and engineering industries, set out to kill inflation, improve productivity and encourage investment by restoring profitability, which had reached vanishing-point in much of British industry. The Labour Party's approach was abandoned in favour of vigorous competition encouraged by lower taxes — financed by the reduction of subsidies to nationalised industries and their eventual privatisation — and the curbing of public expenditure on education, health and social welfare to levels consistent with the real output of the economy. This policy, in a period of general economic recession when most other advanced industrial economies were taking similar steps to avoid economic collapse, inevitably raised the level of unemployment, which reached 3 million by 1982, a figure not seen for 50 years.

However, those who were in employment benefited from the fall in inflation to less than 5 per cent in 1982, and real wages continued to grow. Opinion polls showed that the confidence of many union members in their leadership and in the Labour Party was decreasing, and it came as no surprise when, in June 1983, the Prime Minister, bolstered by her handling of the Falklands conflict, secured a comfortable victory in a general election which gave the Conservatives five more years of power. The Conservatives' manifesto included continuation with the reform of trade union law, the privatisation of nationalised industry and economic policies based upon keeping inflation under control by curbs on public expenditure and the money supply. These policies inevitably had an influence on the evolution of collective bargaining and will continue to do so in the period ahead.

TRADE UNIONS

Changes in trade union membership and effects on the coverage of collective bargaining

Trade union membership rose by over 3.2 million during the 1970s and in 1979 reached a peak of 13.4 million, or 55 per cent of the labour force, in spite of the fact that the numbers employed in such traditionally highly unionised industries as shipbuilding, coal, railways, textiles, clothing and boot and shoe manufacture were falling. The decline in these industries was more than offset by increases in the public sector, notably in national and local government, education and health services, civil aviation and telecommunications. There was also a considerable increase in the employment and union membership of clerical, technical, administrative and professional employees, whose readiness to unionise in order to secure the advantages of collective bargaining was a continuation of a trend that had already become evident in the 1960s.[4] So, too, was the substantial increase in female union membership.

The growth in trade union membership was dramatically checked in 1980 as economic activity plunged downwards and unemployment rose rapidly, especially in those sectors where union membership had been traditionally high. By the end of 1982 total trade union membership was estimated to have fallen by over 2 million and the proportion organised to below 50 per cent of the labour force; the fall continued through 1983 and may well do so for some years.

Although the biggest declines were in the private sector, which bore the main brunt of the recession, there were also sharp drops in the nationalised iron and steel industry and in civil aviation. Perhaps the most significant development for the future was the great difficulty encountered by the unions in organising the rapidly growing high-technology sector. As in the United States, workers in the computer-based industries have shown little interest in joining unions and the unions have not found a way of overcoming this resistance. The precise effect of large-scale movements of union membership on collective bargaining has not been comprehensively researched in Great Britain, but it is assumed by the unions themselves and by employers, politicians and academics that density of union membership is related to coverage and union bargaining power. If the assumption is correct it should be revealed by trends in coverage, strikes, rates of change in pay, hours of work and other conditions of employment. Proving a causal relationship between movements in trade union membership and outputs of the industrial relations system is by no means a simple matter, as the current debate on the impact of unions in the United States shows.[5]

It would be reasonable to expect an expansion of the coverage of collective bargaining in periods of substantial economic growth and the reverse in times of considerable decline in trade union membership. Unfortunately the statistical evidence on which this hypothesis could be tested is not readily available in Great Britain. Gregory and Thomson [6] were, however, able to present some tentative findings on the changes in coverage between 1973 and 1978, since in those two years a question relating to bargaining structure was asked in the annual New Earnings Survey. Unfortunately, since this question has not been repeated, it is difficult to do much more than hazard a guess at what has happened in this respect during the past five years.

Somewhat surprisingly Gregory and Thomson found that between 1973 and 1978 there had been a slight fall in the percentage of employees covered by collective bargaining, from 71.8 to 68.6. This reflected changes in the composition of the workforce and in the structure of collective bargaining. The fall had come predominantly in the coverage of male manual workers — especially in engineering — and in managers of both sexes in agreements made at the national level. At the company and local level there had been significant increases, reflecting the shift towards establishment-based bargaining, but not sufficient to offset entirely the falls resulting from the decline in national bargaining that had been going on for several decades.

The inference that may be drawn from the rapid increase in trade union membership and the virtually unchanged coverage of collective bargaining is that new members of unions were recruited mainly within established collective bargaining units.

During the past five years the numbers of employees covered by collective agreements will have fallen considerably with the rise in unemployment, but the percentage of workers in employment covered by collective agreements has declined very little.

Legislative changes affecting trade unions

Recognition

In the 1970s there was a substantial growth in the number of formal union recognition agreements, stimulated by the Royal Commission on Trade Unions and Employers' Organisations, which strongly advocated the formalisation of agreements at the establishment level. This development was further encouraged by the 1971 Industrial Relations Act which sought to promote union recognition and orderly collective bargaining. The Trades Union Congress (TUC), though opposed to the Act, urged unions to secure voluntary recognition agreements spelling out in detail the rights and duties of the parties and the procedures that should be followed to ensure effective processes of collective bargaining.

The repeal of the 1971 Industrial Relations Act in 1974 and the enactment of the Employment Protection Act in 1975 placed the independent Advisory, Conciliation and Arbitration Service (ACAS) on a statutory basis and charged it with the "general duty of promoting the improvement of industrial relations, and in particular of encouraging the extension of collective bargaining and the development and, where necessary, reform of collective bargaining machinery".[7]

Amongst the responsibilities of ACAS was assisting the unions to gain recognition for collective bargaining purposes, through the conduct of an inquiry into the degree of employee support for a union seeking recognition. If it was satisfied that this was adequate to make collective bargaining viable it could recommend the employer to grant recognition. If the employer failed to comply the union concerned could ask the Central Arbitration Committee established in 1975 to award specified improvements in terms and conditions of employment for the employees involved. In keeping with the voluntary tradition it was not given legal power to enforce recognition.

This procedure was quite extensively used, but it gave rise to many difficulties and both employers and unions eventually accepted that the compulsory element had not worked satisfactorily and did not oppose its repeal in 1980. It was estimated that some 65,000 employees had secured the right to be represented by a union under the statutory procedure, but this was less than the number — some 75,000 — who had done so through voluntary conciliation.

Union membership agreements and union labour only contracts

The formalisation of union recognition was taken a stage further by unions persuading employers to negotiate union membership agreements. Gennard et al.,[8] in a study carried out in 1978, concluded that 5.2 million union members — 23 per cent of the workforce — were covered by formal or informal union membership agreements. A more recent study, made in 1980,[9] suggests that the proportion was possibly 27 per cent.

The growth of compulsory union membership — the closed shop — has undoubtedly contributed to the formalisation of collective bargaining processes, especially in the larger firms and in the public sector, and is seen by some as being due almost as much to the desire of management for orderly industrial relations as to the wish of the unions to achieve greater membership security and bargaining power.

Conservative governments and many workers and managers have viewed the closed shop as a threat to the individual rights of employees, as well as a significant factor in the strength of union opposition to more efficient work practices and the ability to force employers to concede inflationary wage settlements. Under the Industrial Relations Act of 1971 pre-entry closed shops were made void and post-entry closed shops (sometimes called "union shops") unenforceable by giving employees the right to be exempted on the grounds of conscientious objection. Under the Trade Union and Labour Relations Act of 1974 the Labour Government swept away these restrictions, but in 1980 the incoming Conservative Government, in the 1980 Employment Act, again sought to protect employees who had a conscientious objection to the closed shop by giving them the right to claim unfair dismissal. In the case of new closed shops the Act requires a union to secure in a ballot vote a majority of not less than 80 per cent of employees entitled to vote. Without this endorsement any dismissal on grounds of non-membership is unfair and renders the union liable to be joined with the employer and made to share the cost of any compensation and damages awarded to the employee dismissed. Under the 1982 Employment Act these damages have been raised to penal levels.

The 1980 Act, together with the effects of the recession which brought high unemployment in branches such as vehicle manufacture, mechanical engineering and shipbuilding, where the closed shop has traditionally been strong, virtually stopped the making of new closed-shop agreements. In a survey conducted in 1983 for the Department of Employment, Professor Gennard calculates that union membership in closed shops fell from a peak of 5.2 million in 1978 to 4.5 million in 1982 — a decline of 13 per cent.[10]

Gennard suggests that most unions, confronted with matters of more pressing concern to their members, have ceased to accord the closed shop a high priority. It remains to be seen, however, whether this observed drop in union support for the closed shop will encourage union members to reject existing union membership agreements from 1984 onwards if the matter comes to a vote, as it will do under the 1982 Act if there has been no secret ballot endorsing the closed shop in the previous five years.

Where closed shops have been in existence for long periods it is unlikely that employers will actively seek to persuade the unions that they should be abolished, but there is evidence that employers are changing their attitudes towards giving unions the same degree of support as in the past. Feeling that unions have abused their power, many employers are no longer as willing to negotiate union membership agreements, to check off union subscriptions and to provide facilities for what they often regard as an excessive number of shop stewards. Under the pressures of shrinking levels of demand and widespread redundancies shop stewards have put up only limited resistance to these developments unless they have seriously threatened to undermine their ability to represent union members' interests.

With the growth of the closed shop it had become common for unions in the printing industry, the building trade and local government (especially where controlled by Labour councils) to insist that employers should have commercial dealings only with unionised firms which observed conditions of employment the same as, or similar to, those in their own firm. Under this pressure, employers were called upon to refuse to consider tenders for contracts from firms unless they were on a list approved by the unions and to insert in all commercial contracts a requirement that union labour only would be used.

The 1982 Act makes clauses in commercial contracts legally void if they seek to make union membership or non-membership a condition of the contract. It also makes unlawful any other practice designed to exclude firms from contracts on the grounds that they employ or do not employ workers who belong to a union. Those who transgress these prohibitions will be liable to injunctions and to damages, which may be sought by anyone who might be adversely affected, if it can be shown that a loss has been suffered.

Some personnel managers [11] who have favoured closed-shop agreements and other measures to strengthen unions have predicted that the change to a less accommodating policy will produce a backlash when the demand for labour increases. If, however, there is no return in the 1980s to the kind of political and economic environment that existed until the end of the 1970s, there may well be a continued decline in union strength in the private sector. In the public sector, where the trade unions are now most strongly entrenched, their future power is also problematical. A lot will depend on how much of the public sector is dismantled by the Conservatives and whether there is a return to a strong Labour Government in the next decade.

Industrial action

The 1980 and 1982 Employment Acts have had a number of direct effects on industrial action. The 1980 Act redefined the legal limits of picketing during an industrial dispute and the limits of lawful secondary action. Under pressure from employers the 1982 Employment Act removed some of the protection which had been conferred on employees taking part in industrial action by the 1975 Employment Protection Act. The 1982 Act further reshaped the law by changing the definition of a lawful trade dispute and removing the blanket immunity which unions had enjoyed since the 1906 Trade Disputes Act, except for the short period when the 1971 Act was on the statute book.

Taken together, these changes have narrowed the legal limits of strike action. Picketing in an industrial dispute is now lawful only if the pickets are picketing their own place of work, unless they are trade union officials representing those who are in dispute with the employer and are accompanying a member who is employed at the place of work being picketed. The section of the Act regulating picketing does not give rise to any criminal offence, but it does give the employer and other injured parties an opportunity to seek an injunction against the pickets.

Among the main purposes of the 1982 Employment Act were, according to the Department of Employment, to bring the legal immunities for trade unions into line with those for individuals so that trade unions would become liable to pay damages if they organised unlawful industrial action. To be lawful, trade disputes now must be between workers and their own employers and wholly or mainly concerned with terms and conditions of employment; engagement, suspension and termination of employment; allocation of work; matters of discipline; membership or non-membership of a union; facilities for union officials; or recognition of union rights to represent workers and procedures for negotiation and consultation.

The aim of the Act was to deter a union from seeking to bring pressure on an employer to concede union demands by extending a strike or other action to third parties not directly involved in a dispute. The new definition of a "lawful trade dispute" means in effect that sympathy strikes are almost always likely to be unlawful and, if authorised by a union, to render it liable to legal proceedings.

In December 1983 the National Graphical Association was fined a total of £675,000 for violating an injunction granted to an employer which called on the union to refrain from illegal picketing. In addition, the court ordered the seizure of the union's assets until such time as it obeyed the law. When the union appealed to the TUC for help the General Council decided that it could only support union actions that were within the law.

The 1974 Trade Union and Labour Relations Act, as amended in 1976, protected employees taking industrial action called by a union in Great Britain which related to an issue that had arisen abroad. Such action is now lawful only where it can be clearly shown that the employees in Great Britain taking this action are likely to be directly affected in respect of matters that are the object of lawful industrial action.

The Government has indicated that it intends to take reforms in the legal framework of industrial relations still further. In a Bill before Parliament it proposes to remove immunity from legal action in cases where trade unions do not hold a secret ballot before authorising a strike or any other form of industrial action that interferes with or breaks the employment contracts of those called upon to take part in it. The Bill does not require that there must be a majority in favour to sustain the right of immunity.

The Government is also giving consideration to proposals to limit the exercise of the right to strike in industries and services essential to the community; the Prime Minister has stated that further legislation may follow the Bill on ballot voting at present before Parliament.

EMPLOYERS' ORGANISATIONS

With the shift to plant and enterprise systems of collective bargaining the role of employers' organisations has inevitably changed. A recent study [12] suggests that in spite of this development there has been little fall-off in the membership of employers' organisations during the past decade, no doubt because they continue to provide important services which are highly valued and increasingly used. These services include negotiating and administering procedures to deal with disputes, providing information and advice, consultation and representation.

Certain industries, including electrical contracting, sections of port transport and shipping, are covered by comprehensive industry-wide agreements. Employers in textiles, printing, construction and a number of other industries negotiate less comprehensive, but still fairly substantial agreements. At the other extreme are organisations such as the Engineering Employers' Federation and Chemical Industries Association, which negotiate agreements at the industry level covering only minimum rates of pay, length of the working week, annual holidays, and shift and overtime payments.

It is clear that employers' organisations are likely to go on playing an important role, both in the collective bargaining process and in many other aspects of industrial relations. There is some evidence that their influence might begin to grow again if they can take new initiatives. The Engineering Employers' Federation has already embarked on this course, and is trying to negotiate framework agreements that permit member firms to negotiate flexibility between trades and occupations, entry into skilled occupations and training at any age, to introduce flexible working schedules spread over 24 hours and a seven-day week, and to review demarcation agreements that can no longer be justified.

On the whole, employers' organisations and individual employers have given strong support to the 1980 and 1982 Employment Acts, though with some differences of opinion between different categories of managers. The strongest support for the new legislation has come from senior executives and production, finance and marketing managers. Personnel managers have given more cautious support and warned against the dangers of management relying too heavily on the law as a means of reforming industrial relations.

COLLECTIVE BARGAINING

Trends in bargaining structure

There is great diversity in the structure of collective bargaining in Great Britain. The significance of industry-wide negotiation has declined since the Second World War in most of the private sector, but it remains of varied importance in a substantial number of industries. Many employers continue to belong to employers' organisations and in most industries there continue to be negotiations on a limited range of issues between employers' organisations and trade unions at the national or industry level. Below this level bargaining may take place at the district or local level and at the level of the enterprise or plant. In many industries there is bargaining at all these levels.

In the public sector the structure of bargaining is also complex — although perhaps not quite so complex as in the private sector — because the actual employing institutions have differing degrees of autonomy. Generally speaking, the dominant form of bargaining is at the national level, but on certain pay questions and many other matters it also takes place at regional or local levels.

Studies by Daniel and Millward [13] and Brown [14] have shown that in pay bargaining there is a clear correlation between the size of the establishment and the level at which agreements are made. There are, however, differences between industries. The general trend has been towards single-employer bargaining, but in paper, printing, textiles, clothing, footwear, fur and leather, multi-employer bargaining is still the dominant form.

By the beginning of the 1980s more than two-thirds of manual employees and three-quarters of non-manual employees in private manufacturing companies employing more than 50 full-time workers were covered by single-employer agreements.[15] If, however, the economy as a whole is taken a different picture emerges, as Daniel and Millward [16] have shown: the proportion of firms reporting multi-employer bargaining as having the most importance for pay increases was 46 per cent in the private sector and 75 per cent in the public sector.

Brown and Terry [17] have suggested that there are forces, which appear as yet to be only straws in the wind, that are pushing the larger multi-plant enterprises "towards more centralised or higher-level bargaining". British Leyland has been a well-publicised case in which annual pay bargaining was removed from plant to corporate level under pressure from the management.

More recently there have been examples of a shift in the other direction. Particularly dramatic is that of the nationalised British Steel Corporation, which refused in 1981 and 1982 to negotiate any pay agreement at the national level. The Corporation slightly modified this stance in 1983, but it has by no means abandoned the view that pay at plant level should be determined by reference to local labour markets and productivity standards.

The shift to plant-level bargaining was first encouraged by the growth in the power of shop stewards under conditions of full employment, and consolidated by the emergence of professional personnel managers who made common cause with shop stewards in concentrating on issues that were of primary importance to peaceful and efficient management of the plant. Out of this development emerged the full-time shop steward paid by the company to represent the interests of employees who were covered by union membership agreements. Brown [18] has calculated that the number of full-time officials employed by the unions by the end of the 1970s had barely changed over the previous 20 years, but that "the number of full-time shop stewards had soared so as to outnumber them by perhaps as much as two to one in the private sector".

Influence of the recession on plant and enterprise industrial relations

The growth in plant bargaining and the numbers of full-time shop stewards has tended to isolate plant industrial relations from the union organisation outside the plant. This tendency was evident from the number of unofficial strikes in the period up to the beginning of the recession in 1979. Since 1979 strikes have fallen to the lowest level for two decades and unofficial strikes have become much less frequent, especially in the private sector. This has been mainly due to the effect of rising unemployment, but the formalisation of agreements, improvements in pay structures, the widespread use of job evaluation, the growth of single-employer bargaining at plant or company level and the development of procedural agreements, often including provision for third-party intervention, will all have helped, as will the improvement in communications and the extension of employee participation.

During the recession it might have been expected that shop stewards placed in a weak bargaining position would have become more dependent upon full-time union officials. This has not proved to be the case; in fact, union officials seem to be playing a less important role than before, owing to a number of factors.

First, unions are being compelled by falling incomes to economise on staff and services, thus weakening the links between national and regional officials and stewards and plant organisations.

Second, although shop stewards are in a weak bargaining position, some union leaders, influenced by militant minorities, have urged them to fight redundancies, plant closures and much lower levels of pay increase by taking strike action. Quite often rank-and-file members have been reluctant to adopt this type of response. As the employment situation has worsened and employers have insisted on smaller numbers of stewards and set tighter limits on their role, their strength has decreased. Rather than resist contractions in employment by strike action, workers have shown increasing readiness to take redundancy payments and early retirement lump-sum cash payments.

Third, employers have sought by careful selection to retain the more efficient and more co-operative workers. The old demarcation lines drawn by unions between skilled and less skilled workers have grown more blurred.

Internal labour markets have become more important as job evaluation, on-the-job training and greater flexibility have become dominant themes. Advancing technology specific to a particular enterprise has undermined the grip of the craft union on its members in a period when apprenticeship has begun to disappear. Control at the workplace has shown a tendency to pass back to management.

This trend has been reinforced by greater harmonisation of working conditions between manual and non-manual workers. Incremental salary scales, membership of sickness and pension schemes, redundancy and early retirement provisions have all bound shrunken groups of manual workers closer to their employers. The initiative for these changes in conditions of employment and work patterns has generally been taken by management.

The development of workplace-centred industrial relations has meant that collective bargaining has become a more complex activity in terms of the roles of the two parties, of its structural characteristics, and of its relationship to other forms of representation and the evolving pattern of collective and individual legal regulation.

The role of wages councils

Great Britain has never had a statutory minimum wage covering all employees. Since 1909, with the passing of the Trade Boards Act, it has followed a policy, supported by both unions and employers, of buttressing collective bargaining by the establishment of tripartite boards with power to fix legally enforceable minimum wages and related conditions of employment for workers employed in industries and services determined by the Secretary of State, following a public inquiry into the effectiveness of voluntary collective bargaining as a means of ensuring acceptable minimum standards.

After the Second World War unions became less enthusiastic supporters of the wages council system, since they came to believe that a statutory system of wage fixing might be a deterrent to collective bargaining. In 1947 there were 69 wages councils; by 1983 the number had fallen to 26, covering some 2 million workers employed in 350,000 establishments. This decline was due mainly to the growth of trade union membership and the spread of collective bargaining, to the effects of the labour market during the long period of relatively full employment, and to various forms of statutory assistance.

In 1979, in response to the unions' concern, a Wages Councils Act was passed which sought to make wages councils more independent of the State and to give unions a more positive role so as to facilitate an evolution from the tripartite wages council system to a bipartite collective bargaining system. The Act gave the unions that were represented on wages councils the right to appoint their own members, and the powers of the councils were extended to cover a wider range of terms and conditions of employment than the traditional wages, working hours and holidays. Wages councils were no longer required to submit their decisions to the Secretary of State for approval; they were given the power to issue their own wages regulation orders and to decide when these would take effect. As a step towards the replacement of a wages council by voluntary collective bargaining ACAS was given the responsibility, at the request of the Secretary of State for Employment, for carrying out inquiries into the establishment, abolition or revision of wages councils. As an intermediate step towards collective bargaining ACAS was empowered to recommend the conversion of a wages council into a statutory joint industrial council without independent members, but none has so far been established.

The slowing down of the economy and the rise in the level of unemployment since 1979 have made the unions much more reluctant to agree to the abolition of wages councils and other forms of statutory support. Employers, too, have been cautious and those covered by wages councils have made few demands that they should be abolished. This is probably because wages councils protect them on the one hand from more aggressive collective union demands for recognition and bargaining, and on the other hand from competitive wage cutting which might also be damaging to their industrial relations and competitive position.

With the rise in unemployment and the advent of a government that is strongly committed to a free market economy and lower levels of government regulation of business activities, there have been strong attacks on the maintenance of statutory minima as a cause of inflation and higher levels of unemployment. The Government has not yet been persuaded that it should abolish all wages councils at one fell swoop, though it is clearly ready to continue the process of reducing their number when this course has the support of employers and unions.

The role of public policy in private sector bargaining and public sector pay determination

During the 1970s there was growing criticism of the effectiveness of collective bargaining as a system of pay determination. There was also much controversy over the efficacy of the reforms suggested by the Royal Commission report of 1968 with a view to formalising bargaining, creating more effective procedures and generating greater responsiveness to the need to achieve higher productivity and better utilisation of labour and prevent highly inflationary levels of pay settlements.

All parties recognised these problems, but there was no real consensus on how effective reforms could be achieved. The Confederation of British Industry (CBI) argued, first, that the Government should stop trying to regulate pay increases by central controls, as it had done repeatedly since the end of the Second World War, but should set an example by pursuing monetary and fiscal policies consistent with maintaining a stable price level. As the largest employer it should ensure that it did not encourage, through the processes of "comparability", inflationary pay settlements in the private sector. The second requirement was a campaign to bring about a more realistic appreciation of the fundamental factors that were undermining Great Britain's economic performance. Third, there was the urgent need to reorganise the tangles of existing collective bargaining arrangements so as to discourage leap-frogging in the scramble for higher and higher pay packets. Fourth, it was essential for there to be a more even balance of bargaining power between trade unions and employers.

To achieve these objectives the CBI called upon employers and their organisations to seek to rationalise bargaining units between plants, enterprises and industries; to limit the annual pay round to the first three months of the year; and to revise pay structures so that differentials had a rational basis related to skill and responsibility.

This initiative had a cold reception from both the Labour Government and the TUC. The Government did not accept the CBI's belief in the virtues of market forces in circumstances of tighter control of the money supply and public expenditure. It had, moreover, embarked on another attempt to curb runaway inflation by a "social contract" with the TUC, setting a ceiling on pay rises in exchange for increases in social benefits and higher taxes on upper incomes and the wealthy.

The TUC viewed the CBI proposals as utopian, but they may well have encouraged the General and Municipal Workers' Union, whose General Secretary was the current Chairman of the TUC, to put forward proposals for revising and co-ordinating the bargaining arrangements in the public sector. A TUC Public Services Committee was established in 1979, but the change in the political and economic climate over the past four years has frustrated its objectives.

Under the Labour Government's pay policies between 1977 and 1979 public sector employees felt they were being unfairly treated as their pay was more strictly controlled than pay in the private sector. They lost confidence in the social contract and responded by a massive bout of militant strike activity which culminated in 1978-79. Faced with this situation the Labour Government set up a national Commission on Pay Comparability with responsibility for establishing an acceptable basis of pay comparison right across the public services and finding an urgent solution to the bitter disputes that had developed.

Before the Conservatives were elected to office in 1979 they had given a pledge to accept the findings of the Commission in the cases which had been referred to it. These produced an explosion in public sector pay and proved to be extremely inflationary in their effect. The Government responded by abolishing the Commission, and imposed a tighter limit (4 per cent) on annual increases in expenditure, including pay increases.[19] It then abolished the civil service Pay Research Unit and abandoned the principles of comparability on which the Unit had worked.

Although the Pay Research Unit had also been suspended by Labour governments during periods of national incomes policies, these decisions of the Conservative Government led to an angry conflict with the civil service trade unions, which engaged in selective strike action. As part of a settlement to this dispute the Government agreed to set up a committee of inquiry into civil service pay under the chairmanship of Mr. Justice Megaw.

The main recommendation of the Megaw Inquiry was that civil service pay should be more closely related to that prevailing on the general labour market as this was influenced by economic and social forces rather than by detailed occupational comparisons based on analogues fixed, in effect, by a bargaining process within an autonomous pay research unit which were then binding on the Government. The Megaw Committee of Inquiry did not reject the concept of comparability completely, but recommended that in future civil service pay should follow broader pay bands; it proposed in place of the Pay Research Unit's annual review a full review of civil service pay every four years based on surveys commissioned from independent consultants. The report on facts would then provide evidence for use in informed collective bargaining. The Committee did not accept the idea that there should be regional variations in pay but it did propose the introduction of merit pay and bonuses.

The Committee of Inquiry examined the proposition that civil servants should be prepared to sacrifice their right to strike in exchange for guarantees that their relative pay and conditions of employment would be protected. It was considered that such guarantees ought not be given since they would run counter to the Committee's conclusion that civil service pay had to reflect economic and social factors.

Nor was the Committee in favour of unilateral arbitration, which had a long history in civil service pay determination, though it conceded that arbitration jointly agreed upon could have an important role. The Committee was aware that a less regulated system of collective bargaining than had previously existed would involve the risk of higher levels of conflict and even strikes, but believed that it was in the public interest that the bargaining parties should take this risk.

The Government accepted the Megaw Committee's report, but the unions were far from satisfied with it. However, they did not believe that they were in a position to secure a return to the old concepts on which the Pay Research Unit had operated. It is too early to forecast exactly how the new system of civil service pay determination through a more open system of collective bargaining will settle down. If, however, it produces a significant rise in the level of conflict, which is widely felt to be damaging to the public interest, further changes may well be made in the future.

In spite of the revisions that are being made in public sector systems of pay determination, it is difficult, given the degree of fragmentation of the systems, the strength of the unions and the inadequacies of managerial strategies and methods of control, to see how the settlement of public pay can fail to be marked by tension and conflict, which from time to time will result in significant outbreaks of industrial unrest.

Extension and scope of collective bargaining

Until the Second World War collective bargaining had a rather narrow scope, being confined to the basic conditions of employment — pay, hours of work, job content and holidays.

With the growth and formalisation of collective bargaining at the plant level there has been a considerable expansion in the range of issues negotiated. The Workplace Industrial Relations Survey listed ten main items in addition to pay that were the subject of negotiation. This list, which is by no means an exhaustive one, comprises physical working conditions, redeployment within the establishment, manning levels, redundancy, major changes in production methods, recruitment, holiday entitlement, length of the working week, capital investment and pensions.

Bargaining on capital investment and pensions is much less frequent than on the other items. There has been rising pressure from unions to persuade employers to grant them the right to bargain on these items, but many employers are not prepared to yield.

Collective bargaining and workers' participation

It was widely believed during the Second World War and the period following it that any formal procedures to consult with employees on broader issues of work organisation and management should be separate from the bargaining process. Since the 1950s and the growth of plant bargaining and the role of shop stewards, this separation has been less clear-cut, but it has never entirely disappeared. Although the same managers and trade union representatives may often be involved, there are still a large number of enterprises, private and public, which maintain separate bargaining and consultative structures.

This separation was deemed important by managements since it enabled them to discuss issues on which they did not wish to bargain, but to be free to take the final decision after consultation. The unions, too, saw the advantage of avoiding commitment on issues that might have compromised their bargaining role. The same concerns were uppermost when it was decided that divisional employee directors in the nationalised steel industry should not be appointed by, or be directly responsible to, the unions operating in the same workplace. This decision was, however, later changed to permit local union officials to serve on the divisional boards in the areas in which they had their union appointments; the adverse effects which had earlier been thought inevitable did not occur.

There was in fact a significant decline in the number of separate joint consultative committees in the 1960s, but research published in 1972 showed that many companies had nevertheless retained them,[20] and there seems to have been an increase since 1977. The Daniel and Millward survey of workplace industrial relations has shown that almost 40 per cent of a random sample of 3,300 establishments had consultative committees. Establishments of similar size had been affected in the same degree, with slightly more growth in the private sector than in the public sector, and rather more in the services sector. Where trade union membership was strong, as in the case of a closed shop, joint consultative committees tended to become an adjunct to the institutions of collective bargaining; where the unions were weak, the committees provided an alternative channel of representation.

The following ten issues in order of the frequency with which they came up were included in the ambit of these committees: production issues; employment issues; pay issues; working conditions; welfare services; health and safety matters; future company developments; fringe benefits; financial issues; administrative changes. Further survey evidence suggested a significant overlap with collective bargaining.

Under the 1975 Employment Protection Act union representatives are entitled to ask for the disclosure of information without which they would be materially impeded in carrying on collective bargaining and which it would be in accordance with good industrial relations practice to disclose. Further practical guidance on disclosure is given in an ACAS code of practice which may be cited and taken into account should there be a complaint to the Central Arbitration Committee that an employer has unreasonably withheld the information a union representative is entitled to receive under the Act.[21]

The Daniel and Millward survey asked managers and manual and non-manual worker representatives how much information was provided on three items: pay and conditions of service, manpower requirements, and the financial position of the establishment. There were significant differences between managers and workers' representatives in the assessment of the amount of information given. Nevertheless, over 50 per cent of the workers' representatives stated that they received quite a lot, or a great deal, of information on pay and conditions of service, and a little over 40 per cent thought they received a significant amount of information on manpower requirements. However, only 30 per cent said they were given enough information on the financial position of the establishment.

An interesting finding of the survey was that requests for information were considerably more common in establishments where collective bargaining was supplemented by formal consultative machinery.

It is clear from the survey and from evidence from many other sources that there is an important change going on in industrial relations at the level of the plant or enterprise. Unions are still overwhelmingly concerned with securing improvements in pay and reducing hours of work through collective bargaining, but employers are responding to rising pressures from their employees for more consultation and information outside the collective bargaining process. This is taking place not only through formal committees. Briefing groups, departmental meetings, working parties and quality circles are now widely established procedures for the participation of employees and the exchange of information between managers and workers.

OUTLOOK

The future of collective bargaining in Great Britain is clouded by uncertainty. In the shorter term perhaps the most significant question is whether a Conservative Government will again be returned to office in 1988 or whenever the next election is held. Since the Labour Party is pledged to repeal the legal framework enacted since 1980, an electoral defeat for the Conservatives would mean another upheaval in the law. It is impossible to say, however, whether a Labour victory would bring a complete return to the situation that existed before the Conservatives came into power.

Also of great significance will be the extent to which the Conservative Government is able to carry through its programme of denationalisation. This policy could lead to the breaking up of centralised bargaining systems in airways, telecommunications and the gas industry. In most parts of the public sector there is some evidence of pressure for decentralisation, but as yet there is no clear indication that centralised bargaining has had its day. Government policies may, however, encourage this development in the next few years.

One of the most crucial factors in the future is likely to be whether the unions can check the fall in their membership and regain their political influence. There are reasons for believing that this will be difficult, since many union members have serious doubts about the policies pursued in the past. Opinion polls have shown that many of them hold the unions responsible for high levels of inflation, slow economic growth, damaging strikes and undemocratic behaviour.

Structural changes in industry which are reducing the size of employment units are leading to better relations between workers and managers. This improvement in plant and enterprise industrial relations is being encouraged, in spite of multi-unionism, by the development of company-centred ad hoc union organisations and by management strategies which are fostering this trend. The resurgence of joint consultation and the rapid growth of quality circles, though not necessarily as an alternative to collective bargaining, are diminishing the effects of multi-unionism, defusing tensions and creating a more harmonious pattern of industrial relations.

Technological advance is creating a new environment in many industries and services and a new type of skilled worker well aware that the problems of adjustment required by new technology cannot be solved by Luddite methods. Managements are also conscious of the need to provide conditions of employment more akin to those enjoyed by white-collar workers in the past.

There is, of course, resistance on the part of union leaders who see their power and even their organisations disappearing under the combined effects of modern technology, and social, economic and political change. The attempts by the National Graphical Association in Britain to maintain its grip on the closed shop as a means of protecting not only its members but its very existence is a classic example of trying to check an irresistible tide of change. Unless the union can find means of coming to terms with these developments, so as to give it an acceptable role in the printing industry of the future, it is bound to wither away.

The advent of the new legal framework, though contested vigorously by the unions, has not aroused the antipathy of public opinion as did the challenge mounted against the Industrial Relations Act between 1971 and 1974. The attitudes of employers are also different. They are no longer reluctant to use the law against unions refusing to accept the need for change, for greater efficiency and for less inflationary pay settlements. An increasing number of employers, especially from overseas, have become deeply sceptical of the advantages of union recognition and collective bargaining. In the major companies industrial relations management has become much more vigorous, aiming at a tighter control of all aspects of personnel administration which in multi-plant enterprises is generally co-ordinated and directed centrally.

In these circumstances the unions are on the defensive. A good many of their more far-sighted leaders have understood the challenge, but others cling to past beliefs and are convinced that history will repeat itself with the return of a Labour Government in a few years' time. However, in many cases where union leaders have sought to make pay claims that employers have resisted as excessive and have called on their members to strike they have not been followed by the rank and file, although the latter have shown signs of readiness to support more aggressive bargaining tactics when there are indications that demand is recovering. It is nevertheless unlikely that strikes will become more frequent unless there is a significant and sustained drop in the level of unemployment.

In spite of the decline in union militancy it is probable on the evidence of the past four years that the collective bargaining process will continue to produce wage settlements somewhat above the rate of economic growth and above the rates of pay achieved by Great Britain's main competitors. The problem of containing inflation is therefore likely to remain a factor of major significance which may once again bring to the forefront of political debate the issue of curbing collective bargaining as a necessary condition for raising the rate of economic growth and lowering the level of unemployment.

In 1973, as the United Kingdom was about to enter the European Economic Community, it was expected that EEC membership would in the course of time influence collective bargaining and the development of wage and other employment conditions in Great Britain. In the event, however, these expectations have proved largely unfounded. There has been a growing interest in the influence of European directives and decisions of the European Court on such issues as sex discrimination, human rights in relation to the closed shop and the European Commission's proposed directives on employee access to information and consultation and participation in the supervisory and management boards of enterprises. These directives have been supported by the unions, but vigorously opposed by employers. The Conservative Government has indicated in a consultative paper that it does not believe the directives on worker participation will contribute to the improvement of industrial relations in Great Britain and it is likely that it will if necessary exercise its veto if it is still in office when a final decision is made by the Council of Ministers. It has nevertheless urged employers to take the initiative themselves to bring about a greater degree of employee involvement without waiting to be compelled to do so by legislation.

The fundamental thrust of industrial relations in Great Britain is likely to continue to be centred on the establishment and the enterprise. Collective bargaining will inevitably reflect this trend, but with weakened union organisation and more positive and open management it is possible that it will become more narrowly focused on pay, with other aspects of working conditions and work procedures being determined through a greater direct involvement of employees in the decision-making process.

Notes

[1] This article refers principally to collective bargaining practice in Great Britain (i.e. England, Scotland and Wales), although many of the general comments apply equally to Northern Ireland. Where "United Kingdom" is referred to, this specifically includes Northern Ireland, and the term "British" can also be assumed to cover the United Kingdom as a whole.

[2] Professor of Industrial Relations, London School of Economics and Political Science.

[3] B. C. Roberts and S. Rothwell: "Recent trends in collective bargaining in the United Kingdom", in *International Labour Review* (Geneva, ILO), Dec. 1972, pp. 543-571.

[4] R. Price and G. S. Bain: "Union growth in Britain: Retrospect and prospect", in *British Journal of Industrial Relations* (London), Mar. 1979.

[5] See J. T. Addison: "Are unions good for productivity?", in *Journal of Labor Research* (Fairfax, Virginia), spring 1982.

[6] M. B. Gregory and A. W. J. Thomson: "The coverage mark-up, bargaining structure and earnings in Britain, 1973 and 1978", in *British Journal of Industrial Relations*, Mar. 1981, pp. 26-37.

[7] For the text of the substantive provisions of the Act, see *Legislative Series* (Geneva, ILO), 1975—UK 2.

[8] J. Gennard et al.: "The extent of closed shop arrangements in British industry", in *Employment Gazette* (London), Jan. 1980, pp. 16-22.

[9] S. Dunn: "The growth of the post-entry closed shop in Britain since the 1960s: Some theoretical considerations", in *British Journal of Industrial Relations*, Nov. 1981, pp. 275-296.

[10] J. Gennard and S. Dunn: *The closed shop in British industry* (London, Macmillan, 1984), Ch. 8.

[11] See, for example, "Man of the moment — Robert Ramsay", in *Personnel Management* (London), Oct. 1981, pp. 32-35.

[12] K. Sisson: "Employers' organisations", in G. S. Bain (ed.): *Industrial relations in Britain* (Oxford, Blackwell, 1983), p. 121.

[13] W. W. Daniel and N. Millward: *Workplace industrial relations survey* (London, Heinemann Educational Books, 1983), pp. 188-189.

[14] W. Brown: *The changing contours of British industrial relations, A survey of manufacturing industry* (Oxford, Blackwell, 1981), pp. 7-13.

[15] ibid.

[16] Daniel and Millward, op. cit., pp. 187-188.

[17] W. Brown and M. Terry: "The changing nature of national wage agreements", in *Scottish Journal of Political Economy* (Edinburgh), June 1978, pp. 119-133.

[18] W. Brown: "British unions: New pressures and shifting loyalties", in *Personnel Management*, Oct. 1983.

[19] D. Winchester: "Industrial relations in the public sector", in *Industrial relations in Britain* (Oxford, Blackwell, 1983).

[20] R. O. Clarke et al.: *Workers' participation in management in Britain* (London, Heinemann Educational Books, 1972), pp. 72-75.

[21] For a discussion of the operation of the law on disclosure of management information to trade unions, see J. R. Bellace and H. F. Gospel: "Disclosure of information to trade unions: A comparative perspective", in *International Labour Review*, Jan.-Feb. 1983, pp. 57-74.

RECENT TRENDS IN COLLECTIVE BARGAINING IN THE UNITED STATES

Donald E. Cullen [1]

By nearly any measure, the collective bargaining system in the United States has been in retreat during recent years. The unionised share of the private American economy, never large compared with that of most other industrialised countries, has grown even smaller as many unionised companies faltered in their product markets and many unions faltered in organising the unorganised. Within the unionised sector that remains, the customary bargaining process has often been stood on its head as the parties negotiated over the extent to which labour would concede to management's demands. And the Federal Government not only has failed to take certain steps that many unionists and others believe are necessary to halt the decline of collective bargaining, such as amending the basic labour legislation, but has even contributed to it through measures such as the deregulation of key unionised industries. All those trends are reasonably clear. Much less clear is whether this retreat of collective bargaining will prove to be tactical and temporary or far-reaching and permanent. That question has generated a major controversy in the United States, with both practitioners and scholars sharply divided in their predictions of the future course of collective bargaining. This article will describe the recent trends that led to this controversy and will offer an appraisal of where they may be leading.

THE RECENT RECORD: AN OVERVIEW

It is usually impossible to pinpoint the moment when any bargaining trend begins, but a settlement between the United Auto Workers (UAW) and Chrysler Corporation in October 1979 was certainly one of the first of the concession bargains that have become common in American industry in recent years. Indeed it is worth looking at the whole series of UAW-Chrysler negotiations from 1979 to 1984, for they illustrate both the nature of concession bargaining and the controversy it has produced.[2]

The Chrysler case at first appeared to be more an exception to the normal bargaining pattern than the portent of a new trend. For nearly 30 years, the three largest automobile companies — General Motors (GM), Ford and Chrysler — had negotiated separate but nearly identical multi-year agreements with the UAW. These agreements determined wage increases by an unusual formula: a specified percentage amount, called an "annual improvement factor", which was initially designed to reflect the improvement in productivity in the economy as a whole, and had provided annual wage increases of 3 per cent since the mid-1960s; and a variable cost-of-living adjustment (COLA) every three months. When the contracts expired in the fall of 1979, the UAW won new three-year agreements at GM and Ford which continued the traditional wage formula and also provided significant improvements in pensions and paid days off (additional to annual leave). One estimate valued the settlement at 33.4 per cent over three years.[3]

At Chrysler, however, management was demanding a two-year freeze on wages as part of its efforts to stave off bankruptcy. The company had lost $250 million in 1978 and was on its way to losing $1,100 million in 1979 and probably even more in 1980; nearly one of every three Chrysler workers represented by the UAW was on lay-off in 1979; and the company was seeking loan guarantees from the Federal Government (which it eventually secured through special legislation). In response to those pressures, the UAW agreed to three increasingly stringent sets of concessions between October 1979 and January 1981: the elimination or deferral of most of the annual improvement and COLA increases that the usual wage formula would have provided, significantly lower pension increases than those the UAW had won at GM and Ford, and the discontinuance of certain paid days off.

Those concessions, when measured against the GM and Ford settlements, totalled $1,100 million, and by 1982 they had opened a gap of about $2.50 an hour between the average wage at GM and Ford and that at Chrysler. In return, the Chrysler management agreed to take several steps highly unusual in American industry: to invite the UAW's president to join the company's board of directors; to initiate profit-sharing and employee stock-ownership plans once the company began to make profits again; to ensure "equality of sacrifice" by pledging that managers, supervisors and employees not represented by the UAW would not be granted any changes in wages, benefits or other conditions of employment more favourable than those granted to UAW members; to permit, in effect, the union to file grievances (but not take them to arbitration) if it believed that the company retained a disproportionately large number of supervisors during lay-offs; and to invest part of the company's pension fund in "socially desirable projects", such as low-cost housing and non-profit health facilities in communities where many UAW members lived. It soon became evident that the Chrysler case was not as exceptional as it had first appeared. In 1981, as the economy slid into a severe recession and foreign competition continued unabated, profits dropped sharply at GM and disappeared completely at Ford; as a result, both companies pressed the UAW to renegotiate their 1979 contracts, which were not due to expire until the fall of 1982. In early 1982 the union agreed to new GM and Ford contracts with concessions similar to those made at Chrysler: no annual improvement factor for approximately 30 months, the deferral of some cost-of-living adjustments, and the elimination of several paid days off. The companies' concessions included a two-year moratorium on certain plant closings; the guarantee of at least 50 per cent of normal pay up to retirement age for laid-off workers with considerable seniority; and several of the concessions to which Chrysler's management had agreed, including profit-sharing (but not union representation on either company's board of directors).[4]

Bargaining in several other industries soon followed suit. In trucking, the Teamsters concluded a new national agreement in 1982, which provided for no guaranteed wage increase for 37 months and a change from six-monthly to annual cost-of-living adjustments. In 1983 the United Steelworkers agreed to an immediate cut of $1.31 in hourly pay six months before the expiry of their contract (with $1.25 to be restored in stages over the next three years), together with the elimination of five quarterly cost-of-living adjustments and other concessions. Concession bargaining also occurred throughout these years in airlines, meat packing, construction, newspapers, tyres and copper.

At Chrysler, meanwhile, the financial picture had greatly changed for the better. The company had accumulated about $1,000 million from the sale of property and vehicles, and in December 1982 the UAW negotiated with it a new 13-month contract providing for a wage increase of 75 cents per hour and the resumption of quarterly COLA payments; in return, the workers agreed to give up the profit-sharing plan they had gained only the year before. Then, in the first half of 1983, Chrysler earned a profit of $482 million and announced that it would pay back $400 million in federally guaranteed loans seven years ahead of schedule. The UAW promptly pressed the company to renegotiate their new agreement before its scheduled expiry in 1984, and in September 1983 the parties concluded yet another contract, this one restoring an estimated $400 million of the $1,100 million in wage and benefit concessions to which the UAW had earlier agreed.[5]

Profits also recovered strongly in GM and Ford in 1983 and 1984, provoking a rallying cry among union members of "Restore [the concessions] and more in '84". The 1984 negotiations at the two industry leaders by and large followed the pre-1980 pattern: bargaining up to the strike deadline (the date of expiry of the existing contracts); a six-day strike against some but not all GM plants (to put pressure on the company at minimum cost to the workers); a settlement at GM involving no significant union concessions and returning to a variation of the old formula of a three-year contract with specified annual increases and quarterly COLA payments, together with other improvements; and the adoption by Ford of the main features of the settlement.[6]

Recent contracts in other industries have varied greatly, ranging from those involving no concessions to those providing for concessions exceeding — and different from — those negotiated in the automobile industry. Yet, the experience in this sector fairly reflects the most intriguing features of bargaining in this country since the late 1970s. First, as most people know, many American employees and their unions have agreed to far-reaching concessions in wages and other conditions of employment. Second, as perhaps fewer people realise, at least some employers paid for those concessions by agreeing to union gains, such as profit-sharing, union membership on the board of directors, and guarantees of income security, that many American managers would have considered unthinkable a few years ago. In addition, the alacrity with which the parties in the automobile industry resumed "bargaining-as-usual" in 1983 and 1984 raises a question about the durability of the changes, in attitudes and practices, that concession bargaining has produced. To investigate this and related questions, it is necessary to examine in more detail both the changing and the stable aspects of American union-management relations over the past several years.

STABILITY AND CHANGE

Some of the recent bargaining trends can be captured in numbers and some cannot. It may be useful to begin with the two dimensions of bargaining that can be quantified most precisely — wages and strikes — because the data on these subjects show graphically the pattern of recent changes.

Wages

Although the typical union contract in the United States has been extended to cover a large number of non-wage issues, the wage bargain remains of central importance in most negotiations. The contract usually establishes the precise hourly or other rate, and not simply a minimum, for each worker covered by the contract, and the wage change resulting from negotiations is often a good measure of the shifting balance of power between labour and management.

Table 1 shows that union wage settlements, unemployment and price increases struck a precarious balance during the stagflation years of the 1970s. During that decade wage increases averaged 6.8 per cent a year (not counting the variable increases that occurred under COLA clauses), unemployment averaged 6.1 per cent, and annual price increases averaged 7.1 per cent. In the chaotic years beginning with 1980, wage increases at first advanced with inflation and then collapsed under the weight of the sharp rise in unemployment in 1982.

Other measures, not shown in table 1, help to bring out the severity of the recent decline in the rate of negotiated wage changes. Of the workers covered by major settlements (those covering at least 1,000 workers) in 1982, 44 per cent received no wage increase at all in the first year of their contract and 36 per cent received no increase during the life of their contract. Most observers have focused on the declining wage increases in manufacturing, where the average annual rate over the life of the contract dropped from 5.4 per cent in 1980 to 1.4 per cent in 1984. In construction, however, the decline was even greater: from an average of 11.5 per cent in 1980 to 1.0 per cent in 1984.[7]

In addition, there has been increasing recourse to the two-tier wage system. This offers a politically attractive compromise under which management's

Table 1. Trends in union wage settlements, work stoppages, unemployment and prices in the United States, 1970-84

| Year | Average annual wage settlement in private industry [1] (%) | Work stoppages [2] | | Rate of unemployment [3] (%) | Annual rate of increase in consumer prices [4] |
		Involving 6 or more workers	Involving 1,000 or more workers		
1970	8.9	5 716	381	4.8	5.9
1971	8.1	5 138	298	5.8	4.3
1972	6.4	5 010	250	5.5	3.3
1973	5.1	5 353	317	4.8	6.2
1974	7.3	6 074	424	5.5	11.0
1975	7.8	5 031	235	8.3	9.1
1976	6.4	5 648	231	7.6	5.8
1977	5.8	5 506	298	6.9	6.5
1978	6.4	4 230	219	6.0	7.6
1979	6.0	4 827	235	5.8	11.5
1980	7.1	3 885	187	7.0	13.5
1981	7.9	2 568	145	7.5	10.2
1982	3.6	...	96	9.5	6.0
1983	2.8	...	81	9.5	3.0
1984	2.4	...	62	7.4	3.5

[1] The mean annual rate of adjustment in wages over the life of the contract in all union-management settlements that were reached in the year indicated and that covered at least 1,000 workers in private industry. Each settlement is weighted by the number of workers it covers. Account is taken of all decisions to increase, decrease, or not change wages during the term of each agreement, but not of wage changes under COLA clauses. In 1983, when all union settlements averaged 2.8 per cent by this measure, those including a COLA clause averaged 2.0 per cent and those without averaged 3.7 per cent. [2] Data refer to all work stoppages that began in the year indicated and lasted a full shift or longer. Owing to budget stringencies, the Bureau of Labor Statistics (BLS) discontinued collecting data on strikes involving fewer than 1,000 workers after 1981. [3] The number unemployed as a percentage of the labour force, including members of the armed forces stationed in the United States. [4] The percentage change in the consumer price index for urban wage earners and clerical workers.

Sources: BLS: *Current Wage Developments* (Washington), Apr. 1984, table 19; *Monthly Labor Review* (Washington), Apr. 1982, p. 107, and Mar. 1985, various appendix tables; and unpublished data on the number of strikes involving six or more workers in 1981.

demand for wage relief is met by providing that new workers will be hired at lower rates; some contracts require that the new employees' rate must be raised to the full rate within two or three years, but others contain no such provision. Two-tier systems, which have been negotiated in the retail food industry since the late 1970s, and more recently in trucking, airlines, aerospace and the federal postal service, can create problems for everyone involved: employees in the lower tier, who may feel discriminated against; those in the upper tier, who may grow apprehensive that management will seek to replace them with less expensive new recruits; and negotiators, who will certainly find it difficult to agree on a method of returning to a single-tier system.

Further, the table necessarily excludes wage changes that result from COLA clauses since these cannot be measured at the time of settlement. The importance of COLA clauses has fluctuated over the years, but the omission of their effects from the table clearly results in understating both union wage gains in earlier years and union wage losses in recent years. The proportion of workers under major union contracts who were covered by COLA clauses increased from 26 per cent in 1970 to 59 per cent in 1976 and has remained around that level till now. A more inclusive measure — "effective wage adjustments" [8] — shows that of the total wage increases that took place each year under all major union contracts, both newly and previously negotiated, the proportion resulting from COLA clauses averaged 32 per cent in the high-inflation years of 1979-81 and then declined to 18 per cent in 1982-83. That decline reflected both the easing of inflation and the decision of several bargaining units to waive scheduled COLA increases or to tighten their COLA formula in various ways.

This description of wage concessions deserves a few qualifications, however. Although some union-management negotiators, as at Chrysler, were led to freeze or cut wages as early as 1980, the data in table 1 show that the average wage settlement in major units continued to climb in 1981. Also, the drop in the average adjustment after 1981 was not as catastrophic as might have been expected from the publicity surrounding the most extreme cases. In 1982 and 1983, for example, the rate was still at nearly half its average level in the 1970s (3.2 per cent compared with 6.8 per cent). Also, since the rate of inflation had dropped from about 7 per cent in 1970-79 to about 4 per cent in 1982-84, the decline was less severe in real than in current dollars.

In short, the average union wage settlement has certainly declined sharply in recent years, but the precise extent and significance of that decline are open to debate. The same can be said, it will be seen, of other recent bargaining trends.

Strikes

Table 1 shows that the total number of work stoppages in the United States averaged about 5,000 (more precisely, 5,253) per year during the 1970s and then declined abruptly to half that level in 1981, the last year for which all-strike data are available. Similarly, strikes involving 1,000 or more workers averaged 289 per year in 1970-79 and then dropped to half that level in 1981 and even lower in 1982-84. To place these figures in perspective, it should be noted that the number of strikes was *higher* during the 1970s than during any other ten-year period since the end of the Second World War, but it was also probably *lower* during 1980-84 than during any other five-year period in the post-war years.[9] The table shows, not surprisingly, that this reversal in strike activity roughly paralleled the rise in unemployment and the decline in union wage settlements that occurred in the first half of the 1980s.[10]

The all-strike data also offer some tantalising hints that the structure as well as the number of strikes may have radically changed in the past few years. Studies of strike activity in earlier years have shown that strikes have typically lasted longer in the United States than in most other industrialised countries.[11] In the late 1970s the average strike lasted even longer than before. The mean duration of all strikes increased from 23 days during the 1946-75 period to 32 days in 1976-80, by far the longest duration in any five-year period since 1927, when all-strike data were first collected.[12]

These data, together with those in table 1, suggest that as economic conditions worsened in the late 1970s unions grew increasingly reluctant to strike but that once a strike was called the stakes were often so high, involving challenges to long-established practices or even the survival of one or both parties, that it was likely to last longer than before. By this reasoning, the average strike should have lasted even longer during 1981-84, but unfortunately no data are available on strike duration after 1980 to test this hypothesis.

In addition, the proportion of strikes that occurred during the term of a contract suddenly dropped from an average of 33 per cent during 1961-77 to only 15 per cent in 1977-80. The one-third share of such strikes in earlier years is surprising at first glance, since most American contracts contain no-strike clauses. As noted in a previous study,[13] however, this measure is not a reliable indicator of the extent of wildcat strikes in American industry in general. Many no-strike clauses permit strikes in certain circumstances, and a disproportionate number of strikes during the life of the contract occurred over the special problem of work jurisdiction in construction, an industry with many craft unions which was particularly strike-prone during the 1960s and early 1970s. Then, the number of wildcat strikes in bituminous coalmining, always high, doubled during the mid-1970s as a result of upheavals within the miners' union and for other reasons.[14]

The decline in such strikes in the late 1970s has not been systematically studied. It is reasonable to assume, however, that it resulted in large part from the sharp rise in non-union competition that occurred in both construction and coal during the late 1970s, the growing accommodation of the parties in coal in recent years, and the cumulative effect in these and other industries of the relatively high unemployment of the 1970s. Unfortunately, no data are available to show whether strikes during the term of an agreement continued to decline, as seems likely, in the early 1980s.

Will these recent changes in strike activity prove to be transitory, disappearing with the emergence of the economy from the sharp recession of the early 1980s? It is hard to believe otherwise, given the history of strike activity in this country. As Edwards recently noted of the record up to 1974, one of the main features of American strikes has been the "tendency for their 'shape' [their frequency, scale, and duration] to exhibit a marked consistency throughout the period since 1881".[15]

Non-wage subjects of bargaining

Since no agency collects more than a small percentage of the estimated 178,000 union-management agreements negotiated in the United States, no one can describe the content of the typical American labour contract with any precision. Observers agree, however, that it is more comprehensive than the typical contract in most European countries. In unionised factories, for example, the contract usually covers at least the following subjects: the scope of the bargaining unit (the employees covered by the contract); union security; management rights; wages (basic rate by occupation plus shift and overtime and other premium rates); several so-called fringe benefits (employee benefit plans such as health insurance, pensions, paid holidays and vacations); discipline; grievance procedure; contract duration; strikes during the contract; and the role of seniority in lay-offs, promotion and recall.

Studies of major contracts in the private sector have shown the following trends in three non-wage clauses: [16]

1. *Union security.* The share of major contracts requiring all employees to join the union or to pay the equivalent of union dues (the union shop or the agency shop) remained at about 75 per cent from 1958-59 to 1980, reflecting the fact that the spirited battles of earlier years over this subject had been resolved by the mid-1950s in most large bargaining units. In addition, 85 per cent of the major contracts studied in 1980 provided some kind of check-off, that is, automatic deduction by the employer of union dues (and often assessments and initiation fees) from the pay cheques of union members.

Yet the share of major contracts providing only the minimum legal institutional security for unions (aside from check-off) — recognition that the union is the sole representative of all workers in the unit, members and non-members — still stood at a surprisingly high 17 per cent in 1980. The remaining contracts (4 per cent in 1980) called for various compromises, primarily maintenance of membership (workers are free to join or not to join, but once they join, they must remain in the union for the duration of the contract).

2. *Anti-discrimination provisions* have spread rapidly since the early 1960s, reflecting the increasing concern of society with this subject. Thus the share of major contracts forbidding the employer to discriminate on the basis of age rose from 2 per cent in 1961 to 64 per cent in 1980; on the basis of sex, from 10 per cent to 83 per cent; and on the basis of race, from 32 per cent to 86 per cent.

3. *Contract duration* increased significantly in earlier years and then decreased in the 1980s. In 1956, 22 per cent of major contracts ran for three or more years; the proportion had increased to 73 per cent by 1972 and remained at that level in 1980. In 1982, however, it dropped to 43 per cent and in 1983 climbed back to only 50 per cent.

At the other extreme, the share of major contracts running for less than two years declined from 34 per cent in 1956 to 2 per cent in 1980, but it then increased to about 25 per cent in both 1982 and 1983. This shortening of contract duration reflects a logical reaction by many negotiators to the turmoil and uncertainty of the early 1980s.

Though only fragmentary trend data are available on the subject of *seniority*, it is recognised to be a major factor under union contracts in determining the order of lay-offs, in promotions and transfers, in the assignment of staff and overtime work, in improvements in holiday and pension entitlements, and probably in the tempering of disciplinary penalties. The recent spate of concession bargaining does not appear to have weakened this role. Some employers have succeeded in reducing the extent of "bumping" permitted during lay-offs, but many others have agreed to income guarantees for senior employees threatened by changes designed to increase productivity.

In fact, the dominant question in the concession bargaining of recent years has been how best to provide *job security* or *income security*. Collective bargaining has grappled from its earliest days, of course, with the endless task of balancing management's need for innovation and cost control against the need of workers for job security. What many observers believe to be different about bargaining in the 1980s are the severity of the pressures on employers to innovate and otherwise cut costs — probably more intense than at any other time since the 1930s — and the corresponding extent and variety of the bargaining responses.

Many of the concession bargains of the 1980s have drawn on well-known techniques for coping with economic adversity — advance notice of change, retraining, severance pay, early retirement bonuses, work-sharing, interplant transfers, moving allowances, supplementary unemployment benefits, attrition clauses and the guaranteed annual wage; what is novel about the bargains is their number, apparently much larger than in any previous post-war recession. Several other concession bargains have captured attention, however, because they are believed or hoped to be the forerunners of a more co-operative approach to union-management relations than the bargaining norm of the past. These cases involve joint and continuing efforts, often at the shop-floor level, to increase productivity by restructuring work systems and, in the currently fashionable jargon, improving the quality of work life. These programmes have led to changes such as enlarging jobs by adding new duties, cutting crew sizes, combining craft jobs, rotating jobs among team members, and providing more flexibility in daily and weekly working hours.[17]

One of the most remarkable approaches ever taken to job security in the United States is that recently adopted in the automobile industry. This industry is cited again not because the approach adopted here is typical of American bargaining but because it is a highly visible experiment that combines several old and some very new adjustment techniques.

The bargaining parties in the industry had undertaken various co-operative programmes in the 1970s, most of them short-lived, and in the early 1980s they initiated quality circles and other worker participation programmes. The 1984 agreements at GM and Ford have gone still further, to create a "job opportunity bank" for most workers displaced by new technology and similar changes. This scheme, introduced for a six-year period, guarantees that such workers will not be laid off; they will instead draw their normal pay and be provided with retraining, transfer to another plant, or assignment to "non-traditional" jobs (such as charity work) or to replacing workers on leave. The companies also promised to invest considerable funds in projects suggested by labour-management committees for creating new jobs in old or underutilised automobile plants and in communities with many auto company lay-offs.[18] In addition, the agreements require increased company funding of programmes adopted in earlier years that provide income to laid-off employees, and they also contain company commitments to attempt to reduce overtime.[19]

While it might be tempting to dismiss these automobile agreements as anomalies that can be afforded only by a handful of very rich companies, it should be remembered that considerable publicity attends every automobile settlement in the United States, and no industry has had a greater effect on the shape of post-war bargaining in this country.

How widespread at present are the bargaining approaches to job security, such as quality circles, that are less sweeping than the 1984 agreements in the automobile industry but are nevertheless departures from traditional bargaining remedies? And are those new approaches gaining or losing in favour as the American economy recovers in 1985? Unfortunately, there are no certain answers to these questions, leaving everyone free to claim with impunity that the known cases represent either the wave of the future or an aberration of the recent past.

Also unanswered is the question how successful any marriage will be in the long term between the new forms of worker participation, such as quality circles, and the conventional form of worker participation, namely collective bargaining. The parties often attempt to separate the administration of the labour contract from the operation of the new participation schemes, but such separation will be difficult to maintain for long. On the other hand, the parties will face formidable problems if they attempt to integrate the two systems formally. As a recent study of this question concluded:

The most direct effect of expanded worker participation efforts, especially those that involve work reorganisation, is a movement away from the detailed job control form of unionism characteristic of US collective bargaining. This does not mean that the collective bargaining agreement will no longer govern the terms and conditions of employment. However, detailed specification of contractual rules may give way to a more flexible and varied form of work organisation at the plant level. This implies a major change in the roles of the local union, supervisors, and higher levels of management.[20]

Finally, as unions have encountered increasing problems in organising the unorganised (discussed below), several have pressed for "painless organising" provisions. Some employers have agreed, for example, not to initiate "double-breasted" operations during the term of an agreement, that is, not to establish a parallel non-union firm under overlapping but legally distinct ownership, as many unionised employers in construction and trucking have done.

To deal with the related problem that unions call the runaway shop — the opening of new plants, often in the lightly unionised South, by unionised firms often based in the strongly unionised North — some unions have won "accretion clauses" that automatically extend the existing contract to the new plant. Others have won a slightly milder clause under which the employer agrees to recognise and bargain with the union at the new plant without asking for the government-supervised election that an employer can demand under the law (and that unions often lose today). Much milder, but still advantageous to unions, are "neutrality pledges" whereby employers agree not to actively oppose union attempts to organise at new plants.

In addition, several unions have won "successor clauses" to minimise the problems posed by the sale of a unionised firm during the term of its labour contract. If the nature of the business remains unchanged, the law requires the purchaser to recognise and bargain with the existing union but does not require him to accept the previous contract. This can lead to abrupt changes in a bargaining relationship, possibly including a change to non-union status if the purchaser is determined to avoid agreeing to a new contract. A successor clause, if it does not resolve these problems, at least postpones them by requiring, as a condition of sale, the continuation of the existing labour agreement until its expiry date.

Such "painless organising" clauses are still relatively rare in American contracts, in sharp contrast to the practice of contract extension in several European countries. Both the content and the rarity of these clauses reflect the still controversial status of unions in the United States.

The negotiation process

Deadline bargaining has long been, and continues to be, the dominant method of negotiating American labour contracts. Most contracts contain both a no-strike clause and a fixed date of expiry, after which (in the private sector) the union is free to strike. Negotiations typically begin about two months before the strike deadline and usually end in agreement shortly before the contract expires. Although a strike thus occurs in only a small proportion of negotiations (probably a good deal less than 15 per cent),[21] the possibility of a strike on a specific date shapes most bargainers' tactics from the beginning to the end of negotiations.[22]

Some interesting changes have occurred in bargaining practices in recent years, however. First, as noted above, the early 1980s saw the parties in a number of hard-pressed companies depart from the deadline model by engaging in *unscheduled negotiations*, that is, renegotiating their contracts well before they were due to expire. In those cases the usual bargaining process was dramatically reversed: instead of the union pressing a reluctant employer to change the status quo or face the loss of profits imposed by a strike, the employer pressed an often reluctant union to change the status quo or face the loss of even more jobs to lower-cost competitors. Though it is not known how many such renegotiations took place, they probably were both more numerous in the early 1980s than ever before and yet only a small minority of all negotiations even then. They also appear to be dwindling in number as the economy improves in the mid-1980s.

Second, negotiators are undoubtedly relying less on *pattern bargaining*, or follow-the-leader bargaining, in the 1980s than in previous years. Although the

311

formal structure of bargaining has long been less centralised in the United States than in most European countries, informal bargaining patterns had been followed to some extent in many industries and localities throughout the post-war years. The hallmark of concession bargaining in the 1980s, however, has often been its emphasis on relieving the economic problems of specific companies. That emphasis obviously may clash with the pattern bargaining argument that, for reasons of equity, workers in different companies or industries but in the same "orbit of coercive comparison" should be treated equally. As a result, articles have appeared in the past few years with such titles as "Last rites for pattern bargaining" [23] and "The beginning of the end for industrywide wages?".[24]

This development poses the same problem of interpretation as the other changes in bargaining that have occurred in the 1980s. On the one hand, pattern bargaining undoubtedly did break down in several industries in the early years of concession bargaining and has continued to lose ground in at least some. For example, in addition to the disintegration of the pattern in the automobile industry, beginning at Chrysler in 1979, recent bargaining in airlines has been little short of chaotic. Also, in coal and trucking, in which multi-employer bargaining (in a sense, formalised pattern bargaining) has been the norm, employers' associations have suffered serious defections by companies hoping to strike a better bargain on their own; and in steel a co-ordinated bargaining committee of the major producers, established in the 1950s, dwindled from nine members in 1980 to five in 1984 and then, in 1985, was completely disbanded.

On the other hand, obituary notices for pattern bargaining in the unionised sector as a whole are surely premature. Automobile bargaining in 1983 and 1984 showed that fractured patterns can be repaired, at least in part, and in other industries concession bargaining has created its own pattern. Within a bargaining orbit, after all, restrictive agreements by those settling first can be as coercive as liberal agreements in their effects on those settling later.

A third and related development has been the greater willingness of some American employers to *operate during a strike* — through the hiring of strike replacements, perfectly legal in most circumstances; or the employment of non-striking workers; or the use of supervisors and managers to perform strikers' work. Many small employers have operated during strikes in the past, but few large companies attempted to do so from around 1950 until fairly recently when a change is said to have occurred in the thinking of at least some employers on this subject.[25] The possible reasons for that change include the increasing automation of industries such as oil, chemicals and telephones, which enables supervisors and managers alone to maintain operations more easily than before; the loose labour markets of the 1975-85 period which often provided a large supply of strike replacements, from printers to pilots; and the harder line many employers appear to have taken towards unions on several fronts in recent years. Thus management's increased use of this tactic is probably both a cause and an effect, on a minor scale, of labour's declining power in recent years.

Fourth, the rate of *contract rejections* — the proportion of negotiations in which union members vote down tentative bargaining agreements — declined slightly in the 1970s and 1980s. The actual rate of rejections is known only for negotiations in which federal mediators met with the parties, presumably a high-conflict sample. That rate averaged about 13 per cent in the late 1960s, remained relatively stable at around 11 per cent in 1970-79, and declined during 1980 and 1981, the latest years for which data are available.[26] The rejection rate roughly paralleled the strike rate in those negotiations in both level and trend, a result that is mildly surprising. It is understandable, of course, that rejection votes lead to strikes in many cases; in fact, in some unions a vote to reject is automatically a vote to strike. Yet, the folklore of bargaining says that in other cases rejection votes are often a negotiating ploy arranged by union leaders to pressure management into another move, or a genuine message of dissatisfaction from members who want more negotiations but not a strike. Unfortunately, no study has been made of these questions since the early 1970s.[27] When more recent data on mediation disputes become available, they will probably show that both rates continued to decline during 1982-84, just as the more inclusive measure of strike activity in table 1 shows a decline for those years. The remarkable stability of the contract rejection rate during most of the 1965-81 period suggests, however, that any further decline that occurred in 1982-84 will be temporary.

Finally, a novel experiment in *interest arbitration* (the arbitration of new contract terms) enjoyed a brief and instructive vogue in recent years. In 1972 the parties in basic steel concluded an Experimental Negotiating Agreement (ENA), the first time in many years that interest arbitration was voluntarily adopted in a major American industry. The United Steelworkers gave up the right to strike over economic issues in exchange for the right to take any impasse to arbitration *and* for a guaranteed minimum wage increase of 3 per cent per year plus a COLA clause with no ceiling. The parties hoped by that agreement to avoid two problems that had resulted from their deadline bargaining in previous years: the loss of customers who switched to foreign steel sources or domestic steel substitutes, at least partly because of the recurrent threat that a strike would cut off their steel deliveries; and the fluctuations in production and employment (and thus in employer costs and workers' income) that resulted from customers frantically stockpiling steel before a strike deadline and then, even when no strike occurred, ordering little for weeks afterward. The ENA worked well during the remainder of the 1970s in that the parties negotiated their next three agreements without resorting to arbitration. That feat was important because, at least in the United States, a major criticism of interest arbitration has been the chilling effect it may have on negotiations. But a major reason for the parties' avoidance of arbitration was the liberal guarantee the union had won of 3 per cent annual wage increases plus an uncapped COLA. The companies could not win a cheaper settlement in arbitration and the union could not expect to win much more, since the wage formula was providing a better yield during the high-inflation years of the 1970s than many other unions were winning with the right to strike.

The cost in fact proved to be the downfall of interest arbitration in steel. Management concluded that the price of the ENA was too high; the union refused to renew it at a lower price; and the parties therefore dropped it from their agreement in 1980. As far as one can judge from published reports, since 1973 only one other bargaining relationship in the private sector (at National Airlines) has experimented with interest arbitration.

Contract administration

The American bargaining system has long emphasised the day-to-day administration of contracts in a manner that differs from the practice in many other countries. The union is the sole representative of all employees covered by the contract, both union members and non-members, and it therefore has a decisive voice in determining which grievances are to be pressed and which are to be dropped, as well as the terms on which they are settled. In addition, the contract provides the sole procedure available to workers for presenting most grievances; [28] local as well as national unions have large staffs by the standards of many countries, and most local union officials spend a large part of their time handling grievances; and in over 90 per cent of contracts the final step in the grievance procedure is an appeal to a private arbitrator, selected and paid jointly by the parties, who has the power to overturn management decisons found to violate the contract and to order, for example, the reinstatement of a wrongfully discharged worker, with back pay for the time he has lost, or the promotion of one worker over another selected by the employer.[29]

The major features of this process have remained unchanged for many years, but some developments warrant comment. First, for no obvious reason *arbitration activity* appears to have abruptly levelled off in the early 1980s after a long period of rapid growth. (Unfortunately, no data are available on trends in grievance activity short of arbitration.) One measure of arbitration activity indicates that it tripled in the 1960s, tripled again in the 1970s, and then showed almost no increase at all from 1980 to 1984.[30]

One might reasonably have expected the opposite: that in the dark days of 1980-84, with unemployment soaring and wage settlements sagging and workers reluctant to strike, both employees and their unions would be more inclined than before to challenge every income-threatening decision by management through all the steps of the grievance procedures. Perhaps that did not happen because many employers had convinced their employees that they could and must work together co-operatively; or perhaps many workers feared that their employer, tightening up on every front, would be more likely than usual to rid himself of "trouble-makers"; or maybe hard-pressed unions, many of which laid off staff during these years, lacked the staff and money necessary to carry cases through to arbitration. But all that is speculation; at this point no one really knows why the growth of arbitration activity apparently came to a sudden halt in the 1980s or whether it will soon resume.

A second development in contract administration has been the impact in recent years of a legal doctrine known as the union's duty of *fair representation*.

This doctrine states that, because American labour law makes the union the exclusive representative of all workers in a bargaining unit on employment matters, the union has a legally enforceable duty to represent each and every worker "fairly". That doctrine had first been enunciated by the Supreme Court in 1944, but it was not until 1967 that the Court applied it to contract administration.

The result has been a growing number of lawsuits in which workers sue their union for allegedly mishandling their grievances. The charge may be, for example, that union officers did not investigate a lost grievance adequately or chose not to press it to arbitration because the grievant was a political rival within the union or was not a union member. Employers are also often liable for damages for the action, such as a dismissal, that prompted the grievance mishandled by the union.

Unions and employers have won most of the fair-representation cases brought against them but many have clearly become more cautious in administering their contracts. Unions are more inclined than before to take questionable grievances further, and several appear to take to arbitration most or all dismissal cases, no matter how weak. Many practitioners deplore this trend, arguing that it not only wastes time and money but also impairs the effectiveness of the grievance procedure in handling well-founded grievances.[31]

Finally, in the 1970s the parties in a few cases adopted so-called *expedited arbitration* systems to ease three problems afflicting many conventional arbitration systems: excessive delay, cost and legal formalism. The typical expedited system supplements the conventional system, handling relatively simple cases (such as minor disciplinary grievances) within a prescribed few days from filing to award, using a panel of on-call arbitrators, and banning briefs and transcripts (and sometimes lawyers!).

Another minor mystery of the American bargaining scene is the failure of expedited arbitration to spread very far or fast in spite of conditions that appeared propitious. The parties have loudly complained for years of the delay, cost and formalism of conventional arbitration; basic steel and the federal postal service adopted expedited systems in the early 1970s which are still being used; the few studies of expedited arbitration have been laudatory;[32] and the concept has been endorsed by the American Federation of Labor and Congress of Industrial Organizations (AFL-CIO) and promoted by the American Arbitration Association (AAA). Yet expedited arbitration accounted for only 4 per cent of a large sample of AAA cases in 1983-84, the same proportion as in 1982.[33] It is difficult to think of reasons other than the inertia of the parties for the lukewarm reception accorded this promising innovation in contract administration.[34]

The public sector

In the United States, more than in many countries, both the law and the practice of collective bargaining differ significantly between the private sector, on which this article has so far focused, and the sector comprising federal, state and local governments. Strikes by government employees are illegal in most jurisdictions; the law has reserved more prerogatives (declared more subjects non-bargainable) for public employers, particularly at the federal and state levels, than for private employers; and the private sector has no counterpart of the complex and ambiguous relationship in the public sector between labour unions, the executive agencies that do most of the bargaining, the legislative bodies that provide the funds and write the bargaining laws, and the civil service and similar agencies that regulate certain employment decisions.

Since the 1960s, when unionism unexpectedly mushroomed in the public sector, the bargaining differences between the sectors have narrowed but nevertheless remain substantial. One difference that appears to persist results from the lack of a strike deadline in most of the public sector, leading to negotiations that are often much more protracted than is customary in the private sector. To take an extreme example, in the spring of 1985 municipal employees in New York City reached an agreement with the city government only after negotiations had dragged on for a full year beyond the expiry of the parties' previous contract. And in the public schools — suddenly a major unionised "industry" in the United States — piecemeal evidence suggests that of the several hundred teacher negotiations that occur annually at the community level, a large number extend well beyond the expiry of the previous contract.

The lack of the strike weapon in most of the public sector has spurred considerable experimentation in public policy. For example, interest arbitration, anathema to the private sector, was adopted in 1970 for federal postal employees; between 1965 and 1977 it was instituted by 18 states for all or some state and local government employees, particularly police and fire-fighters; and in 1983 two more states adopted such laws. Ten of the state laws call for some form of final-offer arbitration, a procedure in which the arbitrator must select one of the last offers by the parties rather than being free to fashion his own award. The intent of the final-offer procedure is to minimise the possible chilling effect of conventional arbitration on negotiations; by removing the arbitrator's discretion to split the difference between the parties' final positions, the law provides an incentive to the parties to narrow their differences significantly, possibly to the point of agreement, before they turn to an arbitrator. It seems that these laws have indeed been more successful than conventional arbitration laws in encouraging the parties to do this.[35]

Another significant difference between the two sectors in the 1960s that has since persisted lies in the trend of union organisation, and thus of the practice of collective bargaining. According to one set of sources, union members as a proportion of all employees continued to decline in the private sector — a trend that had begun in the mid-1950s — dropping from 31 per cent in 1970 to 23 per cent in 1980 and then to 19 per cent in 1984. In contrast, the rate of unionism in the public sector, which had increased sharply in the 1960s, continued to increase, though more slowly, in the 1970s — rising from 33 per cent in 1970 to 36 per cent in 1980 — and then remained at that level through 1984.[36]

The reasons for the difference in growth rates are not all clear, particularly the reasons for the sudden desire of government employees in the 1960s to join unions or to press their professional and civil service associations to engage in collective bargaining for the first time. Once that shift occurred in employee attitudes, however, a clear difference emerged between the sectors in the reaction of employers to union organisation and demands for recognition. In most of the public sector, management has shown only moderate resistance, if any, but in the private sector the resistance has usually been strong and sometimes virulent.[37]

On the other hand, some convergence has occurred since the 1960s in the legal status and practice of collective bargaining in the two sectors. For example, eight states legalised strikes for certain groups of public employees between 1967 and 1979, and two other states did so in 1983.[38] Also, unions in the public sector have diligently whittled down the scope of management prerogatives in many instances, just as unions in the private sector did earlier. In the celebrated strike by federal air traffic controllers in 1981, for example, most attention understandably focused on the decision by President Reagan to dismiss an unprecedented number (11,301) of strikers. Nearly as significant, however, was this conservative Administration's willingness to bargain with the union before the strike over an array of subjects — salaries, severance pay, and operational and safety policies — that Congress had reserved for determination by itself or by management.[39] Another form of convergence occurred in the 1970s when public sector unions proved to be as vulnerable as private sector unions, at least in large part, to economic pressures. In the 1960s several critics had argued that collective bargaining in the public sector was dangerous because neither employers nor unions in that sector are subject to the discipline of the market-place. In the 1970s, however, taxpayer revolts erupted literally from coast to coast (Massachusetts and California being the prime examples), and concession bargaining came early to the parties in several large cities, such as New York, that found themselves caught between soaring costs and an eroding tax base. As a result, "by the late 1970s, public wages were rising more slowly than private [wages]".[40] Also, several studies have concluded that the union wage effect is no larger in the public sector, and is perhaps smaller, than in the private sector.[41]

THE DETERMINANTS OF RECENT CHANGES

Nearly all analyses of recent bargaining trends in the United States agree on the immediate causes of the wave of concession bargaining that has occurred in the 1980s. The primary cause was the dismal performance of the economy. A recession in 1980 was followed by a weak recovery and then, beginning in August 1981, an even more severe recession, as unemployment, the rate of business failures, and excess manufacturing capacity all reached post-war highs in 1982. The economy recovered strongly in several respects in 1983-84 but, as table 1 shows, unemployment continued well above its 1970-79 average.

Those recessions alone would have been enough to trigger concession bargaining in many industries, but in certain strongly unionised ones other developments aggravated the recession pressures on labour and management. Foreign competition, for example, is certainly not a new phenomenon, but before 1970 the United States usually exported more than it imported. During the 1970-85 period, however, foreign competition became a major factor in union strongholds such as automobiles and steel, accounting in 1984 for as much as 25 per cent of the American market in those industries.

In addition, government deregulation — the removal of some or all government controls over entry into an industry and over pricing and other operating decisions by firms already in the industry — gathered momentum in the late 1970s as Congress deregulated three other union strongholds: airlines in 1978 and railroads and trucking in 1980. In airlines and trucking that action led to lower prices for consumers but also to the bankruptcy of several firms and the entry of many new, usually non-union firms.[42] Those changes in turn led to much of the concession bargaining that has recently occurred in airlines and trucking.[43]

In yet other industries non-union competition grew during the 1970s without the stimulus of deregulation, contributing to the recession pressures on negotiators in the 1980s. In construction, for example, it is estimated that the non-union share of the market rose from about 55 per cent in the mid-1970s to about 70 per cent in the mid-1980s; and over the same period the proportion of bituminous coal mined outside the coverage of the United Mine Workers' national agreement rose from about 50 per cent to about 60 per cent.[44] This growth in non-union competition, like the growth in foreign competition, was partly a result of bargaining gains in earlier years. Indeed, some economists argue that a significant cause of the concessions of the 1980s was the fact that the union/non-union wage differential in the private sector had risen to a post-war high by 1980, triggering a backlash of market forces that took the form of growing non-union and foreign competition.[45]

To some extent, of course, the growth in non-union competition is a manifestation of the trend that has dominated much of the recent discussion of industrial relations in the United States: the decline in the extent of union organisation in American industry. In 1985 the AFL-CIO described that decline as follows:

The proportion of workers who are eligible to join a union and who in fact belong to a union has fallen from close to 45 per cent to under 28 per cent since 1954; using the measure of percentage of the entire workforce, the decline has been from 35 per cent to under 19 per cent.[46]

Another widely used measure of that decline is the rate of union victories in the government-supervised elections held to determine whether particular groups of workers wish to be represented by a union. That rate has steadily dropped, from 80 per cent in 1946 to 46 per cent in 1981.[47] Although the decline in union organisation therefore began long before the recent rounds of concession bargaining, the continuing erosion of the unionised share of the private sector must have added yet further pressure on some union negotiators in the 1980s.[48]

Finally, the role of public policy in recent years deserves a brief comment. As noted above, several state laws governing bargaining in the public sector have introduced new dispute resolution procedures, and the deregulation of airlines and trucking provided a major stimulus to concession bargaining in those industries. In addition, mandatory wage and price controls during the early 1970s undoubtedly exerted some temporary influence on collective bargaining. Conventional labour legislation has not played a significant role, however, in shaping recent bargaining trends in the private sector. The governing statute, the National Labor Relations Act (NLRA), has remained unchanged since it was last amended in 1974 to extend its coverage to non-profit health care facilities. Labour mounted a major effort in 1977-78 to secure amendments aimed primarily at improving unions' organising prospects, but the "reform Bill", after easily passing the House of Representatives, failed by a narrow margin following a 19-day filibuster in the Senate.[49]

SOMETHING NEW OR SOMETHING OLD?

Although analysts generally agree on the causes of the recent trends in collective bargaining in the United States, they agree far less, as might be expected, on the implications of those trends. Derber has well described the conflicting answers being given to the question whether the American bargaining system is entering a new stage:

> Supporters of the new-stage theory fall into two opposing camps. One, reviewing developments in labour-management co-operation [and concession bargaining], has concluded that the long-time adversarial system is being significantly modified, if not replaced, by a more integrative, mutualistic approach. The other camp . . . argues that unions have been losing ground for over two decades . . . and that the dominant trend of industrial relations is union-free [i.e. non-union].
>
> In opposition . . . are the supporters of what may be labelled the "rerun theory". These observers assert that the traditional collective bargaining system is . . . as in the past . . . responding pragmatically to the conditions of the economic environment, and that when the economy regains its health collective bargaining will return to its former aggressive and adversarial self.[50]

As the reader will probably have guessed, I believe the "rerun" school has the better of a close argument. Concession bargaining is far less unusual on the American scene than some contemporary accounts suggest. As others have pointed out, concession bargaining in one form or another occurred in several union-management relationships in the 1920s (then termed union-management co-operation and undertaken in response to an increase in non-union competition and the rise of "scientific management"), in the 1950s and early 1960s (continuous or productivity bargaining, a response to the effects of technological change and recessions), and again during the 1973-75 recession.[51]

Also, in every period, regardless of the health of the economy in general, concession bargaining has occurred in particular relationships under economic stress. In most of those cases, co-operation largely evaporated when economic conditions grew significantly better or worse.[52] In short, concession bargaining and co-operative union-management experiments have often occurred in the past but seldom lasted very long. It is true, as the "new stage" school points out, that concession bargaining has been far more widespread in the 1980s than in any previous round of post-war bargaining. But the pressures to adopt concession bargaining were far greater in the 1980s than before. The 1981-82 recession was the worst of the post-war period, and the level of foreign and non-union competition reached post-war highs in the 1980s. The extent of concession bargaining in the 1980s therefore proves only the extent of its causes and not necessarily its durability.

The "rerun" argument does not predict that bargaining patterns will be the same in the 1990s as they were in the 1970s. Changes occur constantly in most union-management relationships — witness the turbulent record before 1980 in industries as varied as coal, construction, longshoring and airlines — and they will doubtless continue to occur, including some exciting ventures in co-operation. The rerun argument does predict, however, that if the economic recovery of the mid-1980s continues, most unionised industries in the private sector will return to a reliance on the strike-deadline model of bargaining to resolve their major differences. Such a return to "bargaining-as-usual" had already begun in the automobile and some other industries by 1985.

But what if the economy is healthy but foreign competition continues to intensify and the unionised share of the labour force continues to decline? The answer, as usual, will vary with the circumstances. If employment and profits in a particular industry are threatened to the extent they often were in the early 1980s, labour and management in that industry will be likely to engage in concession bargaining and co-operative experiments regardless of the source of the threat. But foreign and non-union competition strikes more selectively (or randomly) than a recession, leaving the parties in many other cases relatively free to engage in the competitive behaviour so dear to the heart of the American negotiator.

The knowledgeable reader will treat these predictions, of course, with the disrespect they deserve. It is well established that American specialists in industrial relations have a record of predicting the future that easily matches that of economists, political scientists and generals.

Notes

[1] Professor, New York State School of Industrial and Labour Relations, Cornell University.

[2] Unless otherwise noted, the data in this section are taken from the excellent articles by George Ruben that appeared in each January issue of the *Monthly Labor Review* (Washington, US Department of Labor, Bureau of Labor Statistics (BLS)) from 1981 to 1985, summarising developments in collective bargaining during the preceding year.

[3] This estimate assumed an annual rate of inflation of 8 per cent during the period of the contract; see "Will the auto pact break pattern bargaining?", in *Business Week* (New York), 1 Oct. 1979, p. 92.

[4] At one point in these negotiations, GM and the UAW announced a tentative agreement that was astonishing in the light of the company's long record as a champion of management rights. GM agreed that it would apply all savings from UAW concessions to reducing the prices of its cars and trucks. For reasons not made public, this agreement was not part of the final contract.

[5] "A pact with the UAW that may backfire on Chrysler", in *Business Week*, 19 Sep. 1983, p. 31.

[6] The annual increases in the GM and Ford settlements averaged only 2.25 per cent and differed by wage level, in contrast to the previous practice of 3 per cent increases for all employees. The parties also agreed to continue the profit-sharing plan adopted in 1982 and to initiate an extensive job security programme, described below.

[7] Unless otherwise indicated, the wage data in this section are taken from various issues of *Current Wage Developments* (Washington, BLS) or *Monthly Labor Review*.
In 1982, 11 per cent of the 578 major settlements were renegotiated before their scheduled expiry date, which is usually a sign of economic distress. The "no wage increase" category includes a small number of contracts in which wages were cut — only 2 per cent of all first-year settlements in 1982, but 15 per cent in 1983 (31 per cent in manufacturing). The average duration of the 1982 settlements was 31 months, which suggests the importance of considering both BLS measures of wage adjustments: changes in the first year of a contract and changes over its entire life.

[8] All the wage increases, decreases, and zero changes occurring under all major contracts in a given year as a result of changes specified or guaranteed in that year's settlements, plus deferred changes specified in settlements reached in previous years, plus contingent changes that resulted from COLA clauses.

[9] The total number of strikes per year averaged 4,328 in 1946-55, 3,619 in 1956-65 and 4,936 in 1966-69. Unless otherwise noted, the data in this section are taken from various issues of *Analysis of Work Stoppages* (Washington, BLS) and *Monthly Labor Review*.

[10] For evidence that unemployment has a more pronounced effect in reducing strike rates in the United States than in several other OECD countries, see M. Paldam and P. J. Pedersen: "The macroeconomic strike model: A study of seventeen countries, 1948-1975", in *Industrial and Labor Relations Review* — hereafter *ILRR* (Ithaca, New York), July 1982, pp. 510-511.

[11] For an interesting attempt to explain this and other aspects of the American strike record, stressing the extent and intensity of the struggle for job control, see P. K. Edwards: *Strikes in the United States, 1881-1974* (Oxford, Basil Blackwell; New York, St. Martin's Press, 1981).

[12] Similarly, the median duration of strikes rose from nine days in 1950-75 (no median data are available for 1946-49) to 15 days in 1976-81.

[13] D. E. Cullen: "Recent trends in collective bargaining in the United States", in *International Labour Review* (Geneva, ILO), June 1972, pp. 519-520.

[14] J. M. Brett and S. B. Goldberg: "Wildcat strikes in bituminous coal mining", in *ILRR*, July 1979, pp. 465-483.

[15] Edwards, op. cit., p. 219.

[16] These studies are summarised in BLS: *Characteristics of major collective bargaining agreements, January 1, 1980*, Bulletin 2095 (Washington, 1981), pp. 2-8. The contract duration data for 1982 and 1983 are taken from *Current Wage Developments*.

[17] "A work revolution in US industry", in *Business Week*, 16 May 1983, pp. 100-110; and I. H. Siegel and E. Weinberg: *Labor-management co-operation: The American experience* (Kalamazoo, Michigan, W. E. Upjohn Institute for Employment Research, 1982). The latter study shows that labour-management co-operation has a long history in the United States.

[18] "The GM settlement is a milestone for both sides", in *Business Week*, 8 Oct. 1984, pp. 160-161. The later Ford settlement paralleled the GM settlement.

[19] G. Ruben: "Modest labor-management bargains continue in 1984 despite the recovery", in *Monthly Labor Review*, Jan. 1985, pp. 4-5.

[20] T. A. Kochan et al.: *Worker participation and American unions: Threat or opportunity?* (Kalamazoo, Michigan, W. E. Upjohn Institute for Employment Research, 1984), p. 194.

[21] A detailed study of this question shows that strikes occurred in 14 per cent of 1,050 negotiations in bargaining units of 1,000 or more workers in manufacturing during the period 1971-80. Since this study and others have found strike incidence to vary directly with unit size, the strike rate in all negotiations, while unknown, is presumably below the rate in the large units studied here. C. Gramm: "Determinants of strike incidence and severity", in *ILRR* (forthcoming).

[22] This does not mean that negotiations are exclusively adversarial or based solely on economic power. For the best description of the complex mixture of forces at work in labour negotiations in the United States, see R. E. Walton and R. B. McKersie: *A behavioral theory of labor negotiations* (New York, McGraw-Hill, 1965).

[23] A. Freedman and W. E. Fulmer, in *Harvard Business Review* (Boston), Mar.-Apr. 1982, pp. 30-48. See also A. Freedman: "A fundamental change in wage bargaining", in *Challenge* (White Plains, New York), July-Aug. 1982, pp. 14-17.

[24] *Business Week*, 5 Mar. 1984, p. 78.

[25] C. R. Perry et al.: *Operating during strikes* (Philadelphia, Wharton School, University of Pennsylvania, 1982).

[26] Federal Mediation and Conciliation Service: *Annual Reports*, 1964-81 (Washington, US Government Printing Office).

[27] For the most recent empirical study, see D. R. Burke and L. Rubin: "Is contract rejection a major collective bargaining problem?", in *ILRR*, Jan. 1973, pp. 820-833.

[28] The principal exceptions are claims that an employer discriminated on grounds prohibited by law, such as age, race, sex or union activity. In such cases the employee may often appeal through the contract procedure or the administrative and judicial procedure established by law, or both.

[29] In 1980, 97 per cent of contracts covering 1,000 or more workers contained grievance arbitration provisions. BLS: *Characteristics of major collective bargaining agreements . . .*, op. cit., p. 112.

[30] Federal Mediation and Conciliation Service: *Annual Reports*, various years.

[31] For an excellent analysis of this subject, see J. T. McKelvey (ed.): *The changing law of fair representation* (Ithaca, New York State School of Industrial and Labor Relations, Cornell University, 1985).

[32] See, for example, M. H. Sandver et al.: "Time and cost savings through expedited arbitration procedures", in *Arbitration Journal* (New York), Dec. 1981, pp. 11-21.

[33] American Arbitration Association: *Study Time* (a newsletter) (New York), Oct. 1984.

[34] Another innovation that has met with limited acceptance is grievance mediation. For a description of the most ambitious application of this technique, see J. M. Brett and S. B. Goldberg: "Grievance mediation in the coal industry: A field experiment", in *ILRR*, Oct. 1983, pp. 49-69.

[35] T. A. Kochan: *Collective bargaining and industrial relations* (Homewood, Illinois, Richard D. Irwin, 1980), p. 295.

[36] These estimates are from BLS data for 1970 and Current Population Survey data for 1980 and 1984, as reported respectively in J. F. Burton, Jr.: "The extent of collective bargaining in the public sector", in B. Aaron et al. (eds): *Public-sector bargaining* (Washington, Bureau of National Affairs, 1979), p. 3; and L. T. Adams: "Changing employment patterns of organized workers", in *Monthly Labor Review*, Feb. 1985, p. 28.

[37] For an excellent analysis of the possible reasons for the trend of unionisation in the public sector, see Burton, op. cit., pp. 1-43. For an analysis of the record of the private sector stressing the effect of management opposition, see R. B. Freeman and J. L. Medoff: *What do unions do?* (New York, Basic Books, 1984), Ch. 15.

[38] The two states that legalised strikes in 1983 — Ohio and Illinois — are the same ones that imposed compulsory arbitration in that year. The explanation of this apparent contradiction is that those states mandated arbitration for some groups of employees (police, fire-fighters, etc.), and the right to strike for others.

[39] H. R. Northrup: "The rise and demise of PATCO", in *ILRR*, Jan. 1984, pp. 167-184. Such substantive bargaining is highly exceptional at the federal level, but it is relatively common at the level of local government.

[40] D. J. B. Mitchell: "The new climate: Implications for research on public sector wage determination and labor relations", in *Labor Law Journal* (Chicago), Aug. 1983, p. 473.

[41] For a persuasive study to the contrary, and references to earlier studies of this subject, see L. N. Edwards and F. R. Edwards: "Wellington-Winter revisited: The case of municipal sanitation collection", in *ILLR*, Apr. 1982, pp. 307-318. The union wage effect is the extent to which, other things being equal, union wages exceed non-union wages.

[42] One estimate is that between 1978 and 1983, 10,000 small new operators entered the trucking industry and 14 new airlines were launched. "Deregulating America", in *Business Week*, 28 Nov. 1983, p. 81.

[43] See, for example, H. R. Northrup: "The new employee-relations climate in airlines", in *ILRR*, Jan. 1983, pp. 167-181.

[44] *Daily Labor Report* (Washington, Bureau of National Affairs), 31 Oct. 1984, p. C-1 (for construction); W. H. Miernyk: "Coal", in G. G. Somers (ed.): *Collective bargaining: Contemporary American experience* (Madison, Wisconsin, Industrial Relations Research Association, 1980), p. 46; and "Chaos in coalfields may finally be over", in *Business Week*, 8 Oct. 1984, p. 162. Even the steel industry, with its high barriers to entry, has not been immune to non-union competition. "Mini-mills", which melt scrap in electric furnaces to produce steel and are largely non-union, reportedly increased their share of the American steel market from less than 3 per cent in 1969 to 18 per cent in 1983; see "Time runs out for steel", ibid., 13 June 1983, p. 86.

[45] See M. H. Kosters: "Disinflation in the labor market", in W. Fellner (ed.): *Essays in contemporary economic problems: Disinflation* (Washington, American Enterprise Institute, 1984), pp. 247-286; and Freeman and Medoff, op. cit., pp. 52-57.

[46] *The changing situation of workers and their unions*, Report by the AFL-CIO Committee on the Evolution of Work (Washington, 1985), p. 5.

[47] National Labor Relations Board: *Annual Reports*, various years (Washington, US Government Printing Office).

[48] The causes of this decline in union organisation are the subject of much debate. For a recent study of the effects of several presumed causes, see W. T. Dickens and J. S. Leonard: "Accounting for the decline in union membership, 1950-1980", in *ILRR*, Apr. 1985, pp. 323-334.

[49] In addition, two amendments to the NLRA to change certain organising and bargaining practices in the construction industry passed Congress in 1975 but were vetoed by President Ford. Also, considerable controversy has developed in the 1980s over the administration of the NLRA by President Reagan's appointees to the National Labor Relations Board.

[50] M. Derber: "Are we in a new stage?", in *Proceedings* of the Thirty-fifth Annual Meeting of the Industrial Relations Research Association (Madison, Wisconsin, 1983), p. 1.

[51] See, for example, D. J. B. Mitchell: "Recent union contract concessions", in *Brookings Papers on Economic Activity* (Washington, The Brookings Institution), 1982, Vol. 1, pp. 172-189.

[52] As Jacoby concludes from his excellent analysis of co-operation experiments in the 1920s: "There may be only an intermediate range . . . in which economic stress prods the parties to work together; the struggle for power can reappear, that is, if there is either a marked improvement or a radical deterioration in the economic environment." S. M. Jacoby: "Union-management cooperation in the United States: Lessons from the 1920s", in *ILRR*, Oct. 1983, p. 31.

LIST OF WORKS CITED IN PART I

Aaron, Benjamin. "Arbitration and the role of courts: The administration of justice in labor law", in *Recht der Arbeit*, Sep.-Oct. 1978. (The same article also appeared in *Comparative Labor Law*, fall 1979.)

Adam, Gérard. "La négociation collective en France: Eléments de diagnostic", in *Droit social*, Dec. 1978.

Adams, Roy J. "The extent of collective bargaining in Canada", in *Relations industrielles*, Vol. 39, No. 4, 1984.

AFL-CIO Committee on the Evolution of Work. *The changing situation of workers and their unions.* Washington, DC, 1985.

Albäge, Lars-Gunnar ("An employer's view"); Fjällström, Harry ("A trade unionist's reply"). "Recent trends in collective bargaining in Sweden", in *International Labour Review*, Jan.-Feb. 1986. Reprinted in the present volume.

Albeda, W. "Recent trends in collective bargaining in the Netherlands", in *International Labour Review*, Jan.-Feb. 1985. Reprinted in the present volume.

Anderson, John C. "The structure of collective bargaining", in Anderson and Gunderson (eds.). *Union-management relations in Canada* (see below).

——; Gunderson, Morley (eds.). *Union-management relations in Canada.* Don Mills, Ontario, Addison-Wesley, 1982.

Armstrong, E. G. A. "Employers associations in Great Britain", in Windmuller and Gladstone (eds.). *Employers associations and industrial relations: A comparative study* (see below).

——. "Evaluating the advisory work of ACAS", in *Employment Gazette*, Apr. 1985.

——; Lucas, Rosemary. *Improving industrial relations: The advisory role of ACAS.* London, Croom Helm, 1985.

Arthurs, H. W.; Carter, D. D.; Glasbeek, H. J. "Canada" (1984), in Blanpain (ed.). *International encyclopaedia for labour law and industrial relations*, Vol. 3 (see below).

Australian industrial relations law and systems, Report of the Committee of Review (Hancock Report). Canberra, Australian Government Printing Society, 1985, 3 vols.

Bain, George S. (ed.). *Industrial relations in Britain.* Oxford, Basil Blackwell, 1983.

——; Price, Robert. *Profiles of union growth: A comparative statistical portrait of eight countries.* Oxford, Basil Blackwell, 1980.

Barbash, Jack. "Collective bargaining: Contemporary American experience — A commentary", in Somers (ed.). *Collective bargaining: Contemporary American experience* (see below).

——. "Trade unionism from Roosevelt to Reagan", in Ferman (ed.). "The future of American unionism" (see below).

Barkin, Solomon (ed.). *Worker militancy and its consequences*. New York, Praeger, 2nd ed., 1983.

Beal, Edwin F.; Begin, James P. *The practice of collective bargaining*. Homewood, Illinois, Irwin, 1982.

Bean, Ron. *Comparative industrial relations: An introduction to cross-national perspectives*. London, Croom Helm, 1985.

Beaupain, Thérèse. "Belgium", in Barkin (ed.). *Worker militancy and its consequences* (see above).

Bellace, Janice R.; Gospel, Howard F. "Disclosure of information to trade unions: A comparative perspective", in *International Labour Review*, Jan.-Feb. 1983.

Bergmann, Joachim; Müller-Jentsch, Walther. "The Federal Republic of Germany", in Barkin (ed.). *Worker militancy and its consequences* (see above).

Blanpain, Roger (ed.). *International encyclopaedia for labour law and industrial relations*. Deventer, Kluwer, 1977 onwards.

——. "Belgium" (1985), in idem. *International encyclopaedia for labour law and industrial relations*, Vol. 2 (see above).

——. *Comparative labour law and industrial relations*. Deventer, Kluwer, 1982.

——. "Recent trends in collective bargaining in Belgium", in *International Labour Review*, May-June 1984. Reprinted in the present volume.

Blum, Albert A. (ed.). *International handbook of industrial relations*. London, Aldwych Press, 1981.

Brandini, Pietro Merli. "Italy", in Barkin (ed.). *Worker militancy and its consequences* (see above).

Brown, William (ed.). *The changing contours of British industrial relations*. Oxford, Basil Blackwell, 1981.

—— et al. "Factors shaping shop steward organization in Britain", in *British Journal of Industrial Relations*, July 1978.

Bunn, Ronald F. "Employers associations in the Federal Republic of Germany", in Windmuller and Gladstone (eds.). *Employers associations and industrial relations: A comparative study* (see below).

Caire, Guy. "Recent trends in collective bargaining in France", in *International Labour Review*, Nov.-Dec. 1984. Reprinted in the present volume.

Canada, Privy Council Office. *Canadian industrial relations: The report of the Task Force on Labour Relations*. Ottawa, 1968.

Carew, Anthony. *Democracy and government in European trade unions*. London, Allen & Unwin, 1976.

Chamberlain, Neil W.; Kuhn, James W. *Collective bargaining*. New York, McGraw-Hill, 2nd ed., 1965.

Clarke, R. Oliver. "Collective bargaining and the economic recovery", in *OECD Observer*, July 1984.

——. "The development of industrial relations in European market economies", in *Proceedings of the Industrial Relations Research Association, 1980*. Madison, Wisconsin, 1981.

Clegg, H. A. *The changing system of industrial relations in Great Britain*. Oxford, Basil Blackwell, 1979.

——. *Trade unionism under collective bargaining: A theory based on comparisons of six countries.* Oxford, Basil Blackwell, 1976.

Córdova, Efrén. "Collective bargaining", in Blanpain (ed.). *Comparative labour law and industrial relations* (see above).

——. "A comparative view of collective bargaining in industrialised countries", in *International Labour Review*, July-Aug. 1978.

——. Introductory chapter in ILO: *Selected basic agreements and joint declarations on labour-management relations* (see below).

Craig, Alton W. J. *The system of industrial relations in Canada.* Scarborough, Ontario, Prentice-Hall, 1983.

Cullen, Donald E. "Recent trends in collective bargaining in the United States", in *International Labour Review*, May-June 1985. Reprinted in the present volume.

Dabschek, Braham; Niland, John. *Industrial relations in Australia.* Sydney, McGraw-Hill, 1981.

——;——. "Recent trends in collective bargaining in Australia", in *International Labour Review*, Sep.-Oct. 1984. Reprinted in the present volume.

Daniel, W. W.; Millward, Neil. *Workplace industrial relations in Britain: The DE/PSI/SSRC Survey.* London, Heinemann Educational Books, 1983.

Davey, Harold W.; Bognanno, Mario F.; Estenson, David L. *Contemporary collective bargaining.* Englewood Cliffs, New Jersey, Prentice Hall, 4th ed., 1982.

Deaton, D. R.; Beaumont, P. B. *Determinants of bargaining structure: Some large scale survey evidence for Britain.* Coventry, Warwick University, 1979.

Delamotte, Yves. "Recent trends in the statutory regulation of industrial relations in France", in *Labour and Society*, Jan. 1985.

Desolre, Guy G. "Belgium", in Blum (ed.). *International handbook of industrial relations* (see above).

Despax, Michel; Rojot, Jacques. "France" (1979), in Blanpain (ed.). *International encyclopaedia for labour law and industrial relations*, Vol. 4 (see above).

Dion, Gérard. *Dictionnaire canadien des relations du travail.* Quebec, Presses de l'Université Laval, 1976.

Doeringer, Peter B. (ed.). *Industrial relations in international perspective.* London, Macmillan, 1981.

Dufty, Norman. "Australia", in Blum (ed.). *International handbook of industrial relations* (see above).

Dunlop, John T.; Galenson, Walter. *Labor in the twentieth century.* New York, Academic Press, 1978.

Elvander, Nils. "Sweden", in Roberts (ed.). *Towards industrial democracy: Europe, Japan and the United States* (see below).

European Communities. *Problems and prospects of collective bargaining in the EEC member states.* Luxembourg, 1980.

European Industrial Relations Review, various issues.

European Trade Union Institute. *Collective bargaining in Western Europe 1978-1978 and prospects for 1980.* Brussels, 1980.

Farnham, David; Pimlott, John. *Understanding industrial relations.* London, Cassell, 2nd (revised) ed., 1983.

Ferman, Louis A. (ed.). "The future of American unionism", Special edition of the *Annals of the American Academy of Political and Social Science*, May 1984.

Flanagan, Robert J.; Soskice, David W.; Ulman, Lloyd. *Unionism, economic stabilization and incomes policies.* Washington, DC, The Brookings Institution, 1983.

Flanders, Allan. "The changing character of collective bargaining", in *Department of Employment and Productivity Gazette*, Dec. 1969.

——. "Collective bargaining: A theoretical analysis", in *British Journal of Industrial Relations*, Mar. 1968.

Forsebäck, Lennart. *Industrial relations and employment in Sweden*. Stockholm, Swedish Institute, 1981.

Freeman, Richard B.; Medoff, James L. "New estimates of private sector unionism in the United States", in *Industrial and Labor Relations Review*, Jan. 1979.

——. *What do unions do?* New York, Basic Books, 1984.

Fürstenberg, Friedrich. "Recent trends in collective bargaining in the Federal Republic of Germany", in *International Labour Review*, Sep.-Oct. 1984. Reprinted in the present volume.

Gifford, Courtney D. *Directory of U.S. Labor Organizations: 1984-85 Edition.* Washington, DC, Bureau of National Affairs, 1984.

Gill, Colin. "Industrial relations in Denmark: Problems and perspectives", in *Industrial Relations Journal*, spring 1984.

Giugni, Gino. "The Italian system of industrial relations", in Doeringer (ed.). *Industrial relations in international perspective* (see above).

——. "Recent trends in collective bargaining in Italy", in *International Labour Review*, Sep.-Oct. 1984. Reprinted in the present volume.

Gladstone, Alan; Ozaki, Muneto. "Trade union recognition for collective bargaining purposes", in *International Labour Review*, Aug.-Sep. 1975.

Glendon, Mary Ann. "French labor law reform 1982-1983: The struggle for collective bargaining", in *American Journal of Comparative Law*, summer 1984.

Gospel, Howard F. "Trade unions and the legal obligation to bargain: An American, Swedish and British comparison", in *British Journal of Industrial Relations*, Nov. 1984.

Günter, Hans; Leminsky, Gerhard. "The Federal Republic of Germany", in Dunlop and Galenson (eds.). *Labor in the twentieth century* (see above).

Hamburger, L. "The extension of collective agreements to cover entire trades and industries", in *International Labour Review*, Aug. 1939.

Healy, James J. (ed.). *Creative collective bargaining*. Englewood Cliffs, New Jersey, Prentice Hall, 1965.

Heither, Friedrich H. *Das kollektive Arbeitsrecht der Schweiz*. Stuttgart, Gustav Fischer Verlag, 1964.

Hudson, Michael. "Concerted action: Wages policies in West Germany, 1967-1977", in *Industrial Relations Journal*, Sep.-Oct. 1980.

Hussey, Roger; Marsh, Arthur. *Disclosure of information and employee reporting*. London, Gower, 1983.

ILO. *Collective agreements*, Studies and Reports, Series A (Industrial Relations), No. 39. Geneva, 1936.

——. *Collective bargaining: A response to the recession in industrialised market economy countries*. Geneva, 1984.

——. *Conciliation and arbitration procedures in labour disputes*. Geneva, 1980.

——. *Freedom of association and procedures for determining conditions of employment in the public service*, Report VII (1 and 2), International Labour Conference, 63rd Session, Geneva, 1977.

——. *International standards and guiding principles, 1944-1973*. Labour-Management Relations Series, No. 44. Geneva, 1975.

——. *Report of the Director-General*, International Labour Conference, 71st Session, Geneva, 1985.

——. *Selected basic agreements and joint declarations on labour-management relations*, Labour-Management Relations Series, No. 63. Geneva, 1983.

——. *The trade union situation and industrial relations in Austria*. Geneva, 1986.

——. *Workers' participation in decisions within undertakings*. Geneva, 1981.

——. *World Labour Report 2*. Geneva, 1985.

"Indexierung wirtschaftlich relevanter Grössen", in *Recht der Arbeit*, No. 5, 1975.

Industrial Relations Europe, various issues.

Jacoby, Sanford J. "Union-management cooperation in the United States: Lessons from the 1920s", in *Industrial and Labor Relations Review*, Oct. 1983.

Javillier, Jean-Claude. *Droit du travail*. Paris, Librairie générale de Droit et de Jurisprudence, 1981.

——. *Les réformes du droit du travail depuis le 10 mai*. Paris, Librairie générale de Droit et de Jurisprudence, 1984.

Jenkins, Clive; Sherman, Barrie. *Computers and the unions*. London, Longman, 1977.

Jensen, Vernon, H. "Notes on the beginnings of collective bargaining", in *Industrial and Labor Relations Review*, Jan. 1956.

——. "The process of collective bargaining and the question of its obsolescence", ibid., July 1963.

Kahn-Freund, Otto (ed.). *Labour relations and the law*. London, Stevens, 1965.

Kassalow, Everett M. "Industrial democracy and collective bargaining: A comparative view", in *Labour and Society*, July-Sep. 1982.

Katzenstein, Peter J. *Corporatism and change: Austria, Switzerland and the politics of industry*. Ithaca, New York, Cornell University Press, 1984.

Kennedy, Thomas. *European labor relations*. Lexington, Massachusetts, D. C. Heath, 1980.

Kinnie, N. J. "Single employer bargaining: Structures and strategies", in *Industrial Relations Journal*, autumn 1983.

Kittner, Michael (ed.). *Gewerkschaftsjahrbuch 1984*. Cologne, Bund-Verlag, 1984.

Kochan, Thomas, A. *Collective bargaining and industrial relations: From theory to policy and practice*. Homewood, Illinois, Irwin, 1980.

——; McKersie, Robert B. "Collective bargaining — Pressures for change", in *Sloan Management Review*, summer 1983.

—— et al. *Worker participation and American unions: Threat or opportunity?* Kalamazoo, Michigan, W. E. Upjohn Institute for Employment Research, 1984.

——; McKersie, Robert B.; Cappelli, Peter. "Strategic choice and industrial relations theory", in *Industrial Relations*, winter 1984.

Koshiro, Kazutoshi. "Development of collective bargaining in postwar Japan", in Shirai (ed.). *Contemporary industrial relations in Japan* (see below).

Kozo, Kikuchi. "The Japanese enterprise union and its functions", in Shigeyoshi and Bergmann (eds.) *Industrial relations in transition: The cases of Japan and the Federal Republic of Germany* (see below).

Lacombe, John J. II; Conley, James R. "Major agreements in 1984 provide record low wage increases", in *Monthly Labor Review*, Apr. 1985.

Lange, Peter; Ross, George; Vannicelli, Maurizio. *Unions, change and crisis: French and Italian union strategy and the political economy, 1945-1980*. London, Allen & Unwin, 1982.

Lash, Scott. "The end of neo-corporatism? The breakdown of centralised bargaining in Sweden", in *British Journal of Industrial Relations*, July 1985.

Legislative Series (Geneva, ILO), various years.

Lerner, Shirley W. *The impact of technological and economic change on the structure of British trade unions*, Paper submitted to the First World Congress of the International Industrial Relations Association, Geneva, 4-9 September 1967. Doc. IC-67/8-3, mimeographed.

Lester, Richard A. "Reflections on collective bargaining in Britain and Sweden", in *Industrial and Labor Relations Review*, Apr. 1957.

Levenbach, M. G. "The law relating to collective agreements in the Netherlands", in Kahn-Freund (ed.). *Labour relations and the law* (see above).

Levine, Solomon. "Employers associations in Japan", in Windmuller and Gladstone (eds.). *Employers associations and industrial relations: A comparative study* (see below).

——. "Japan", in Blum (ed.). *International handbook of industrial relations* (see above).

Lewis, Roy. "Collective labour law", in Bain (ed.). *Industrial relations in Britain* (see above).

LLE Journal, various issues.

LO News (Sweden), various issues.

Marsh, A. I.; Evans, E. O. *The dictionary of industrial relations*. London, Hutchinson, 1973.

Martinelli, Alberto; Treu, Tiziano. "Employers associations in Italy", in Windmuller and Gladstone (eds.). *Employers associations and industrial relations: A comparative study* (see below).

McIlroy, John A. "Education for the labor movement: United Kingdom experience past and present", in *Labor Studies Journal*, winter 1980.

McPherson, William H. *Public employee relations in West Germany*. Ann Arbor, University of Michigan, Institute of Labor and Industrial Relations, 1971.

Mire, Joseph. "Industrial relations in Austria", in *New Zealand Journal of Industrial Relations*, Dec. 1981.

Mitbestimmung im Unternehmen: Bericht der Sachverständingenkommission (Biedenkopf Report). Deutscher Bundestag — 6. Wahlperiode, Drucksache VI/334.

Niland, John. *Collective bargaining and compulsory arbitration in Australia*. Kensington, New South Wales, New South Wales University Press, 1978.

——. "Research and reform in industrial relations", in *Journal of Industrial Relations*, Dec. 1981.

Northrup, Herbert R.; Rowan, Richard L. *Multinational collective bargaining attempts*. Philadelphia, Pennsylvania, University of Pennsylvania, The Wharton School, Industrial Research Unit, 1979.

OECD. *Collective bargaining and government policies in ten OECD countries*. Paris, 1979.

Pélissier, J. *Documents de droit du travail*. Paris, Editions Montchrestien, 1971.

Peper, Bram; van Kooten, Gerrit. "The Netherlands: From an ordered harmonic to a bargaining relationship", in Barkin (ed.). *Worker militancy and its consequences* (see above.)

Phelps Brown, E. H. *The growth of British industrial relations*. London, Macmillan, 1957.

——. *The origins of trade union power*. Oxford, Clarendon Press, 1983.

Plowman, D.; Deery, S.; Fisher, C. *Australian industrial relations*. Sydney, Allen & Unwin, 1980.

Purcell, John; Sisson, Keith. "Strategies and practice in the management of industrial relations", in Bain (ed.). *Industrial relations in Britain* (see above).

Quinn Mills, D. "Management performance", in Stieber et al. (eds.). *U.S industrial relations 1950-1980* (see below).

Rehmus, Charles M. (ed.). *Public employment labor relations: An overview of eleven nations*. Ann Arbor, Michigan, University of Michigan, Institute of Labor and Industrial Relations, 1975.

Reuther, Walter, P. "Labor's role in 1975", in Stieber (ed.). *U.S. industrial relations: The next twenty years* (see below).

Rivero, Jean; Savatier, Jean. *Droit du travail*. Paris, Presses universitaires de France, 1970.

Roberts, Benjamin C. (ed.). *Towards industrial democracy: Europe, Japan and the United States*. London, Croom Helm, 1979.

——. "Recent trends in collective bargaining in the United Kingdom", in *International Labour Review*, May-June 1984. Reprinted in the present volume.

Roberts, Higdon C. Jr. "Steward training in Great Britain", in *Labor Studies Journal*, spring 1979.

Ruben, George. "Modest labor-management bargains continue in 1984 despite the recovery", in *Monthly Labor Review*, Jan. 1985.

Savas, Emanuel S. et al. *Computers in collective bargaining: The Adelphi experience*, Report to the Carnegie Corporation. New York, n.p., Jan. 1974.

Schönhoven, Klaus. *Expansion und Konzentration: Studien zur Entwicklung der freien Gewerkschaften im Wilhelminischen Deutschland 1890 bis 1919*. Stuttgart, Klett-Cotta, 1980.

Sellier, François. "France", in Dunlop and Galenson (eds.). *Labor in the twentieth century* (see above).

Shigeyoshi, Tokunaga; Bergmann, Joachim (eds.). *Industrial relations in transition: The cases of Japan and the Federal Republic of Germany*. Tokyo, University of Tokyo Press, 1984.

Shirai, Taishiro (ed.). *Contemporary industrial relations in Japan*. Madison, Wisconsin, University of Wisconsin Press, 1983.

——. "Recent trends in collective bargaining in Japan", in *International Labour Review*, May-June 1984. Reprinted in the present volume.

Siegel, Abraham J. (ed.). *The impact of computers on collective bargaining*. Cambridge, Massachusetts Institute of Technology, 1969.

Sisson, Keith. "Employers' organisations", in Bain (ed.). *Industrial relations in Britain* (see above).

Skögh, Goran. "Employers associations in Sweden", in Windmuller and Gladstone (eds.). *Employers associations and industrial relations: A comparative study* (see below).

Social and Labour Bulletin (Geneva, ILO), various issues.

Somers, Gerald G. (ed.). *Collective bargaining: Contemporary American experience*. Madison, Wisconsin, Industrial Relations Research Association, 1980.

Stieber, Jack (ed.). *U.S. industrial relations: The next twenty years*. East Lansing, Michigan State University Press, 1958.

—— et al. (eds.). *U.S. industrial relations 1950-1980: A critical assessment*. Madison, Wisconsin, Industrial Relations Research Association, 1981.

Streeck, Wolfgang. *Industrial relations in West Germany: A case study of the car industry*. London, Heinemann Educational Books, 1984.

——. "Politischer Wandel und organisatorische Reformen", in *Gewerkschaftliche Monatshefte*, Oct. 1978.

Thomson, Andrew. "A view from abroad", in Stieber (ed.). *U.S industrial relations 1950-1980: A critical assessment* (see above).

——; Hunter, L. C. "Great Britain", in Dunlop and Galenson (eds.). *Labor in the twentieth century* (see above).

Towy-Evans, M. "The personnel management advisory service in Great Britain", in *International Labour Review*, Feb. 1960.

Treu, Tiziano. "Italy", in Roberts (ed.). *Towards industrial democracy: Europe, Japan and the United States* (see above).

——. "Italy" (1981), in Blanpain (ed.). *International encyclopaedia for labour law and industrial relations*, Vol. 6 (see above).

——. "Recent development of Italian labour law", in *Labour and Society*, Jan. 1985.

Ulman, Lloyd (ed.). *Challenges to collective bargaining.* Englewood Cliffs, New Jersey, Prentice-Hall, 1967.

——. *The rise of the national union.* Cambridge, Massachusetts, Harvard University Press, 1955.

United Kingdom, Advisory, Conciliation and Arbitration Service. *Industrial relations handbook.* London, HM Stationery Office, 1980.

United Kingdom, Royal Commission on Trade Unions and Employers' Associations, 1965-68. *Report* ("The Donovan Report"), Cmnd. 3623. London, HM Stationery Office, 1968.

United States, Department of Labor, Bureau of Labor Statistics. *Characteristics of major collective bargaining agreements, January 1, 1980*, Bulletin No. 2095. Washington, DC, 1981.

——. *Directory of trade unions and employee associations*, Bulletin No. 1750. Washington, DC, 1972.

——. *Directory of national unions and employee associations, 1979*, Bulletin 2079. Washington, DC, 1980.

United States, Bureau of National Affairs. *Collective bargaining negotiations and contracts.* Washington, DC, 1983.

United States, Federal Mediation and Conciliation Service. *Annual Reports.* Washington, DC, various years.

Valticos, N. "International labour law" (1984), in Blanpain (ed.). *International encyclopaedia for labour law and industrial relations*, Vol. 1 (see above).

van Voorden, William. "Employers associations in the Netherlands", in Windmuller and Gladstone (eds.). *Employers associations and industrial relations: A comparative study* (see below).

Verdier, Jean-Maurice. "Labour relations in the public sector of France", in Rehmus (ed.). *Public employment and industrial relations: An overview of eleven nations* (see above).

Walton, Richard E.; McKersie, Robert B. *A behavioral theory of labor negotiations.* New York, McGraw-Hill, 1965.

Webb, Sidney and Beatrice. *Industrial democracy.* London, Longmans, Green, 1920.

Weber, Arnold R. "Stability and change in the structure of collective bargaining", in Ulman (ed.). *Challenges to collective bargaining* (see above).

Wedderburn, Lord. "The new industrial relations laws in Great Britain", in *Labour and Society*, Jan. 1985.

White, Harold C.; Meyer, Lynn M. "Employer obligation to provide information", in *Labor Law Journal*, Oct. 1984.

Widermann, Herbert; Stumpf, Hermann. *Tarifvertragsgesetz*. Munich, C. H. Beck'sche Verlagsbuchhandlung, 5th ed., 1977.

Wilke, Manfred. *Die Funktionäre: Apparat und Demokratie im Deutschen Gewerkschaftsbund*. Munich/Zurich, Piper Verlag, 1979.

Williams, Alan. "International perspective: Labor education and labor relations in New Zealand", in *Labor Studies Journal*, May 1976.

Windmuller, John P. "Concentration trends in union structure: An international comparison", in *Industrial and Labor Relations Review*, Oct. 1981.

——. *Labor relations in the Netherlands*. Ithaca, New York, Cornell University Press, 1969.

——; Gladstone, Alan (eds.). *Employers associations and industrial relations: A comparative study*. Oxford, Clarendon Press, 1984.

Wohlert, Klaus. "Vergleich des Tarifverhandlungssystems in Schweden und der Bundesrepublik Deutschland", in *WSI Mitteilungen*, Aug. 1976.

Wood, W. D.; Kumar, Pradeep (eds.). *The current industrial relations scene in Canada 1984*. Kingston, Ontario, Queen's University at Kingston, Industrial Relations Centre, 1984.